Baseball's Shooting Stars

ALSO BY DAVID J. GORDON
AND FROM MCFARLAND

*The American Cardiovascular Pandemic:
A 100-Year History* by David Gordon;
Series Editor Elaine A. Moore (2021)

Baseball's Shooting Stars

*Improbable Ascents
and Burnouts
in the National Pastime*

DAVID J. GORDON

McFarland & Company, Inc., Publishers
Jefferson, North Carolina

LIBRARY OF CONGRESS CATALOGING-IN-PUBLICATION DATA

Names: Gordon, David J. (Special Assistant for Clinical Studies), author.
Title: Baseball's shooting stars : improbable ascents and burnouts in the national pastime / David J. Gordon.
Description: Jefferson, North Carolina : McFarland & Company, Inc., Publishers, 2024. | Includes bibliographical references and index.
Identifiers: LCCN 2024032016 | ISBN 9781476694894 (paperback : acid free paper) ∞
ISBN 9781476653525 (ebook)
Subjects: LCSH: Baseball players—United States—Biography. | Baseball players—United States—History.
Classification: LCC GV865.A1 G67 2024 | DDC 796.357092/273—dc23/eng/20240808
LC record available at https://lccn.loc.gov/2024032016

BRITISH LIBRARY CATALOGUING DATA ARE AVAILABLE

ISBN (print) 978-1-4766-9489-4
ISBN (ebook) 978-1-4766-5352-5

© 2024 David J. Gordon. All rights reserved

No part of this book may be reproduced or transmitted in any form or by any means, electronic or mechanical, including photocopying or recording, or by any information storage and retrieval system, without permission in writing from the publisher.

Front cover: (inset) New York Giants player Cy Seymour on an American Tobacco Company baseball card, circa 1910 (Library of Congress)

Printed in the United States of America

McFarland & Company, Inc., Publishers
 Box 611, Jefferson, North Carolina 28640
  www.mcfarlandpub.com

Table of Contents

Acknowledgments   vii
Preface: The Allure of Shooting Stars   1

1. Introduction   3
2. The King of Second Base: Frederick C. Dunlap (1884)   10
3. The Other Cy: James Bentley "Cy" Seymour (1905)   19
4. The Reluctant Star: George Robert Stone (1906)   25
5. California Dutch: Hubert Benjamin "Dutch" Leonard (1914)   30
6. Windfall: William Wilcy Moore (1927)   37
7. The Left-Handed Satchel Paige: Stewart "Slim" Jones (1934)   42
8. The Pride of the Jury Box: Thomas Francis "Tommy" Holmes (1945)   49
9. Harry the Cat: Harry David Brecheen (1948)   55
10. The Little Pitcher Who Could: Robert Clayton "Bobby" Shantz (1952)   61
11. The Hebrew Hammer: Albert Leonard "Al" Rosen (1953)   68
12. Diamond Jim: James Edward "Jim" Gentile (1961)   75
13. Stormin' Norman: Norman Dalton "Norm" Cash (1961)   80
14. The World's Most Horrible Hitter: Henry John "Hank" Aguirre (1962)   87
15. Bonus Baby: Richard Clark "Dick" Ellsworth (1963)   92
16. The Mark of Zoilo: Zoilo Casanova Versalles (1965)   98
17. Angleworm: Theodore Wade "Ted" Abernathy (1967)   105
18. Fenway Power: Americo Peter "Rico" Petrocelli (1969)   111

19.	Billy Sunday: Billy Cordell Grabarkewitz (1970)	118
20.	The Comeback Kid: John Frederick Hiller (1973)	124
21.	The Bird Is the Word: Mark Steven "The Bird" Fidrych (1976)	131
22.	Imperfect: Darrell Ray Porter (1979)	138
23.	Doctor K: Dwight Eugene "Doc" Gooden (1985)	146
24.	The Last 150-Inning Reliever: Mark Anthony Eichhorn (1986)	156
25.	Skates: Lonnie Smith (1989)	161
26.	Journeyman: Richard David "Rick" Wilkins (1993)	170
27.	Bad Boy: Esteban Antonio Loaiza (2003)	175
28.	Brian's Little Brother: Marcus William Giles (2003)	181
29.	The Perfect Pitching Prospect: Mark William Prior (2003)	186
30.	The Natural: Joshua Holt (Josh) Hamilton (2010)	192
31.	The Next Dave Winfield: Matthew Ryan "Matt" Kemp (2011)	200
32.	Wrap-Up	207

Glossary of Terms and Abbreviations	211
Chapter Notes	215
Bibliography	243
Index	253

Acknowledgments

I am grateful to the Research Department at the National Baseball Hall of Fame, specifically Rachel Wells and John Horne, for providing access to their files of news clippings and photos of the players profiled in this book. I am also grateful to my wife Susan, my son Sam, and my daughter Emily for their unflagging love and support.

Preface
The Allure of Shooting Stars

"The skies are painted with unnumber'd sparks.
They are all fire and every one doth shine."
—William Shakespeare, *Julius Caesar*, Act 3, Scene 1

Although my earliest childhood memories include playing baseball and softball with my father and brother, I did not become fully aware of professional baseball until 1954, when I was turning eight years old. I collected a few baseball cards and vaguely remember watching the Giants sweep the Indians in the World Series. By 1956, I was completely hooked and had chosen Mickey Mantle as my favorite player and his team, the Yankees, as my favorite team. Little boys love shiny toys, and such was the case for me with Mantle, who exuded power and confidence and put up stellar stats every year, including the 1956 Triple Crown, and with the Yankees, who regularly reached the World Series and won it as often as not. I devoured the biographies of the storied Yankee greats, like Ruth, Gehrig, and DiMaggio, as they piled accomplishment upon accomplishment. While it is true that their successes eventually came to an end—a tragic one in Gehrig's case—the end came only after they had built a lasting body of work leading to enshrinement in the Hall of Fame.

But while vicariously enjoying the seemingly endless successes of Mantle and the Yankees, I also adopted my hometown Cubs and their star SS Ernie Banks as my co-favorites. This hapless team was never a threat to beat the Yankees—they only met occasionally in meaningless exhibition games—but they were always on WGN-TV and were lovable losers. And somehow, perhaps because their triumphs were rare and short-lived, the Cubs eclipsed the Yankees in my affections as I went through adolescence. (Psychologists say that intermittent reinforcement is the strongest.) Then, as Mantle and Banks declined in the mid to late 1960s, I developed a broader appreciation for the players whose success came less easily and didn't last as long. Unlike the Mantles of the world, their stories are bittersweet and fraught with "what-ifs" and "could-haves." It is these players, who struggled to achieve and sustain stardom and acclaim, to whom I dedicate this book.

I have chosen to profile thirty of the clearest and most poignant examples—I call them "shooting stars"—who achieved the highest peaks and suffered the sharpest declines. The Cubs have had their fair share of such players; I have profiled three of them here—Dick Ellsworth (1963), Rick Wilkins (1993), and Mark Prior (2003). Each had a singular spectacular season, and each faded quickly to mediocrity or oblivion. But every team has had players like this, who exemplify how difficult it is to achieve lasting stardom. For some shooting stars, stardom came and faded early; for others, it came only after a prolonged struggle. Some were brought down by injuries, and others by drugs, alcohol, or personal shortcomings. Their stories are many and varied, but there are no "happily-ever-after" fairy tales among them.

We can all stand back and admire the breadth and magnitude of the accomplishments of the Yankees over many decades. But when you ask fans which teams they really loved, they are more likely to point to underdog teams like the 1914 Braves, the 1955 Dodgers, the 1960 Pirates, the 1967 Red Sox, the 1969 Mets, and the 2016 Cubs. In the same way, we can easily read the biographies of baseball's iconic superstars and admire their bronze plaques in the Hall of Fame. But it is much harder to discover and appreciate the struggles and short-lived triumphs of the shooting stars, many of whom are all but forgotten. Yet it is these shooting stars to whom we can most closely relate and with whom we can most easily identify on a human level. In the coming chapters, I hope you will find that their short-lived triumphs are our triumphs, that their struggles are our struggles, and that their stories are our stories.

◆ 1 ◆

Introduction

Before we set out to explore the stories of baseball's shooting stars, let us define our terms. I will primarily rely on the Baseball-Reference.com version of Wins Above Replacement (WAR) as a global measure of the quality of a season, where 2.0–4.0 WAR signifies a solid regular performer, ≥ 5.0 WAR signifies All-Star level, and ≥ 7.5 WAR signifies a candidate for an MVP or Cy Young award.[1] When an explicit distinction is necessary, I will refer to WAR for position players as WAR (H) and WAR for pitchers as WAR (P). In general, the type of player who is a candidate for this book is one whose peak season was at least 7.2 WAR and who had no other seasons exceeding 6.0 WAR—at least not within five years of his peak. However, since one would not regard a player whose best year was 7.2 WAR and whose second best season was 6.0 WAR as a shooting star, I also require that a player's best one-season WAR must be at least 1.5 times higher than his second best WAR. Thus, I considered Al Rosen, whose 10.1 WAR in 1953 was 1.68 times greater than his 6.0 WAR in 1952, as a shooting star, but not Lloyd Moseby, whose 7.3 WAR career year in 1984 was only 1.17 times greater than his 6.0 WAR in 1983.

One also must consider positional differences and temporal changes in the number of games per season over a century and a half of MLB history. Position players who played before 1900 or in the Negro Leagues (which scheduled many fewer games than contemporary major leagues) and catchers of all eras (typically batting later in the lineup and needing more days off) generally received fewer PA than contemporary non-catchers. Therefore, in general, I considered players in these categories if their WAR (H) per 650 PA was 7.2 or greater in their peak season, even if their raw WAR was < 7.2.

Temporal changes are an even greater issue for pitchers. Despite the shorter seasons, pitchers in the 19th and early 20th centuries pitched far more innings and faced far more batters per season than the roughly 1000 batters per season typically faced by rotation starters who pitched between 1909 and 1988. For example, Old Hoss Radbourn accrued 678.2 IP and 2672 BF in his 19.2 WAR (P) 1883 season, but that translates to only 7.2 WAR (P) per 1000 BF. Conversely, due to the increasing prominence of relief pitchers and near-extinction of complete games, late 20th- and early 21st-century pitchers have tended to shoulder increasingly lighter workloads, typically < 850 BF per season in 2021–23. For example, future Hall of Famer Clayton Kershaw has never faced > 912 batters in a season and has not faced as many as 750 batters since 2017. Therefore, I have turned to prorating WAR (P) per 1000 BF—a typical workload for rotation starters between 1909 and 1988—to level the playing field for pitchers who performed in other eras. Thus, I have required that pitchers have at least 7.2 WAR (P) per 1000 BF *and* at least 6.0 WAR (P) at their peak to qualify as shooting stars. Note that this still excludes most relief pitchers, except for the pre–1990 Rich Gossage–type multi-inning workhorses.

Another factor that I considered was the percentage of a player's career WAR that is attributable to his peak season. However, this factor cannot be determinative, since nearly every player with a brief career would qualify, while a player who otherwise fits the one-off profile with a single 7.5-WAR season plus a dozen 3–4 WAR seasons might be disqualified.

Many more players met the criteria I have outlined than could be included in this book, I have selected an "all-star" team of sixteen hitters (a starter at each position and a backup at catcher, every infield position, and CF plus two backup corner outfielders) and fourteen pitchers (ten starters and four relievers). I have used the following factors to winnow the field:

1. I tried to balance the representation of position players and pitchers. Because of the inherent volatility of pitching performance, shooting star candidates are far more frequent among pitchers than hitters. Many such pitchers excelled as rookies, then damaged their arms and faded quickly from the scene. I have included a few of these here (e.g., Slim Jones and Mark Fidrych) but limited myself to the most compelling examples.
2. I tried to balance the representation of different eras. However, I avoided pre–1908 pitchers, because they often pitched 350-plus innings in a season and accrued correspondingly large WAR (P) totals. I am looking for quality, not mere quantity.
3. I did not consider players strongly suspected of PED use in their

1. Introduction

peak season. Rich Aurilia (2001), Bret Boone (2001), and Javy Lopez (2003) are examples of suspected PED users whom I have excluded.

4. I have not considered any active players (as of 2023). Their stories are unfinished.
5. I tried to select players with the most compelling and varied stories to tell. So I have chosen some excellent players who had a single spectacular peak season and some one-year wonders, whose peaks were not as high but whose careers were otherwise mediocre. Some of my shooting stars struggled for many years before achieving their year of glory; others achieved success early, then flamed out.

Tables 1A and 1B list the position players and pitchers, respectively, whom I have selected and the chapters in which they are profiled. They will be presented in chronological order. I apologize in advance if I have left out any of your personal favorites.

Table 1A: Shooting Star Position Players

Chapter	Starting Lineup	Peak Season				Second Best Season			Career	
		Year	WAR (H)	PA	per 650 PA	Year	WAR (H)	Ratio	WAR (H)	% in Peak
22	Darrell Porter (C)	1979	7.6	679	7.3	1978	4.2	1.81	40.8	19%
13	Norm Cash (1B)	1961	9.2	673	8.9	1965	5.4	1.70	52.0	18%
2	Fred Dunlap (2B)	1884	7.9	478	10.7	1883	4.5	1.76	37.1	21%
18	Rico Petrocelli (SS)	1969	10.0	643	10.1	1971	4.9	2.04	39.1	26%
11	Al Rosen (3B)	1953	10.1	688	9.5	1952	6.0	1.68	32.3	31%
25	Lonnie Smith (LF)	1989	8.8	577	9.9	1982	6.2	1.42	38.5	23%
31	Matt Kemp (CF)	2011	8.0	689	7.5	2009	4.9	1.63	21.4	37%
8	Tommy Holmes (RF)	1945	8.4	714	7.6	1944	5.0	1.68	35.6	24%
	Reserves									
26	Rick Wilkins (C)	1993	6.6	500	8.6	1992	1.9	3.47	14.0	47%
12	Jim Gentile (1B)	1961	6.9	601	7.5	1960	3.1	2.23	17.0	41%
28	Marcus Giles (2B)	2003	7.9	635	8.1	2005	4.0	1.98	16.7	47%
16	Zoilo Versalles (SS)	1965	7.2	728	6.4	1963	2.6	2.77	12.6	57%
19	Billy Grabarkewitz (3B)	1970	6.5	640	6.6	1973	0.4	16.25	5.8	112%
4	George Stone (LF)	1906	8.8	662	8.6	1907	5.4	1.63	26.2	34%
30	Josh Hamilton (LF)	2010	8.7	571	9.9	2008	5.5	1.58	28.2	31%
3	Cy Seymour (CF)	1905	8.0	646	8.0	1904	4.5	1.78	31.6	25%

Table 1B: Shooting Star Pitchers

Chapter	Starting Pitchers	Peak Season Year	Peak Season WAR (P)	Peak Season BF	Peak Season per 1000 BF	Second Best Season Year	Second Best Season WAR (P)	Second Best Season Ratio	Career WAR (P)	Career % in Peak
23	Dwight Gooden	1985	12.2	1065	11.5	1984	5.3	2.30	48.1	25%
15	Dick Ellsworth	1963	10.2	1160	8.8	1961	3.7	2.76	23.3	44%
5	Hubert "Dutch" Leonard	1914	9.6	842	11.4	1917	5.2	1.85	37.4	26%
21	Mark Fidrych	1976	9.6	996	9.6	1977	2.4	4.00	11.3	85%
10	Bobby Shantz	1952	8.8	1103	8.0	1957	3.1	2.84	32.1	27%
9	Harry Brecheen	1948	8.7	931	9.3	1946	5.5	1.58	41.3	21%
7	Slim Jones	1934	8.4	789	10.6	1933	0.5	16.80	9.4	89%
29	Mark Prior	2003	7.4	863	8.6	2005	3.6	2.06	15.7	47%
14	Hank Aguirre	1962	7.4	877	8.4	1964	2.9	2.55	21.0	35%
27	Esteban Loaiza	2003	7.2	922	7.8	2005	3.8	1.89	22.9	31%
	Relief Pitchers									
20	John Hiller	1973	7.9	498	15.9	1974	4.1	1.93	31.1	25%
24	Mark Eichhorn	1986	7.3	612	11.9	1991	2.9	2.52	19.2	38%
6	Wilcy Moore	1927	6.6	870	7.6	1931	4.3	1.53	9.3	71%
17	Ted Abernathy	1967	6.2	427	14.5	1965	3.2	1.94	16.6	37%

All of the listed players except Wilkins, Gentile, Grabarkewitz, Moore, and Abernathy have at least 7.2 WAR in their peak season. However, the peak seasons for Wilkins, Gentile, Moore, and Abernathy each have at least 7.2 WAR when prorated to 650 PA or 1000 BF. Although Grabarkewitz's peak season was slightly substandard, the contrast between his peak season and the remainder of his career was the most extreme of any player I considered.

All of the listed players except Lonnie Smith have ≤ 6.0 WAR in their second best season and a peak-to-runner-up ratio of at least 1.5. I included Smith because his 6.2 WAR runner-up season in 1982 was seven years removed from his 1989 peak and because his career was on life support going into the 1989 season. In the instances of Smith and Grabarkewitz, I thought it was more important to tell the best stories than to be rigid about fitting everyone to the exact same mold.

Another way of looking at our collection of shooting stars is to compare their performance in their peak season to their composite performance across the remaining years of their careers (Figures 1A-B). Since the off-peak performance of each player encompasses many years' worth of PA or BF, it is necessary to normalize WAR to a fixed number of PA (650) or BF (1000) to provide a fair comparison.

1. Introduction

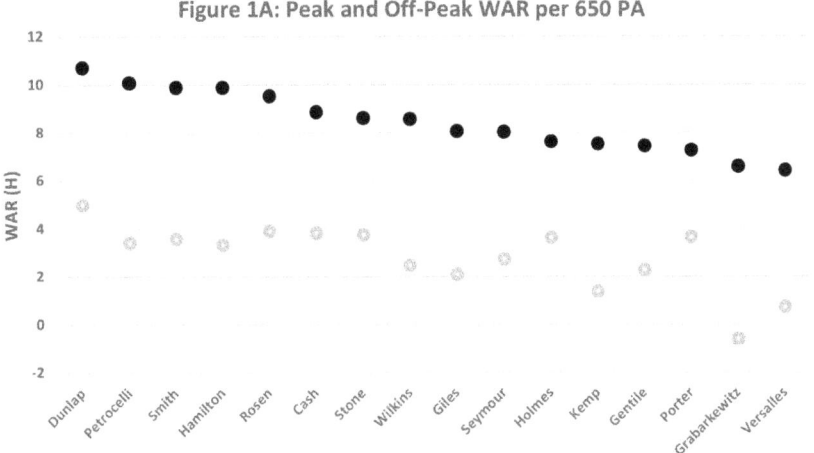

Figure 1A: Peak and Off-Peak WAR per 650 PA

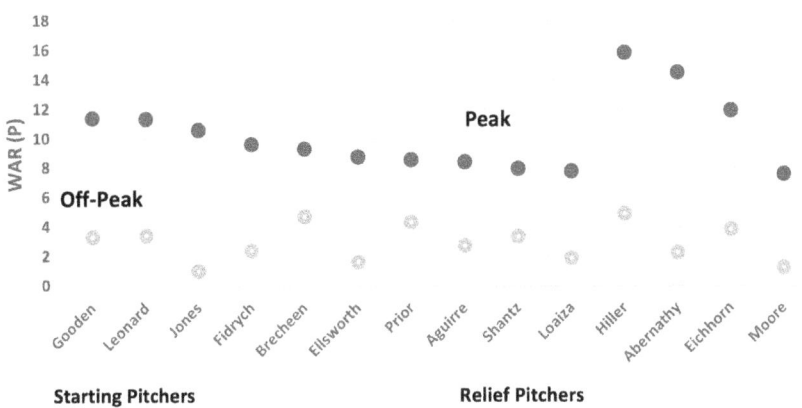

Figure 1B: Peak and Off-Peak WAR per 1000 BF

The peak and composite off-peak WAR (H) per 650 PA for each of the sixteen position players in Table 1A are plotted in Figure 1A. One can see at a glance the large gap between the peak and off-peak WAR (H) per 650 PA of each position player. The peak WAR (H) values vary from 11.4 for Fred Dunlap to 6.4 for Zoilo Versalles. Except for Dunlap, who had 5.0 off-peak WAR (H) per 650 PA, no position player had ≥ 4.0 off-peak WAR per 650 PA. Versalles and Grabarkewitz had only 0.7 and -0.6 off-peak WAR (H), respectively, per 650 PA.

The peak and composite off-peak WAR (P) per 1000 BF for the fourteen pitchers in Table 1B are similarly plotted in Figure 1B. The four relief pitchers (who tend to have the fewest BF per season) are shown at the right. Because of their smaller seasonal workload, relievers tend to have the highest peak WAR (P) per 1000 BF. Dwight Gooden (11.5), Dutch Leonard (11.4), and Slim Jones (11.2) had the highest peak WAR (P) per 1000 BF among the starting pitchers; the other seven starters had peak WAR (P) between 7.8 and 9.6 per 1000 BF. Hiller (4.9), Brecheen (4.7), and Prior (4.4) were the only pitchers with ≥ 4.0 off-peak WAR per 1000 BF. Slim Jones had only 0.6 off-peak WAR per 1000 BF.

I have allocated a chapter in this book for each of the thirty players I selected. These chapters are each written in the style of a magazine article, focusing on the statistical contrast between each player's peak season and the remainder of his career. I have striven to provide sufficient biographical and historical background for the players I have profiled and the teams they played for to create a contextual framework for their statistical accomplishments. However, I have not personally interviewed any of these players (many of whom are deceased) or their families. Readers who are interested in the in-depth biography of any of the players I have profiled are encouraged to read the many articles and online sources—particularly the SABR BioProject pieces (see below)—cited in the chapter notes.

Housekeeping Details

I assume that all of my readers are familiar with standard baseball abbreviations. But just in case an abbreviation puzzles you, I have included a glossary at the end of this book.

Although the WAR values I have used in this book are accurate as of October 2023, Baseball-Reference.com is constantly revising the historical record and tweaking their WAR calculations. It is possible—even likely—that some of the WAR values in this book will have changed by the time you read it. Usually the changes are minor—no more than 0.2 WAR for any player in any season.

My chief sources of biographical information are as follows:

1. SABR BioProject, which has excellent online biographies of most of the pre–2000 players profiled in this book (except Hank Aguirre, Ted Abernathy, and Lonnie Smith) but none of those whose peak years came after 2000.[2]
2. B-R Bullpen, which has biographical information ranging from sketchy to detailed.[3]
3. Other online sources like BaseballPlayerProfiles.com.[4]
4. Player files from the Baseball Hall of Fame Library, generously

1. Introduction

provided by the HOF research department, which contain illuminating clippings of contemporary newspaper and magazine articles about the players.[5]

In every instance, I have cited these sources in the text after the first sentence where information from the source is used. If the biographic material derived from a particular source was several sentences long, I did not repeat the citation after every sentence.

All statistics and analyses cited (except where otherwise indicated) come from Baseball-Reference.com and its companion statistical database analysis site, Stathead Baseball.[6] I have not specifically cited the sources of statistics and biographic information which come directly from a player's home page on Baseball-Reference.com. Citing players' Baseball-Reference.com home pages would have been unwieldy and unnecessary, since readers can easily find these player pages on their own. However, I have included specific citations for all Stathead analyses and for references to box scores, schedules, etc., that require navigation away from a player's Baseball-Reference.com home page.

◆ 2 ◆

The King of Second Base
Frederick C. Dunlap (1884)

On December 1, 1902, an indigent, emaciated 43-year-old man, ravaged by intestinal tuberculosis, died in Philadelphia Hospital.[1] Although he had a wife and three young children in Pittsburgh, he had been living in obscurity in a Philadelphia boarding house. His abject poverty had undoubtedly accelerated the course of his terminal illness. However, since the mean life expectancy for U.S. men was only 49.8 years in 1902 and tuberculosis was their leading cause of death, his death did not attract much notice until someone at the morgue recognized him as ex-ballplayer Fred Dunlap.[2] Still, his funeral was so sparsely attended that strangers had to be hired as pallbearers.

There was nothing about his shabby appearance to suggest that this was once an elegant man who had risen from the streets of Philadelphia to sit atop the baseball world as one of its most celebrated stars less than two decades earlier. Back then, he had been known as "Sure Shot" Dunlap (a nickname bestowed on him by King Kelly for his rifle arm) and the "King of Second Base." For six years (1884–89), he had been the highest paid player in baseball, and he looked and acted the part to the hilt. And in one of those years (1884), he compiled one of the most remarkable and unexpected seasons in baseball history, hitting .412 (MLB's first .400 season), scoring 160 runs and posting 7.4 WAR (10.7 WAR per 650 PA) in only 101 games. His 256 adjusted on-base-plus-slugging percentage (OPS+) was higher than any Babe Ruth season. Indeed, only Josh Gibson (281 in 302 PA in 1943 and 273 in 183 PA in 1937) and Barry Bonds on PED (268 in 2002, 263 in 2004, and 259 in 2001) ever posted a higher OPS+ than Dunlap's 256. Yet Dunlap never had another season in which he posted even 5 WAR or a 160 OPS+, and his career averages were only 134 OPS+ and 5.66 WAR per 650 PA.

Dunlap came from the humblest of beginnings.[3] Born in Philadelphia

2. The King of Second Base

on May 21, 1859, he was orphaned at the age of ten. Although a middle-aged couple took him in and provided food and shelter, they neglected his education and allowed him to roam the streets of Philadelphia, eschewing school for baseball. He never learned to read or write. By age 15 he was playing semi-pro baseball. He graduated to minor league baseball in 1877, playing with three New York teams—Auburn, Hornellsville, and 1879 National Association champion Albany. He made his major league debut, not as a player but as an umpire, for one game in 1879.

In 1880, Dunlap joined the Cleveland Blues (NL), a middle-of-the-pack team, where he teamed with John "Pebbly Jack" Glasscock, the "King of Shortstops" (and an unfairly overlooked HOF candidate) for four years to anchor one of the best defensive infields of his day. He even managed the Blues for most of the 1882 season (when he was just 23 years old), compiling a 42–36–2 record. As a 21-year-old rookie, Dunlap hit a solid .276/.289/.429 (142 OPS+) in 380 PA and led the NL with 27 doubles and 44 DP turned at 2B. He improved to .325/.358/.444 (156 OPS+) in 1881, .280/.323/.354 (120 OPS+) in 1882, and .326/.361/.452 (146 OPS+)

In this Old Judge Cigarettes Trading Card photograph (circa 1888–89), Fred Dunlap, now captain of the Pittsburgh Alleghenys, was past his prime but still the reigning King of 2B. Here he shows off his no-glove backhanded fielding technique (Benjamin K. Edwards Baseball Cards Collection, Library of Congress, Digital ID bbc 0352f, https://www.loc.gov/pictures/resource/bbc.0352f/?co=bbc).

in 1883, his second-best season. He led NL 2B with 297 assists and 62 DP in 1882, building a reputation as the best 2B in the NL. Although Dunlap primarily hit and threw right-handed, he was in fact ambidextrous and could throw runners out with either arm, a distinct advantage when one plays (as Dunlap and Glasscock did) without a fielding glove. He compiled 15.5 WAR in 1554 PA (approximately 6.5 WAR per 650 PA) during his first four seasons, establishing himself as a sure-handed strong armed infielder and a solid hitter, who ranked among the better players in the National League. But he was definitely not a superstar.

However, when Dunlap accepted a $3400 contract from St. Louis millionaire Henry Lucas to play in his "outlaw league" the Union Association (UA) in 1884, he instantly became the highest paid player in baseball, a crown that he would wear for the rest of the decade.[4] Dunlap rewarded this investment with not just a breakout season, but a season for the ages (Table 2). On its face, his 7.9 WAR in 1884 was not extraordinary by current standards, but it was unprecedented in the context of his team's 113-game schedule, surpassing the previous 5.9 mark, set by Cap Anson in 1881 and equaled by Dan Brouthers in 1883, by 35 percent. Pro-rated to the roughly 650 PA available to a modern hitter, Dunlap's 10.74 WAR per 650 PA in 1884 ranks as the 32nd greatest batting season in the history of MLB. Among players with at least 400 PA, only Babe Ruth (1919–21, 1923–24, 1926–27), Barry Bonds (2001–04), Rogers Hornsby (1917, 1924–25), George Brett (1980), Carl Yastrzemski (1967), Mickey Mantle (1956–57), Honus Wagner (1908), Mike Schmidt (1981), Ted Williams (1941, 1957), Ty Cobb (1910, 1917), Willie Mays (1964–65), Mookie Betts (2018), Joe Morgan (1975), Andre Dawson (1981), Jeff Bagwell (1994), and Rickey Henderson (1990) have done better. Although Dunlap had a fine career, it does not measure up to any of these sixteen elite players, of whom all but Bonds and Betts are in the Hall of Fame. Dunlap posted 76 percent more WAR in 1884 than in his next best season (1883) and was more than twice as productive (7.9 WAR in 472 PA) as in the rest of his career (29.2 WAR in 3786 PA, or 5.0 WAR per 650 PA).

Turning from WAR and OPS+ to the more traditional stats, Dunlap also led his league in all three "slash line" categories in 1884, as well as total bases, hits, runs, and home runs, scoring an incredible 160 runs in only 101 games. (The Union Association did not track RBI.) Only 13 players in MLB history have scored more than Dunlap's 160 runs—none of them in so few PA. Tip O'Neill with 167 R in 629 PA (151 more PA than Dunlap) in 1887 had the fewest PA of anyone with > 160 R. Looked at another way, Dunlap scored a run in 33 percent of his 478 PA and in almost 75 percent of the 204 times he reached base via hit or BB. That is simply not done! Even Billy Hamilton's record 198 runs scored in 1894 represented "only" 28 percent of his 702 PA and 56 percent of his 353 times on base via hit or BB.

Table 2: Selected Stats for Fred Dunlap's Peak and Runner-Up Seasons and His Career*

Season	Age	PA	AVG	OBP	SLG	OPS+	TB	H	R	HR	WAR (H)
Peak 1884	25	478	0.412	0.448	0.621	256	279	185	160	13	7.9
per 650 PA							379	252	218	18	10.7
Runner-Up 1883	24	418	0.326	0.361	0.452	146	179	129	81	4	4.5
per 650 PA							278	201	126	6	7.0
Career (1880–91)		4264	0.292	0.340	0.406	134	1612	1159	759	41	37.1
per 650 PA							246	177	116	6	5.7

*League leading totals are shown in boldface type.

Dunlap's .412 AVG in 1884 (which broke Cap Anson' MLB record of .399 in 1881) was 56 points higher than any other player in any major league that year. He also played his typical strong defense at 2B (1.4 dWAR). His 51 errors held his fielding percentage to only .926, but this was above average in an era when infielders played barehanded. And if that weren't enough, the 25-year-old Dunlap managed the Maroons to a 66–16–1 record in their last 83 games as they cruised to a 94–19–1 record and the first and only UA championship.

Although Dunlap remained an everyday player through 1889, he never again came close to matching his 1884 performance. The UA folded after the 1884 season. League founder Henry Lucas had hoarded the league's best players for his own franchise, without regard for the well-being of the other seven franchises, four of which (Altoona, Chicago, Philadelphia, and Washington) moved and/or disbanded during the season.[5] Only the St. Louis Maroons survived the demise of the UA; with Dunlap in tow, they joined the NL in 1885. Unfortunately, neither Dunlap nor the Maroons could sustain their success against the stiffer competition in the older established NL. The Maroons finished eighth and last (36–72) in 1885. Dunlap fell to .270/.354/.333 (119 OPS+) in 464 PA, although, thanks to his outstanding defense (1.5 dWAR), his 4.3 WAR was more than respectable. Nevertheless, a rift emerged between Dunlap and his team, and he was replaced as manager by Alex McKinnon after a 30–40–2 start. The Maroons totally collapsed in their final 39 games under McKinnon, going only 6–32–1. As Lucas's personal fortune dwindled, the faltering Maroons could not compete financially with the powerful St. Louis Browns (AA) and were replaced by Indianapolis after the 1886 season. Today's St. Louis Cardinals trace their lineage back not to the Maroons, but to the Browns, who joined the NL in 1892 after the AA folded.

Off the field, Dunlap did his best to live up to his status as baseball's highest paid player. Despite (or perhaps, to compensate for) his humble beginnings, he outfitted himself with an elegant, expensive wardrobe and comported himself as a gentleman of means. At a time when ballplayers were widely regarded as uncouth ruffians, Dunlap was polite and businesslike. But he was never one to back down from a fight. Although he stood just 5'8" and weighed 165 pounds, his compact muscularity made him more than a match for far bigger men. But more importantly, despite his lack of education, Dunlap taught himself to be a shrewd negotiator, unafraid to speak out and to stand up for himself against ownership. I suspect that his toughness and candor in salary matters lay behind the insinuations in the press later in his career that he was a difficult teammate.

Dunlap was never the same potent offensive force after 1885, hitting only .258/.321/.347 (104 OPS+) for the last six years of his career (1886–91) with 9.4 WAR in 1768 PA. Dunlap's performance on May 24, 1886, was a notable exception. On that day, he became the tenth MLB player to hit for the cycle, scoring three runs and driving in five in an 11–8 loss to the New York Giants.[6] But on August 6, with his team foundering and his finances crumbling, Henry Lucas sold Dunlap's expensive contract to the powerful Detroit Wolverines (NL) for the record price of $4700. There Dunlap joined a star-studded lineup, featuring future Hall of Famers 1B Dan Brouthers, 3B Deacon White, and OF Sam Thompson, as well as Ned Hanlon, Hardy Richardson, Jack Rowe, and Charlie Bennett. Dunlap received a then exorbitant two-year contract for $4500 annually and publicly pronounced himself glad to be free of the failing Maroons. While Detroit fans cheered his arrival, his comments sat poorly with the *Detroit Free Press*, which called him a "disorganizer" and "mischief maker."[7]

Although Detroit won the 1887 NL pennant and dominated their 15-game "World Series" exhibition match-up against the AA champion St. Louis Browns, 10 games to 5, Dunlap hit a disappointing .265/.327/.441 (108 OPS+) and got only 6 hits—5 singles and a triple—in 40 post-season AB. His strong defensive play was still important to his team's success, but his on-field performance no longer justified his salary. So, Detroit (which was also struggling financially) unloaded Dunlap's contract to the Pittsburgh Alleghenys (NL) for $5000 after the season. But Dunlap, foreshadowing the stance taken by Curt Flood 83 years later, would not approve the deal until Pittsburgh agreed to pay him a half-share of the sale price, in addition to his $4500 salary for

1888. "I am sick and tired of being sold without gaining anything by it.... The Detroit managers will have to do one of three things—give me half of the money secured for my release, allow me to go where I please, or fulfill the contract made with me for next year."[8] Dunlap's bold stance paid off, at least in the short term, but it cemented his reputation as a troublemaker.

Although Dunlap had not quite turned 29 when he joined Pittsburgh in 1888, his most productive years lay behind him. A leg injury, suffered in a collision with Detroit teammate Sam Thompson had robbed him of speed and range at 2B, although his hands were still sure and his arm was as strong as ever. The Alleghenys were a mediocre team, whose most notable players were either past their prime (Pud Galvin, Deacon White, and Dunlap) or had not yet reached it (Jake Beckley). Still, Dunlap's reliable defense justified his place in the lineup. Dunlap even managed the 1889 team to a 7–10 record in an interim appointment. However, when he hit only .172/.264/.219 in the first 17 games of the 1890 season, Pittsburgh unceremoniously released him. On his way out, Pittsburgh manager, Guy Hecker, pronounced Dunlap "certainly the worst man to get along with that I ever met."[9]

After his release in 1890, Dunlap, who had been active in the Players Brotherhood (an early baseball players' union), turned to the New York Giants of the newly formed Players League. However, he played in only one game before leaving the team in June. He caught on with the Washington Statesmen (AA) in 1891 but broke his leg sliding into 2B in his eighth game of the season. When Washington discontinued his salary in early June, Dunlap quit and filed an unsuccessful grievance claim.

Still, by the end of his MLB career, Dunlap had accumulated a $100,000 "fortune" and should have been well situated for the next phase of his life. Unfortunately, Dunlap's shrewdness on the baseball field and as a tough negotiator did not translate to the business world. After several real estate and stock investments went sour, Dunlap increasingly poured his money into his second passion—betting on the horses. Dunlap wound up losing his entire fortune within ten years after leaving baseball. Although he married in 1898 and left three surviving children, he died penniless and alone.

Why Was Fred Dunlap a Shooting Star?

Improbable as it was, Fred Dunlap's career year in 1884 did not come completely out of the blue. In 1880–83, he was regarded well enough to be offered the highest salary in baseball to jump to the UA, and he remained a remained a 4-WAR player for two years after he returned to the NL following the demise of the UA. However, His 7.9 WAR in 1884 stands far above the rest of his career (Figure 2).

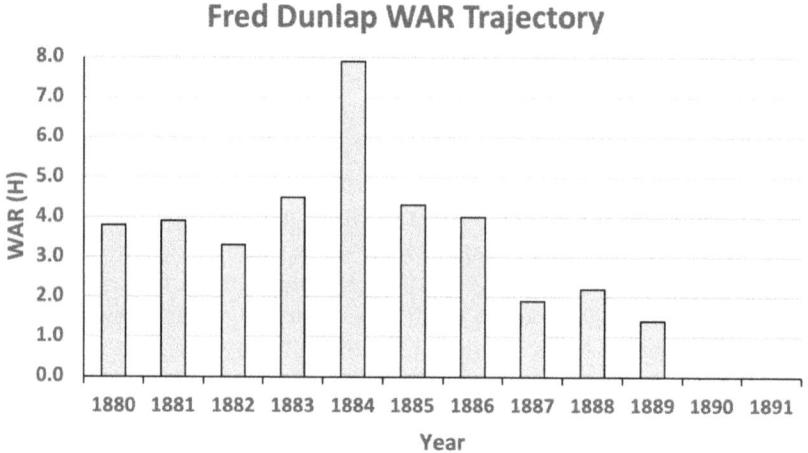

The elephant in the room is that Dunlap's 7.9 WAR season was achieved in an unstable league with subpar talent. Indeed, the UA's dearth of established major league talent, the instability of its franchises (several in small towns), and its lack of competitive balance has led Bill James to argue forcefully that the UA was not a true major league.[10] So was Dunlap's 1884 stat line for real, or was he just (as Bill James contended) a big fish in a very small pond and "never a legitimate star in a legitimate major league?"[11]

In defense of the UA, many of James's harsh critiques could be just as aptly applied to the more established leagues of the 1870s and 1880s.[12] In 1871–75, the National Association (NA) fielded an ever-changing array of teams, representing towns like Elizabeth, Fort Wayne, Hartford, Keokuk, Middletown, New Haven, Rockford, and Troy, and played an unbalanced schedule. In 1875, for example, the Boston Red Stockings went 71–8, while the Keokuk Westerns went 1–12 and folded in June. The American Association had franchises in Boston, Brooklyn, Cincinnati, Indianapolis, Milwaukee, Richmond, Toledo, and Washington that each lasted less than two years; the Richmond franchise lasted only twelve games. Even the venerable National League featured an ever-changing cast of franchises, including minor league cities like Buffalo, Hartford, Indianapolis, Louisville, Providence, Syracuse, Troy, and Worcester, and dipped to six

2. The King of Second Base

franchises in 1877–78 before stabilizing at eight teams. Why single out the UA?

But James's most telling critique of the UA is its subpar talent level. Tommy McCarthy, then a 20-year-old rookie, was the only Hall of Famer who ever played in the UA, and his 14.6 career WAR is the lowest for anyone voted into the HOF primarily for his stats as a player. James counts only fourteen "legitimate major leaguers" who played in the UA in their prime. The best were Tommy Bond, Jim McCormick, Jack Glasscock, and Dunlap. Glasscock and McCormick, who split their 1884 seasons between the NL and UA; each performed significantly better in the UA. James also points to the regression of the St. Louis Maroons from 94–19–1 in the UA in 1884 to 36–72–3 in the NL in 1885 with mostly the same roster as *prima facie* evidence that the UA was a minor league. However, more than twenty years after James's critique, MLB still recognizes the Union Association as a major league.

In truth, there is no bright red line distinguishing major from minor leagues. Although Dunlap's 7.9 WAR in 478 PA in the 1884 UA was undoubtedly inflated by its substandard level of competition, his dominance was remarkable even in a weak league. His WAR was 65 percent better than the UA's next best position player, his teammate Orator Shafer (4.8 WAR in 497 PA), who faced the same weak pitching as Dunlap. Indeed, Dunlap stood as far above his peers as Babe Ruth did in the early 1920s.

The depletion of major league talent in other historical settings has not led to a spate of seasons with > 10 WAR per 650 PA by average players. In 1914–15, the Federal League (FL) was only slightly more successful than the UA in attracting established major leaguers; its most recognizable names were either past their prime (Eddie Plank, Mordecai Brown, Joe Tinker, Johnny Evers) or rookies (Edd Roush). Yet only Benny Kauff (who also enjoyed considerable success with the NL's New York Giants in 1916–17) accrued > 7 WAR (7.8 in 2014), and he needed 669 PA to do it. During World War II (1942–45), the AL and NL rosters were famously depleted by the enlistment of young able-bodied players in the military, with the 1944 AL champion Browns even employing a one-armed OF named Pete Gray. Ted Williams (10.5 WAR in 1942) and Stan Musial (9.5 WAR in 1943 and 8.9 WAR in 1944) reigned supreme in three of those seasons, but of course also enjoyed multiple elite seasons when MLB was at full strength. The Braves' Tommy Holmes (see Chapter 8), who posted 8.4 WAR in 714 PA in 1945 but never > 5 WAR in any other season, comes closest to Dunlap's achievement, but he did not dominate the wartime NL like Dunlap dominated the UA in 1884.

The bottom line is that putting a slightly above average player in a talent-depleted league does *not* automatically produce a season like Dunlap's. No subsequent performances by players in talent-depleted leagues—not even those of Williams or Musial—match Fred Dunlap's 10.74 WAR per 650 PA in 1884. Dunlap may have been a big fish in a small pond, but he was a very big fish indeed!

Our statistical evidence says that Fred Dunlap was an excellent player, even before joining the UA. Furthermore, Dunlap was undeniably one of the best-known and most influential players of his time, even if his 1884 stats are inflated. As late as 1910, Al Spink called Dunlap (not future Hall of Famers Nap Lajoie or Bid McPhee) "the best 2B who ever lived."[13] While he did not play at a high enough level for long enough to be a legitimate candidate for a plaque in Cooperstown, the steep arc of his ascent to the pinnacle of his profession at age 25, the brevity of his stay at the top, and the rapidity of his subsequent professional and tragic personal decline made him a shooting star.

◆ 3 ◆

The Other Cy
James Bentley "Cy" Seymour (1905)

Before Babe Ruth, there was Cy Seymour, whom his biographer Bill Kirwin called "perhaps the greatest forgotten name in baseball."[1] Of course, Seymour was no Babe Ruth, but he stands high in the annals of players who began as pitchers and converted to another position in mid-career. Actually, Cy Seymour's career arc as a pitcher-turned-position player was not that rare, especially in baseball's early days. Hall of Famers John Montgomery Ward (SS), Bobby Wallace (SS), Jesse Burkett (OF), George Sisler (1B), and Sam Rice (OF), as well as Babe Ruth, all began their major league careers as pitchers. On a less lofty level, Rick Ankiel is a recent example of a pitcher who achieved some success after becoming an outfielder. However, Seymour, Ruth, and Negro Leaguer Bullet Rogan are the only players to have collected at least 50 W and hit at least 50 HR in currently recognized major leagues (although Martin Dihigo would also qualify if you include his five seasons in the Mexican League at ages 35–39).

James Bentley Seymore was born in Albany, NY, on December 9, 1872. He began his career with his hometown semipro team (Ridgeway) and then reportedly earned $1000 per month pitching for Plattsburgh in the Northern New York League in 1895. When he reached the major leagues at age 23 with the New York Giants in 1896, sportswriters gave him the nickname "Cy" (short for Cyclone—like the nickname of his better known contemporary, Cy Young) because of the speed and unpredictability of his fastball.[2] Seymour, who claimed to be related to the Duke of Somerset, preferred to be called James or J. Bentley.

In New York, the big lefty (6 feet and 200 pounds) was a good pitcher on a mediocre team. Seymour's peak seasons on the mound came in 1897–99, when he went 57–51 with a 3.32 ERA (114 ERA+) in 911.2 IP, a 1.501 WHIP (reflecting 8.1 hits plus 5.4 walks per 9 IP), 5.3 strikeouts per 9 IP and 11.5 WAR in 4050 BF (2.8 WAR per 1000 BF). His pitching stats are better than they appear at first glance, since 1893–99 was the highest scoring era in baseball history, largely because pitchers hadn't fully acclimated to the new 60'6" distance from the mound to home plate and because foul balls did not yet count as strikes.[3] Seymour led the NL in fewest hits per 9 IP (8.1) in 1897 and in strikeout rate in all three seasons, but (like Nolan Ryan in his early days) walks were his Achilles heel. He led the league in walks all three seasons. Despite his shaky control, Seymour's ERA was 14 percent better than the league average, and he enjoyed a reputation as one of the hardest throwers in the NL and one of the most difficult to hit. In that brief period, he was considered the near-equal of teammate (and eventual Hall of Famer) Amos Rusie. He was also a workhorse. When interviewed twenty years later about how Seymour pitched three games in two days against his Baltimore Orioles in 1897, John McGraw reminisced that Seymour deserved the nickname "Iron Man" as much as Joe McGinnity.[4]

SEYMOUR, N. Y. NAT'L

American Tobacco Trading Card portrait of Cy Seymour at bat during his second stint with the New York Giants (1906–10). He joined the Giants too late for their 1905 World Series Championship and left too soon for their string of NL pennants in 1911–13 (Benjamin K. Edwards Baseball Cards Collection, Library of Congress, Digital ID bbc 0814f, https://loc.gov/pictures/resource/bbc.0814f/).

3. The Other Cy

The 1899 season, Seymour's best as a pitcher, began inauspiciously. He held out for the first month when the Giants refused to raise his salary after he had posted 356.2 IP and 3.0 WAR in 1898. But when he finally got a $500 raise and returned to action on May 11, he responded by posting another 268.1 IP (in only five months) and a career high 4.6 pitching WAR and led the NL in walks and in strikeouts per 9 IP. One can only imagine what his pitch counts must have been. Seymour would pay the price the following season.

Seymour's 1900 season was an unmitigated disaster. He appeared in only thirteen games, made only seven starts, and won only two, posting a 6.96 ERA in 53.0 IP. Giants owner Andrew Freedman questioned his fitness and sent him to the minors (Worcester) in June.[5] Worcester management concurred and returned him to New York. I strongly suspect that his "unfitness" reflected a sore arm from his excessive workload in previous seasons. He was finally sent on loan to Charles Comiskey's Chicago White Sox (who were still a minor league team) and pitched a few games there while remaining on the Giants' reserve list.

In 1901, at age 28, Cy Seymour jumped to the Baltimore Orioles (another mediocre team) in the newly constituted American League and re-invented himself as an outfielder. Seymour had appeared in 53 games as an outfielder in his five years with the Giants and had hit a weak .280/.301/.350 (82 OPS+) in 698 PA during those seasons, posting a composite 1.2 WAR. He hit a respectable but modest .303/.337/.373 (93 OPS+) with 1.6 WAR in 586 PA during his first season, but was released in July 1902 after hitting only .268/.317/.386 (90 OPS+) in 310 PA. However, he immediately improved to .340/.378/.414 (135 OPS+) when he returned to the NL with the Cincinnati Reds. He became a fixture in CF with the Reds for the next four seasons. The Reds were his first good team, winning more games than they lost each year, but never seriously contending for the NL pennant. In 1903–04, Seymour hit a combined .328/.367/.459 (134 OPS+) in 1184 PA and averaged 6 HR, 65 RBI, 78 R and 18 SB per season. His 8.4 WAR (which included 0.5 dWAR) over two seasons pegs him as a well above average hitter and an adequate defender in CF.

But nothing in his nine major league seasons foretold his superstar performance in 1905, one of the best single season performances of the early "deadball era" (Table 3).

With leaguewide scoring trending steadily downward, Seymour led the NL in AVG, SLG, OPS+, TB, hits, doubles, and triples and fell a single HR shy of the NL Triple Crown. Not only did Seymour lead the NL in all these categories in 1905, his totals represented the highest single season marks during the seven years spanning the 1903–1909 seasons.[6] Honus Wagner won six of the seven NL batting titles during this period; Cy Seymour in 1905 was the only exception.[7] Seymour excelled consistently in every month of the 1905 season, hitting .347/.418/.510 in April, .317/.367/.446 in May, .390/.437/.632 in June, .365/389/.481 in July, .385/.472/.517 in August, and a scorching .426/.481/.695 in September (when he hit 4 of his 8 HR and stole 10 of his 21 bases).[8] However, the Reds finished fifth in the NL in 1905 at 79–74–2, their worst finish since 1902.

Table 3: Selected Stats for Cy Seymour's Peak and Runner-Up Seasons and His Career*

Season	Age	PA	AVG	OBP	SLG	OPS+	TB	H	2B	3B	RBI	WAR (H)
Peak 1905	32	646	**0.377**	0.429	**0.559**	181	325	219	40	21	121	8.0
per 650 PA							327	220	40	21	122	8.0
Runner-Up 1904	31	577	0.313	0.352	0.439	134	233	166	26	13	58	4.5
per 650 PA							262	187	29	15	65	5.1
Career (1896–1911)		6227	0.303	0.347	0.405	118	2301	1724	229	96	799	31.6
per 650 PA							240	180	24	10	83	3.3

*League leading totals are shown in boldface type.

In the first half of 1906, Seymour's newfound magic seemed to vanish as quickly as it had arrived a year earlier. In his first 79 games, he hit only .257/.317/.332 (98 OPS+) in 340 PA, good for only 1.4 WAR. After Seymour, now 33 years old, went 0-for-4 in a 2–1 loss to the defending World Series champion Giants on July 12, the struggling fifth place Reds sold his contract to the Giants for $12,000. Reunited with his old team and manager John McGraw, Seymour rebounded nicely to hit .320/.365/.431 (145 OPS+) with 2.4 WAR for the remainder of the season. The installation of Seymour in CF allowed the Giants to make Roger Bresnahan (who had been splitting time between catcher and CF) their full time catcher and helped the Giants go 49–29 in their remaining games and finish 96–56–1. However that was not nearly enough to catch the Cubs who finished with a historic 116–36–3 record before getting upset by the "hitless wonder" White Sox in the World Series.

Seymour gently declined in 1907–09 but remained a solid regular, hitting a composite .286/.335/.373 (119 OPS+) with 7.6 WAR in 1496 PA (2.9 WAR per 650 PA). His offensive production remained well above average, but his defense declined appreciably (-0.7 dWAR). Indeed, Seymour is often remembered as the goat of the October 8, 1908, playoff game between the Giants and Cubs, which had been necessitated by the infamous "Merkel's boner" tie game just over two weeks earlier.[9]

In that game, Seymour misplayed a second-inning Joe Tinker flyball and allowed three unearned runs to score, leading to a 4–2 defeat for Christy Mathewson and costing the Giants the NL pennant.

Seymour finally ran out of gas in 1910. He hit only .265/.324/.334 (91 OPS+) with -0.3 WAR in 322 PA in 1910 and was sold to Baltimore (Easter League) on August 24. He resurfaced at age 40 in 1913, playing in 39 games for the mediocre Boston Braves, but was released on July 19 after hitting only .178/.259/.205 (34 OPS+) in 84 PA.

After pitching for losing teams in New York in 1896–1900, Seymour played for some fairly good teams in Cincinnati and New York in his "second career" as a CF. However, he was perversely unlucky in never playing on a pennant winner. His second tour of duty in New York began one year after the Giants' 1905 championship and ended one year before the Giants embarked on a run of three consecutive pennants in 1911–13. His brief stay in Boston came one year before the "Miracle Braves" stunned the baseball world by storming back from last place to win the 1914 NL pennant and stunning the powerful Philadelphia Athletics in the World Series.

Cy Seymour did not live to enjoy a long retirement. He tried unsuccessfully to catch on in the minor leagues as a player or manager for years.[10] When he finally signed to play with Newark of the International League in 1918 at age 45, he lasted only thirteen games. World War I and the influenza pandemic had pushed baseball to the back burner that year. Seymour was by then a heavy drinker and was too old and not fit enough for military service. He earned a marginal living working in the New York shipyards and contracted tuberculosis. He died on September 20, 1919, at age 46.

Why Was Cy Seymour a Shooting Star?

Like Fred Dunlap and many others profiled in this book, Cy Seymour had a good career, highlighted by a single great season (Figure 3). He was a 4-WAR pitcher in 1897–1899 and a 4-WAR position player in 1903–04 and 1906–07, but he was an 8-WAR player only in 1905.

While I agree with his biographer Bill Kirwin that Seymour has gotten less credit than he deserves, I would not consider him a serious candidate for the Hall of Fame.[11] It is true that Seymour's raw stats might appear less impressive than they should, because he pitched in a high-scoring era and hit in a low-scoring era. However, his ERA+, OPS+ and WAR stats are adjusted for scoring environment. In fact, Cy Seymour was only a true star for one season (1905) and was never

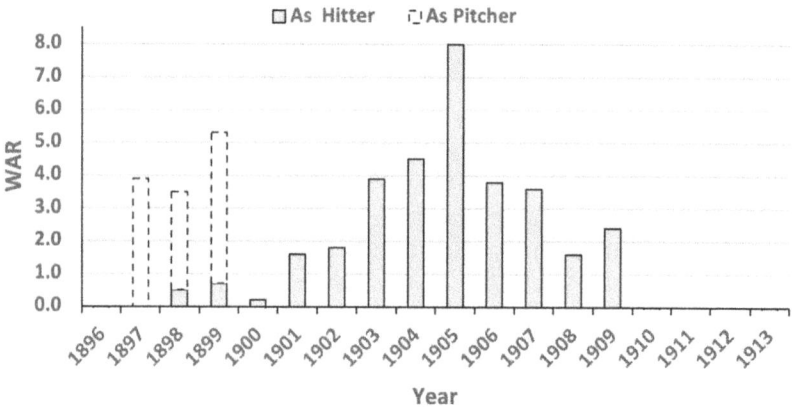

a "difference maker" for any winning team. He scores only 40.2 on my career value index metric (CVI), which combines hitting and pitching value and awards extra credit for seasons with pro-rated WAR > 5.0.[12] This places him outside the top 500 players and in the neighborhood of Rico Petrocelli (40.5, Chapter 18). His CVI does rank higher than six Hall of Famers who were elected by the BBWAA—Lou Brock, Bruce Sutter, Catfish Hunter, Rabbit Maranville, Rollie Fingers, and Pie Traynor—as well as twenty-two non–Negro Leaguers who were elected by various iterations of the Veterans Committee (VC). But the vast majority of players with CVI < 55 are NOT in the Hall of Fame.

While players who excel both as pitchers and hitters don't come along every day, Seymour is not unique in this regard. As noted in the opening paragraph, there is a substantial list of pitchers who hurt their arms and reinvented themselves as position players and a shorter list of so-so position players (including Hall of Famer Bob Lemon) who reinvented themselves as pitchers. What is truly rare—at least outside of the Negro Leagues—is the Shohei Ohtani type of two-way player who excels *both* as a hitter and pitcher simultaneously. Looking back a decade before Cy Seymour, one finds an example, pitcher-outfielder Bob Caruthers, who amassed 218 wins and 44.7 WAR as a pitcher and 14.1 WAR as an outfielder in 1884–92. His 50.7 CVI makes him a more credible HOF candidate than Seymour. However, the fact that Seymour's career was not worthy of the HOF ought not stop us from honoring his remarkable 1905 season, when he played like a Hall of Famer.

◆ 4 ◆

The Reluctant Star
George Robert Stone (1906)

Although George Stone never threw a major league pitch, he was in many other ways the AL counterpart of Cy Seymour. While Seymour's 1905 NL batting title interrupted what would have been a streak of seven consecutive batting titles by future Hall of Famer Honus Wagner, Stone's 1906 AL batting title interrupted a run of 19 consecutive seasons (1901–19) in which the AL batting title was monopolized by four future Hall of Famers, Ty Cobb (11), Nap Lajoie (5), Tris Speaker (1), and Elmer Flick (1).[1] Like Seymour, Stone never played for a pennant winner. Yet George Stone, whose nickname was "Silent George," was a reticent and reluctant star, whose first love was playing the violin and who, even at the height of his career, was eager to leave baseball and start a career in business.[2]

George Robert Stone, one of baseball's earliest Jewish stars, was born in Lost Nation, IA, on September 3, 1876 (according to Baseball-Reference .com) or 1877 (according to his obituary in the *Clinton Herald*).[3] I have used the 1877 date for this chapter. Stone first began take baseball very seriously when he got five hits, including 3 HR, in a local amateur game as a 16-year-old clerk in Coleridge, NE. The speedy 5'9" 175 pound lefty, who hit out of a deep crouch, first played professionally in 1902 for Peoria and Omaha in the Western Association and led the league with 198 hits. He made his major league debut at age 25 with the Boston Americans (later to become the Red Sox) in 1903, but struck out in his only two PA before getting sent to the Milwaukee Brewers of the (minor league) American Association. He remained with the Brewers in 1904 and put together a terrific season, hitting .404 with 256 hits, which set a record that stood until the league folded in 1997. On August 9, the Brewers tried to trade him to Washington in a three-way deal for a sum the *Washington Post* called "as large as was ever paid for a minor league ball player."⁴ The Post even called him "the premier batter of the world." But when the deal fell through and Stone's contract was re-acquired by Boston, Stone refused to report and sat out the rest of the season.

Boston, whose manager Jimmy Collins did not like Stone's unusual crouching batting stance, traded him to the last place St. Louis Browns for fading future Hall of Famer Jesse Burkett the following December.⁵ Stone was an immediate hit for the Browns, batting .296/.347/.410 (146 OPS+) with 5.0 WAR in 696 PA and leading the AL with 187 hits and 26 SB. Although he posted a negative dWAR (-1.0), he was (according to a contemporary writer) a "reliable fielder" who "covers a great deal of territory."⁶

Stone truly blossomed in 1906, leading the AL in AVG, OBP, SLG, and OPS+ and finishing third behind Nap Lajoie and Terry Turner with 8.8 WAR (Table 4). His 208 hits included 25 doubles, 20 triples, and 6 HR, enough to lead the AL with 291 total bases. His 8.0 oWAR led the AL.

Stone started hot, hitting .468/.519/.638 in 53 PA in April, and stayed hot all year.⁷ His best month was July, when he hit .379/.433/.568 in 108 PA. August (.295/.362/.381) was the only month in which he didn't hit at least .340. The lowly Browns benefited from Stone's success, finishing 76–73–5—a 23 game improvement over 1905 and good for fifth place. But even at the end of this banner season, Stone commented in an interview with *The Sporting Life*, "I realize

This American Tobacco Trading Card portrait showing St. Louis Browns speedster George Stone running the bases utterly fails to capture how dynamic he was in his heyday (1905–08). At least you can see what he looked like (Benjamin K. Edwards Baseball Cards Collection, Library of Congress, Digital ID bbc 1728f, https://www.loc.gov/pictures/resource/bbc.1728f/?co=bbc).

4. The Reluctant Star

that each year I continue in baseball sets me just that much further back in a business career.... How many promising men have grown old in baseball and found their usefulness on the diamond gone and their ability to earn a respectable salary lessened through lack of experience in the business world. No, in a few years, you will see me hustling for myself in my Nebraska home, trying to work up a business that by and by will work for me."[8] His words were both wise and prophetic.

Table 4: Selected Stats for George Stone's Peak and Runner-Up Seasons and His Career*

Season	Age	PA	AVG	OBP	SLG	OPS+	TB	H	SB	R	WAR (H)
Peak 1906	28	662	**0.358**	0.417	0.501	193	**291**	208	35	91	8.8
per 650 PA							286	204	34	89	8.6
Runner-Up 1907	29	672	0.320	0.387	0.399	132	238	191	23	77	5.4
per 650 PA							230	185	22	74	5.2
Career (1903–1910)		3677	0.301	0.360	0.396	144	1295	984	132	426	26.2
per 650 PA							229	174	23	75	4.6

*League leading totals are shown in boldface type.

Determined to capitalize on his 1906 success and to make the most of whatever time he had in baseball, Stone asked for a $5000 salary—$1500 more than the $3500 Browns owner Robert Hedges had offered—and refused to report until Hedges met his demands. Stone had a good season but fell short of his 1906 performance. His slash line dropped to .320/.387/.399 (152 OPS+) in 672 PA and his WAR fell from 8.8 to 5.4. His dWAR, which was an acceptable -0.2 in 1906, fell to -0.7 in 1907. Although there were no formal All-Star teams in 1907, his WAR and OPS+ ranked fourth behind Ty Cobb, Sam Crawford, and Elmer Flick among AL outfielders.[9] Nevertheless, the Browns regressed to 68–83–3 and finished sixth.

Stone's performance declined further in 1908, when he hit .281/.345/.369 (132 OPS+) with 4.1 WAR in 662 PA. He was still well above average, but St. Louis ownership (who were paying him top dollar) and fans (who expected a .300 hitter) were becoming disenchanted. There were unsubstantiated rumors that Stone had contracted malaria.[10] Still, the Browns improved to 83–69–3 and finished fourth. This would be their high-water mark during Stone's tenure with the team.

But in 1909–10, there could be no denying that Stone was not the player he once was. The turning point was a serious ankle injury in 1909, which sidelined him from May 11 through June 19 and again from

September 10 through October 2.[11] This slowed him down, both on the bases (where he could no longer beat out bunts and infield hits) and in the field (where he could no longer reach balls he used to catch easily).[12] He hurt his throwing arm trying to compensate. The injury limited him to 83 games and 350 PA, although he remained an above average hitter when he was able to play. He hit .287/.340/.339 (121 OPS+), but his 1.6 WAR suffered from his loss of fielding range (-0.5 dWAR). Although he recovered to play 152 games in 1910, he was only a shell of his former self, especially in the field. He hit only .256/.315/.329 (108 OPS+) with 1.3 WAR, reflecting a horrendous -1.5 dWAR. With the decline of their one-time star, the Browns stumbled to 61–84–4 in 1909 and a dismal 47–107–4 in 1910. Although Stone played briefly for the minor league Milwaukee Brewers in 1911, he was washed up as a major leaguer at age 33.

Unlike Dunlap and Seymour, George Stone prospered after he left baseball, entering the banking industry in Coleridge, NE, and enjoying his violin in his spare time. He even owned a minor league baseball team briefly. He and his wife had a son, who became a doctor. George Stone retired to Clinton, IA, in 1940 and died there of a heart attack at age 67 in 1945.

Why Was George Stone a Shooting Star?

George Stone arrived late to the major leagues and shot quickly to the top. But his star burned out just as quickly, and he was soon forgotten. He was clearly more than a one-year wonder, since he enjoyed 5.0-WAR seasons on either side of his peak season (Figure 4). But his 8.8 WAR performance in 1906 stood far above the rest and comprised 34 percent of his 26.2 career WAR. His seven-year career was too short to qualify for HOF consideration.

One common thread in the baseball careers of the three players profiled so far is the impact of the oppressive system in which they worked. Each did battle with ownership at some point in his career—holding out for better pay, objecting to having no say in where they were traded, protesting the lack of compensation for workplace injuries. Injuries prematurely ended the careers of Dunlap and Stone, as well as the pitching career of Cy Seymour before he re-emerged as a CF, and each eventually found himself on the scrap heap with no pension and without a second thought from the teams they served. Ultimately, the team owners held all the cards. The fact that Stone was a far more successful man and led a longer and happier life than Dunlap or Seymour can be

directly attributed to the fact that he never pinned his aspirations in life to his success as a ballplayer. Modern ballplayers are fortunate to work in a far more humane system and owe a debt of gratitude to their predecessors who made this possible.

◈ 5 ◈

California Dutch
Hubert Benjamin "Dutch" Leonard (1914)

Emerging at last from the era of iron-man pitchers, who routinely compiled 350+ IP, completed almost every start, and sometimes even pitched two games in one day, we come now to our first shooting star pitcher, Hubert "Dutch" Leonard. This stocky Red Sox lefty of the deadball era is not to be confused with right-handed knuckleballer Emil "Dutch" Leonard, who posted 51.7 pitching WAR in 1933–53. (Neither pitcher had any Dutch ancestry.) Our man Hubert was born in Ohio on April 16, 1892, and grew up in Fresno, CA. In fact, he attended the same high school (Fresno HS) that produced Hall of Famer Tom Seaver and major league aces Dick Ellsworth (Chapter 15) and Jim Maloney a half century later.[1] In any case, Leonard pitched like a Hall of Famer at the tender age of 22 in 1914 but was never again more than a solid mid-rotation starter. He was his own worst enemy.

Dutch Leonard's extraordinary 1914 season followed a promising but not especially memorable rookie season in which he went-14–17 with a 2.39 ERA (121 ERA+) and posted 4.3 WAR in 1079 BF at age 21. However, this solid performance gave little hint of what was to come in 1914, when he posted a whopping 9.6 WAR in only 842 BF (Table 5).

On a prorated basis, this translates to 11.4 WAR per 1000 BF, the second best of any starting pitcher in this book (behind Dwight Gooden's 11.5 in 1985) and comparable to the best seasons of Greg Maddux (1995) and Roger Clemens (1997). Pedro Martinez (2000 and 1999), Walter Johnson (1913), and Gooden are the only starters to have posted ≥ 11.5 WAR per 1000 BF in a season. Leonard's 0.96 ERA in 1914 was the best single-season ERA for any qualifying 20th (or 21st) century pitcher and trails only Tim Keefe (who posted a 0.86 ERA in only 105 IP in 1880) on the all-time leaderboard. His 279 ERA+ indicates that his minuscule ERA was not a mere statistical artifact of pitching in the deadball era; he was almost three times stingier than the league-average (2.73 ERA) AL pitcher.² His 0.886 WHIP, while less extraordinary than his ERA, was also well under the league average (1.244).

Table 5: Selected Stats for Dutch Leonard's Peak and Runner-Up Seasons and His Career*

Season	Age	BF	ERA	WHIP	ERA+	W-L	SO	BB	SHO	WAR (P)
Peak 1914	22	842	**0.96**	**0.886**	**279**	19–5	176	60	7	9.6
per 1000 BF							209	71	8	11.4
Runner-Up 1917	25	1168	2.17	1.114	119	16–17	144	71	4	5.2
per 1000 BF							123	61	3	4.5
Career (1913–25)		8928	2.76	1.225	115	139–114	1160	664	33	37.4
per 1000 BF							130	74	4	4.2

*League leading totals are shown in boldface type.

Hubert "Dutch" Leonard enjoying a quiet moment alone on a chilly, gray day at Fenway Park. During his six years (1913–18) with the Red Sox, Leonard was a stalwart in rotations featuring Babe Ruth, Smoky Joe Wood, Carl Mays, Ernie Shore, and Rube Foster, which helped win three World Series (Harris & Ewing Collection, Library of Congress, Digital ID hec 03129, http://hdl.loc.gov/loc.pnp/hec.03129).

Leonard was a model of consistency. In his 25 starts in 2014, 17 of which he completed, he yielded 4 ER once (8 IP with no decision), 3 ER once (1 IP with no decision—his worst start of the year), 2 ER three times (1–2), 1 ER 11 times (7–3–1), and no ER nine times (7–0–2), including a 13-inning tie versus Philadelphia's Bob Shawkey.[3] To apply an anachronistic twenty-first-century construct, 21 of his 25 starts were quality starts (≥ 6 IP, ≤ 3 ER). Except for the aforementioned 4-ER-in-8-IP outing, when he gave up 11 hits, he did not yield < 3 or > 8 hits in any start. He was even better in his 11 relief appearances, yielding no ER and only five hits in 26 IP and posting four wins (including the last eight innings of a 16-inning game against Detroit on July 20) and three saves (including Babe Ruth's first major league win on July 11). His 7.1 SO per 9 IP led the AL. His season might have been even more impressive had he not missed the entire month of September with a wrist injury. Although Boston could not keep pace with Connie Mack's Philadelphia Athletics, then in the final year of their AL dynasty, Leonard, who finished 16th in the MVP voting, did his part. Unfortunately, 1914 was as good as it got for Dutch Leonard.

In 1915, Leonard reported to spring camp out of shape and made only three starts before July, but then came on strong to finish 15–7 with a 2.68 ERA (119 ERA+) and a 1.075 WHIP in 183.1 IP.[4] His strikeout rate fell to 5.7 per 9 IP but was still good enough to lead the AL. His 3.8 WAR was very respectable, given that it was accomplished in only 705 BF, but his pro-rated 5.4 WAR per 1000 BF was still less than half as good as it had been the previous year. The good news was that the Red Sox, taking full advantage of the Athletics' collapse to last place after Connie Mack's financially motivated sell-off of his star players after their shocking sweep at the hands of the "Miracle Braves" in the 1914 World Series, began their own four-year dynasty by winning the AL pennant and beat the Phillies in the 1915 World Series in five games. Leonard was only the fourth-ranked starter on that team by WAR (behind Ernie Shore, Smoky Joe Wood, and Rube Foster, but ahead of Babe Ruth). However, he contributed a 2–1 complete-game victory over Pete Alexander in Game 3 to put the Sox ahead of the Phillies for good.[5]

Leonard finally put together full seasons for the Red Sox in 1916–17 and became a solid but unspectacular mid-rotation starter, compiling a combined 34–29 record in 568.1 IP with a 2.26 ERA (118 ERA+), 1.124 WHIP, 4.6 SO per 9 IP, and 10.3 WAR (4.6 WAR per 1000 BF). He even pitched his first no hitter against the Browns on August 30, 1916.[6] He outpitched Rube Marquard in Game 4 of the 1916 World Series to give the Red Sox a 3–1 lead over the Brooklyn Robins en route to a second consecutive World Series championship.[7] However, the Red Sox finished second to the White Sox in 1917. Although the Red Sox would return to win another AL pennant and World Series in 1918, Leonard was mediocre that year (8–6, 99 ERA+, more BB than SO), although he did pitch his second no-hitter. Like many MLB ballplayers in that war year, his season was cut short when he took a defense-related job at the end of July in lieu of military service. He was unable to participate in the World Series. By this time, Leonard had developed a spitball, on which he relied increasingly, as his fastball and curveball were losing their bite. (Leonard was in fact one of the 17 pitchers who were allowed to continue throwing the spitball under a grandfather clause when the spitball was outlawed in 1920.[8]) Spitballs notwithstanding, Leonard was never again a top-tier pitcher. In his last five years in Detroit, he was thoroughly mediocre, going 49–50 with a 3.79 ERA (102 ERA+), 1.372 WHIP, 4.2 SO per 9 IP, and 9.4 WAR (2.7 per 1000 BF).

So, what stopped Hubert "Dutch" Leonard from fulfilling the promise of his age 22 superstar season? There is no doubt that Leonard had extraordinary ability, but it requires a combination of hard work, an even temperament, and good fortune to parlay short-term brilliance into a Hall of Fame career. Leonard had none of these. He was a widely disliked player, who feuded constantly with management and his peers. Speaking on behalf of umpires around the league, Hall of Fame umpire Billy Evans called him "gutless" and someone who "whined on every pitch called against him."[9] Ty Cobb called him a dirty player who deserved to get hurt. This was pretty rich coming from Cobb, who made a practice of intimidating opponents by playing (to put it euphemistically) with reckless disregard for their safety and welfare. But in this case, Cobb, who claimed that Leonard was one of only two players he ever intentionally spiked, was in the majority.

We can look to David Jones's thorough and well-researched SABR biography for insight into the man behind the stats.[10] I will summarize only the highlights below. Unlike most of his peers, Leonard was an educated man from a large, cultured, middle-class California family, including an older brother Cuyler, who was an accomplished musician and composer. Hubert (the youngest of six) focused on baseball, first attracting notice while taking classes and pitching at St. Mary's College. However, he had a strong stubborn streak and a contrarian personality that frequently erupted into confrontations that undermined and eventually ended his career. For example:

- As a 20-year-old minor leaguer at Worcester in 1912, Leonard walked out on his team, claiming that it was a "rotten" league and that he got no support. He was initially suspended for

insubordination, but Boston management relented when he refused to return and re-assigned him to their Denver affiliate.
- Coming off his breakout 1914 season, he reported to spring training disgruntled with his contract and out of shape and started only three of the Red Sox's first 36 games. He then created a media firestorm by publicly blasting team president Joseph Lannin and manager Bill Carrigan. He finally rejoined the Boston rotation on July 7, their 69th game. Although he salvaged his season with a strong second half, his lack of discipline and commitment had cost him the opportunity to build on his success and establish himself as an ace.
- When cash-strapped Red Sox owner Harry Frasee traded him to the Yankees along with Ernie Shore and Duffy Lewis for four lesser players and cash following a down season, Leonard refused to report to his new team and eventually forced a trade to Detroit. He did not start a game until the end of May.
- After three solid but unspectacular seasons in 1919–21 in Detroit, Leonard held out for a higher salary in 1922 and jumped to an independent league in California when Detroit owner Frank Navin refused to meet his demands. He was suspended for two years. When he was finally reinstated in 1924 at age 32, he was a shell of his former self.

Unfortunately, Leonard's return to Detroit meant a reunion with player-manager Ty Cobb, with whom he shared a longstanding intense mutual antipathy.[11] Cobb repeatedly overused him and berated him in front of his teammates when he was ineffective. Matters came to a head on July 14, 1925, when Cobb sadistically left Leonard in the game for nine full innings to absorb a 12-run, 20-hit drubbing by the Athletics, even laughing when A's manager Connie Mack pleaded with Cobb to remove Leonard before he damaged his arm. A week later, Leonard was waived, and Cobb trashed him to ensure that no MLB team would claim him. He was eventually traded to Vernon (PCL) but refused to report.

Leonard of course was furious—not just at Cobb, but at Cleveland manager Tris Speaker, his ex-teammate in Boston, who declined to claim him from the waiver wire—and bent on revenge. For most players, revenge would have meant getting himself into excellent shape, finding a new team that would give him an opportunity to prove himself, and sticking it to his old team by defeating them on the field. Not so for Leonard. Instead, early in the 1926 season, Leonard filed an allegation to the Commissioner's Office that Cobb and Speaker, along with Smoky Joe Wood (the one-time flame-throwing pitcher who was finishing out his career as an outfielder with Cleveland), had conspired to fix the outcome of a game played on September 24, 1919—the day after the White Sox (soon to become the infamous Black Sox) clinched the pennant—that would help the Tigers to beat out the Yankees for third place.[12] Cobb, Speaker, Wood, and Leonard allegedly placed bets with professional bookmakers on the outcome of that game; Leonard (who did not pitch that day) claimed that he personally won $130. Although Leonard documented his accusation with letters signed by Cobb and Wood, the evidence was ambiguous as to whether any bets were actually placed and by whom, and the trail was cold. When Leonard refused to testify in person, Commissioner Landis, who was not eager to rekindle the public memory of the Black Sox scandal more than six years after the fact, did not pursue the matter further. However, Leonard's allegations were credible enough to bring about the quiet dismissal of Cobb and Speaker from their managerial positions after the 1926 season. If similar allegations had come from a more respected source in a timelier fashion, Cobb and Speaker might have met a harsher fate. In any case, by making these allegations and admitting his own complicity, Leonard had burnt his last bridge. His MLB career was now over.

Leonard landed on his feet, retiring with his wife (a former vaudeville dancer who eventually divorced him) to his lucrative vineyard in central California and enjoying his lavish home and swimming pool, where he entertained ex-baseball players and other celebrities, and his extensive record collection.[13] Like his nemesis Ty Cobb, with whom he had more in common than either would have cared to admit, Leonard was a shrewd businessman; he left a $2.2 million-dollar estate when he died of a stroke in 1952 at age 60.

Why Was Dutch Leonard a Shooting Star?

Leonard was obviously a gifted pitcher, who had five other solid 4-to-5 WAR seasons and posted 37.4 WAR (P) over the course of his 11-year career. But he never again came even close to his dominant performance in 1914 (Figure 5). There was nothing dicey about his 9.6 WAR performance that year. The AL was the strongest of the three major leagues in 1914, and Fenway Park played as a neutral park.[14] The deadball environment in which he pitched in 1914 was similar to that in his other prime years (1913–17).

Although Leonard was also victimized by MLB and its highhanded and oppressive reserve clause, it is hard to muster much sympathy for him. The setbacks he suffered were largely the product of his own

selfishness and stubbornness. He repeatedly sabotaged his own career. His nephew described him perfectly to baseball researcher Joseph Simenic, who asked why Leonard refused to go on the record regarding his allegations against Cobb and Speaker: "When he was not in the mood, he was not about to do anything, regardless of what it might be."[15] He is destined to be remembered as one of baseball's early shooting stars, who had a fine career—but one that fell short of his early promise.

◈ 6 ◈

Windfall
William Wilcy Moore (1927)

The 110-win 1927 New York Yankees are regarded by many as the greatest team of all time. Their lineup, which was nicknamed "murderers row," included Hall of Famers Babe Ruth, Lou Gehrig, Tony Lazzeri, and Earle Combs, as well as slugging LF Bob Muesel. Their pitching staff was fronted by Hall of Famers Waite Hoyt and Herb Pennock, as well as 18-game winner Urban Shocker. So, it hardly seems fair that the Yankees, a team already blessed with an abundance of riches, should be the beneficiaries of the colossal windfall by which a 30-year old Oklahoma farmer and journeyman minor league right-handed pitcher whom no one wanted simply fell into their laps and emerged as one of MLB's first star relief pitchers. Yet that is how Wilcy Moore became a Yankee.

William Wilcy Moore was born on May 20, 1897, in Bonita, TX. Shortly after he was born, his parents moved their large family (seven sons and two daughters) to Hollis, OK, where they had filed a homestead claim on 160 acres of farmland on which they could grow cotton.[1] When Wilcy was old enough, he began to play semi-pro baseball for a local team when he wasn't needed on the farm. He did not begin his professional career until 1922, when he was 25 years old. He pitched well enough in the low minor leagues but was not even remotely regarded as a major league prospect.

The turning point of his career came in 1925 when he was pitching for the Greenville Spinners in the Class B South Atlantic (Sally) League and a line drive fractured his right arm.[2] When he recovered, he found that it hurt to throw overhand. However, he discovered that he could comfortably throw sidearm and that his new sidearm delivery caused his pitches to break sharply downward. Thus, the run-of-the-mill over hand pitcher Wilcy Moore, transformed into side-arming "Sinker Cy." In 1926, he completely dominated Sally League hitters, going 30–4 with a 2.86 ERA in 305 IP. When Yankee GM Ed Barrow saw an article about Moore in the Sporting News, he sent scout Bob Gilks down to Greensville to take a look. Gilks was unimpressed and dismissed Moore as too old to start a major league career. Moore himself had planned to retire to his farm after the season. But essentially on a whim, Barrow talked Moore out of retirement and signed him. Yankees manager Miller Huggins was also skeptical at first, but Moore pitched well enough in spring training to make the team. What followed was one of the most surprising performances in the history of the Yankees (Table 6). In 50 games, 12 as a starter and 38 as a reliever, Moore's 6.6 WAR (P) led the Yankees and ranked third in the AL, behind White Sox aces Tommy Thomas (8.3) and Ted Lyons (7.3).

Table 6. Selected Stats for Wilcy Moore's Peak and Runner-Up Seasons and His Career*

Season	Age	BF	ERA	WHIP	ERA+	W-L	SV	SO	CG	SHO	WAR (P)
Peak 1927	30	870	2.28	1.146	**171**	19–7	**13**	75	6	1	6.6
per 1000 BF								86	7	1	7.6
Runner-Up 1931	34	798	3.88	1.361	111	11–13	**8**	37	8	1	4.3
per 1000 BF								46	10	1	5.4
Career (1927–33)		3025	3.70	1.395	110	51–44	37	204	14	2	9.3
per 1000 BF								67	5	1	3.1

*League-leading totals are shown in boldface type.

In his twelve spot starts, Moore went 6–4 with a 2.61 ERA and a 1.237 WHIP in 93.0 IP.[3] Ten of these were quality starts, including six complete games, one of which was shutout. He pitched at least six innings in all but one start—2 ER in 5.0 IP against Washington on July 14.[4] Only once did he yield more than 3 ER—allowing 5 ER in 8.1 IP in a win over Detroit on September 22. Moore was even better in his 38 relief appearances, totaling 120.1 IP (3.17 IP per appearance), going 13–3 with 13 saves, a 1.80 ERA, and a 1.089 WHIP.[5] After getting hit hard in his first appearance on April 14, giving up 4 ER in 4.2 IP in a 9–9 tie with Philadelphia, he did not yield another ER in his next eight appearances.[6] Altogether, he held the opposition to no ER in 28 of his 38 relief appearances, which ranged from 0.2 to 7.1 IP. He yielded 5 ER once (4.1 IP in a 10–8 win at Detroit on July 8) and 4 ER twice (in the April 14 game and in 4.0 IP of a 12–11 win over Chicago on June 8). He yielded 2 ER four times (including in a 9–8 win over Philadelphia where he relieved Urban Shocker with a 9–3 lead in the ninth inning and gave up run-scoring singles to the only two batters he faced).

6. Windfall

Moore also contributed significantly to the Yankees four-game sweep of the Pirates in the 1927 World Series with an 0.84 ERA and 1.219 WHIP in 10.2 IP.[7] He picked up a 1.2 IP scoreless save in relief of Waite Hoyt in the Yankees' 5–4 win in Game 1, and wrapped up the sweep with a complete game 4–3 win in Game 4 (where two of the three Pittsburgh runs were unearned). Moore was not the MVP of this Yankee powerhouse and the Cy Young award did not yet exist, but baseball writers voted him the AL's top pitcher of 1927.[8]

Moore, who batted only .102 for his career, was also famous for his ineptitude as a hitter, although he was not as bad as Hank Aguirre 35 years later (Chapter 14). When his teammate Babe Ruth saw him in spring training, he bet $300 that Moore would not get three hits all year.[9] When Moore got his third hit in Detroit on August 26 on a little squib down the third base line that somehow did not roll foul, Ruth groaned in disbelief but paid up. Moore later added three more hits including a home run in his final game of the season, also in Detroit. The following spring, Moore told Ruth in front of reporters that he had used the $300 to purchase two mules, which he named Babe and Ruth. He was joking at the time, but after the story received widespread coverage, Moore followed through and bought two mules.

Unfortunately, Moore was basically a one-year wonder, who never repeated his 1927 success. He hurt his shoulder in a fall at his farm that winter, and could not regain his form. He averaged only 5 W and 6 SV with a 4.15 ERA (93 ERA+) and 1.525 WHIP in 121.1 IP in 1928–29, good for -1.1 WAR (P). The Yankees then traded him to St. Paul of the American Association, where he temporarily revived his career, going 22–9 in 1930 while leading the league in innings pitched.[10] When the Red Sox drafted him in 1931, Moore responded with his best season since 1927, going 11–13 with 8 saves, a 3.88 ERA (111 ER+), a 1.249 WIP, and 4.3 WAR.

Unfortunately, Moore regressed again in 1932, compiling a miserable 5.23 ERA (85 ERA+), 1.660 WHIP, and 0.1 WAR in 84.1 IP before an August 1 trade sent him back to New York. He pitched much better in the last two months, finishing with a 4.61 ERA (95 ERA+), a 1,582 WHIP, and 1.0 WAR. Then he topped off his brief resurgence by finishing off the Yankees' four-game World Series sweep of the Cubs with a sterling 5.1 IP Game 4 win in relief of Johnny Allen, in which Moore yielded only two hits and an unearned run as the Yankees overcame a 4–1 first inning deficit to win 13–6.[11]

However, Moore could not sustain this brief comeback. He was terrible in 1933 (5.52 ERA, 71 ERA+, 1.806 WHIP, -1.6 WAR), and the Yankees released him after the season. Surprisingly for a guy who was ready to go home after a 30–4 minor league season in 1926, Moore pitched for another four years in the minor leagues before retiring to his farm for good at age 40. In retirement, He returned to New York for the occasional old-timers game but mostly enjoyed a quiet life. He died on March 29, 1963, at age 65.

Why Was Wilcy Moore a Shooting Star?

At the advanced age of 30, Wilcy Moore came out of the low minor leagues to become the 1927 AL pitcher of the year and a valuable piece of one of baseball's most iconic champions. Except for a partial resurgence in 1931, he never again was more than an average pitcher. His major league career lasted only six years, and 71 percent (6.6/9.3) of his career WAR (P) came in 1927 (Figure 6).

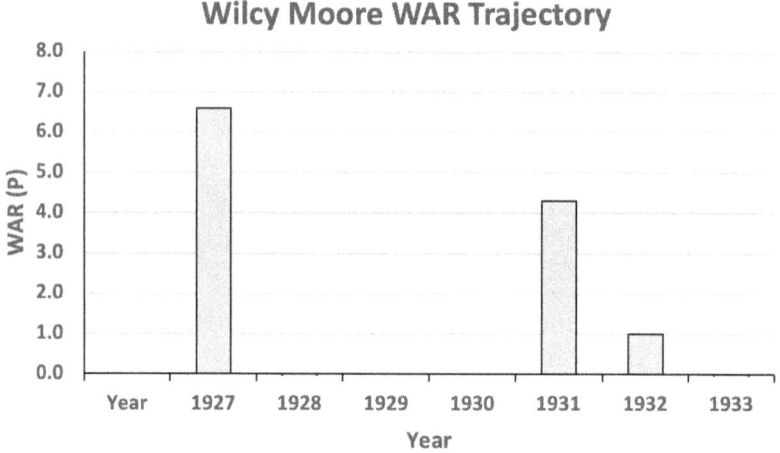

Moore also paved the way as one of MLB's earliest relief specialists. When he arrived in the AL in 1927, four decades before the "save" was invented as a statistic, AL pitchers completed 47 percent (584/1238) of their starts.[12] Moore and his contemporary, Washington's Firpo Marberry, were the first front line pitchers to be used primarily out of the bullpen. Moore's usage bore little resemblance to that of late 20th or early twenty-first-century relievers. He was not used primarily to preserve late inning leads. He was more similar to workhorse relievers like John Hiller (Chapter 20) and Mark Eichhorn (Chapter 24), who might enter a game in the first or second inning and pitch multiple innings or even the rest of the game. He also started several games every year and completed 50 percent (6) of his twelve starts in 1927 and 44 percent (14) of his 32 career starts. While baseball and its strategies have changed radically in the past 100 years, Wilcy Moore remains one of baseball's most storied one-year wonders. We are unlikely to see anyone like him again.

⋄ 7 ⋄

The Left-Handed Satchel Paige

Stewart "Slim" Jones (1934)

Although I am not old enough to remember the Negro Leagues, I do remember some of the ex–Negro League stars, like Roy Campanella, Larry Doby, Monte Irvin, Minnie Minoso, and Satchel Paige, who played in the newly integrated National and American Leagues in the 1950s. The colorful stories that players like Paige and Buck O'Neil told about their Negro League experiences, where the stars performed Bunyanesque feats and everyone seemingly had a glorious time, have always captured my imagination.

But the reality—much of which is lost to history—was really quite another matter. The seven Negro Leagues that are now recognized as major leagues were shoestring enterprises, none lasting more than 16 years, which operated under the twin burdens of economic hardship and racial segregation in a time of economic depression and world war. They played a limited schedule (generally 50–100 games) with frequent interruptions for more lucrative exhibition games and could not afford to pay players fairly for their services. Players supplemented their incomes by playing in winter leagues in Cuba, Mexico, and South America, where they could also enjoy being treated like human beings. Some (including Satchel Paige) played several seasons in better-paying independent leagues, but at the cost of leaving no documentation of their achievements in some of their prime seasons. Their record keeping was sketchy with many omissions and discrepancies. The happy face that players like Satchel Paige and Buck O'Neil painted on their Negro League experiences attests more to their optimism and resiliency than to the actual conditions in which they played.

With this backdrop, we come to the tragic tale of Stewart "Slim"

7. The Left-Handed Satchel Paige

Jones, the 6'6" 180-pound Philadelphia Stars fastballer who was anointed in 1934 as the left-handed Satchel Paige or (if you prefer) the black Lefty Grove at the tender age of 21.[1] Jones was a true one-year wonder; 8.7 of his 9.4 career WAR (8.4 pitching WAR and 0.3 hitting WAR) were achieved in a single season. But what a season that was! Prorated to 1000 BF, Jones's 10.65 pitching WAR per 1000 BF in 1934 has been surpassed by only 13 starting pitchers in MLB history—Pedro Martinez (1999–2000, 2003), Greg Maddux (1994–95), Bill Foster (1926), Bullet Rogan (1925), Walter Johnson (1913), Aaron Nola (2018), Dwight Gooden (1985), Hubert "Dutch" Leonard (1914), Roger Clemens (1990, 1997), Jacob deGrom (2018), Zack Grienke (2015), Satchel Paige (1934), and Lefty Grove (1936). Paige himself, not one for false modesty, called Jones the best pitcher he ever saw.[2] But only four years later, Slim Jones was dead from complications of alcoholism. He left no wife or children to tell his story and is largely forgotten today.

In this 1934 photograph of the Philadelphia Stars' 6'6" one-year wonder Slim Jones in happy times, there is no mistaking where he got his nickname (National Baseball Hall of Fame Museum).

Slim Jones was born on May 6, 1913, and grew up in Baltimore living with his father, a divorced mill worker, and his uncle and older sister. By the time he was 16, he had dropped out of school and was playing local semipro baseball. In 1932, he pitched 25 forgettable innings (0–3, 3.96 ERA) for the Baltimore Black Sox of the short-lived East-West League (EWL), and performed only slightly better (5–3, 4.23 ERA) in 1933, when his team moved to the second Negro National League (NN2) after the EWL folded. However, the Black Sox, struggling financially under the Great Depression, scheduled only 31 league games that year. So, Jones pitched in a Puerto Rican league the following winter, under the tutelage of veteran Black Sox catcher Tex Burnett, where he found new confidence and command and struck out 210 batters.[3] Still, when he reported to the newly formed Philadelphia Stars in 1934, little was expected.

From 1933 to 1936, the second Negro National League (NN2) was the only active major Negro League. It was more of a loose conglomeration of teams that scheduled official games as best it could afford at the height of the Great Depression, than a league in the traditional sense of the word. It did not bother with such niceties as equitable distribution of talent or a balanced schedule to ensure integrity of competition. The only real contenders in that top-heavy league were the Pittsburgh Crawfords (who played 77 games), the Philadelphia Stars (67 games), and the Chicago American Giants (51 games); the remaining teams played 47, 35, 25, 25, and 13 games and were there mainly to provide the "Big 3" with some variety in their opponents. To stimulate interest, the NN2 used a split season format in 1934, in which the first-half winner and second-half winner met in September in a seven-game showdown for the league championship.[4]

Going into the 1934 season, the Pittsburgh Crawfords, who had won the pennant in 1933, were the obvious favorites. Their lineup was stacked with future Hall of Famers, including Josh Gibson (C), Oscar Charleston (1B/manager), Judy Johnson (3B), Cool Papa Bell (CF), and Satchel Paige (P). Other stars included 2022 Hall of Fame finalist Victor Harris (LF) and William Bell (P). The Chicago American Giants, who had finished second in 1933, had four Hall of Famers: Mule Suttles (1B), Willie Wells (SS), Turkey Stearnes (CF), and Bill Foster (P). But the only Hall of Famer on the Philadelphia Stars (who were not even in the league in 1933) was 36-year-old reserve Biz Mackey. Needless to say, the Stars were a heavy underdog. But somehow, after finishing third behind Chicago and Pittsburgh in the first half, Philadelphia managed to beat out Pittsburgh in the second half and upset Chicago 4–3 to win the league championship. The player who was almost single-handedly responsible for the Stars' pennant was Slim Jones.

Jones pitched in nearly half (30) of the Stars' 67 league games, starting 22, and was credited with 20 of their 39 wins, as well as 2 SV. No other Stars pitcher had more than 8 wins. While daily box scores are not available, we can surmise than he pitched many of those games against the stacked Pittsburgh and Chicago lineups, including several duels against Satchel Paige, who was then 27 years old and in his prime (13–3, 1.54 ERA, 0.872 WHIP, 268 ERA+, 6.1 WAR in 561 BF). But the

7. The Left-Handed Satchel Paige

21-year-old Jones was even better. He led the league in almost every pitching category (Table 7).

Table 7: Selected Stats for Slim Jones's Peak
and Runner-Up Seasons and His Career*

Season	Age	BF	ERA	WHIP	ERA+	W–L	SO	BB	CG	SHO	WAR (P)
Peak 1934	21	789	1.29	0.926	323	20–4	**164**	47	**20**	**6**	8.4
per 1000 BF							208	60	25	8	10.6
Runner-Up 1933	20	273	4.23	1.197	102	5–3	51	27	4	0	0.5
per 1000 BF							187	99	15	0	1.8
Career (1932–38)		1755	3.26	1.192	136	32–21	295	130	30	6	9.4
per 1000 BF							168	74	17	3	5.4

*League leading totals are shown in boldface type.

Jones's SABR biography has accounts of five games in which Jones and Paige appeared together in 1934.[5]

- Pittsburgh, May 20: Jones beats Paige 10–5 on a seven-run 9th inning comeback from a 5–3 deficit. One of the five Pittsburgh runs came on a Josh Gibson HR.
- Philadelphia, May 23: Jones wins 3–0 with 11 strikeouts. Paige also fanned 11.
- Chicago, August 26: Pitching on the same (East) team in the East-West All-Star Game, Jones pitches the first three innings and Paige the last 4 of a 1–0 victory over the West team.
- New York, September 9: In an exhibition game at Yankee Stadium, featuring clutch pitching and multiple fielding gems, Jones and Paige dueled to a 1–1 tie. Monte Irvin called it the greatest game he ever saw.[6]
- New York, September 30: In another exhibition game at Yankee Stadium, on the eve of the seventh game of the league championship series, Paige outdueled Jones 3–1.

As Jim Croce might have commented, "you don't mess around with Slim."[7]

Jones also played a pivotal role in Philadelphia's 4–3 win over Chicago in the championship series. The series began inauspiciously with Jones entering in relief and coughing up two ninth inning runs that turned a 3–2 lead into a 4–3 loss. Jones came back the next day to start Game 2 and took a tough 3–0 loss. After splitting the next two games and falling behind three games to one, the Stars took games 5 and 6 to even the series. The series then paused for an exhibition double-header on September 30, which featured the aforementioned 3–1 Paige-Jones duel (won by Paige) and a win by the New York Black Yankees over the Chicago American Giants. The Championship Series resumed on October 1 with a 4–4 tie which was called because of darkness. Finally, Jones ended the series the next day with a five-hit 2–0 shutout. Jones even iced the game with an RBI single in the seventh inning. Jones then added a coda to his career year on October 16 by pitching the Stars to a 4–3 victory to complete a double-header sweep of the newly crowned major league World Series champion St. Louis Cardinals.

Every baseball fan knows that Satchel Paige went on to pitch for another 20 years—31 years if you count his one-game cameo with the Kansas City Athletics in 1965 at age 59—and to earn a place in the Hall of Fame. The Pittsburgh Crawfords would come to win NN2 pennants in 1935–36, even with Satchel Paige taking a hiatus to play for independent teams in Bismarck and Kansas City in 1935. But what happened to the young lefty who was his equal in 1934?

Sadly, injuries and alcoholism prevented Jones from ever pitching more than 67.1 innings or posting more than 0.5 WAR again. The seeds of Slim Jones's precipitous decline were almost certainly sown by his immense workload in 1934. His 30 appearances and 203 IP may not sound so bad, but those appearances (plus several more in exhibition games) were packed into four months (May 6–September 3) and were followed by appearances in the championship series and exhibition games against Pittsburgh and the St. Louis Cardinals in September-October. Jones had also pitched an unknown number of innings in Puerto Rico in the winter of 1933–34 and returned there for an encore in the winter of 1934–35.

By the time, Jones reported to the Stars in 1935 his arm was sore, although one press report called him cocky and out of shape.[8] He began the new season with a 5–1 victory in the six-inning nightcap of a double header to earn a split against the Brooklyn Eagles but went quickly downhill from there, finishing the season with a 4–5 record and a miserable 5.88 ERA, while striking out only 36 batters in 67.1 IP. Along the way, Stars owner Ed Bolden suspended him without pay for failing to maintain a satisfactory conditioning regimen during his rehabilitation. That seems harsh, considering what the ailing Jones had done for his team, but perhaps Bolden (who was also black) was indirectly calling him out for his increasing reliance on alcohol to numb his pain. The lone highlight of his 1935 season came in the East-West All-Star game on August 11, where (for old times' sake) Jones was given the opportunity to start; he responded with three innings of one-hit shutout ball, adding a solo home run that staked his team to a 3–0 lead.

7. The Left-Handed Satchel Paige

The rest of Jones's story is not pretty. He returned to Puerto Rico after the 1935 season to try to regain his form but only aggravated his arm troubles. He was even worse in 1936, finishing 2–4 with a 6.96 ERA in only 14 appearances. In 1937 he only made one (ineffective) pitching appearance and served mainly as a part-time first baseman and pinch hitter. In 1938, his final attempt to regain his pitching form fizzled. Although he was still only 25 years old, there would be no more comeback attempts.

The melodramatic "Hollywood" version of Slim Jones's death on November 19, 1938, is that he pawned his overcoat to buy a bottle of booze on a bitter cold night, then caught pneumonia and died.[9] The truth is that he died of kidney failure and other complications of chronic alcoholism.[10] His death was not the result of one foolish drunken act, but of a chronic pattern of alcohol abuse over years. Thus, although the role of alcoholism in his on-field decline is not well documented, one cannot help but infer that what may have begun as an attempt to self-medicate his arm pain sped his downfall. There is no doubt that a modern player in Jones's predicament would receive more humane and effective treatment for his pain and addiction, if for no other reason than that he was a valuable asset. But in a league that could barely stay afloat in hard economic times, players were fodder, and compassion was a luxury they could not afford.

Why Was Slim Jones a Shooting Star?

Slim Jones is perhaps the most extreme shooting star in this book. He had a single terrific year and produced little or no value in any other of his six years in the major leagues (Figure 7).

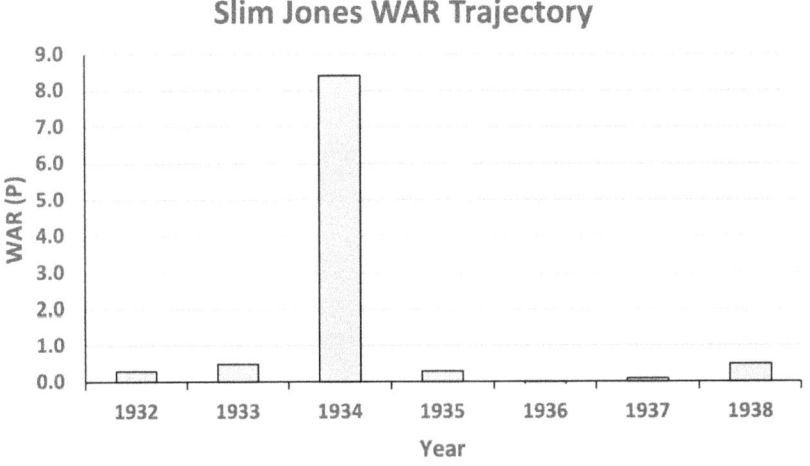

It is well known that the performance of pitchers is inherently more volatile than that of hitters. One could fill a book with pitching careers that began brilliantly and then went sideways due to some combination of injury, alcohol/drug problems, or simple ineffectiveness. But the rapid ascent and precipitous decline of Slim Jones under conditions that no one should be forced to tolerate is especially compelling. Even with only that single great 1934 season and nothing else to show for his brief career, Slim Jones was regarded in sufficient esteem to make the third team in a 1952 Pittsburgh Courier poll of the best Black players of all-time.[11] I'm afraid that his name would elicit only a blank stare if a similar poll were taken in 2023.

❖ 8 ❖

The Pride of the Jury Box
Thomas Francis "Tommy" Holmes (1945)

On July 25, 1978, the Reds were playing a night game against the Mets, as Pete Rose took his record-tying 37-game hitting streak into Shea Stadium. Tommy Holmes, the previous record holder and now a Mets adviser, was watching from the Mets box as Rose broke his 33-year-old record with a third-inning single. The game was stopped, and Holmes came out to congratulate Rose on breaking the record that was his signature achievement, thanking Rose for "making him a big-leaguer again."[1] Such was the grace and humility of the man, who was beloved in baseball from the moment he set foot in Boston Braves Field in 1942 until his death in 2008 at age 91.

When Tommy Holmes arrived in Boston, the woebegone Braves were mired in nearly three decades of futility and played second fiddle in Boston to the more popular Red Sox (who were hardly world beaters themselves). Attendance at Braves Field was so sparse, that the bleachers in RF (where Holmes played in his prime) were often called the "jury box" because a sportswriter once counted only 12 fans sitting there.[2] But when Tommy Holmes moved into RF, he became the most popular man to ever play for the Boston Braves.[3]

Thomas Francis Holmes (whose childhood nickname "Kelly" did not accompany him to the major leagues) was born in Brooklyn, NY, on March 29, 1917, into a large Irish family. Starting at age five he aspired to be a prizefighter and won several boxing prizes in elementary school, but his father discouraged this pursuit. He turned his attention to baseball setting his eyes on CF where his favorite Dodger Johnny Cooney played.[4] As a senior at Brooklyn Technical High School, under the tutelage of Coach Anthony Tarantino, who called him "the best high school player in Brooklyn," he hit .635.[5] In 1937, while playing with the semipro Brooklyn Bushwicks, Holmes got the opportunity to play against the Pittsburgh Crawfords, whose roster still included Satchel Paige, Josh Gibson, and several other stars. Famed Yankees scout Paul Krichell (who had signed Lou Gehrig in 1923) watched Holmes get a couple of hits against Paige and signed him for a $500 bonus.

Unfortunately, Holmes was stuck in the Yankees minor league system for five years (1937–41), while Charlie Keller, Joe DiMaggio, and Tommy Henrichs patrolled the outfield in Yankee Stadium. The powerful Yankees, who won the World Series in four of these five years (except 1940), had no use for Holmes, despite the fact that he hit above .300 in every minor league stop and slugged at least .420 in every year but 1941. At least, Holmes quipped, he was being blocked in CF by the best baseball player in the world (DiMaggio). Finally, on December 9, 1941, Yankees manager Joe McCarthy, who had promised Holmes that spring to trade him to an organization that had an opening for him at the major league level, sent him to the lowly Boston Braves.[6]

Now 25 years old and recently married, Holmes seized his opportunity. Braves manager Casey Stengel immediately installed Holmes as his everyday CF and leadoff hitter, and 39-year-old future Hall of Famer Paul Waner (then in his final season) took him under his wing. In 1942–43, Holmes hit a solid .274/.343/.368 (109 OPS+) with 6.9 WAR in 1330 PA (or 3.4 WAR per 650 PA) while skillfully patrolling the spacious CF at Braves Park (1.0 dWAR). Holmes was summoned by his draft board in March 1944, but was exempted from military service because of a bad sinus condition.[7] He returned to the Braves and improved to .309/.372/.456 (128 OPS+) with 13 HR—four HR more than he had hit in 1942–43 combined. It was the first of five consecutive years when his AVG would exceed .300. He also set new highs in R (93) and RBI (71) and WAR (5.0). But his defense regressed (-0.1 WAR) and he did not make the NL All-Star team. Despite Holmes's development, the Braves remained a losing team, finishing sixth or below in all three seasons.

Having established himself as a sold major league contributor, Holmes's performance reached a whole new level in 1945 (Table 8). Now manning RF, Holmes led the NL in TB (367), hits, doubles, HR, SLG, OPS+, and WAR, while finishing second in AVG and RBI and third in runs scored. However, although Holmes had the better overall season by far, he finished a distant second to NL batting champion Phil Cavaretta in the NL MVP voting, because Cavaretta played for the first-place Cubs while Holmes played for the sixth place Braves.

Holmes began the 1945 season red hot, hitting .426/.500/.553 in April, .390/.431/.610 in May, and .390/.482/.610 in June.[8] On June 5, he began the 37-game hitting streak that would become his signature achievement. The streak ran through July 10 and broke Rogers Hornsby's previous NL record of 33 games. Willie Keeler had once hit in 45 consecutive games, but that streak was spread over two seasons (1896–97). When Holmes's hitting streak ended, he was hitting .401. He was easily elected to the NL All-Star team, but the game itself was not played because of the war. However, he gradually tailed off to .323/.413/.608 in July, .353/.392/.672 in August, and .294/.349/.395 in September-October. While the lefty hitter's home run total (more than twice as many as in any other season) undoubtedly got a significant boost from Braves management's decision to bring in the right field fence by 20 feet in mid–1944, Holmes's remarkable all-around performance made him a legitimate star, as well as the pride of the RF "jury box."

Table 8: Selected Stats for Tommy Holmes's Peak and Runner-Up Seasons and His Career*

Season	Age	PA	AVG	OBP	SLG	OPS+	H	2B	HR	R	RBI	SB	WAR (H)
Peak 1945	28	714	0.352	0.420	**0.577**	175	**224**	47	28	**125**	117	15	8.4
per 650 PA							204	43	25	114	107	14	7.6
Runner-Up 1944	27	705	0.309	0.372	0.456	128	195	**42**	13	93	73	4	5.0
per 650 PA							180	39	12	86	67	4	4.6
Career (1942–52)		5566	0.302	0.366	0.432	122	1507	292	88	698	581	40	35.6
per 650 PA							176	34	10	82	68	5	4.2

*League leading totals are shown in boldface type.

It is also noteworthy how rarely Holmes struck out that year. Holmes was extremely difficult to strike out throughout his career. His lifetime 40.92 AB/SO (4992 AB/122 SO) is the seventh best of all time, trailing only Willie Keeler, Joe Sewell, Lloyd Waner, Joe Start, Nellie Fox, and Lave Cross.[9] Keeler, Start, and Cross aren't really comparable, because they played before the foul-strike rule was adopted in 1901 (NL) and 1903 (AL).[10] Amazingly, in 1945, Holmes did even better, striking out only nine times in 636 AB (70.7 AB/SO). Since the implementation of the foul strike rule, only seven players—Sewell (6 times), Keeler (twice), Stuffy McInnis (twice), Charlie Hollocher, Lloyd Waner, Pie Traynor, and Edd Roush—have ever done better.[11]

Although Holmes never again reached the heights of his 1945 season, he remained one of the Braves steadiest and most popular players from 1946 to 1948, averaging .315/.370/.426 (118 OPS+) with 7 HR, 64 RBI, 85 R, and 4.1 WAR in 652 PA per season. The Braves finally won more games than they lost (81–72–1, fourth place) in 1946, then improved to 86–68 (second place) in 1947. Finally, in 1948, the Braves finished 91–62–1 and won their first pennant since the "Miracle Braves" of 1914. Now age 31, Holmes played in his first All-Star game, making the NL team as a reserve, entering the game in the sixth inning, and grounding out in his only PA.[12] But more importantly, he also played in his first World Series. Although he got only five hits (all singles) in 26 AB, the first one—in the eighth-inning off future Hall of Famer Bob Feller—gave Boston a 1–0 victory in Game 1.[13] However, the Indians won four of the next five games to win the Series. Holmes was rushed to the hospital for an emergency appendectomy the day after the Series ended.[14]

As it turned out, 1948 was Holmes's last good season. In 1949–50, he fell to .281/.353/.425 (110 OPS+) with 3.8 WAR in 788 PA and was relegated to platoon duty in RF. The Braves, racked with dissension, fell to fourth place in 1949 and tumbled all the way to seventh place in 1950. The following year, the Braves, believing that Holmes had reached the end of the line as a player, offered him the opportunity to become the player-manager for their minor league affiliate in Hartford. However, when manager Billy Southworth unexpectedly resigned on June 19 with the Braves struggling at 38–41–1, Holmes was suddenly brought in to replace him.[15] The Braves went 48–47 under Holmes's stewardship and finished fourth—not bad, considering his relative youth and managerial inexperience. But the bottom dropped out in 1952, and veteran manager Charlie Grimm was brought in to replace Holmes after only 35 games (of which the Braves lost 22).[16] The Braves had a good young core, including rookie Eddie Mathews, but would not blossom until they moved to Milwaukee in 1953. Holmes never managed in the major leagues again.

After his dismissal as the Braves manager, Holmes finished the 1952 season and his playing career in his hometown with the NL champion Brooklyn Dodgers, where he hit a dismal .111/.200/.139 (-5 OPS+) in 40 PA. He did get to play in his second World Series, but was hitless in his only PA, as the Yankees beat the Dodgers 4–2.

Not embittered by his unceremonious dismissal in 1952, Holmes returned to the Braves organization as a minor league manager in 1953 and spent the next six years hopping back and forth between managerial and scouting jobs in the Braves and Dodgers organizations. In 1959, he became the director of the *New York Journal-American*'s sandlot baseball program (a job once held by his mentor Paul Waner) and thrived there for the next 15 years as he cheered on each of his 85 players who reached the major leagues.[17] In 1973, he took on an additional public relations job for the Mets, where he remained for the next three decades. He was a frequent guest at old-timers functions and charitable events. Tommy Holmes remained in baseball until he was 85 years old and died on April 14, 2008, at age 91.[18]

8. The Pride of the Jury Box

Why Was Tommy Holmes a Shooting Star?

Tommy Holmes was a good player (≥ 3.4 WAR), for seven years (1942–48), but his 1945 season stands well above the other six (Figure 8). Not only was his 8.4 WAR 68 percent higher than his next best season, his run production, home runs, and stolen bases far outstripped any other season in his career.

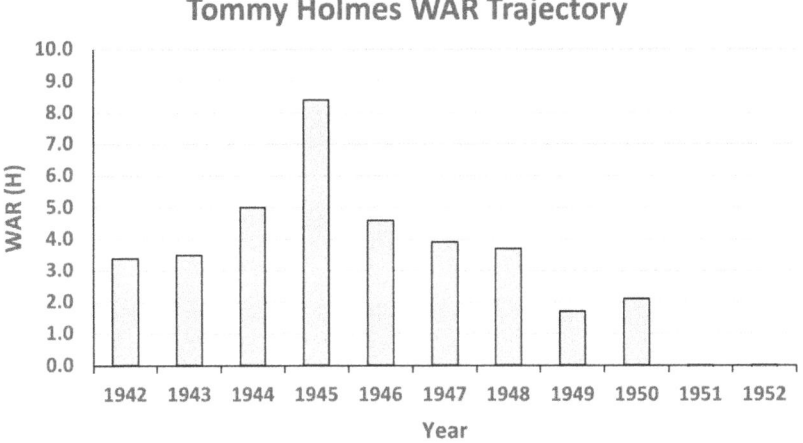

A skeptic might question whether Holmes's 1945 season was really that much better than his "runner-up" 1944 season, when he had 5.0 WAR. Certainly, his career high water mark of 28 HR in 1945 was inflated by the Braves decision to shorten their RF fence by 20' in mid-1944. But while shortened fences may have turned some of his extra base hits into home runs in 1945, Holmes had 29 more hits, including 20 more extra base hits in 1945 than in 1944 in only nine more PA. Furthermore, when Holmes's HR total regressed to single digits after the RF fence was moved back to its original depth in 1946, his hit total also fell by 48 and his extra base bit total fell by 34. Clearly, Holmes was a far better hitter in 1945 than in 1944, 1946, or any other season in his career, irrespective of the distance to the RF fence.

There is also no evidence that Holmes's 8.4 WAR in 1945 was artificially inflated by the absence of star players who served in the wartime military. Most of the players who missed the 1945 season also missed the 1944 season (when Holmes had only 5.0 WAR). Stan Musial, who missed only the 1945 season, did just as well in 1946 (9.3 WAR), when the NL was at full strength, as in 1944 (8.9 WAR). Holmes was clearly a legitimate shooting star—a good player, who accrued a solid 35.6 career WAR total but attained greatness just for one single season.

Tommy Holmes was a wonderful example of a "baseball lifer," a rarity among shooting stars. Most shooting stars do not go on to long careers in baseball management or administration. Almost every player's career ultimately ends in failure, but the aftertaste of that failure can be particularly bitter in players who had tasted spectacular success but didn't get to enjoy it for long. Dunlap, Seymour, and Jones all died young and in poverty. Leonard, Moore, and Stone lived long full lives but (each for his own reasons) were glad to put baseball in their rearview mirrors. Among the players featured in subsequent chapters, only Harry Brecheen (Chapter 9) and Al Rosen (Chapter 11) had impactful careers in organized baseball after their playing days were over, and even they were not lifers. Tommy Holmes was blessed with an even temperament and a small ego, which enabled him to enjoy the good times and to absorb the setbacks with equanimity. Being one of baseball's most likeable men is a great asset when you hang in the same circles for almost 70 years.

◆ 9 ◆

Harry the Cat
Harry David Brecheen (1948)

Many shooting star pitchers made their big splash before age 27 but then were unable to sustain a high level of performance due to injuries, personal issues, or plain loss of effectiveness. Harry Brecheen was a different kind of cat. He was a late bloomer, who knocked around in the minor leagues until he was nearly 30, then had his career year at age 33. Actually, he had been a very good pitcher for several years before that, but his diminutive stature (5'10" and 160 pounds) and the glut of big power pitchers in the Cardinals' extensive farm system, which peaked at 31 minor league teams in 1940, had denied him a chance to shine in his twenties.[1] Thus, Brecheen's 41.3 career pitching WAR is respectable enough, but he might have accrued 50–60 WAR and become a borderline HOF candidate had he received an earlier big-league opportunity.

Harry Brecheen was born on October 14, 1914, and grew up on a farm outside of Ada, OK, a small town near the Texas border. He was a small wiry kid, who loved baseball, fishing, and hunting and idolized fellow Oklahoma lefty Carl Hubbell.[2] He was a straight fastball-curveball pitcher in his teens, where his outstanding 65–3 record in American Legion baseball earned him a tryout with the Tulsa Oilers (a Pirates affiliate) in 1933 at age 18.[3] The Pirates did not offer Brecheen a contract due to his small size and poor command, but he did get lowball offers from the Cardinals and Yankees. He declined and returned to Ada to marry his sweetheart Vera. He took a construction job in Ada to supplement his income from semipro baseball. Two years later, with Vera's encouragement, he relented and signed on with unaffiliated Class A Galveston. But he struggled there and subsequently for two Class C teams in 1936, where he went 6–22 with 132 walks in 266 IP. Although by then he had developed a screwball like his idol Carl Hubbell, he could not throw it for strikes. However, in 1937, he finally learned to control his screwball and mix it successfully with his curveball. He went 21–6 with the Class B Portsmouth Cubs, with only 69 BB in 249 IP. The Cardinals acquired his contract from the Cubs at the end of the season.

Although Brecheen won 82 games in the next five years as he slowly ascended through the many-layered maze of Branch Rickey's extensive farm system, going 13–10 (3.06 ERA), 18–7 (2.31 ERA), 16–9 (2.75 ERA), 16–6 (3.64 ERA), and 19–10 (2.09 ERA) in 1938–1942, he entered the 1943 season with only a three-game "cup of coffee" in St. Louis in 1940 to show for his efforts.[4] With big hard-throwing aces like Mort Cooper, Johnny Beazley, and Max Lanier anchoring a World Series championship team in 1942 and several similar minor league prospects knocking on the door, there had been no room for a slim 5'10" finesse pitcher like Brecheen on the parent club. So, from 1940 to 1942, he was stuck in AAA Columbus. By 1943, the Cardinals had exhausted their three options on Brecheen and were required to add him to the major league roster or risk losing him. The decimation of the organization by World War II—specifically the departure of 21-game winner Johnny Beazley—finally opened a spot for Brecheen, who had a 4-F exemption for a congenital spinal malformation.[5] He was 28 years old.

Brecheen was an instant favorite in St. Louis. Used as a "swingman" between the starting rotation and bullpen, he made 13 starts and 16 relief appearances in 1943, going 9–6 with a 2.26 ERA (150 ERA+), a 1.012 WHIP, 4 saves,

Small, wiry, and intense, Harry "The Cat" Brecheen, who pitched for the St. Louis Cardinals in 1940 and 1943–52, was always ready to pounce on any ball hit his way (National Baseball Hall of Fame Museum).

and 3.1 WAR in 527 BF. Brecheen quickly developed a reputation as a tough clutch pitcher and a superlative fielder. He committed only eight errors in his 1907.2 IP career. His small size and quick feline reflexes earned him the nickname "Harry the Cat"; no surname was required to identify him. Red Smith admiringly called him "a scrawny little scrap of meat, just a fragment of whalebone and rawhide."[6] But there he was, on the mound in critical situations in Games 1, 3, and 4 of the World Series (which they lost four games to one to the Yankees).

Brecheen proceeded to build on his 1943 success. From 1944 to 1947, mostly as a starter, he went 62–35 with a 2.81 ERA (133 ERA+), a 1.204 WHIP, 6 saves, and 17.4 WAR in 3284 BF (5.3 WAR per 1000 BF). He also won Game 4 of the 4–2 World Series triumph over the St. Louis Browns in 1944, saved the Game 2 clincher of their 2–0 play-off series sweep over the Dodgers for the 1946 NL pennant, and won Games 2, 6, and 7 of their 4–3 World Series victory over the Red Sox in 1946. Brecheen is probably best known for his Series-clinching 1946 victory, which came in a 2-inning relief appearance on the day after he had pitched a 5–1 complete game victory and cemented his reputation for toughness under pressure. Brecheen, who was suffering from a bad cold, entered the game with baserunners on second and third base and nobody out in the eighth inning to try to protect a 3–1 lead.[7] After striking out Wally Moses and getting Johnny Pesky to line out to RF, Dom DiMaggio doubled to tie the game. Brecheen then bore down to retire Ted Williams on an infield popup. After the Cardinals came back to take the lead on one of baseball's most memorable plays, Enos Slaughter's "mad dash" from 1B to score on what looked like a routine two-out single, Brecheen yielded two singles to start the ninth inning. He then recovered to put down the next three Sox hitters and seal the victory. That would be his final World Series appearance. Overall, Brecheen went 4–1 with an 0.83 ERA and 1.224 WHIP in 32.2 IP in three World Series.

Another aspect of Brecheen's toughness is that since early in the 1945 season, he had been pitching with a painful left elbow that swelled up after every game (probably the result of throwing too many screwballs).[8] He learned to pitch through the pain but could no longer fill his customary swingman role and now worked almost exclusively as a starter. Unlike his contemporaries, he was used sparingly and was never allowed to face as many as 1000 batters in a season. Brecheen had struggled in the last two months of the 1947 season after a strong start and seemed to have begun the gradual decline typical of 32-year-old pitchers. Although he still won 16 games that year, his ERA and WHIP had risen to career highs of 3.30 and 1.281, respectively, and the Cardinals finished five games behind the Dodgers. So, when he entered the 1948 season as a 33-year-old soft-tossing lefty with a precarious elbow, whose glory days were probably behind him, Harry the Cat was an unlikely candidate for a superstar season. But that is exactly what happened.

Brecheen began the 1948 season pitching at weekly intervals to nurse his tender elbow and rattled off three straight complete game shutouts, including a one-hitter against the Phillies, where the only hit came on a close call on an infield grounder.[9] He finally yielded his first run on May 15 an 8–3 complete game win over Pittsburgh. When his elbow began to feel better as the weather warmed up in June, he picked up the pace, finishing with 30 starts. Brecheen logged at least 6 IP in 26 of those starts, which included 23 "quality starts" and 21 complete games, seven of them shutouts. He yielded no ER eight times, 1 ER seven times, 2 ER four times, and 3 ER five times. Uncharacteristically, he struck out seven or more batters in nine starts—all wins— and led the NL in strikeouts for the only time in his career. His 1-H, 8-SO shutout of the Phillies was his best outing, but his 2-H, 7-SO shutout of the Giants on August 4 was a close second. Brecheen made only five ineffective starts—against the Phillies on June 8 (5 ER in 5.0 IP in a 7–5 win), the Giants on June 13 (5 ER in 2.0 IP in an 8–7 loss), the Reds on July 9 (4 ER in 5.0 IP in a 6–4 win), the Braves on August 24 (7 ER in 6.1 IP in a 9–3 loss), and the Dodgers on August 29 (3 ER in 0.0 IP in a 12–7 loss). Brecheen was also nearly perfect in three relief appearances, yielding no ER, 1 H, and 1 BB in 4.2 IP. Brecheen wound up winning 20 games and leading the NL in WAR, ERA, WHIP, ERA+, SHO, and SO (Table 9). He also led the NL with 5.7 SO per 9 IP while walking only 1.9 per 9 IP.

Table 9: Selected Stats for Harry Brecheen's Peak and Runner-Up Seasons and His Career*

Season	Age	BF	ERA	WHIP	ERA+	W-L	SO	BB	CG	SHO	WAR (P)
Peak 1948	33	931	**2.24**	**1.037**	**182**	20–7	**149**	49	21	7	**8.7**
per 1000 BF							160	53	23	8	9.3
Runner-Up 1946	31	954	2.49	1.206	139	15–15	117	67	14	5	5.5
per 1000 BF							123	70	15	5	5.8
Career (1940–53)		7821	2.92	1.188	133	133–92	901	536	125	25	41.3
per 1000 BF							115	69	16	3	5.3

*League leading totals are shown in boldface type.

The Cardinals entered September in a tight four-team race, trailing the Dodgers and Braves by 1.5 games and leading the Pirates by

0.5 games Living up to his clutch reputation, Brecheen went 5–1 that month. Following a tough 3–1 complete game loss to the Reds, he finished with five straight complete game wins over the Cubs, Phillies, Giants, Cubs and Pirates, in which he yielded a total of two runs,[10] Unfortunately, Brecheen's heroic efforts were not enough, and the Cardinals finished second, 6.5 games behind Boston.

Over the next four years, age and elbow problems gradually overtook Brecheen. Although he remained reasonably effective with ERA between 3.25 and 3.80 and WAR between 1.4 and 3.0 in 1949–52, he could no longer carry his accustomed workload, and his IP steadily declined from 233.1 in 1948 to 214.2 in 1949 to 163.1 in 1950 to 138.2 in 1951 to 100.2 in 1952. When the Cardinals moved to release Brecheen after the 1952 season, he signed with the last place St. Louis Browns as a player-coach amid tampering charges, which were rejected by Commissioner Ford Frick.[11] Although the 38-year-old Brecheen finished only 5–13 for the hapless Browns, he was still able to post a more than respectable 3.07 ERA and 1.304 WHIP in 117.1 IP in his final season. His ERA never exceeded 3.80 in any season.

The transfer across town paid off in 1954, both for Brecheen and the Browns, when the Browns (now the Orioles) moved to Baltimore and installed Brecheen as their full-time pitching coach. During his 13-year tenure at that position, under managers Jimmy Dykes, Paul Richards, Billy Hitchcock, and Hank Bauer, he presided over the gradual development of a perennial contender built on strong pitching and defense.[12] In 1960, the Orioles, featuring young pitchers like Milt Pappas, Chuck Estrada, Steve Barber, and Jack Fisher, finished a surprising second behind the Yankees. By 1964, under new manager Hank Bauer, when they lost a tight three-team race to the Yankees and White Sox, Dave McNally, Wally Bunker, and veteran Robin Roberts had joined the rotation. In 1966, Brecheen's last year as pitching coach, the Orioles finally won the AL pennant with a four-man rotation of McNally, Jim Palmer, Bunker, and Barber—all of whom Brecheen had developed and mentored. Another Brecheen protégé, Milt Pappas, had been traded for 1966 MVP and triple crown winner Frank Robinson the previous winter. The upstart Orioles then upset Koufax, Drysdale, and the Dodgers in a pitching-dominated 4–0 sweep of the World Series, behind 6.2 innings of scoreless relief by Moe Drabowski in Game 1 and shutouts by Palmer, Bunker, McNally in Games 2–4. The Dodgers fell behind by three runs before their first AB and never led in any game. Although Brecheen was still not quite 52 years old when the Series ended, he decided to retire with his wife in Ada, Oklahoma, where he could hunt and fish to his heart's content. He was 89 when he died in 2004.

Why Was Harry Brecheen a Shooting Star?

Once he got his belated big league opportunity, Harry Brecheen was a consistently excellent pitcher. His WAR (P) never fell below 2.6 over the nine years spanning 1943–51, and his ERA never rose above 3.80 in any of his 12 major league seasons. He will certainly be remembered for far more than his star turn in 1948, which indeed takes a back seat to his three wins in the 1946 World Series in his obituaries.[13] But post-season heroics aside, his 8.7 WAR in 1948 clearly stands well above all the other seasons in his career (Figure 9).

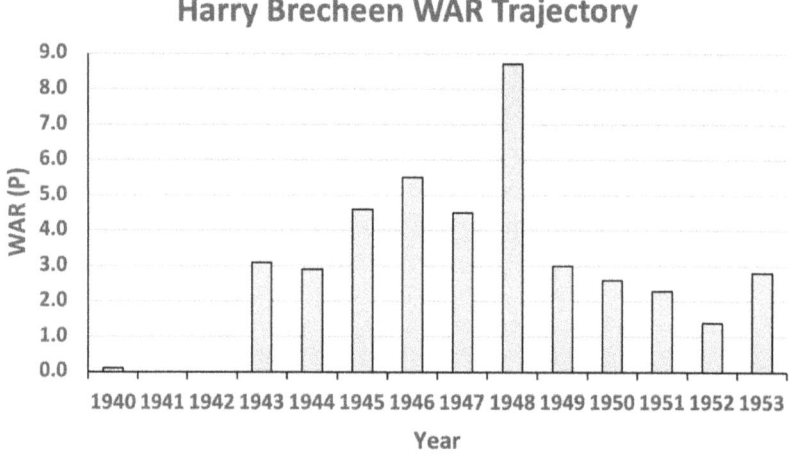

Brecheen's anomalous 1948 season was more of a respite from the elbow issues that had plagued him for most of his long-delayed major league career than a true breakout season. In a more just world, he might have had a 15-year instead of a 12-year MLB career, and he might have racked up one or two more seasons with 7+ WAR in his mid–20s when he was young and healthy, instead of toiling away unnoticed in the Cardinals farm system. He might even have been a Hall of Fame contender. His career trajectory is a monument to grit and perseverance, rather than a tale of one great single-season performance. His 8.7 WAR season was but one of many notable accomplishments of Harry the Cat. Indeed, Brecheen's greatest impact on the game may have been his prominent role in building the fledgling Orioles from the ashes of the decrepit 1953 St. Louis Browns into a pitching-rich dynasty that lasted almost 20 years after he retired.

◆ 10 ◆

The Little Pitcher Who Could

Robert Clayton "Bobby" Shantz (1952)

"Mighty Mite," "sawed off little character," "midget southpaw," "batboy," and "toy pitcher"—Bobby Shantz had to listen to all of these insults and more from scouts and managers who took one look at him and decided he could not possibly pitch in the major leagues.[1] Even his high school coach told him he was too small to be a pitcher and assigned him to the outfield. His draft board rejected him in early 1944 because, at age 18, he stood only 4'11"—one inch shy of the army's minimum height requirement. But appearances can be deceiving. Eight years later, having grown to 5'6½" and 139 pounds, Bobby Shantz was the toast of baseball and the AL MVP. Although injuries prevented a repeat performance, he stubbornly refused to go away and enjoyed a highly successful 16-year major league career.

Robert Clayton Shantz was born on September 26, 1925, in Pottstown, PA. His father Wilmer Shantz was a fine semipro third baseman, and his younger brother Billy would become a major league catcher.[2] Bobby's diminutive stature may have resulted from a near fatal childhood fever at age 6. It was apparently not genetic, since his brother Billy stood 6'1" and weighed 160 pounds. Notwithstanding his size, Bobby was an excellent athlete who excelled at bowling, ping pong, diving, gymnastics, and kicking a football. But his first love was always baseball.

Bobby Shantz had grown enough to be drafted into the army in December 1944 and was sent to the Philippines in July 1945, as the war was ending.[3] He got an opportunity to pitch for his squad team and did well enough against a team of touring major leaguers to earn a tryout with the Dodgers. They didn't want him. In 1947, after his discharge from the army, Shantz (now having reached his full adult height) signed with a sandlot team in the East Penn League and pitched them to the league championship. His admirers arranged an exhibition game where he would face recent league alumnus Curt Simmons, who had received a $65,000 bonus to sign with the Phillies and had just won his major league debut against the Giants. Shantz won the match-up 4–1 while allowing eight hits and striking out 14. Although most scouts remained skeptical, A's scout Harry O'Donnell signed the Shantz brothers to play for Lincoln, NE, in the Class A Western League in 1948. An 18–7 record with a 2.82 ERA and 212 strikeouts in 214 IP in Lincoln earned Bobby an express ticket to the major leagues.

Shantz, who was recovering from off-season surgery for a bone spur in his shoulder, did not get into a game until May 1. Although he gave up only one hit in 0.2 IP, Connie Mack optioned him to AAA Buffalo after the game.[4] However, Mack was forced to quickly reverse himself when two of his top pitchers from 1948, Dick Fowler and Phil Marchildon, were sidelined. He sent a police car to intercept Shantz, who was en route to Buffalo, but Shantz pulled off onto a side road when he heard the sirens and drove on when they passed. Upon reaching Buffalo, he learned he had been recalled and took a train to join the A's for a three-game series in Detroit. In his next appearance on May 6, Shantz was called in to relieve starter Carl

In six years (1949–54) with the Philadelphia Athletics, 5'6" Bobby Shantz repeatedly showed his detractors that very good things can come in small packages (National Baseball Hall of Fame Museum).

10. The Little Pitcher Who Could

Schieb in the fourth inning with no one out and the A's trailing 3–1 after a three-run HR by Vic Wertz. Shantz then pitched nine no-hit innings, echoing Ernie Shore's 9 perfect innings in relief of Babe Ruth in 1917. The A's finally staked Shantz to a 5–3 lead in the top of the 13th inning. Shantz gave up a double and a run-scoring single to start the bottom of the 13th inning, but then saved the day with a spectacular diving catch on a popped up bunt, leaping over his fallen catcher Buddy Rosar, then firing to 1B to complete the double play. He struck out Bob Swift for the final out to wrap up his first major league win and cement his spot on the major league roster.

Despite this flashy beginning, Shantz experienced more lows than highs during his first two seasons with the A's. He made 30 starts and 39 relief appearances in 1949–50 and struggled to a 14–22 record with a 4.16 ERA (105 ERA+) and 1.493 WHIP while striking out 151 in 341.2 IP. His 4.5 WAR in 1494 BF (3.0 WAR per 1000 BF) was decent but nothing special. Then, appearing mostly as a starter, he took a significant step forward in 1951, going 18–10 with a 3.94 ERA (108 ERA+) and 1.378 WHIP in 205.1 IP. He made the AL All-Star team—largely on the strength of his 18 wins for a sixth place team—but did not pitch in the game. Although he finished strong by winning 10 of his last 12 games, his 2.4 WAR in 869 BF was really no better than in 1949–50, and his strikeout rate declined. At age 25, Shantz had established himself as a solid swingman on a second-division team. Nothing about his performance said that this was a rising star.

However, Shantz would shock all of his naysayers in 1952 (Table 10).

Table 10: Selected Stats for Bobby Shantz's Peak and Runner-Up Seasons and His Career*

Season	Age	BF	ERA	WHIP	ERA+	W-L	SO	BB	CG	SHO	WAR (P)
Peak 1952	26	1103	2.48	**1.048**	159	24–7	152	63	27	5	**8.8**
per 1000 BF							138	57	24	5	8.0
Runner-Up 1957	31	688	**2.45**	1.139	148	11–5	72	40	9	1	3.1
per 1000 BF							105	58	13	1	4.5
Career (1949–64)		8045	3.38	1.260	119	119–99	1072	643	78	15	32.1
per 1000 BF							133	80	10	2	4.0

*League leading totals are shown in boldface type.

In 33 starts and a career-high 279.2 IP for the fourth place A's, Shantz won an AL-leading 24 games—more than 30 percent of his team's 79 win total—and also led the AL in WHIP and WAR (P). His 24 wins were surpassed only by Robin Roberts, who won 28 for the

NL Phillies. Shantz was an All-Star again, but this time he got into the game in the fifth inning and struck out the only three batters he faced—Whitey Lockman, Jackie Robinson, and Stan Musial—before rain ended the game.[5] Despite playing on a fourth place team, Shantz easily won the AL MVP award with 280 vote points, far outdistancing the next three finishers—Allie Reynolds (183), Mickey Mantle (143), and Yogi Berra (104)—who split the "Yankee vote."[6]

A more granular look at Shantz's 33 starts in 1952—27 of them complete games—reveals how dominant he was.[7] He pitched at least six innings in 31 of his 33 starts. One of the two exceptions was the September 23 game where an errant second inning pitch by the Senators' Walt Masterman broke Shantz's wrist and ended his season. He gave up 3 ER or fewer in 24 of those 31 long starts ("quality starts" in modern parlance), including five complete game shutouts. He gave up no ER in three other CG starts and 1 ER in 7 other CG starts (including a 14-inning 2–1 victory over the Yankees on May 20, in which he struck out 11). The A's went 25–8 in Shantz's starts versus 54–67–1 in games started by other pitchers. Shantz was torrid in the first four months, going 20–3 with a 1.55 ERA and 0.908 WHIP through August 5.[8] However, he tailed off sharply in August-September, going 4–4 with a 4.93 ERA and 1.427 WHIP in his last 10 starts. At one point, he lost three consecutive decisions between August 31 and September 9 by a combined score of 29–4 while getting torched for 23 ER and 24 H in 21.2 IP. His worst clunker during this 10-day stretch was an 11-run pasting in 6.2 IP against the Yankees on September 4. However, Shantz was 4–3 against the AL champs overall, including CG shutouts in Yankee Stadium on June 28 (12–0) and September 19 (2–0). Because of this late-season slump, Shantz's 1952 performance was not quite as dominant as Dutch Leonard's and Slim Jones's peak seasons, but he definitely earned his MVP award.

Perhaps, the heavy workload in 1952 took its toll, but for whatever reason, Shantz was not the same pitcher in 1953. After breaking even with a respectable 3.44 ERA and 1.147 WHIP in 34 IP in his four April starts, the wheels came off in May.[9] He lost three of four decisions with a 4.94 ERA and 1.469 WHIP in 34.2 ERA, before being removed from a May 23 game against the Red Sox with a severely injured left shoulder. A tendon had separated from the bone.[10] Tendon transplant surgery was recommended, but Shantz opted for rest and rehabilitation. Somehow he returned to the mound in July and made seven more starts. He finished the season 5–9 with a respectable 4.09 ERA (105 ERA+), a 1.259 WHIP, and 1.8 WAR. But his shoulder never fully recovered.

Shantz continued to struggle as a part-time starter in 1954–55 and as a reliever in 1956, compiling a composite 8–17 record with a mediocre 4.57 ERA (93 ERA+), 1.438 WHIP, and 1.7 WAR in 234.1 IP (1013 BF). The A's, who had moved to Kansas City in 1955, fell to the AL cellar with a 52–102 record in 1956, and no longer had a place for a 31-year-old gimpy lefty bullpen arm four years removed from glory. So on February 19, 1957, the A's, who established a cozy trading relationship with the Yankees in the late 1950s (some called them a glorified Yankee farm team), sent Shantz to New York in a 13-player trade, in which the AL champs also came away with Art Ditmar and Clete Boyer and the A's received no one of consequence.

Perhaps rejuvenated by his first opportunity to pitch for a winning team, Shantz returned to the starting rotation and had a strong comeback season in 1957, the second-best season of his career. In 21 starts and 9 relief appearances, he went 11–5 with a sparkling 2.45 ERA and 148 ERA+ (both of which led the AL), a 1.139 WHIP, and 3.1 WAR in 173.0 IP (688 BF). Finally receiving recognition for his fielding prowess, he also became the first Yankee to win a Gold Glove, an honor he would receive in each of the final eight seasons of his career. Although he was no longer the workhorse of 1952, his 148 ERA+ was not that far short of his 159 ERA+ in his MVP season. With Whitey Ford sidelined early in the season and their other pitchers struggling, Shantz almost single-handedly kept the Yankees afloat thru June with a 9–1 record with a 2.25 ERA and 1.149 WHIP at the All-Star break, before fading to 2–4 with a 3.42 ERA and 1.215 WHIP in the second half.[11] Shantz was rewarded with his first and only World Series start, a 4–2 loss to Lew Burdette, who beat the Yankees three times that October to lead the Braves to the World Series Championship.[12] Shantz lasted only three innings and gave up 3 ER and 6 H. He came back in relief of Tom Sturdivant in Game 4 and pitched three hitless scoreless innings in a 7–5 loss to Warren Spahn. He also yielded an unearned run in relief in the Game 7 loss to Burdette.

Shantz was a valuable swingman for the Yankees in 1958–60, making 17 starts (13 of them in 1958) and 91 relief appearances and earning 19 wins and 14 saves, with a 2.90 ERA (124 ERA+), 1.179 WHIP, and 3.2 WAR in 288.1 IP (1187 BF). He did not pitch in the Yankees' 1958 4–3 World Series comeback win over the Braves, but he made three relief appearances in the 4–3 1960 World Series loss to Pittsburgh. He was credited with a very cheap save for inducing Don Hoak (the only batter he faced) to ground into a game ending double play in the Yankees 16–3 Game 2 rout. He also faced two batters, retiring both, to close out the seventh inning of their 3–2 loss to Vern Law in Game 4. Finally, in perhaps the most exciting Game 7 in World Series history, Shantz entered in the third inning with the Yankees trailing 4–0 and held Pittsburgh scoreless through the 7th inning while the Yankees scored seven unanswered runs.[13] However, the tiring Shantz gave up three consecutive hits to start the eighth inning and was replaced by Jim Coates with the Yankees still clinging to a 7–5 lead. After retiring two batters, Coates gave up an RBI single to Roberto Clemente and a three-run HR to journeyman catcher Hal Smith. Although the Yankees came back to tie the game in the top of the ninth, Bill Mazeroski famously ended the game with walk-off HR off Ralph Terry. The decision by Casey Stengel to allow Shantz to go three batters too long probably contributed to Stengel's subsequent dismissal as Yankees manager.

Game 7 was the last game of the 35-year-old Shantz's Yankee career. The Washington Senators claimed him in the 1960 expansion draft and promptly flipped him to Pittsburgh for Bennie Daniels (who led the team with 12 wins in 1961) and two others. Shantz remained a durable and effective reliever in 1961 with 6 W, 2 SV, a 3.32 ERA (119 ERA+), a 1.310 WHIP, and 1.6 WAR in 89.1 IP. After Houston claimed him from the Pirates in the 1961 expansion draft, Shantz bounced to the Cardinals to the Cubs to the Phillies—all contenders looking to add a bullpen arm—in 1962–64. (Shantz was one of the players the Cubs acquired in the infamous 1964 Brock-Broglio trade—see Chapter 15.) He continued to pitch effectively in limited action, with a composite 14 W, 16 SV, 2.51 ERA (152 ERA+), 1.044 WHIP, and 5.0 WAR in 218.1 IP (877 BF). He retired after the 1964 season, leaving the game on his own terms. He returned to Chalfont, PA, to manage a dairy bar and restaurant.[14] At age 98 as of October 2023, Shantz is currently the oldest living MVP.

Why Was Bobby Shantz a Shooting Star?

Bobby Shantz was a unique player, a survivor, who did not let his small stature keep him from becoming an MVP quality starting pitcher nor let what might have been a career ending injury keep him from reinventing himself as a highly effective relief pitcher. Although he chose to retire at age 39, he probably could have pitched well into his forties.

There is no question that Shantz fulfills the defining attributes of a "shooting star." His 8.8 pitching WAR in 1952 was nearly three times the 3.1 WAR of his runner-up 1957 season and comprised 27 percent of his 32.1 career WAR (Figure 10).

But when you look closely at his 1957, 1959, and 1962 seasons (when his ERA+ was 148, 153, and 214, respectively), the difference

10. The Little Pitcher Who Could

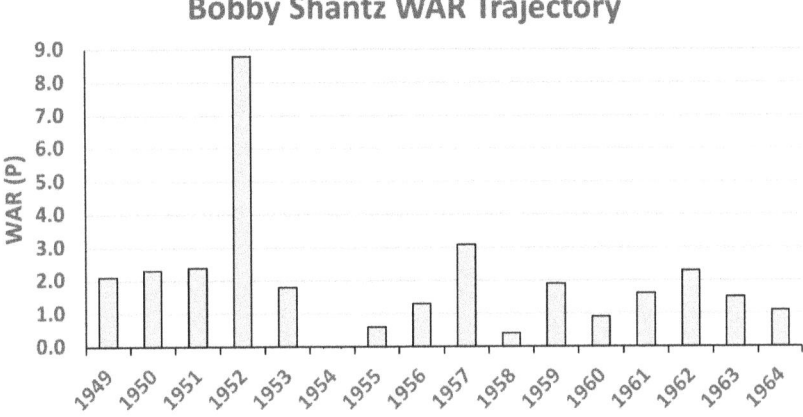

from 1952 (159 ERA+) was one of quantity more than quality. Bobby Shantz was no Hall of Famer, but he was an excellent and durable pitcher, who repeatedly confounded his many doubters and got the most out of his ability.

◈ 11 ◈

The Hebrew Hammer
Albert Leonard "Al" Rosen (1953)

Which third baseman do you suppose produced the highest WAR for a single major league season?[1] You might guess George Brett, who hit .388 in 1980, but painful hemorrhoids, which required in-season surgery, limited him to 515 PA and 9.4 WAR that year. What about Mike Schmidt, who leads all 3B with 106.8 career WAR? Schmidt maxed out at 9.8 WAR in 1974, but might have accrued at least 10 WAR in 1981, were it not for the strike that wiped out one-third of the season and limited him to 434 PA and 7.7 WAR. Perhaps another Hall of Famer like Ron Santo (9.8 in 1967), Home Run Baker (9.3 in 1912), Scott Rolen (9.2 in 2002), Wade Boggs (9.1 in 1985), Brooks Robinson (8.4 in 1964), or Eddie Mathews (8.2 WAR in 1959)? What about A-Rod (9.4 in 2005 and 2007) or recently inducted Hall of Famer Adrian Beltre (9.6 in 2004)? No, Al Rosen, who played only seven full seasons and accrued only 32.3 WAR in his career, has them all beat with his 10.1-WAR MVP season for the 1953 Cleveland Indians.

Nothing in life came easy for Albert Leonard Rosen, who was born in Spartanburg, SC, on February 29, 1924. Abandoned by his father as a small child, his mother Rose moved the family to the Little Havana section of Miami, FL, where his grandmother could watch Al and his younger brother Jerry while Rose worked in a dress shop to support them.[2] Since his was the only Jewish family in Little Havana, Al—despite his severe asthma (which he eventually outgrew)—learned toughness at an early age. He channeled his aggression into sports and excelled in boxing, football, basketball, and (of course) baseball. His friends and family called him "Flip," but he was just "Al" when he reached the major leagues. After starring on his high school baseball team, Rosen briefly attended the University of Florida before signing a minor league contract with Thomasville (an Indians Class D affiliate in

11. The Hebrew Hammer

the North Carolina State League) in 1942. But before the year was out, he joined the Navy and was sent to the Pacific theater, where he navigated an assault boat in the landing on Okinawa. He left the Navy as a lieutenant in 1946.

Over the next 3.5 seasons, the right-handed slugger methodically advanced up the Cleveland organizational chain, pulverizing minor league pitching at every level and earning the nickname "The Hebrew Hammer," which echoed the nickname of "Hammerin' Hank" Greenberg, the Jewish star in whose footsteps he hoped to follow.[3] He hit 79 HR with 360 R and 388 RBI, and never hit less than .319/.410/.524 in any season. In July 1948, he homered in five consecutive AB for AAA Kansas City. But all this slugging only got him two brief promotions to Cleveland in 1948–49, where he got 2 H in 14 PA and a single unsuccessful pinch hit AB in the 1948 World Series. The problem was that Cleveland already had All-Star 3B Ken Keltner, who hit 31 HR with 119 RBI in 1948 and was far better defensively than Rosen. Rosen got an extended call-up in July 1949, as the 32-year-old Keltner began to decline, but he saw only sporadic action (23 G, 51 PA) and got only two doubles, five singles, and seven walks. Rosen finally got his break on April 18, 1950, when the Indians released Keltner and made Rosen their everyday third baseman.

There was never any doubt that Rosen could slug. In his first full major league season, he hit .287/.405/.543 (145 OPS+) with 5.9 WAR in 668 PA. He led the AL with 37 HR and

Al Rosen of the Cleveland Indians, posing bare-armed and holding a bat with a backdrop of appreciative female fans, was one of the AL's most prolific power hitters in 1950–54 (National Baseball Hall of Fame Museum).

added 100 R, 116 RBI, and 100 BB for good measure. He took a step back in 1951, hitting .265/.362/.447 (124 OPS+) with 24 HR, 82 R, 102 RBI, and 3.5 WAR. His defense at 3B also regressed; his fielding average and dWAR fell from .969 and 0.8, respectively, in 1950 to .958 and -0.3 in 1951. In 1952, Rosen's offensive production returned to its 1950 level. He hit .302/.387/.524 (160 OPS+) with 28 HR, 101 R, 105 RBI, and 6.0 WAR and was elected to start his first All-Star game, walking and scoring a run in 2 PA. However, his defense at 3B remained shaky. On August 19, with the Indians trailing the first place Yankees by only two games, the Indians blew a 5–2 lead to the Red Sox in which Rosen went 0-for-5, grounded into two double plays, and interfered with pitcher Early Wynn who was trying to field a ninth inning bunt.[4] Indians manager Al Lopez benched Rosen in favor of Hank Majeski for the rest of the series.[5] The move worked, as Majeski went 4-for-5 with 2 R and 1 RBI in an 18–8 rout the next day to cut the lead to one game. Still, Rosen was back two days later against the Yankees as the Indians won to pull into a first place tie. However, the Indians lost the next day, and the Yankees held on to win their fourth consecutive pennant by two games over the frustrated Indians. It was the second consecutive year in which the Indians won 93 games but finished second.

Rosen worked hard over the off-season to improve his game, fielding hundreds of groundballs and giving up golf to focus on his baseball swing. His efforts paid off in 1953 with the best season not only of his career but arguably, of any third baseman in MLB history (Table 11).

Table 11: Selected Stats for Al Rosen's Peak and Runner-Up Seasons and His Career*

Season	Age	PA	AVG	OBP	SLG	OPS+	TB	HR	R	RBI	WAR (H)	dWAR
Peak 1953	29	688	0.336	0.422	**0.613**	**180**	**367**	**43**	**115**	**145**	10.1	1.0
per 650 PA							347	41	109	137	9.5	0.9
Runner-Up 1952	28	649	0.302	0.387	0.524	160	297	28	101	**105**	6.0	-0.3
per 650 PA							297	28	101	105	6.0	-0.3
Career (1946–56)		4374	0.285	0.384	0.495	137	1844	192	603	717	32.3	0.4
per 650 PA							274	29	90	107	4.8	0.1

*League leading totals are shown in boldface type.

Rosen, who led the AL in HR, R, RBI, TB, SLG, OPS+, and WAR, was the unanimous choice for MVP.[6] He just missed winning the AL Triple Crown when he barely failed to beat out an infield grounder on the season's final day, ceding the batting title to Mickey Vernon, .337 to .336.[7] Furthermore, his fielding improved dramatically. His fielding average and dWAR improved to .964 and 1.0, respectively, and for the

11. The Hebrew Hammer 71

first time, he led AL 3B in assists after finishing sixth in 1952. Rosen also finished fourth in range factor (his first top 10 finish). He was elected to start the All-Star game again, but was hitless in 4 PA.

Rosen was outstanding in every month of the 1953 season.[8] His worst month was June, when he hit .292/.389/.540 with 7 HR and 25 RBI in 131 PA. He saved his best month for last, hitting .392/491/.680 with 8 HR and 23 RBI in September. However, the Indians once again fell short by 8.5 games in their annual quest to dethrone the Yankees as AL champions, finishing second for the third straight year. The Yankees won their fifth consecutive AL pennant and WS championship.

Rosen picked up where he left off in the first two months of the 1954 season, hitting .361/.429/.660 with 13 HR and 49 RBI in 178 PA in April-May, as Cleveland raced to a first place 28–13 record en route to an AL record-setting 111 wins (eight more than the Yankees).[9] However, held back by a broken finger that sidelined him from June 5–14, he slumped to .264/.371/.340 with only 1 HR and 7 RBI in 62 PA in June.[10] He was still elected to start the 1954 All-Star Game, where his 2 HR and 5 RBI led the AL to an 11–9 victory and earned All-Star MVP recognition.[11] Rosen improved to .304/.404/.518 with 5 HR and 22 RBI in 136 PA in July, although his finger still bothered him. He remained in the lineup but slumped terribly in August to .194/.317/.350 with 3 HR and 14 RBI in 123 PA. He played sparingly (19 G, 67 PA) in September, hitting .373/.522/.579, but with only 2 HR and 10 RBI. Despite his injury and uneven performance, Rosen enjoyed an excellent 4.4 WAR season, hitting .300/.404/.506 (147 OPS+) with 24 HR, 76 R, and 102 RBI. However, he was outshone on his own team by Bobby Avila (7.1 WAR), Larry Doby (5.7 WAR), and pitchers Early Wynn (5.5 WAR), Bob Lemon (4.9 WAR), and Mike Garcia (4.6 WAR). Yogi Berra (5.3 WAR) was named the AL MVP. Rosen finally got his first (and only) opportunity to participate meaningfully in the World Series in 1954. Unfortunately, he could only muster three harmless singles and a walk in 13 PA, as Willie Mays, Dusty Rhodes, and the underdog New York Giants swept the Indians 4–0.[12]

Although Rosen was still only 30 years old, 1954 would be his last good season. Hampered by a back injury suffered in a traffic accident, Rosen hit only .254/.358/.414 (103 OPS+) in 1955–56 and averaged only 538 PA, 18 HR, 62 R, 71 RBI, and 1.6 WAR per season. The Indians reverted to their pre–1954 status, finishing second to the Yankees each year. Balking at the prospect of a second $5000 pay cut and frustrated by his inability to play up to the standards he had set in 1950–54, Rosen announced his retirement from baseball after the season.[13]

Rosen then left baseball for a 17-year career as an investment banker in the Cleveland office of Bache and Company, although he kept his hand in as a spring batting instructor for the Indians.[14] However, his life changed in March 1971 when his wife of 19 years, Teresa, died in a fall from the 19th floor of the Warwick Hotel in Philadelphia—an apparent suicide.[15] He married his second wife Rita less than a year later.[16] In 1973, Rosen left investment banking for a job in the business office of Caesar's Palace in Las Vegas, which he occupied for five years.[17]

But even after 22 years away from the game, Al Rosen was not done with baseball. In 1978, his old friend George Steinbrenner (with whom he had become friendly when he was an investment banker and Steinbrenner was a shipbuilding executive in Cleveland) hired Rosen as president of the Yankees.[18] There he found himself in the uncomfortable position of go-between between Steinbrenner and another strong personality, manager Billy Martin, with whom he often clashed. Things came to a head on July 24, with the Yankees trailing the Red Sox by 10.5 games, when Martin was forced to resign after famously saying of Reggie Jackson and Steinbrenner, "One's a born liar and the other's convicted."[19] Forced to find a new manager, Rosen called on his old Cleveland teammate Bob Lemon, who calmed the waters and managed the Yankees to a stirring comeback, which culminated in a memorable playoff win over the Red Sox for the AL pennant, decided by an unlikely walk-off HR by light-hitting Bucky Dent, and a 4–2 World Series victory over the Dodgers.[20] However, nothing ever lasted long in Steinbrenner world. In 1979, Martin was back in, Lemon was out, and Rosen was shunted to the sidelines, dealing only with business matters. Rosen resigned in September.[21] He accepted an executive position at Bally's Casino in Atlantic City but had to resign in October 1980 after authorizing $2.5 million in bad loans.[22]

Undaunted, Rosen returned to baseball in November 1980 when Houston owner John McMullin hired him to replace Tal Smith as the Astros president and general manager. Again, he walked into a firestorm, since Smith, who had just presided over Houston's first playoff team, was very popular and McMullin was feuding with his partners, many of whom wanted to retain Smith.[23] Shortly after joining the Astros, Rosen had to undergo open heart surgery. Although the Astros were a winning team under Rosen's stewardship, they failed to reach the postseason.

When the Astros replaced Rosen in September 1985, he immediately accepted a position as president and general manager of the San Francisco Giants, who were coming off a 100-loss season and consecutive last-place finishes.[24] Finally given a free hand, Rosen installed Roger Craig as the manager and set about returning the Giants to respectability. Sparked by the addition of rookies Will Clark and Robby Thompson and a career year from veteran ace Mike Krukow, the Giants improved to 83–79 in 1986 and then won the NL West Division pennant (90–72) in 1987. Rosen won the 1987 Executive of the Year award, becoming the only former MVP to be so honored. After regressing to 83–79 in 1988, the Giants won the NL pennant in 1989, but got swept by the Oakland A's in the World Series (which was interrupted by an earthquake). Rosen remained with the Giants through 1992, when he and Rita retired for good to Rancho Mirage, CA. Rosen was 91 years old when he died on March 13, 2015.

Why Was Al Rosen a Shooting Star?

Rosen qualifies as a shooting star because his 10.1 WAR in 1953—the highest of any position player profiled in this book—was 68 percent higher than in his runner-up 1952 season (Figure 11).

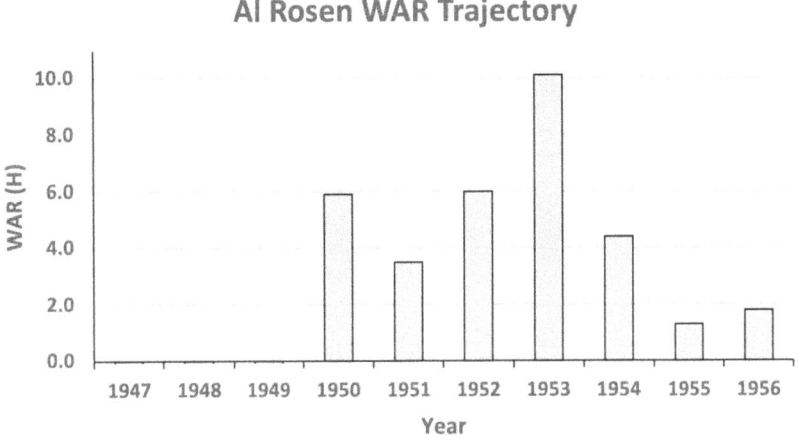

However, as one of the AL's premier sluggers for an uninterrupted five year period (1950–54), Rosen's career arc stretches the boundary of the shooting star rubric. Although 1953 was clearly his best season, with an MVP and uncontested career highs in every offensive category, he was good for too long to fit the typical mold. However, what made his 1953 MVP season an outlier was his uncharacteristically strong defensive performance at 3B. It was as if Harmon Killebrew (an HOF slugger, whose defensive struggles forced a mid-career move from 3B to 1B)

suddenly turned into Mike Schmidt for one season. Because his career was so short, Rosen's 10.1 WAR in 1953 accounted for 31 percent of his 32.3 career WAR. However, it was only the brevity of his career, delayed by lack of a major league opportunity until age 26 and ended prematurely by a back injury that limited his mobility, which prevented him from compiling far more impressive career totals.

Al Rosen had to overcome many hardships to accomplish what he did—poverty, an absent father, wasting four years destroying minor league pitching while being denied a major league opportunity, his wife's suicide, and having his hands tied as a GM by two of MLB's more mercurial team owners. He was also a fighter, who forcefully stood up against the antisemitism he encountered along the way.[25] Whatever the obstacles, Al Rosen persevered until he eventually reached the peak of his profession both as a player and executive. That, if nothing else, makes him worth remembering.

◆ 12 ◆

Diamond Jim
James Edward "Jim" Gentile (1961)

From the proliferation of farm systems in the 1930s until the expansion of the 1960s it was not unusual for "quadruple A" players who had proven all they could in the minor leagues to be denied a legitimate major league opportunity. We have already seen in recent chapters how this issue held back the careers of Tommy Holmes, Harry Brecheen, and Al Rosen. But no one's career was more profoundly affected than lefty slugger Jim Gentile, who had been stuck in the Dodgers' farm system from 1953 to 1959 despite pummeling minor league pitchers for 208 HR and 702 RBI over the course of seven seasons at 1B. Finally, Gentile got a reprieve when the rebuilding Orioles acquired his services in 1960. With the Dodgers, he was blocked at 1B by future Hall of Famer Gil Hodges, with OF/1B Ron Fairly (who was four years younger than Gentile) waiting in the wings as Hodges turned 35. With the Orioles, Gentile only had to beat out 40-year-old incumbent 1B Bob Boyd, who had hit only 3 HR with 41 RBI in 1959. By 1961, Gentile was a shooting star.

James Edward Gentile was born into an Italian-American family in San Francisco on June 3, 1934, and was raised, along with his three siblings, by his maternal grandmother after his parents' marriage fell apart.[1] He became interested in baseball at an early age and served as a batboy for his favorite minor league team, the San Francisco Seals. He starred for his high school team (Sacred Heart Cathedral Preparatory) as a pitcher and right fielder and helped the team win two city championships in 1951–52. He was only 18 when he signed with the Brooklyn Dodgers out of high school as a pitcher. After he went 2–6 with a 3.65 ERA in 1952, the Dodgers converted him to 1B.

Gentile spent the rest of the 1950s in the minor leagues, making only two forgettable cameo appearances, totaling 41 PA, with the parent club in 1957–58. In the minors, he developed a reputation as a fearsome power hitter with an equally fearsome temper. In 1953–56, he smacked 136 HR and drove in 452 runs in Class A and AA leagues, while batting between .270 and .297. After hitting 40 HR in the pitcher-friendly Texas League in 1956, Gentile joined the NL Champion Dodgers in a successful (14–4–1) post-season tour of Japan and contributed 8 HR.[2] Gentile was a bit less productive at AAA Montreal in 1957, hitting only 24 HR with 90 RBI, but made his major league debut on September 10, drawing a walk in a 9–2 loss to the Cubs. On September 22, his first major league hit was a home run against Robin Roberts in a 7–3 win over the Phillies. Two days later, he was the starting 1B in the Dodgers' final game at Ebbets Field. But in 1958, he found himself back at AAA Spokane. He had a terrible season, hitting only .249/.338/.432 and injuring his hand punching a water cooler. His lackadaisical performance landed him back in AAA in 1959 after a trade to the White Sox fell through.[3] Although he clashed with St. Paul manager Max Macon, he recovered to hit .288/.389/.512 with 27 HR and 87 RBI. This was enough to attract the interest of the Baltimore Orioles who acquired him conditionally for $50,000 and two players to be named (PTBN) if he stuck with the team.

Coming off an impressive offseason performance in the Panamanian winter league, Gentile arrived in the Orioles training camp in spring 1960 with a clear shot at earning the starting 1B job. The Orioles, who were coming off a sixth place finish in 1959, had not had a winning record since 1945 and were desperate for power. Their team HR leader was catcher Gus Triandos with 25. Gentile had a terrible spring, but manager Paul Richards gave him 120 AB to prove himself and avoid being returned to the Dodgers.[4] Gentile rose to the challenge, hitting .322/.469/.519 with 4 HR and 26 RBI in 113 PA through the end of May.[5] The power then kicked in in June, when he hit .351/.485/.730 with 8 HR and 28 RBI. He made the AL All-Star team as a reserve, but did not play in either game. Needless to say, the Orioles opted to hold onto their new slugger and gladly sent the two PTBN (Wille Miranda and Bill Lajoie) and perhaps a nice thank you note to the Dodgers to complete the trade. Gentile cooled off somewhat in the second half to finish at .292/.403/.500 (145 OPS+), with 21 HR, 98 RBI, 67 R, and 3.1 WAR. With the infusion of power from Gentile and Rookie of the Year SS Ron Hansen, who hit 22 HR, the Orioles hit 22 more HR (123 vs 101) and scored 131 more runs (682 vs 551) than in 1959, and improved to second place at 89–65, eight games behind the Yankees.

However, what Gentile did in 1961 leaves his fine rookie season in the dust (Table 12).

12. Diamond Jim

Table 12: Selected Stats for Jim Gentile's Peak and Runner-Up Seasons and His Career*

Season	Age	PA	AVG	OBP	SLG	OPS+	TB	HR	R	RBI	WAR (H)
Peak 1961	27	601	0.302	0.423	0.646	187	314	46	96	**141**	6.9
per 650 PA							340	50	104	152	7.5
Runner-Up 1960	26	464	0.292	0.403	0.500	145	192	21	67	98	3.1
per 650 PA							269	29	94	137	4.3
Career (1957–66)		3479	0.260	0.368	0.486	136	1421	179	434	549	17.0
per 650 PA							265	33	81	103	3.2

*League leading totals are shown in boldface type.

Gentile absolutely pulverized AL pitching. He led the AL only in RBI (tied with Maris at 141) but finished third behind the Yankees' "M-boys" in HR and third behind Mantle and Norm Cash (but ahead of Maris) in SLG and OPS+. His performance included an AL record-tying four grand slam HR, two of them coming in consecutive AB in consecutive innings—an unprecedented feat.[6] However, Gentile's tour de force season was overshadowed by the Maris-Mantle race to 61 HR, and he finished third behind the two Yankee stars (but ahead of Cash) in the MVP voting. Gentile was especially torrid in July and August, when he hit .378/.505/.872 with 25 HR and 56 RBI, but slumped badly to a tepid .184/.282/.368 in September.[7] He was again selected as an All-Star reserve (behind Cash) but played only in Game 1, going hitless in 2 AB.[8] Although the Orioles improved to 95 wins, they could do no better than third place, 14 games behind the Yankees 109-win juggernaut and 6 games behind the 101-win Tigers. In an interesting footnote to the 1961 season, Maris was originally credited with 142 RBI, one more than Gentile. It was not until a scoring correction in 2010, which took 1 RBI away from Maris, that Gentile was credited with a share of the 1961 RBI championship. The Orioles invited him to Camden Yard that year and surprised Gentile by presenting him with a giant $5000 bonus check, recognizing his accomplishment 39 years after the fact.[9]

After the season, a *Sport Magazine* article compared Gentile's first two major league seasons favorably to those of Hall of Fame sluggers like Babe Ruth, Jimmy Foxx, and Hank Greenberg.[10] These comparisons were clearly ridiculous, even without the benefit of hindsight. Gentile continued to provide solid power numbers and made his only All-Star start in 1962 (going hitless in 3 AB), but he hit only .250/.349/.453 (124 OPS+) in 1221 PA in 1962–63, while averaging 28 HR, 80 RBI, 72 R, and 2.4 WAR per season.[11] He did not get along with the new Orioles manager, Billy Hitchcock, who tried to get Gentile to pull the ball more.[12] The Orioles plummeted to seventh place (77–85) in 1962. Although they rebounded to fourth (86–76) in 1963, they had failed to fulfill the promise of 1960–61. Changes were in order.

On November 27, 1963, the Orioles traded Gentile to Kansas City for steadier (but less powerful) 1B Norm Siebern. The deal made sense for the Orioles, who had a similar but younger lefty slugger, Boog Powell, playing out of position in LF. Although new manager Hank Bauer did not move Powell to 1B immediately, the replacement of Gentile with Siebern at 1B gave the Orioles a more balanced lineup.[13] Meanwhile, the eighth place A's also brought in slugging Rocky Colavito from Detroit, who with Gentile, would hopefully give them a formidable righty-lefty middle-of-the-order power pairing.[14] The moves didn't work. Although Gentile and Colavito combined for 62 HR and 173 RBI, the A's lost 105 games and fell to 10th place. Gentile specifically remained stuck at his 1962–63 performance level, hitting .251/.372/.465 (128 OPS+) with 28 HR, 71 RBI, 71 R, and 1.5 WAR. The drop in WAR reflected Gentile's defensive deterioration to -1.0 dWAR; he had previously been considered an above average defensive 1B.

The abject failure of the 1964 restructuring prompted the A's to reverse course, trading Colavito to Cleveland during the off-season and sending Gentile to Houston in May 1965 to make room for young 1B Ken Harrelson. Although the A's again lost > 100 games and finished last, youngsters like Bert Campaneris and Catfish Hunter began to lay the groundwork for their championship teams of the early 1970s. Over in Houston, however, the move to the Astrodome was Kryptonite for Gentile. In 81 games with the Astros, Gentile hit only .242/.352/.392 (117 OPS+) and managed only 7 HR and 31 RBI in the cavernous Astrodome. Things got no better in 1966. When umpire Ed Vargo ejected Gentile for twice tossing a bat in his direction on June 24, the Astros demoted him to AAA Oklahoma City.[15] A few weeks later, Gentile was traded to Cleveland, where he finished out his major league career as a backup to Fred Whitfield at 1B. Gentile tried unsuccessfully to make the Phillies in 1968, and accepted $25,000 to play in Japan in 1969.[16] However, he missed two months with a ruptured Achilles tendon and hit only 8 HR with 16 RBI for Otsuka. He was not invited back.

After he left baseball, Gentile mostly worked in the automotive business, selling tires and briefly operating a Midas Mufflers franchise.[17] He also managed two independent baseball teams—the Fort Worth Cats (2001–02) and Mid–Missouri Mavericks (2004–05) and ran a baseball camp in Chandler, OK. He is now retired and lives in Oklahoma with Paula, his wife of fifty years.

Why Was Jim Gentile a Shooting Star?

Jim Gentile was a solid slugging first basement, whose outstanding 1961 season was clearly an outlier, abetted perhaps by the dilution of pitching talent following expansion of the AL from eight to ten teams. His 6.9 WAR (H) that season represented 41 percent of his career total; he never posted more than 3.1 WAR in any other season (Figure 12).

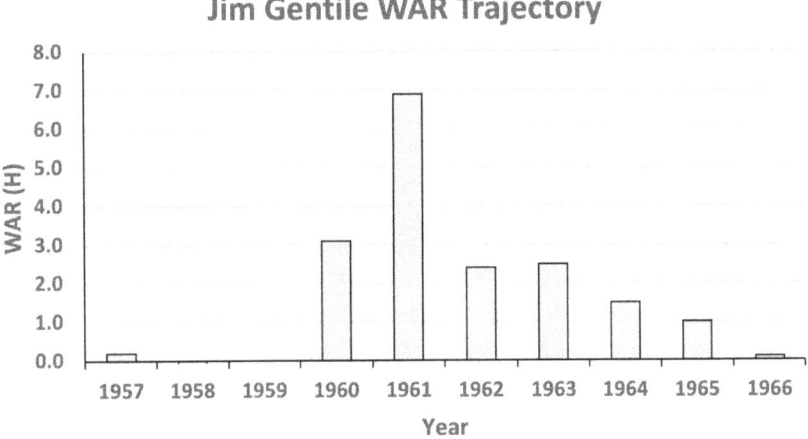

Gentile was clearly no Hall of Famer, not even close. That being said, the fact that he spent seven prime years stuck in the Dodgers' minor league system undoubtedly held him back from attaining a far more impressive career total than his actual 17.0 WAR. Opportunity came too late for Jim Gentile to be more than a shooting star. One wonders how many other all-but-forgotten players who were born before 1940 might have achieved stardom if there had been more MLB teams, if these teams had been open to all comers, and if the reserve clause had not buried so many major league ready players in the overstocked minor league farm systems of teams like the Yankees, Dodgers and Cardinals, who had "No Vacancy" signs at the major league level.

◈ 13 ◈

Stormin' Norman
Norman Dalton "Norm" Cash (1961)

The dawn of the expansion era in 1961 was a vintage year for memorable batting seasons. Cash's 9.2 WAR was only the third best of 1961, trailing Mickey Mantle (10.5 WAR, his third best season) and Henry Aaron (9.4 WAR, his personal best). Willie Mays (8.7 WAR) also had a terrific season (only his 10th best!). The 1961 season also featured Roger Maris's record-breaking 61 HR (6.9 WAR, his second best season), Al Kaline's (8.4 WAR, his third best season) and Frank Robinson's 7.7 WAR (his third best season). Ken Boyer (8.0 WAR), Vada Pinson (7.5 WAR), and Rocky Colavito (7.6 WAR), as well as Jim Gentile (Chapter 12), all had career years.

Cash was no one-year wonder. The burly lefty-hitting 1B had a fine 17-year major league career; his 52.0 career WAR is the second highest of the 30 players featured in this book, behind only Dwight Gooden's 53.0 WAR (48.1 for pitching and 4.8 for hitting—see Chapter 23). While Cash received only six Hall of Fame votes from the BBWAA in 1980 (his lone appearance on the ballot), he had a strong case for the hypothetical "Hall of the Very Good." His 373 HR in a Detroit uniform is tied with Miguel Cabrera for second on the Tigers' all-time list—between Al Kaline (399) and Hank Greenberg (366). But after slashing .361/.487/.662 (201 OPS+) in 1961, he would never again hit ≥.283 or reach 150 OPS+. Indeed, perhaps unfairly, the good-natured fun-loving Texan would be remembered more for his pranks and uninhibited personality than his considerable prowess on the diamond. After all, it was Norm Cash who stepped to the plate carrying a table leg instead of a bat with two out in the ninth inning of a Nolan Ryan no-hitter on July 15, 1973, claiming that he stood no chance against Ryan with a conventional bat.[1] When the umpire made him get a bat, Cash struck out meekly on three pitches.

13. Stormin' Norman

Norm Cash was born in tiny Justiceburg, TX, about 60 miles southeast of Lubbock, on November 10, 1934.² His family owned a 250-acre cotton farm, where young Norman helped out from an early age by hoeing and driving a tractor. He starred in football at Sul Ross State college setting the school rushing record with 1255 yards in his senior year (1955). He was drafted by the Chicago Bears, but he chose baseball and signed with the White Sox. After showing good power in Class B in 1955–56, hitting 40 HR in 906 PA, he served in the military for most of 1957–58. He returned for 29 games in AAA in August 1958, following a brief June stint with the White Sox. Cash spent the entire 1959 season with the AL Champion "Go-Go" White Sox as a pinch-hitter and backup 1B behind Earl Torgeson and slugging mid-season acquisition Ted Kluszewski. Although Cash was their best defender at 1B, he hit only .240/.372/.375 (107 OPS+) with 4 HR in 130 PA and was included as a throw-in a short-sighted trade to bring back aging fan-favorite Minnie Minoso from Cleveland to bolster their team for 1960. On April 12, 1960, before he had played a game for them, the Indians flipped Cash to Detroit for Steve Demeter, who disappeared from MLB after going 0-for-5 in four games in 1960.

When the 1960 season began, the Tigers had a few prominent stars like Al Kaline, Rocky Colavito, Jim Bunning, and Frank Lary, but were otherwise mediocre. Although Cash, who hit .286/.402/.501 (140 OPS+) with 18 HR and 63 RBI in 428 PA, was a distinct upgrade over 1959 incumbent 1B Gail Harris, the Tigers actually finished four

This late career photograph of Norm Cash, probably from the early 1970s, captured the usually happy-go-lucky Detroit first baseman in a contemplative mood in the Tiger dugout (Doug McWilliams/National Baseball Hall of Fame Museum).

games worse (71–83) than they had done in 1959 (75–79) and fell from fourth to sixth place. But 1961 was a different story.

When new Detroit manager Bob Scheffing pointed to the obscure 26-year-old Cash in spring training of 1961 as the next AL batting champion, no one took it as more than the usual spring hype.[3] After losing to Cleveland 9–5 on opening Day, the Tigers rattled off an eight-game winning streak, including a 4–3 win over the Yankees by notorious "Yankee killer" Frank Lary, in which Cash's fourth inning HR put the Tigers ahead for good.[4] They remained in first place through May and after a June 4 double header sweep of Minnesota stood at 33–16 with a lead of 2.0 games over Cleveland and 5.5 games over the Yankees. On that date, Norm Cash, who went 5–7 in that double-header, led the AL with a .345 AVG and had 12 HR with 44 RBI. After a three-game losing streak knocked them out of first place, the Tigers regained the lead on June 14 and held it through July 6. A blistering stretch by Cash, who hit .413/.506/.947 with 11 HR and 22 RBI in 89 PA between June 10 and July 1, fueled the Tigers' 15–6 hot streak during this 3-week stretch.[5] Although Cash slumped in early July and his AVG fell from off a bit from a peak of .373 on July 1, the Tigers were 55–30 and still led the second-place Yankees (who were hitting HR at a record pace) by 1.5 games at the All-Star break on July 9. Cash, now hitting .355/.483/.666 with 24 HR and 75 RBI, was elected to start the All-Star game at 1B over Jim Gentile and Harmon Killebrew.

Unfortunately for the Tigers, the Yankees (led by Maris, Mantle, and four others who each hit at least 20 HR) were just heating up, and the Tigers could not keep pace. The Yankees passed the Tigers for good on July 25, although the Tigers remained very close (1.5 games) through August 31.[6] But after the Yankees swept a critical three-game series with the Tigers on September 1–3, the Tigers lost five more games in a row to fall a full 10 games out of first place. Cash held his own during this streak, batting .276/.344/.517 with 2 HR, but it was not enough. The Tigers finished 101–61, 8.0 games behind the Yankees. But Cash easily won the major league batting championship, outhitting AL runner-up Al Kaline by 37 points and NL champion Roberto Clemente by 9 points. Cash's 1961 stats (Table 13) all represented career bests.

Cash's .361 AVG was the not only the highest of 1961, it was the highest in more than a decade, spanning 1958–69. His 41 HR ranked sixth in the AL and seventh in MLB, his 132 RBI ranked fourth in the AL and fifth in MLB, and his 201 OPS+ ranked second in MLB (behind only Mantle's 206). Cash even posted 11 of his 43 career SB in 1961.

Cash and the Tigers entered 1962 with high hopes, but they were quickly dashed. They never stood higher than fourth place after May 3, and never got closer than 9.0 games out of first place after July 15.[7] They struggled to remain above .500, and stood at 73–73 as late as September 15, before rallying in the final two weeks to finish fourth at 85–76, 10.5 games behind the pennant winning Yankees. While Cash continued to hit with power (39 HR, 89 RBI, 135 OPS+), his batting average fell by more than 100 points to .243. Although the productivity of 1961 stalwarts Colavito, Kaline, and Frank Lary also declined in 1962, and Cash's 3.6 WAR still ranked third among Tiger position players, it was Cash who received the lion's share of the blame for the Tigers' failure to contend. But in truth, 1962 was a better gauge than 1961 of Cash's true ability. As Cash himself said, every ball he hit in 1961 seemed to drop in, but he was not so lucky in 1962.[8] Still, while his 3.6 WAR and a 135 OPS+ of 1962 stacked up poorly against his 9.2 WAR and a 202 OPS+ of 1961, Cash remained a valuable player.

Table 13: Selected Stats for Norm Cash's Peak and Runner-Up Seasons and His Career*

Season	Age	PA	AVG	OBP	SLG	OPS+	TB	H	HR	R	RBI	BB	WAR (H)
Peak 1961	26	673	**0.361**	**0.487**	0.662	201	354	**193**	41	119	132	124	9.2
per 650 PA							342	186	40	115	127	120	8.9
Runner-Up 1965	30	553	0.266	0.371	0.512	148	239	124	30	79	83	77	5.4
per 650 PA							281	146	35	93	98	91	6.3
Career (1958–74)		7914	0.271	0.374	0.488	139	3274	1820	377	1045	1104	1043	52.0
per 650 PA							269	149	31	86	91	86	4.3

*League leading totals are shown in boldface type.

In the mid-1960s, Cash remained a solid middle-of-the-order slugger on a gradually improving Tigers team. From 1963 to 1967, he hit .263/.362/.469 (133 OPS+) and averaged 27 HR, 82 RBI, 74 R, and 4.1 WAR in 593 PA. In the best of those seasons (1965), he posted a 148 OPS+ and 5.4 WAR (see Table 13). By 1967, the Tigers had developed the core of a championship team (Denny McLain, Mickey Lolich, Earl Wilson, Bill Freehan, Dick McAuliffe, Willie Horton, Jim Northrup, Mickey Stanley, in addition to old standbys Cash and Kaline) and barely lost out to Boston in a close four-team pennant race on the final day of the season. However, Cash, who was now 32 years old, slumped at the end of the season and lost playing time to late-season acquisition Eddie Mathews (who was nearing the end of his Hall of Fame career).

Cash began the 1968 World Series championship season in a horrific slump and was hitting only .195/.289/.419 after a fruitless pinch-hitting appearance on July 24.[9] Al Kaline had essentially replaced him as the everyday first baseman. After riding the bench for the next three days, Cash finally got a start at 1B on July 27 and broke out with a 4-for-5 performance in a 9–0 win over Baltimore. After sitting out the series finale against lefty Dave McNally, he returned to the starting lineup on July 29 and got his 14th HR and 31st RBI. He went on from there to hit to hit .326/.389/.535 with 11 HR and 32 RBI in the last two months to finish at.263/.329/.487 (142 OPS+) with 25 HR, 63 RBI, and 3.5 WAR in 458 PA.[10] Cash stayed hot in the World Series, hitting .385/.433/.500 in 30 PA against the Cardinals, including a leadoff HR off Nelson Briles in the sixth inning of Game 2 to extend a 2–0 lead in a must-win game and two key RBI that helped bring back the Tigers from the brink of defeat in Game 5 when they were down three games to one.[11] The Tigers came back to win the Series in seven games.

Although Cash continued to be benched often against lefties, he remained an above average player at ages 34–36 in 1969–71, batting .275/.373/.481 (134 OPS+) and averaging 23 HR, 73 RBI, 70 R, and 2.9 WAR in 510 PA—just a notch below his 1962–68 performance level. In 1971, he started the season so well that the fans voted him into the All-Star Game. Although he fell off somewhat in the second half, he still finished with 32 HR—one behind AL leader Bill Melton—and 91 RBI and batted .283. It was his second highest AVG for a full season.

Cash declined considerably in 1972–73, hitting only .260/.347/.457 (128 OPS+) and averaging 20 HR, 50 RBI, 51 R, and 1.8 WAR in 460 PA. Still, he managed to hit .267/.353/.467 in the 1972 ALCS, including a HR off Catfish Hunter that gave the Tigers an early lead in Game 1 and a bases-loaded tenth-inning walk that tied Game 4 ahead of Northrup's game-winning single.[12] On August 12, 1973, the Tigers held a Norm Cash Day at Tiger Stadium to salute his 14 distinguished seasons as a Tiger.[13] At Cash's request, he received only symbolic gifts; fan contributions were directed to the Police Athletic League for the support of youth sports programs.

The end came abruptly in 1974, starting with the spring training announcement that another Cash—24-year-old Ron—would platoon with 39-year-old Norm at 1B.[14] Neither Cash would hold the job. Ron was a flop, appearing in only 20 games in 1974 and never playing in the major leagues again. Norm slumped badly and played only 44 games at 1B, losing his starting job to Bill Freehan, then was unceremoniously released on August 6. The 1974 season was also Al Kaline's swan song, but he was allowed to retire gracefully. The Tigers, who had been a steady contender (except for one season) since 1967, finished at 72–90, last in the AL East Division.

Norm Cash did not live to enjoy a long retirement. Capitalizing on his Detroit connections and his outgoing personality, Cash took a job as an automobile sales rep but became bored and moved into broadcasting. He worked briefly in 1976 as a commentator on ABC's Monday Night Baseball, but his pungent and irreverent humor offended some viewers and led to his dismissal.[15] He also played professional slow-pitch softball with the Detroit Caesars in 1977–78.[16] However, Cash, who had a longstanding fondness for the bottle, suffered a significant stroke in 1979.[17] By 1981 he had recovered enough to provide color commentary on Tigers cable TV telecasts but had to step down in 1983 because his advancing cerebrovascular disease had slurred his speech. When he appeared at an old-timers' game at Tiger Stadium in 1986, his physical condition had deteriorated to the point where he could not field routine groundballs, and he was embarrassed when a one-hop throw to 1B bounced off his head.[18] On Columbus Day weekend that year, after he had been drinking heavily, he lost his balance on a wet dock while trying to board his 30-foot cabin cruiser, slipped into the water, and drowned. Cash's advanced cerebrovascular disease and his inebriation both probably contributed to his inability to climb out of the water and save himself.[19] He was a month shy of his 52nd birthday.

Why Was Norm Cash a Shooting Star?

Norm Cash is remembered in his obituaries mainly for his flukish .361 batting average in 1961–90 points above his career AVG—and for the time he carried a table leg to home plate to face Nolan Ryan, but he was much more than a fluke or a clown. Cash had an excellent 17-year career, with 52.0 WAR and nine seasons with ≥ 3.0 WAR. He was no Hall of Famer, but his 52.0 career WAR stands 31st among all 1B—similar to that of Fred McGriff (52.6) and above Hall of Famers Orlando Cepeda, Frank Chance, Gil Hodges, Jim Bottomley, and High Pockets Kelly.[20] My own Career Value Index (CVI) metric ranks him as the 329th best player of all time though the end of the 2023 season.[21] To put this ranking in context, consider that 77 of the 273 men who have been elected to the Hall of Fame as players through January 2024 rank below Cash in CVI.

Cash was a five-time All-Star and finished fourth in the MVP voting in 1961 and twelfth in 1966 and 1971. While he was generally not a prodigious home run hitter, he hit 20 or more home runs every year from 1961 to 1969, a decade when offense was down throughout baseball. Although six players—Harmon Killebrew, Henry Aaron, Willie Mays, Willie McCovey, Frank Robinson, and Frank Howard—hit more than Cash's 260 HR during these nine years, only Cash, Aaron, and Billy Williams hit at least 20 HR *every* year.[22]

All this notwithstanding, Cash's 1961 season, when he set career highs in every significant offensive category, clearly far outshone the rest of his career (Figure 13).

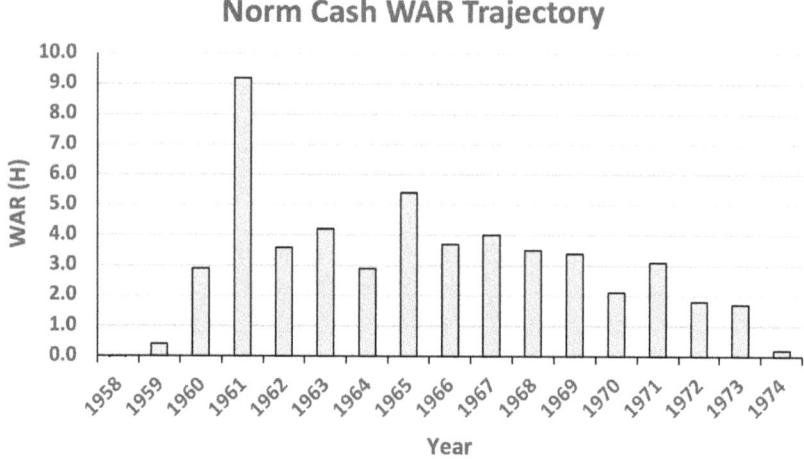

Some have pointed to Cash's admitted use of a corked bat in 1961, as a factor in his anomalous offensive totals that year, but this is unlikely, since he also used a corked bat in 1962, when he hit only .243.[23] Besides, replacing wood with the lighter cork increases bat speed, but the decrease in mass has an offsetting effect on exit velocity. Cash was a consistent power hitter and a mainstay of a good Detroit lineup from 1960 through 1973. His nickname "Stormin' Norman" notwithstanding, Tigers president Jim Campbell eulogized him as "a well-liked free spirit. He was everybody's friend and ... one of the greatest players ever to wear a Tiger uniform. Norm loved life. He would occasionally get his nights and days mixed up, but he never missed a ballgame."[24] The term "shooting star" does not do full justice to this larger-than-life baseball character.

◆ 14 ◆

The World's Most Horrible Hitter[1]
Henry John "Hank" Aguirre (1962)

In 150+ years of MLB history, there have been a few pitchers with lower batting averages than Hank Aguirre's .085, but none looked more helpless at the plate than poor Hank. Watching a major league pitcher face Hank Aguirre was like watching a cat toying with a mouse. If you are old enough to remember John Kruk's comical turn at bat against Randy Johnson in the 1993 All-Star Game, you may be able to conjure up an image of how pathetic the 6'4" Aguirre looked with a bat in his hands against pitchers far less fearsome than the Big Unit. After he hit .027 (2-for-75) n 1962—his peak pitching season—the Detroit press honored this "achievement" by presenting him with a miniature bat with a half-dozen holes drilled in it.[2] Aguirre laughed good-naturedly. When the designated hitter rule was introduced in 1973, Aguirre quipped that this rule could have spared him much embarrassment had it been in effect during his 16-year career. But despite his ineptitude as a hitter, Aguirre was a good lefty pitcher and an even better human being.

Henry John Aguirre was born on January 31, 1931, in Azusa, CA, where his parents had migrated from Jalisco, Mexico, as itinerant farm workers several years earlier. From an early age, he and his six siblings helped his parents pick vegetables to earn a meager living. He loved music and baseball. He learned to play the saxophone and earned an associate degree in music from Pasadena's East Los Angeles Junior College in 1952.[3] After graduation, Aguirre signed a contract to pitch for the Cleveland Indians.

Aguirre gradually worked his way up the minor league chain from 1952 to 1955 and made his major league debut in September 1955 after going 11–9 with a 3.24 ERA in 186 IP with AAA Indianapolis. Although he was effective in his four appearances (2–0, 1.42 ERA), he returned to AAA in 1956 and shuttled between the majors and minors for the rest of 1956 and 1957. He got a break in 1958 when Cleveland GM Frank "Trader" Lane dealt Aguirre and veteran catcher Jim Hegan to Detroit for bonus baby catcher Jay Porter and pitcher Hal Woodeschick. Aguirre spent the 1958 season in the Tiger bullpen, notching 3 W and 5 SV in 69.2 IP (0.7 WAR), but spent almost the entire 1959 season in the minors, posting 8 W and a 3.73 ERA as a starter. His career seemed to be going nowhere.

Relying heavily on his screwball to neutralize right-handed hitters, the left-handed Aguirre finally established himself as a reliable bullpen asset in 1960 at age 29. In 1960–61, he went 9–7 with a 3.00 ERA (135 ERA+), 1.247 WHIP, 18 SV, 112 SO versus 68 BB, and 3.9 WAR in 150 IP (630 BF). In their 101-win 1961 season, Aguirre was the Tigers' second best reliever behind Terry Fox. Aguirre seemed to have carved out a modest but useful niche for himself for the next few years. However, fate held something better in store.

Coming off their highest winning percentage since 1935, the Tigers simply could not get going in 1962.[4] Although Jim Bunning continued to pitch like an ace, sore-armed co-ace Frank Lary was terrible and third and fourth starters Don Mossi and Paul Foytack were only so-so. By May 25, the Tigers were treading water at 18–17.[5] Desperate to find someone to take up the slack, the Tigers turned to Aguirre, who had been moderately effective in ten bullpen appearances (1–2 with 3 SV and a 4.00 ERA in 18 IP), to start against the Yankees on May 26.[6] Aguirre was terrific, yielding only one run and five hits in a complete game 2–1 victory over the defending World Series champions. Aguirre would make 21 more starts and 30 more relief appearances that season, amassing 216.0 IP. After pitching mostly out of the bullpen in April-May, he made three starts and three relief appearances in June, going 4–0 with a 1.79 ERA and 0.793 WHIP in 40.1 IP.[7] In the second half, pitching as a starter in 16 of 22 appearances, he went 9–5 with a 2.29 ERA and 1.165 WHIP in 129.2 IP.[8] Taking up the mantle of injured teammate Frank Lary, Aguirre pitched particularly well against the Yankees, winning three of four starts, and yielding only 3 R and 7 H in 8.1 IP in his only defeat. Perhaps the highlight of his season (although it was far from his best pitched game) was a 7–5 win over the Yankees on June 22, when Aguirre's sixth-inning single off Hal Reniff—one of only two hits he got all season—drove in what turned out to be the winning run.[9] Unfortunately, the Tigers finished a disappointing fourth in the AL that year with an 85–76 record, despite Aguirre's best efforts. Aguirre

14. The World's Most Horrible Hitter

was selected to the 1962 AL All-Star team, and yielded two runs in 3.0 IP in the AL's 9–4 Game 2 victory in his only All-Star appearance.[10] Aguirre wound up leading all AL pitchers in WHIP and all MLB pitchers in ERA, ERA+, and WAR (P) in 1962 (Table 14), but he received no Cy Young award votes and only a smattering of MVP votes.[11]

Table 14: Selected Stats for Hank Aguirre's Peak and Runner-Up Seasons and His Career*

Season	Age	BF	ERA	WHIP	ERA+	W-L	SO	BB	CG	WAR (P)
Peak 1962	31	877	**2.21**	**1.051**	**185**	16–8	156	65	11	7.4
per 1000 BF							178	74	13	8.4
Runner-Up 1963	32	954	3.67	1.285	102	14–15	134	68	14	2.9
per 1000 BF							140	71	15	3.0
Career (1955–70)		5790	3.25	1.232	117	75–72	856	479	44	21.0
per 1000 BF							148	83	8	3.6

*League leading totals are shown in boldface type.

Cinderella's coach would turn back into a pumpkin as the calendar rolled into 1963. Although Aguirre would go on to enjoy five more successful seasons in Detroit, he would never come close to replicating his 1962 success. He enjoyed three more solid years as a starter in 1963–65 with the best being a 2.9 WAR season in 1963 (see Table 14). He could muster only a combined 19–20 with a 3.67 ERA (97 ERA+), a 1.184 WHIP, and 2.6 WAR in 370 IP 1964–65, which made him a slightly below average starting pitcher in those low-scoring seasons. He initially didn't get along with Chuck Dressen when he became the Tigers' manager in mid–1963, but the two men made their peace when Dressen returned after a heart attack in 1965.[12] Aguirre's decline accelerated in 1966, when he went 3–9 with a 3.82 ERA (91 ERA+), 1.254 WHIP, and -0.7 WAR in 103.2 IP, and finished the year in the bullpen. He was used sparingly out of the Tigers bullpen in 1967 and posted a 2.40 ERA in 41.1 IP as the Tigers fell just one game short of the AL pennant.

Unfortunately, Aguirre, now 37 years old did not get to stick around in 1968 for the Tigers' first pennant since 1945 and their exciting come-from-behind World Series victory over St. Louis. His contract was sold to the Dodgers that spring, and he finished out his career with the Dodgers (1968) and Cubs (1969–70) as a lefty bullpen specialist. Although he was quite effective in that role (172 ERA+ in 98.0 IP), the Cubs released him on July 6, 1970. But that was not quite the end of Aguirre's baseball career. Phil Wrigley, always thinking out of the box, brought back Aguirre in 1972 as an "assistant manager" to Leo

Durocher, perhaps a forerunner to the modern "bench coach." After Durocher was replaced, he remained a Cubs coach under Whitey Lockman in 1973–74.

However, Hank Aguirre's 16-year pitching career was not his greatest achievement in life. In 1979, he returned to southwest Detroit (their largest Hispanic community) and invested his entire personal savings plus loans from the Small Business Administration and local community leaders (including Tigers owner John Fetzer) to build an automotive supplies business called Mexican Industries, which provided jobs to Hispanics and (after early struggles) became one of the premier ethnic minority firms in the U.S.[13] By 1990, Aguirre had amassed a fortune of $25 million and ranked 46th on *Hispanic Business Magazine*'s listing of America's wealthiest Hispanics. He even put together a group of investors that made a bid to buy the Tigers in 1990. When Hank Aguirre died of prostate cancer on September 5, 1994, at age 63, his obituaries were less about his prowess on the diamond, than about his vision, philanthropy, and humility.[14] He had only one great year on the mound, but he brought joy every day.

Why Was Hank Aguirre a Shooting Star?

There have been hundreds of pitchers who had more impressive careers than Hank Aguirre. After all, he was a shooting star, who was essentially a league average pitcher for all but one season—four months, really—of his 16-year major league career (Figure 14).

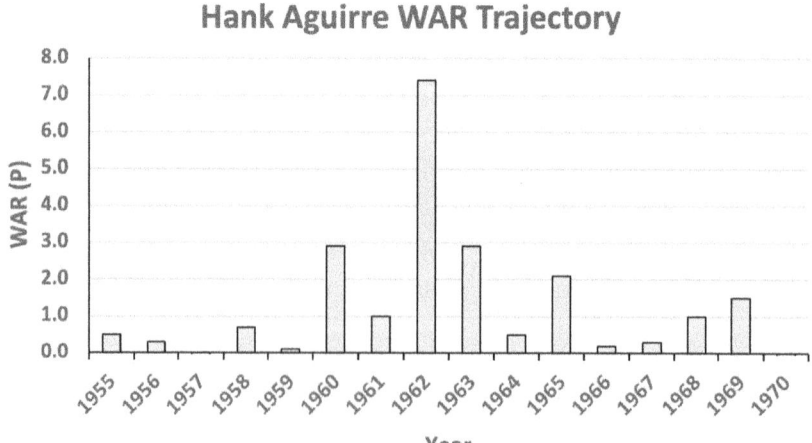

He accrued only 21.0 pitching WAR and 17.8 total WAR during those 16 years. He made only one All-Star team and never pitched in a post-season game. Although Aguirre was a fan favorite and was well-liked by his teammates, his baseball career as a whole was not impactful. Yet, through hard work and an abiding sense of purpose, Hank Aguirre rose from humble beginnings to leave an indelible mark on his community and to win the love and gratitude of his people. There have been many ballplayers with greater on-field accomplishments who cannot say the same.

◈ 15 ◈

Bonus Baby
Richard Clark "Dick" Ellsworth (1963)

As a Cubs fan, I remember 1963 as the first season in my lifetime when the Cubs won more games (82) that they lost (80). True, they finished a lowly seventh in a 10-team league, but surely there would be better things to come, with an emerging core of young stars—Ron Santo, Billy Williams, Lou Brock, Ken Hubbs, and brilliant young lefty Dick Ellsworth—joining still-potent veterans Ernie Banks, Larry Jackson, Lindy McDaniel, and Bob Buhl. No one was more responsible for the Cubs' dramatic improvement from their 103-loss 1962 team than one-time bonus baby Ellsworth, who had finally come into his own after three uneven seasons, including a horrendous 20-loss season in 1962. But nothing is ever that easy for the Cubs. It would be four more years (including a last place 103-loss 1966 season) until the Cubs would again win more games than they lost. By then, Ellsworth was gone, and only Banks, Santo, and Williams remained from 1963.

Dick Ellsworth was born in Lusk, Wyoming, on March 22, 1940, but he and his family moved to Fresno, CA, when he was just three years old.[1] He went 15–0 as the ace of a great 1958 Fresno High School team that would send five players to the major leagues, including mid–1960s Cincinnati ace pitcher Jim Maloney and catcher Pat Corrales, who managed three MLB teams in 1978–87, as well as Ellsworth.[2] (Tom Seaver also starred at Fresno high school a few years later.) The Cubs won a fierce competition for his services with a $60,000 signing bonus. Three days after his graduation, Ellsworth took the mound for the Cubs in an exhibition game against the White Sox. The bonus rule requiring teams to carry prospects who received large signing bonuses—i.e., "bonus babies"—on their major league roster for two years, which impeded the development of Sandy Koufax and Harmon Killebrew and ruined the careers of many less talented prospects, had been rescinded earlier that year, so this exhibition appearance was intended only as a one-off showcase to tantalize hungry Cubs fans.[3] But Ellsworth pitched a four-hit complete-game shutout against a lineup that would finish second to the Yankees in 1958 and dethrone them as AL champions a year later. His performance earned him a start against the Reds in a real game on June 22. However, Ellsworth did not survive the third inning of his major league debut, yielding 4 ER, 4 H, 3 BB, 1 HBP, and 2 WP in 2.1 IP.[4] So, Ellsworth would have to pay his minor league dues.

Ellsworth didn't fare well at AA Fort Worth in 1958, but improved dramatically at AAA Houston in 1959 (10–14, 2.60 ERA). A 2–0, 0.86 ERA start in his first three games (21.0 IP) at Houston in 1960 put him back in the majors for good at age 20. But there would be growing pains. The young lefty held his own in 1960–61, going a combined 17–24, with a 3.79 ERA (105 ERA+), a 1.384 WHIP, and 5.8 WAR in 363.1 IP (1543 BF). The Cubs finished seventh in both years, winning about 40 percent of their games. But Ellsworth and the Cubs both regressed badly in 1962. Foundering under P.K. Wrigley's bizarre "college of coaches" system, in which there was no permanent manager, just a succession of "head coaches" who rotated at irregular intervals to other assignments in the organization, the Cubs fell to 59–103, finishing in ninth place, six games behind the Houston Colt 45s expansion team and ahead of only the historically awful (40–120) New York Mets.[5] The tightly wound Ellsworth, now 22 and suffering perhaps from the absence of consistent mentoring to help channel his fiery temper, fell to 9–20 with a 5.09 ERA (81 ERA+) and a 1.524 WHIP. He was a hot mess, and so were the Cubs. It appeared that Ellsworth was doomed to follow in the footsteps of one-time aspiring Cubs aces like Warren Hacker, Dick Drott, and Glen Hobbie, who failed to fulfill their early promise in the 1950s.

However, the fortunes of Ellsworth and the Cubs took an abrupt upturn in 1963 when owner P.K. Wrigley tacitly admitted the failure of his rotating head coaches by appointing Bob Kennedy as the head coach for the entire season. (The college-of-coaches concept would not disappear entirely until the Cubs hired Leo Durocher as their manager in 1966.) The Cubs also brought in a full-time veteran pitching coach, Fred Martin, and two veteran pitchers, Larry Jackson and Bob Buhl, who could mentor Ellsworth and teach him to throw an effective slider and change-up and to master the art of pitching. The effects of the makeover were immediately apparent.

Ellsworth opened the season with a three-hit 2–0 shutout of the eventual World Series champion Dodgers and lost a 10-inning 1–0 heartbreaker to the Dodgers in Los Angeles six days later.[6] By June 6, Ellsworth's record stood at 8–3 with a 1.51 ERA in 12 starts, and the

Cubs, after sweeping a four-game series from the Giants, stood at 31–23, tied with the Giants and Cardinals for first place. The Cubs could not sustain that lofty position but did climb as high as 10 games over .500 (50–40, second place) on July 18, before eventually fading to 82–80 (seventh place) at the end.

However, Ellsworth did not fade (Table 15).

Table 15: Selected Stats for Dick Ellsworth's Peak and Runner-Up Seasons and His Career*

Season	Age	BF	ERA	WHIP	ERA+	W-L	SO	BB	CG	SHO	WAR (P)
Peak 1963	23	1160	2.11	1.025	**167**	22–10	185	75	19	4	10.2
per 1000 BF							159	65	16	3	8.8
Runner-Up 1961	21	799	3.86	1.398	108	10–11	91	48	7	1	3.7
per 1000 BF							114	60	9	1	4.6
Career (1958–71)		9156	3.72	1.331	100	115–137	1140	595	87	9	23.3
per 1000 BF							125	65	10	1	2.5

*League leading totals are shown in boldface type.

Although he finished second in WAR and ERA to Cy Young award winner Sandy Koufax (who performed in pitcher-friendly Dodgers Stadium), he led the NL in ERA+. He also finished fourth in WHIP (behind Koufax, Juan Marichal, and Houston's Turk Farrell). He completed 19 of his 37 starts and gave up three or fewer ER in 31/37 starts—29 of them "quality starts" (≥ 6 IP, ≤ 3 ER)—including four complete game shutouts and four other games when he was removed before yielding an ER.[7] He even yielded three or fewer ER in seven of his 10 defeats. His best outing was a 2–0 one-hit shutout against the Phillies on June 1, in which he came within a Wes Covington drag bunt of a no-hitter.[8] But he also pitched a two-hit shutout against the Pirates and three-hit shutouts against the Dodgers and Braves. After they could muster only a single unearned run in six innings the first time they faced him on April 21, the Giants gave Ellsworth the most trouble, tagging him for 5 ER in 7.0 IP on June 5, 4 ER in 6.0 IP on September 2 (both games that Ellsworth won) and for 5 ER in 2.2 IP (Ellsworth's worst outing of the season) on August 2. His two other bad outings came in a loss to LA on June 9 (6 ER in 5.2 IP) and a no-decision against Pittsburgh on August 21 (5 ER in 6.1 IP). Ellsworth received no votes for the 1963 Cy Young award, which was won unanimously by Sandy Koufax, and only a smattering of MVP votes. However, his remarkable feat of following a 20-loss season with a 20-win season—the first pitcher to do so since Paul Derringer in 1934—earned him Comeback of the Year honors, perhaps a misnomer for a 22-year-old pitcher who had no great prior major league success to come back to.⁹ In contemporaneous interviews, Ellsworth attributed his turnaround to learning to control his temper, learning to throw a slider and changeup, improving his curveball, and gaining experience. He was also grateful for the mentorship of his teammates Larry Jackson and Bob Buhl and for the installation of the steady Bob Kennedy as full-time head coach and the savvy Fred Martin as pitching coach.¹⁰

Unfortunately, Ellsworth's and the Cubs' newfound success did not carry over to 1964, which began ominously with the death of rising star 2B Ken Hubbs in the crash of his small airplane on February 13. Ellsworth got off to a strong start, standing 8–5 with a 3.05 ERA after a complete game victory over Pittsburgh on June 14.¹¹ He was even selected to the NL All-Star team for the only time in his career, but he did not get into the game. However, the Cubs struggled to keep their heads above water and stood only 27–27, in sixth place on the morning of June 15.¹² Frustrated with the inconsistency of 25-year-old CF Lou Brock, who was hitting a lackluster .251/.300/.340, the Cubs traded him to their archrivals, the St. Louis Cardinals, for sore-armed pitcher Ernie Broglio, in what turned out to be a blunder of historic proportion. Broglio, who had won 21 games in 1960 and 18 in 1963, would win only seven games in his 2.5-years with the Cubs (which closed out his career), while Brock went on to set major league stolen base records as the St. Louis leadoff hitter through 1979 and was elected to the Hall of Fame in 1985. During the two weeks after the trade, the Cubs hovered briefly around .500, like Wile E. Coyote suspended in mid-air churning his legs before realizing that he had run off a cliff, and then sank like a stone to finish 76–86 and in eighth place. Meanwhile, the Cardinals—who actually were a game *behind* the Cubs on June 15—overtook the collapsing Phillies in the final week of the season to capture the NL pennant and beat the Yankees in the World Series. As for Ellsworth himself, he fought the good fight through July, at which point he stood 12–12 with a 2.93 ERA and 1.197 WHIP.¹³ But he too ran out of steam in the final two months, going 2–6 with a 5.73 ERA and 1.606 WHIP (uncannily similar to his 1962 stat line) to finish 14–18 with a 3.75 ERA (99 ERA+), 1.137 WHIP, and 1.6 WAR.

Ellsworth's 1965 stat line was a near-duplicate of 1964. This time, he went 14–15, with a 3.81 ERA (97 ERA+), a 1.277 WHIP, with 2.2 WAR. While a sub-4.0 ERA and a sub-1.3 WHIP seem pretty respectable, they were league-average for the mid–1960s. Although Ellsworth was still only 25 years old, he was now no more than a middling innings-eater, a far cry from his star turn in 1963. The Cubs finished eighth again, and Lou Klein replaced Bob Kennedy as the head coach. Things got much worse under new manager Leo Durocher in 1966, as the Cubs plunged to the cellar, losing 103 games. Ellsworth was no longer even a league average pitcher that year, finishing 8–22 with a 3.98 ERA (93 ERA+), a 1.381 WHIP, and 0.5 WAR. He did not hit it off with Durocher, but there was no open break. Still, it was time for a change of scenery. So, on December 7, Ellsworth was traded to Philadelphia—a team that had coveted him since they were outbid for his services back in 1958—for another change-of-scenery candidate, 25-year-old righthanded pitcher Ray Culp.

Although the Phillies and their manager Gene Mauch were ecstatic to add Ellsworth to a rotation that already featured future Hall of Famer Jim Bunning, Chris Short, Rick Wise and Larry Jackson, things didn't go any better for Ellsworth with the fifth-place Phillies in 1967 than they had with the Cubs in 1966.[14] By June 30, his record stood at 2–4 with a horrendous 6.02 ERA and 1.739 WHIP.[15] He improved in July and August before posting another 6.57 ERA in September, mostly from the bullpen. He finished 6–7 with a 4.38 ERA (78 ERA+), a 1.500 WHIP, and -0.9 WAR. Although this was probably his worst season to date, the fact that he made only 21 starts and had decent offensive support spared him the ignominy of a third 20-loss season. The Phillies sent him to Boston, the defending AL champions who had taken the Cardinals to seven games in the World Series, that winter for backup catcher Mike Ryan.

Pitching with a contending team for the first time in his career, Ellsworth went 16–7, with a 3.03 ERA (105 ERA+), a 1.189 WHIP, and 2.2 WAR in 808 BF in 1968—his best year since 1963—despite missing five August starts with the mumps,. His co-ace and fellow 16-game-winner that year was none other than Ray Culp, the man for whom he had been traded in 1966. Although Ellsworth's performance won him Comeback of the Year accolades from the Chicago press corps, Ellsworth's stats were not as shiny as they looked.[16] In 1968, the "Year of the Pitcher," the ERA and WHIP for the AL as a whole were 2.98 and 1.185, respectively.[17] Despite the worthy efforts of Ellsworth and Culp, the Red Sox finished fourth at 86–76, 17 games behind the AL-champion Tigers.

Although Ellsworth was still only 28 years old, 1968 was his last hurrah. He developed bone chips in his left elbow in 1969 and could no longer sustain his accustomed workload. In his final three seasons, with Boston, Cleveland and Milwaukee, Ellsworth pitched mainly out of the bullpen, making only 25 starts out of 90 appearances. He went a combined 9–13 with 3 saves, a 4.07 ERA (93 ERA+), a 1.484 WHIP, and 1.7 WAR in 965 BF. He was released by the Brewers at age 31 on June 30, 1971. He returned to Fresno and embarked on a successful career in real estate. In 1988, he was part of the ownership group that purchased the Tucson Toros and brought them to Fresno as the Grizzlies, a Giants farm team until 2014. His son Steve pitched briefly for the Red Sox in 1988. Dick Ellsworth died at age 82 in Fresno on October 10, 2022.[18]

Why Was Dick Ellsworth a Shooting Star?

Dick Ellsworth was an unusually gifted pitcher, but one whose solid 13-year major league career failed to fulfill the greatness that had been forecast for him as an 18-year-old high school phenom and $60,000 bonus baby. Except for his 10.2 WAR in 1963, stardom remained tantalizingly out of reach (Figure 15).

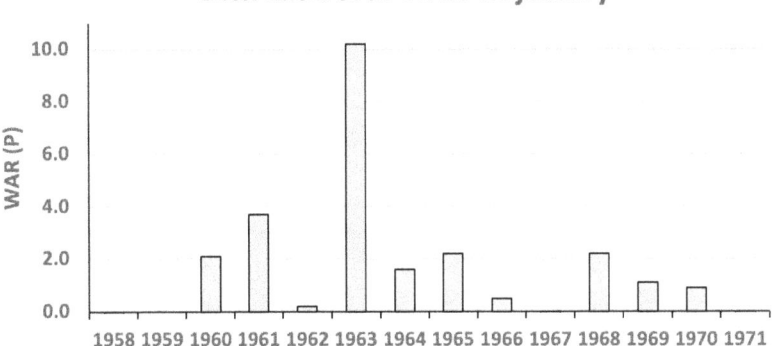

Why did Ellsworth struggle so much while players with lesser ability found sustained success? Unlike some other shooting stars profiled in this book, Ellsworth was a sober man who was physically sound for the first 10 years of his career. While free spirits like Norm Cash (Chapter 13) and Mark Fidrych (Chapter 21) reveled in their time in the sun, the pressure of lofty expectations seemed to crush the joy out of Ellsworth's baseball career. He thrived only after he retired to private life. Dick Ellsworth seems fated to be remembered more for the player he wasn't than for the player he was.

◈ 16 ◈

The Mark of Zoilo
Zoilo Casanova Versalles (1965)

Some called him "Zorro," but Zoilo Versalles bore not even the slightest resemblance to the fictional Mexican Robin Hood–like swashbuckling masked swordsman, played by the likes of Douglas Fairbanks and Tyrone Power in the movies and by Guy Williams in a popular late fifties TV series.[1] Versalles was a skinny bespectacled righty-hitting 5'10" shortstop, who was plagued throughout his short life by the insecurities arising from his impoverished childhood in the slums of Havana.[2] Even at the pinnacle of his 12-year career, he was like a fish out of water in a country whose language he could barely speak and whose culture he could never quite adjust to.

Zoilo Casanova Versalles was born on December 18, 1939, in the poor Marianao section of Havana, Cuba. His father, an itinerant laborer, barely scratched out enough of a living to feed his wife and two sons.[3] His childhood hero was Willy Miranda, a good-field-no-hit Cuban SS of the 1950s.[4] At age 16, Versalles joined the Fortuna Sports Club team in the Cuban Athletic Union League and quickly became one of their top hitters. After he played professionally in the Cuban winter league in 1957–58, Washington Senators scout Joe Cambria, signed him to a contract.

Unlike some of the pre-expansion "shooting stars" of the 1940s and 50s, like Holmes, Brecheen, Rosen, Gentile, and Aguirre, who served extended minor league apprenticeships, Versalles was rushed to the major leagues while he was still raw and immature. Although he spoke almost no English and was terribly homesick, he hit .292/.370/.386 in 568 PA for Class D Elmira (NY) in 1958, after nearly quitting when his mother died one month into the season. He made his major league debut at age 19 on August 1, 1959, after hitting .278/.317/.416 in 400 PA at Class B Fox City and leading the league with 34 errors. Clearly overmatched, he struck out three times in his first major league game and went on to hit only .153/.219/.203 in 64 PA in his first taste of major league pitching. He spent most of the 1960 season at AAA Charleston (SC), hitting .278/.320/.424 in 596 PA and once more leading his league with 42 errors, and again struggled in 47 September PA with the Senators. But with the move to Minnesota in 1961, the rebuilding Twins installed the 22-year-old prospect, now newly married, as their everyday SS, replacing fellow Cuban Jose Valdevielso. Fidel Castro had now banned professional sports in Cuba. So, for better or worse, Zoilo Versalles's future lay in the U.S.

Versalles's rookie season was surprisingly successful, considering his tender age and inexperience. He hit .280/.314/.390 (84 OPS+) with 16 SB and 1.3 WAR in 542 PA and fielded his position adequately (0.5 dWAR), although he hit only 7 HR. Although the Twins finished in seventh place (70–90–1) that year, they had established a promising young core, built around Harmon Killebrew, Bob Allison and Earl Battey and ace pitchers Camilo Pascual, Pedro Ramos, and Jim Kaat.

Bespectacled Minnesota Twins SS Zoilo Versalles flawlessly turning a double play, perhaps during his MVP season in 1965 (National Baseball Hall of Fame Museum).

Versalles's batting average dipped by 39 points in 1962, but this was offset by a marked increase in power. He hit .241/.287/.373 (74 OPS+) in 624 PA with 17 HR, 67 RBI, 69 R, but only 5 SB, which translated to 2.0 WAR. His defense was spectacular at times but inconsistent (dWAR = 2.0), characterized by an AL-leading 501 assists and 5.22 range factor per game but a tendency to get sloppy on routine plays.[5] The Twins had improved by 21 wins over 1961, finishing second to the Yankees, and had emerged as one of the AL's up and coming teams. Versalles, already a solid major league SS with outstanding defensive skills and some pop at age 22, was shaping up to be a valuable piece on a contending team.

Versalles continued to progress in 1963–64, hitting a composite .260/.307/.416 (99 OPS+) and averaging 15, HR, 84 R, 59 RBI, 32 2B, 12 3B, 10 SB, and 2.5 WAR (including 0.6 dWAR) in 692 PA. He led the AL in triples in both seasons. Versalles earned his first All-Star Selection as the AL starter in 1963 and singled in his only at-bat.[6] On defense, he continued to vacillate between outstanding and erratic. He earned his first Gold Glove award in 1963, but he also made five of his 30 errors that season in one night—a July 5 double header against the Orioles.[7] Versalles's defensive play dropped off from 1.0 to 0.1 dWAR in 1964. The Twins, who won 91 games in 1963 but finished a distant third behind the Yankees and White Sox, dropped to 79 wins in 1964. In short, while Versalles had established himself as a definite asset at SS with some upside because of his youth, nothing about his uneven performance in his first four big league seasons indicated that an MVP season was just around the corner.

The 1965 season began inauspiciously when Versalles was fined by manager Sam Mele for failure to hustle on fielding a ground ball in spring training.[8] Chastened by the experience and working hard under the mentorship of Twins infield coach Billy Martin (who had played 2B alongside Versalles for the Twins in 1961), Versalles entered the 1965 season determined to prove his worth.[9] He started well, hitting .277/.303/.516 with 15 doubles, 6 triples, 6 HR, 31 R, and 28 RBI, in 198 PA in 42 April-May games.[10] This was not the stuff that MVP awards are made of, but it was a distinct step up from his prior offensive performance. Meanwhile, with the sudden collapse of the Yankees dynasty, the Twins found themselves atop the AL standings by a half-game with a 27–15 record on May 31.[11] However, Versalles slumped badly in June-July hitting only .197/.260/.307 in 267 PA. Still, he hit 5 HR and scored 42 R despite the slump and continued to play strong defense. In the meantime, sluggers like Tony Oliva, Killebrew, Jimmy Hall, Allison, and Battey carried the offense, as the Twins cruised to a comfortable six-game lead over second place Baltimore on July 31. Versalles was

16. The Mark of Zoilo

selected as an All-Star reserve and went hitless in a single AB.[12] Then, as the calendar turned to August, Versalles suddenly caught fire and hit .346/.389/.575 in 263 PA over the final two months with 23 doubles, 4 triples, 8 HR, 28 RBI, and 53 R, as the Twins coasted to the pennant with a 102–60 record. Versalles's overall stat line (Table 16) was enough to seal his overwhelming selection as AL MVP.

Table 16: Selected Stats for Zoilo Versalles's Peak and Runner-Up Seasons and His Career*

Season	Age	PA	AVG	OBP	SLG	OPS+	TB	2B	3B	SB	R	WAR (H)	dWAR
Peak 1965	25						**308**	**45**	**12**	27	**126**	7.2	3.0
		728	0.273	0.319	0.462	115							
per 650 PA							275	40	11	24	113	6.4	2.7
Runner-Up 1963	23						249	31	**13**	7	74	2.6	1.0
		667	0.261	0.303	0.401	94							
per 650 PA							243	30	13	7	72	2.5	1.0
Career (1959–71)							1887	230	63	97	650	12.6	8.0
		5578	0.242	0.290	0.367	82							
per 650 PA							220	27	7	11	76	1.5	0.9

League leading totals are shown in boldface type.

Although his slash line was nothing special, Versalles dominated the 1965 AL leaderboards, leading the league in PA, TB, 2B, 3B, R, WAR, and dWAR and adding 19 HR, 77 RBI, and 27 SB for good measure. Although some MVP voters supported repeat AL batting champion Tony Oliva, who hit .321/.378/.491 (141 OPS+) and was clearly the superior offensive player, WAR and the intangibles clearly favored Versalles, who had his best defensive season and won his second Gold Glove. According to 1965 Twins 2B Frank Quilici, who watched Versalles close-up every day, his performance was "the greatest display of shortstop I've ever seen played on a day-to-day basis .. he was unbelievable that year."[13] Quilici continued, "Whenever we needed to have a run in scoring position, he could steal a base or take another base…. I'll bet he turned 20 singles into doubles that year." Along the same lines, Billy Martin recalled that Versalles had scored from 1B on singles several times that season.[14]

The Twins were distinct underdogs against the formidable Dodgers pitching staff in the 1965 World Series, but caught a break when Game 1 fell on Yom Kippur and Jewish Dodger ace Sandy Koufax's start was delayed until Game 2. Versalles and the Twins came out swinging against Dodger co-ace Don Drysdale, driving him from the mound in a six-run third inning featuring a three-run HR by Versalles, and going on to win 8–2 behind Mudcat Grant.[15] They followed by nicking Koufax for two runs (one of them unearned) and defeating the Dodgers 5–1 behind Jim Kaat the next day. But the Twins bats fell silent when the Series moved to LA, and the Dodgers ultimately prevailed in seven games. Although Versalles hit a solid .286/.333/.500 during the Series, he did not score or drive in a run in Games 3–7 after scoring three and driving in four in the first two games.

Unfortunately, the rest of Versalles's career was a total washout. His fall was sudden and calamitous. He hit only .249/.307/.346 (83 OPS+) with 1.3 WAR in 596 PA in 1966. His doubles (20), triples (6), HR (7), RBI (36), and SB (10) each fell by at least half from their 1965 highs, and he scored 53 fewer runs (73) than in 1965. The fact that Versalles missed 25 games (including a two-week stint on the disabled list with a hematoma in his back on June 12–25) does not explain this steep decline, since he was hitting only .249/,290/.386 *before* the injury.[16] Although he committed fewer errors (35) in 1966 than his 39 in 1965, he also made many fewer plays, declining in assists, range factor, fielding percentage, and dWAR (1.2). Meanwhile, the Twins started poorly, reaching a nadir of 35–43 on July 3, before recovering to finish second at 89–73, eight games behind the World Series champion Orioles.[17]

Attributing his 1966 woes to too much time (and food) on the banquet circuit following his MVP season, Versalles was determined to come back strong in 1967 and reported to spring training refreshed and 15 pounds lighter.[18] But the results only got worse. Although he played 160 games, he hit a horrendous .200/.249/.282 (51 OPS+) in 626 PA with little power and only 3 SB. His -1.6 WAR (which included -1.1 dWAR) was the worst of any everyday player in the major leagues.[19] He rode the bench for much of September. Despite Versalles's lack of production, the Twins came within one game of the AL pennant, losing both games of a decisive two-game series to the "Impossible Dream" Red Sox on the season's final weekend after entering the weekend with a one-game lead.

Seeing an opportunity to fill their hole at SS with a 28-year-old former MVP, the Dodgers sent three veteran players—Bob Miller, Ron Perranoski, and John Roseboro—to acquire 1965 heroes Versalles and Mudcat Grant in a blockbuster trade that headlined the 1967 winter meetings.[20] Although Versalles had problems with Twins manager Cal Ermer in 1967 and proclaimed that he had always wanted to play for the Dodgers, the trade did not revitalize his career.[21] He could do no better than .196/.244/.266 (59 OPS+) in 436 PA, again without power, speed, or good defense. Even in the "Year of the Pitcher," this was unacceptable. His -1.1 WAR was again below replacement level. A lumbar disk injury suffered when he stumbled awkwardly over 1B while running out a grounder limited his range and his playing time and would bother him for the rest of his life, but the games he missed in 1968 probably just protected his WAR from falling even further below replacement level.[22] In any case, by the end of the year, the Dodgers were ready to move on and left Versalles exposed in the expansion draft. He was taken by San Diego, who flipped him to Cleveland. After splitting another unproductive season (0.7 WAR) between the Indians and Senators in 1969, Versalles played in Mexico in 1970, then caught on as a reserve with Atlanta in 1971. When he hit only .191/.233/.325 (53 OPS+) with another sub-zero WAR in 66 games, the Braves released him.

Versalles led a marginal existence after leaving baseball. His limited skills and chronic back condition prevented him holding down a full-time job. He subsisted on his baseball pension, supplemented by a small income from odd jobs along with the occasional "loan" from Twins owner Cal Griffith, who still had a soft spot in his heart for his one-time SS prodigy.[23] A 1981 World Series Time Capsule feature in The Sporting News described Versalles as "a bitter, angry man" about his inability to land a job in baseball.[24] He sold his MVP trophy and other memorabilia, not only to raise money, but to rid himself of reminders of better times. He and his wife Josefa, mother of his six daughters, separated.[25] In his final years, Versalles suffered from serious stomach and heart problems. Versalles was alone when he died of atherosclerotic cardiovascular disease in June 1995 at age 55.

Why Was Zoilo Versalles a Shooting Star?

There is no doubt that Zoilo Versalles's MVP 1965 season far outstrips the rest of his career (Figure 16). Although his pro-rated 6.4 WAR per 650 PA (7.2 WAR in 728 PA) that season is the lowest among the 30 players I have selected for this book, his WAR was no better than average in 1962–64 and well below average in his other eight major league seasons. In fact, he was among the worst players in MLB in 1967–68. Versalles's career arc exemplifies the term "one-year wonder."

Even in Versalles's MVP season, his offensive performance had a gaping two-month hole in June-July, when he hit below .200 before surging in August-September. The inconsistency of Versalles's signature season mirrors that of his career as a whole. Versalles simply played with a desperate intensity that was unsustainable. When his head was really in the game, as it was during those magical final two months of 1965, he was nearly unbeatable—a tenacious hitter, an aggressive baserunner, and a rangy SS with a penchant for the

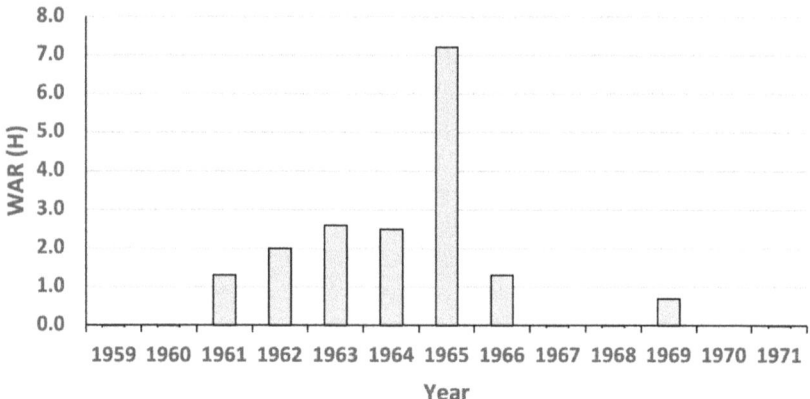

spectacular. But too often, when he wasn't fully engaged, he would give away outs and muff easy grounders. It is easy to understand why teams kept giving him second and third chances, but once he hurt his back in 1968, he finally ran out of chances.

◈ 17 ◈

Angleworm
Theodore Wade "Ted" Abernathy (1967)

When the Cincinnati Reds picked up 34-year-old journeyman pitcher Ted Abernathy, a failed starter turned reliever with a gimpy shoulder and a funky right-handed submarine delivery, in the 1966 Rule 5 Draft, he was a most unlikely shooting star candidate. After all, Abernathy had bounced between the major and minor leagues (mostly the latter) from 1955 to 1963 and had posted only one decent major league season in his career—a 31-Save 3.2-WAR performance with the eighth-place 1965 Cubs. But he followed that performance with a horrible (-0.9 WAR) 1966 season that got him traded to the Braves and then outrighted to Richmond (AAA) in October. Of all the shooting stars profiled in this book, none had a worse prior track record than Abernathy's 15-year struggle (mostly unsuccessful) to stick in the major leagues. But in 1967, Abernathy broke the mold and stepped up as the closer and stabilizing force for a young Cincinnati rotation. Thanks in part to Abernathy, the Reds, who were still three years away from becoming the powerful Big Red Machine, finished fourth in the NL at 87–75 in 1967—an 11-game improvement over their seventh-place 1966 finish.

Ted Abernathy was born on March 6, 1933, in Stanley, NC, a small town in Gaston County, about 21 miles northwest of Charlotte.[1] His two loves were hotrod cars and baseball. He originally threw with a conventional overhand motion but learned to throw sidearm after he tore his rotator cuff as a high school freshman in 1948. He starred in high school and American Legion baseball in 1949–51 but received no bonus when he signed with the Washington Senators in 1952. He was assigned to Class D Roanoke Rapids where he went 20–13 with a 1.69 ERA and 293 SO in 255.0 IP as a side-arming starting pitcher and earned a promotion to AA Chattanooga in 1953. There he went 4–1 in six starts until he was drafted into the army, where he was assigned to the medical corps and drove an ambulance. He was discharged in time for spring training in 1955 and spent the entire season in the major leagues, going 5–9 with a 5.96 ERA (66 ERA+) in 14 starts and 26 relief appearances totaling 119.1 IP for the Senators. He returned to the minors in 1956, going 12–16 with a 3.90 ERA as a starter in Louisville (AAA), and earned a late-season call-up. However, he injured his elbow on a cold September day in Boston and was unable to pitch without pain for the next three years. Nevertheless, he did continue to pitch, struggling to a 2–10 record with a 6.78 ERA (57 ERA+) with the Senators in 1957 and returning to the minors in 1958. At this point, he was a sore-armed 25-year-old minor league pitcher whose career was going nowhere.

Ted Abernathy, pitching for Cleveland Indians in 1963–64, demonstrates his extreme submarine delivery, in which the ball appeared to rise out of the ground. His unorthodox delivery would make him a shooting star a few years later (National Baseball Hall of Fame Museum).

The Senators tried to rehabilitate Abernathy's arm in the Florida Instruction League and then Charlotte (AAA) in 1959, but nothing worked. Finally, he was sent to an orthopedic surgeon, Dr. Richard Wrenn, who removed a handful of calcified debris from his shoulder and reattached the two muscles that had torn loose in 1948.[2] When Abernathy reported to spring training in 1960, he was throwing pain-free using a submarine motion, which earned him the nickname "Angleworm" because his pitches seemed to rise up out of the ground. However, the Senators released him after only two relief appearances in which he yielded 4 ER in 3.0 IP. He signed with Milwaukee in June and spent the rest of the season in the Braves' minor league system, where he had a 2.44 ERA in 70.0 IP, all in relief. He moved on to Cleveland in 1961–63 and finally resurfaced in the major leagues for the last four months of the 1963 season. In 1963–64 with Cleveland, he posted a 9–8 record with 23 saves, a 3.68 ERA (99 ERA+), and 1.477 WHIP, and 0.5 WAR in 132.0 IP. He was finally healthy, but at age 31, his prospects were dim.

Abernathy got his big break when the Chicago Cubs acquired his contract from Cleveland and paired him with Lindy McDaniel at the back of their bullpen. The bullpen was the bright spot of this otherwise sorry 90-loss team. Abernathy made a record-setting 84 appearances, 62 of them closing out the game, and went 4–6 with a major league-leading 31 saves in 38 opportunities and compiling a 2.57 ERA (143 ERA+), 1.240 WHIP, 3.2 WAR in 136.1 IP. McDaniel was similarly dominant in a set-up role—5–6 with 2 saves, a 2.59 ERA (143 ERA+), a 1.259 WHIP, and 2.9 WAR in 129.0 IP. Abernathy was particularly strong in April-July, with a 1.91 ERA and 1.071 WHIP in 94.1 IP and succeeding in 22/27 save opportunities.[3] However, he tailed off to a 3.27 ERA and 1.500 WHIP in August and a 4.95 ERA and 1.750 WHIP in September, blowing two of his final six save opportunities. Although, Abernathy won the NL Fireman of the Year award, 1965 was a good, but not dominant, season.[4]

Abernathy could not replicate this success in 1966. After earning a save with 2.1 scoreless inning in his first appearance, he was battered for two blown saves and losses in two of his next three appearances, giving up 6 ER in 1.2 IP.[5] By May 27, Abernathy was 1–3 with a 6.18 ERA and had converted only 5/8 save opportunities. By this time, the Cubs, under new manager Leo Durocher, had fallen to 10–27 and were buried in tenth place 4.5 games behind the ninth place Mets. A debacle against St. Louis two days earlier in which Abernathy gave up 6 ER on 6 H and 3 BB in 0.1 IP had sealed his fate. So, Abernathy was sent to the Braves for journeyman OF/1B Lee Thomas. He pitched better for the Braves and brought his season record up to 5–7 with 9 SV, a 4.55 ERA (82 ERA+), a 1.473 WHIP, and -0.9 WAR in 93.0 IP. But that was not enough to save his spot on the Braves' 40-man major league roster after the season. As he turned 34, Abernathy's fine 1965 season seemed like a one-off.

When Cincinnati took a flyer on Abernathy in the 1966 Rule 5 Draft, Manager Dave Bristol hoped to reinforce a bullpen that had been overworked behind a starting rotation that had finished tied for last in the NL in complete games (28) that season.[6] They hit the jackpot (Table 17).

Table 17: Selected Stats for Ted Abernathy's Peak and Runner-Up Seasons and His Career*

Season	Age	BF	ERA	WHIP	ERA+	W-L	SV	SO	BB	WAR (P)
Peak 1967	34	427	1.27	0.978	**299**	6–3	**28**	88	41	6.2
per 1000 BF								206	96	14.5
Runner-Up 1965	32	572	2.57	1.240	143	4–6	**31**	104	56	3.2
per 1000 BF								182	98	5.6
Career (1955–72)		4963	3.46	1.395	107	63–69	149	765	592	16.6
per 1000 BF								154	119	3.3

*League leading totals are shown in boldface type.

Abernathy not only rebounded from his off-year, but he also significantly surpassed his 1965 dominance in the bullpen. Although a pulled muscle, which sidelined him for 19 days in late May and early June, limited him to 14 fewer appearances and 30 fewer IP in 1967 than he had in 1965, he still got a league-leading 28 saves while pitching to a microscopic 1.27 ERA—almost 200 percent better than the league average—and a 0.978 WHIP. His 6.2 WAR was the sixth best ever for any pitcher who made at least 75 percent of his appearances in relief—behind Rich Gossage (8.2 in 1975), John Hiller (7.9 in 1973), Mark Eichhorn (7.3 in 1986), Wilcy Moore (6.6 in 1927) and Bruce Sutter (6.5 in 1977).[7] (Profiles of Hiller, Eichhorn, and Moore appear in Chapters 20, 24, and 6.) Abernathy held the opposition scoreless in 61 of his 70 appearances, including each of his last 21 appearances (August 19–September 29).[8] He yielded a total of 15 ER all season—1 ER in five games, 2 ER in three games, and 4 ER in his lone true clunker—a 7–2 loss to the Dodgers on April 18, in which he entered in seventh inning with the Reds trailing 3–2 and gave up a single, a HIP, and three walks after getting the first two batters out. He finished the season 6–3 with 28 saves and only three blown saves.[9] Those saves came in very handy, since the Reds finished dead last in the NL with 34 complete games, but still managed to win 87 games and finish fourth. Abernathy was again selected NL Fireman of the Year and received a smattering of MVP votes.

Abernathy continued to be a bullpen mainstay for several teams over the next five years, bouncing from the Reds (1968) to the Cubs (1969–70) to the Cardinals (1970) and finally to the Royals (1970–72). He averaged a 6–5 record with 12 saves and 1.9 WAR in 89 IP per season, with a 2.54 ERA (138 ERA+) and a 1.300 WHIP. He was especially popular with the overachieving expansion Royals.[10] However, although he was still pitching well at age 39 in 1972 (1.74 ERA in 58.1 IP), the Royals released him the following spring to make room for younger pitchers. Unable to catch on with another team, he retired to North Carolina. After he left baseball, Abernathy worked for his son's landscaping business in Gastonia. In his declining years he suffered from Alzheimer's Disease.[11] He died in a nursing home on December 19, 2004.

Why Was Ted Abernathy a Shooting Star?

While Abernathy was honored twice as Fireman of the Year, his 6.2-WAR 1967 season was nearly twice as good as his 3.2-WAR 1965 season and far surpassed any other season in his 14-year career (Figure 17).

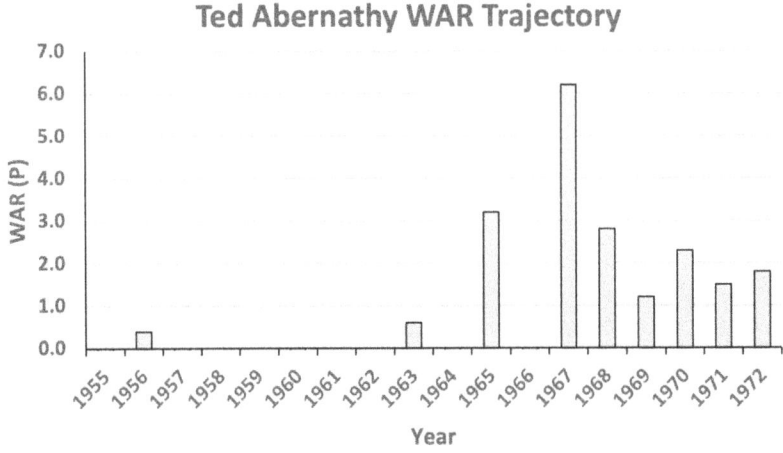

The stats say that Ted Abernathy was no more than a journeyman with 16.6 career WAR, but his career tells a remarkable story of desire and persistence in the face of adversity that would have derailed almost anyone else. He persevered through painful injuries—the first coming when he was a high school freshman—and totally re-engineered his pitching delivery twice rather than go home and lick his wounds. He endured repeated rejections and pitched mostly in the minor leagues for 12 years before finally establishing himself as a major leaguer in his thirties. Then, after he was ignominiously released only a year after leading all NL relief pitchers, he came back in 1967 to win his second NL Fireman of the Year award and continued to pitch effectively until age 39. Ted Abernathy was no superstar, but he got the most out of his modest abilities.

❖ 18 ❖

Fenway Power
Americo Peter "Rico" Petrocelli (1969)

Rico Petrocelli, who anchored the left side of the Boston Red Sox infield from 1965 to 1974, was a key element in their transition from a clownish 100-loss ninth place team to an AL East power. Although he was originally touted as a defense-first SS who would struggle to hit, his right-handed power was so well suited to the dimensions of Fenway Park that he flipped the script. He even broke Vern Stephens's AL record of 39 HR by a SS in 1969. Meanwhile, the Red Sox grew dissatisfied with his diminishing range at SS and moved him to 3B in 1971. Although Petrocelli did not always see eye-to-eye with Red Sox management and once requested a mid-career trade, he spent his entire major league career in Boston and still retains close ties to the city.

Rico Petrocelli was born on June 27, 1943, and grew up as the youngest of seven children in a large close-knit Italian-American family in the Sheepshead Bay area of Brooklyn, NY.[1] His father and cousins operated a shop in New York City's Garment District. Rico showed exceptional athletic ability early on and starred in both basketball and baseball at Sheepshead Bay High School. His parents exempted him from helping in the shop so that he could concentrate on athletics. He was heavily scouted as a pitcher and outfielder until he injured his right elbow in 1961. But the Red Sox still liked what they saw, offered him a contract, and converted him to SS.

At Winston-Salem (Class B) in 1962, Petrocelli struggled to adjust to SS and made 48 errors. However, he hit ,277/.379/.460 with 17 HR and 80 RBI. That was good enough to earn a promotion to Reading (AA) in 1963, where his fielding improved but he hit only .239. Still, he continued to show good power (19 HR and 78 RBI) and was rewarded with a one-game cup of coffee with the Red Sox in late September, where he hit an RBI-double off the Green Monster in his first AB. However, he struggled badly in Seattle (AAA) in 1964, missing many games with seemingly minor injuries and hitting only .231/.290/.337. Homesick and worried about his ill parents, he flew home to New York in mid-season, thereby earning a reputation as unreliable.[2] Nevertheless, the Red Sox installed him as their starting SS at the start of the 1965 season, two months shy of his 22nd birthday.

Going into the 1965 season, the Red Sox were a terrible team, particularly on defense. They had lost 90 games in 1964 and had the lowest defensive efficiency (0.683) in the AL.[3] Dick Stuart (aka Dr. Strangeglove), a power-hitting 1B who was historically inept defensively, was emblematic of the team's personality, but was by no means the only offender. Manager Billy Herman was so eager to upgrade the infield defense that he was willing to install an immature rookie at SS and live with his ups and downs. Petrocelli filled the bill defensively, providing 1.4 dWAR in 1965, despite chronic elbow problems that hampered his throwing. Unfortunately, he was the only Red Sox regular with a dWAR > 0.4 that year, and the team lost 100 games.[4] But Herman also had to suffer through his moody shortstop's many downs, as Petrocelli got off to a miserable start, hitting only .174 in his first 20 games and even experimented briefly with switch-hitting.[5] Furthermore, elbow pain and a variety of minor injuries limited him to 103 games. However, it was a positive season overall. Petrocelli gradually learned to take advantage of Fenway Park's short left-field wall and finished at .232/.309/.412 (99 OPS+) with 13 HR and 33 RBI and 2.0 WAR in 363 PA.

Petrocelli had a similar season in 1966, hitting .238/.295/.383 (85 OPS+) with 18 HR, 59 RBI, and 2.8 WAR in 573 PA. Most of his value was on defense (2.4 dWAR), although he did provide occasional welcome pop from the sixth or seventh slot in the batting order—especially at Fenway Park. The team also showed signs of improvement, as youngsters like Jim Lonborg, Reggie Smith, George Scott, and Joe Foy joined Yastrzemski and Conigliaro to form a solid core. However, Petrocelli's relationship with Billy Herman, who had grown impatient with his young shortstop's moodiness and self-doubt, soured irrevocably when Petrocelli, upset by the quality of his play and his aching elbow, left the team abruptly in mid-game on August 13 and did not return until September 2.[6] Herman was furious and demanded that Petrocelli be suspended; instead, the Red Sox merely fined him $1000. Less than a week later, Herman was fired, and Pete Runnels managed the last 16 games of the season. The Red Sox again finished in ninth place at 72–90.

Petrocelli took a big step forward in 1967 under the more patient managerial hand of Dick Williams, who brought in Petrocelli's minor league manager and mentor, Eddie Popowski, to give him special attention. Petrocelli thrived, batting .259/.330/.420 (113 OPS+) with 17 HR, 66 RBI, and 4.1 WAR (2.4 dWAR) in 556 PA, mostly out of the seventh slot in the batting order, and was selected to start the All-Star Game for the AL. He popped out in his only AB.[7] Of course, 1967 was also the year of the "Impossible Dream," when the Red Sox, led by Carl Yastrzemski's monster 12.4 WAR Triple Crown season, emerged from the nether regions of the AL and came from one game behind on the last weekend of the season to finish at 92–70, a single game ahead of the Twins and Tigers, to take the AL pennant. Petrocelli got only four hits against the Cardinals in the World Series, but two of them were solo home runs in Game 6—a game the Red Sox had to win to stay alive.[8] His first HR staked the Sox to a 1–0 lead, and the second gave the Sox a 3–2 lead they would not relinquish in a Series-tying 8–4 win. Unfortunately for the Red Sox, Bob Gibson would end the Impossible Dream the next day, but Petrocelli (who had struck out in his first two AB) did nick Gibson for a leadoff double in the eighth inning and scored a cosmetic run in a 7–2 defeat. Overall, Petrocelli had established himself as a top-tier SS.

However, Petrocelli and the Red Sox both regressed in 1968. Petrocelli was limited to 123 games by chronic elbow issues and hit only .234/.292/.374 (96 OPS+) with 12 HR, 46 RBI, and 3.8 WAR (2.1 dWAR) in 451 PA, as the Red Sox finished fourth, 17 games behind Detroit. With the Red Sox already out of contention, he sat for most of September. He was still a major defensive asset at SS, despite his balky elbow, but offensively he was average at best, with decent power but below average on-base skills. Nothing in his four full major league seasons suggested that he was on the verge of superstardom in 1969.

In 1969, Rico Petrocelli put together one of the best seasons ever by an MLB SS (Table 18).

Table 18: Selected Stats for Rico Petrocelli's Peak and Runner-Up Seasons and His Career*

Season	Age	PA	AVG	OBP	SLG	OPS+	TB	HR	R	RBI	WAR (H)	dWAR
Peak 1969	26	643	0.297	0.403	0.589	168	315	40	92	97	**10.0**	2.7
per 650 PA							318	40	93	98	10.1	2.7
Runner-Up 1971	28	661	0.251	0.354	0.461	123	255	28	82	89	4.9	0.7
per 650 PA							251	28	81	88	4.8	0.7
Career (1963–76)		6171	0.251	0.332	0.420	108	2263	210	653	773	39.1	14.4
per 650 PA							238	22	69	81	4.1	1.5

*League leading totals are shown in boldface type.

His MLB-leading 10.0 WAR in 1969 was tied with Cal Ripken, Jr., for the eighth best season of all time for any SS. Only Ripken, Honus

Wagner (twice), Rogers Hornsby, Robin Yount, Arky Vaughan, and Lou Boudreau—all Hall of Famers—ever did better.[9] He continued to shine on defense (2.7 dWAR), but his OBP suddenly soared by nearly 100 points to .403 after averaging a .307 OBP in 4+ seasons. Furthermore, he more than doubled his best previous seasonal outputs in HR (40 versus 18) and BB (98 versus 49), and amassed 643 PA in 154 games. His performance earned him an All-Star start; he had one single in 3 AB.[10] He also finished seventh in the AL MVP voting, although the Red Sox finished a distant third in the AL East with 87 wins, 22 fewer than Baltimore. Petrocelli started the season red hot, hitting .408/.506/.775 in April.[11] He fell off to .258/.406/.613 in May-June, but slugged 17 HR with 39 RBI. He rebounded to .304/.396/.554 in July-August, although his power output fell to 10 HR and 28 RBI. He hit .274/.344/.496 in September-October and added 7 HR and 21 RBI.

Petrocelli did some of his best hitting against two of the AL's best teams in 1969, hitting .313/.395/.642 with 5 HR and 11 RBI against the 109-win Orioles and .353/.405/.559 against the 90-win Tigers, but his favorite opponent was Kansas City (.357/.449/.857 with 5 HR and 12 RBI).[12] Highlights of his season included:[13]

- On April 13, his 2-run HR in the 4th inning off Luis Tiant sparked Boston to a 3–1 win over Cleveland.
- On April 25, his 7th inning solo HR off Mickey Lolich helped secure a 5–4 Boston win over Detroit.
- On May 4, his walk-off 2-run HR in the 11th inning gave Boston a 4–2 win over Detroit.
- On May 11, his two 2-run HR sparked Boston to a 7–3 win over the Angels.
- On May 28, his 2-run second inning HR staked Boston to a 2–1 lead in a 4–3 win over Kansas City.
- On June 8, his 2 HR and 3 RBI keyed an 8–2 rout of Kansas City.
- On July 19, his eighth inning solo HR helped insure a 5–3 win over Baltimore.
- On August 3, his fourth inning solo HR off Catfish Hunter gave Boston a 2–0 lead en route to a 3–2 win over Oakland.
- On September 1, he hit a first inning grand slam HR that sparked Boston to a 6–2 win over Oakland.
- On September 5 against Washington, he hit a three-run seventh inning HR that put the Red Sox up 8–7 and then drove in the winning run with a walk-off BB.

Although Rico Petrocelli would never again produce a WAR even half as good as his 10.0 in 1969, he continued to excel in 1970–71, missing only nine games while hitting .256/.344/.467 (118 OPS+) and averaging 28 HR, 96 RBI, 82 R, and 4.8 WAR in 662 PA. However, after leading all major league SS in fielding percentage at .9813 in 1969 (and finishing second in 1968), Petrocelli's fielding percentage fell out of the top 10 in 1970 at .9701, and his dWAR fell to 1.3. Since he was never the rangiest of SS, the Red Sox jumped at the chance to acquire defensive whiz Luis Aparicio from Baltimore, and obtained Petrocelli's consent to move to 3B. He made the transition seamlessly and led all major league 3B in fielding percentage with .9762 in 1971. He even set a major league record with 77 consecutive errorless games.[14] However, the Orioles continued to own the AL East with 108 wins in 1970 and 101 in 1971, while the Red Sox remained stuck in third place with 87 and 85 wins.

Off the field, the picture was not so bright. Petrocelli and the Red Sox were sued for of a $1.25 million by an airline stewardess who claimed that he had groped and punched her on the team's April 12, 1970, cross-country charter flight.[15] Petrocelli denied the allegations.[16] The lawsuit was quietly settled in 1974. In the 2020s, a situation like this would receive closer scrutiny from the Commissioner's office.

Petrocelli's performance declined rapidly as he neared and entered his 30s. Although his August hot streak helped propel the Red Sox to a close second place finish behind Detroit in the AL East in 1972, he finished the season hitting only .240/.339/.363 (104 OPS+) with 15 HR and 75 RBI. His elbow issues flared up in 1973 and required season-ending surgery on August 29. He requested a trade after the season but changed his mind. In 1974, a September 15 beaning by Milwaukee's Jim Slaton ended his season and led to chronic dizziness and balance issues that would plague the rest of his career. Overall, he averaged only .243/.327/.367 (95 OPS+) and 1.3 WAR in 451 PA from 1972 to 1976. He never hit more than 15 HR or batted in more than 76 runs in any of those five seasons. The highlight of his late career was Boston's unexpected run to the 1975 pennant, which was fueled by their marvelous young outfielders—MVP Fred Lynn, Jim Rice, and Dwight Evans—and the clutch pitching of Luis Tiant. Petrocelli played only a small supporting role. Although he got just two hits in the ALCS, one of them was a solo HR off Rollie Fingers in the seventh inning of Game 2, which helped cement a 6–3 lead over defending World Series Champion Oakland en route to a 3–0 series sweep.[17] He then went on to hit .309 in the heartbreaking 4–3 loss to the Big Red Machine in the World Series. However, plagued by the aftereffects of his 1974 beaning and problems with his medications, Petrocelli was unproductive in 1976, gradually losing playing time to rookie Butch Hobson. The Red Sox released him at the end of spring training in 1977.

Petrocelli went into sports journalism after his playing career ended, writing a regular column in the *Boston Herald* and co-hosting a local sports talk radio show with Glenn Ordway.[18] In 1979, he joined veteran Red Sox broadcaster Ken Coleman in the radio booth, but was let go after only one year. After several years out of baseball, he caught on as a manager in the White Sox organization in 1986–89, advancing as far as AA, then returned home as sports director for the Jimmy Fund in 1989–91. He then returned to the Red Sox, first as the manager of their AAA affiliate in Pawtucket and then as a roving instructor. In 1998, he left the Red Sox to establish the Petrocelli Marketing Group, but has remained active in the baseball community. Recently, he co-hosted Sirius/XM's *Remember When* weekly radio show.

Why Was Rico Petrocelli a Shooting Star?

There is no doubt that Rico Petrocelli qualifies as a shooting star. Not only was his 10.0 WAR in 1969 more than double that of any other season in his career, he was also at his defensive peak as a SS (Figure 18).

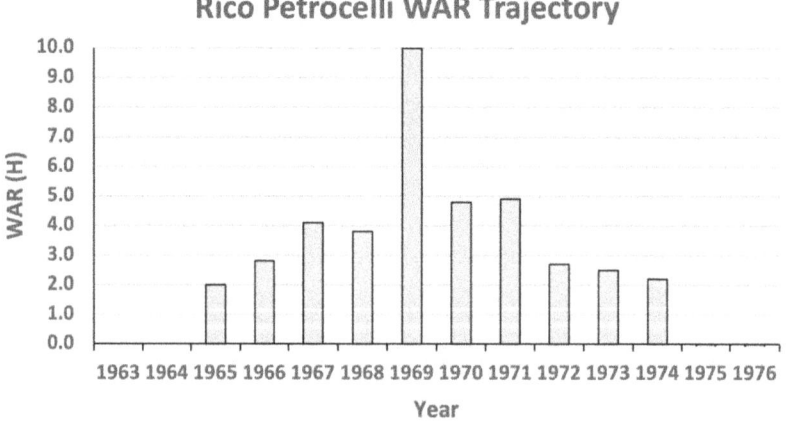

Looking at his career as a whole, Rico Petrocelli was a dependable but unspectacular SS/3B with decent power for most of his career, with 39.1 career WAR in 12 full seasons. Superficially, one might view him as a poor man's Cal Ripken, but without the incredible durability and longevity that made Ripken special. But unlike Ripken, Petrocelli's power stats were greatly exaggerated by playing half his games in Fenway Park. Over the course of his career, Petrocelli hit .272/.354/.489 with 134 HR and 465 RBI in Boston, but only .230/.312/.355 with 76 HR and 306 RBI on the road.[19] But his prowess at Fenway Park was not what made his 1969 season special. Petrocelli's home-away split was actually *less* pronounced in 1969 (.313/.424/.641 with 22 HR and 57 RBI at home versus .283/.383/.540 with 18 HR and 39 RBI on the road) than in the remainder of his career.[20] Furthermore, although Fenway Park did play as a hitter's park in 1969, the 106 Park Factor that year was no greater than in other years in Petrocelli's career.[21] Thus, while Petrocelli's power stats were undoubtedly enhanced over the course of his career by playing his home games in Fenway Park, the contrast between 1969 and the rest of his career clearly represented a genuine performance peak, not a ballpark effect.

◆ 19 ◆

Billy Sunday
Billy Cordell Grabarkewitz (1970)

Chatty and quick with a quip, Billy Grabarkewitz—the man who led the league in consonants—was a favorite of LA fans and of sportswriters everywhere during the early 1970s, but his once promising career was stymied by badly timed injuries. Although his 6.5 WAR in his career year is the lowest of the 16 position players I have selected as shooting stars, I just had to find room for a player who may have been the most extreme one-year wonder of any non-pitcher in MLB history. While it is not that difficult to find pitchers who starred for a single season and then washed out—Slim Jones (Chapter 7) and Mark Fidrych (Chapter 21) are two examples—position players like this are rare. Every other position player in this book had at least 1.9 WAR in one or more seasons beside his career year—but not Billy G. He never posted as much as 1 WAR in any single season except 1970, and he totaled -0.7 WAR for the other six seasons of his career. I can find no other historical example of a position player with a career lasting at least five years who posted ≥ 6.5 WAR in one season, but played at or below replacement level for the remainder of his career.

Billy Cordell Grabarkewitz was born of mixed Polish and Irish heritage in Lockhart, TX, on January 18, 1946. Like his father, he was a big Brooklyn Dodger fan; Pee Wee Reese was his favorite player.[1] Although his adult height was only 5'10", he was an outstanding all-around athlete at Alamo Heights High School in San Antonio, lettering in baseball, basketball, football, golf, and track. After two years at St. Mary's University in San Antonio, where he starred at 3B, he was chosen by the Dodgers in the twelfth round of the 1966 amateur draft.

Grabarkewitz, who batted right-handed, began at low A Tri-City in 1966 and hit a solid .258/.449/.472 with 11 HR and 21 SB in 342 PA. He advanced to Class A Santa Barbara in 1967, where he played SS

19. Billy Sunday

and hit .281/.430/.476 in 788 PA with 27 HR and 87 RBI, while leading his league with 149 R, 158 BB, and 48 SB. This breakout performance established him as the Dodgers' top prospect.[2] It was in Santa Barbara that Grabarkewitz earned the nickname "Billy Sunday" after hitting a game-winning ninth-inning grand-slam HR to defeat the Fresno Giants.[3] He hit 14 of his 27 HR that year on Sundays. The only flaw in his game was his 150 strikeouts. He was on this way to even better things with Class AA Albuquerque in 1968, hitting .308/.455/.512 in 370 PA as of August 3 and in line for a major league promotion to replace slumping SS Zoilo Versalles, when he sustained a grisly compound fracture of his right ankle in a collision at home plate. Although he was still on crutches, the Dodgers protected him in the 1969 expansion draft while exposing Versalles and thereby creating an opening for Grabarkewitz to became the Dodgers' starting SS in 1969.

However, the 1969 season did not go as planned. Grabarkewitz, now 23 years old, still had a pronounced limp when he reported to spring training and began the year at AAA Spokane.[4] He was recalled after hitting .432 in his first nine games but went hitless in 4 AB in his April 22 major league debut. He got his first major league hit—an infield single—the next day, while tying a major league record by playing a full nine innings without a single fielding chance at SS. However, he subsequently struggled badly and was demoted to Spokane on June 11 when the Dodgers brought back Maury Wills. Grabarkewitz returned to the Dodgers a month later, but finished the season with only four singles, a double, a triple, and 4 BB in 70 PA. With the Dodgers now sporting a bumper crop of young infielders in the majors or knocking on the door—including Steve Garvey, Ted Sizemore, Bill Russell, Ron Cey, Bobby Valentine, and Bill Sudakis—Grabarkewitz's standing on what fans were calling the "Mod Squad" (named after a popular late sixties TV show) had become less secure. Still, the Dodgers refused all trade offers for Billy G., including one which would have brought future Hall of Fame reliever Hoyt Wilhelm from the Angels.[5]

Although Grabarkewitz, now healthy, earned a spot on the Dodgers 1970 Opening Day roster with a strong performance in spring training, he had no defined role. The Dodgers' starting infield that day had Wes Parker at 1B, 1969 Rookie of the Year Ted Sizemore at 2B, Maury Wills at SS, and rookie Steve Garvey at 3B.[6] Grabarkewitz, Bill Sudakis, and veteran Jim LeFebvre were the infield reserves. But when Sizemore sustained a minor leg injury in the season's fifth game on April 11, Grabarkewitz filled in at 2B. The next day was a Sunday, and "Billy Sunday" got his first hit of the season, a two-run seventh inning HR.[7] Although Sizemore returned to action on April 19, Grabarkewitz never relinquished his place in the starting lineup, first shifting to 3B to replace slumping Steve Garvey, later filling in at SS when Maury Wills got hurt, and occasionally spelling Sizemore at 2B.

Looking at his season month by month, Grabarkewitz hit .333/.464/.533 in 57 PA in April, then really heated up in May, hitting .394/.479/.564 in 117 PA.[8] As the calendar turned to June, Dodger fans organized a write-in All-Star campaign for Billy G., who had been left off the NL ballot. But that was never going to work for a player who played multiple positions, whose name most fans could not spell or pronounce, and who usually appeared in Dodgers box scores as something like "Grbkwtz" to save space.[9] Although Grabarkewitz cooled off a bit in June to hit .292/.398/.417, he was selected as an All Star reserve and got one hit—an 11th inning single—in 3 AB as a mid-game replacement for Tony Perez at 3B.[10] It was Billy G.'s single that advanced Pete Rose to 2B and set up the memorable collision at home plate between Rose and catcher Ray Fosse on the next play. Fosse was never the same again. After hitting .280/.396/.430 in July, Grabarkewitz slumped to .174/.311/.378 in August, but finished strong with .291/.380/.447 in September-October. Altogether, it was a remarkable season (Table 19).

Table 19: Selected Stats for Billy Grabarkewitz's Peak and Runner-Up Seasons and His Career

Season	Age	PA	AVG	OBP	SLG	OPS+	TB	HR	R	RBI	SB	WAR (H)
Peak 1970	24	640	0.289	0.399	0.454	134	240	17	92	84	19	6.5
per 650 PA							244	17	93	85	19	6.6
Runner-Up* 1973	27	238	0.205	0.343	0.333	95	65	5	39	16	5	0.4
per 650 PA							178	14	107	44	14	1.1
Career (1969–75)		1390	0.236	0.351	0.364	101	423	28	189	141	33	5.8
per 650 PA							198	13	88	66	15	2.7

*Minimum 200 PA.

Grabarkewitz played 97 games at 3B, 50 games at SS, and 20 games at 2B in 1970. While he did not lead the NL in any category, he led the second place Dodgers in HR, BB, OBP, OPS+, and WAR and tied Willie Davis for the team lead in runs scored. The one weakness in his game remained strikeouts; his 149 SO led the Dodgers by far and was the fourth highest total in MLB behind Bobby Bonds, Tommy Agee, and Nate Colbert.[11] Nowadays, in the age of analytics, we would forgive his high strikeout rate as an acceptable price of the selectivity that enabled him to lead his team in BB and OBP.

The following winter, the Dodgers traded Ted Sizemore for star third baseman Dick Allen, pushing Grabarkewitz off of 3B, but clearing the way for him to take over for Sizemore at 2B. However, the injury jinx reared its ugly head again. Reportedly, on the second day of spring training 1971, Dodgers VP Al Campanis ordered Grabarkewitz and prospect Marv Gallaher to remain on the field after a full workout to practice the double play.[12] Both walked away afterwards with sore arms. Grabarkewitz had only 62 PA before hitting the disabled list on May 17. Although he managed to collect another 25 PA in June-July, he returned for another long stint on the disabled list before submitting to off-season shoulder surgery. It was a lost season, although Billy G. quipped that he had earned a promised raise by cutting down on his strikeouts; "you can't strike out when you don't play."[13]

Garbarkewitz was physically sound when reported for spring training in 1972, but the competition for playing time in the Dodger infield had gotten more congested. Steve Garvey had taken over at 3B and would soon be pushed to 1B by Ron Cey. Bill Russell had replaced Wills at SS. That left Billy G. to compete with veteran Jim Lefebvre and youngsters Lee Lacy and Davey Lopes at 2B. Grabarkewitz fell flat, hitting only .167/.265/.278 (56 OPS+) with -1.0 WAR in 166 PA. Again injuries—specifically a fractured finger that sidelined him for most of August—compounded his struggles, but he had hit poorly even before he got hurt.[14]

Finally willing to trade their once untouchable prospect, the Dodgers packaged Billy G. with Frank Robinson, Bobby Valentine, Mike Strahler, and former ace Bill Singer in a trade with the Angels that netted them ace Andy Messersmith and 3B Ken McMullen.[15] Grabarkewitz, still only 27 years old, looked forward to an opportunity to revive his once promising career with the fifth place Angels, who had no one of consequence blocking his pathway to playing time at any infield position. He began the season at 3B but did not hit and was again relegated to a utility role. He hit only .163/.316/.295 (81 OPS+) in 159 PA with the Angels before they traded him to the Phillies on August 14 for a player to be named later (who turned out to be incumbent 2B Denny Doyle). Although he improved to .288/.397/.409 in 79 PA for the Phillies, any hopes he may have had to compete for the vacated starting job at 2B in 1974 were dashed when the Phillies acquired 2B Dave Cash from the Pirates. Instead, after a slow start in 1974, the Phillies sold his contract to the Cubs, where he saw only limited duty in a utility role and hit only .248/.358/.328 in 149 PA (91 OPS+). By now, Billy G. was basically a replacement level player with little power or speed. After the Cubs released him at the end of the 1974 season, Grabarkewitz signed a minor league contract with Oakland and appeared in six games with the A's (going 0-for-2) after spending most of the season at AAA. His career was over at age 29. He had amassed only 0.3 WAR in 1971–75 following his 6.5 WAR season in 1970.

After his baseball career was over, Grabarkewitz returned to Texas with his wife and two sons and started an insurance business.[16] He divorced in 1976 but remarried 20 years later and has a daughter by his second wife.

Why Was Billy Grabarkewitz a Shooting Star?

Although Billy Grabarkewitz's 6.5 peak WAR is slightly below my standard for a shooting star, the contrast between that season and the rest of his career is stark (Figure 19).

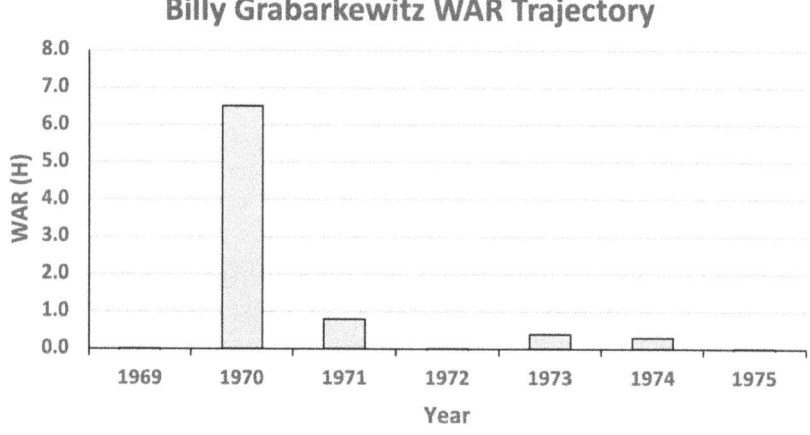

My reflexive take on one-year wonders like Graborkewitz, who attained stardom for a single season but were no better than mediocre for the rest of their careers, is that their career years were flukes and that the law of averages (i.e., regression to the mean) caught up with them. But Grabarkewitz was something else. He was a legitimate prospect with impressive minor league stats. The Dodgers and the many teams that tried to trade for him believed with good reason that he would become a star. Although the horrific ankle injury he suffered in 1968 when he was on the verge of a major league promotion probably diminished his speed and agility, he achieved stardom in 1970 even in that diminished state. Nothing about his sterling 1970 season seems lucky or flukish. A combination of lesser injuries and an overloaded Dodgers farm system—not regression to the mean—conspired to prevent him from becoming the player everyone thought he would be for more than one season. In short, I view Billy Grabarkewitz mainly as a very unlucky player, who might very well have achieved long-term success on a different team and under more favorable circumstances.

◈ 20 ◈

The Comeback Kid
John Frederick Hiller (1973)

John Hiller was in some respects an even less likely candidate than the first two relief pitchers profiled in this book for a superstar season in his thirties. While Hiller had a far better track record going into his 1973 career year than either Wilcy Moore (Chapter 6) or Ted Abernathy (Chapter 17), the seven-year major league veteran was lucky to be alive after suffering a near-fatal heart attack two years earlier and subsequently undergoing major abdominal surgery. Hiller was sidelined for the entire 1971 and most of the 1972 season. While other athletes in baseball and other sports have returned from serious physical injuries, Hiller is the only player I know of who came back to play in the major leagues after such a medical catastrophe. Yet Hiller not only resurrected his career in 1973, but his 7.9 WAR was the second highest ever for a relief pitcher, trailing only Hall of Famer Rich Gossage (8.2 WAR in 1975).[1] He even went on to pitch effectively for seven more years and to post 31.1 career pitching WAR—the fifth highest total of all time (behind only Rivera, Wilhelm, Gossage, and Tom Gordon) for any pitcher who made at least 75 percent of his appearances in relief.[2]

John Hiller was born on April 8, 1943, in Toronto, Ontario. He grew up an avid hockey fan, who took up baseball only to have a sport to play between hockey seasons.[3] Although the 6'1" lefty failed to impress Dodger coach (and ex-manager) Chuck Dressen at a local tryout camp in 1960, he continued to play amateur baseball and improved to the point where Detroit scout Cy Williams signed him to a minor league contract in 1962. After two moderately successful years as a starting pitcher in the lower minors in 1963–64, he moved to the Montgomery (AA) bullpen in 1965 and compiled a 2.53 ERA in 103.0 IP, thereby earning a six-inning cup of coffee with the Tigers in September. He spent most of the 1966 season in Toledo (AAA), with somewhat less success (4.45 ERA in 87.0 IP) and appeared in one game for the Tigers. In 1967, he moved back into the Toledo rotation and went 9–3 with a 2.73 ERA in 99.0 IP over the first three months. The Tigers recalled him in late June, and he went 4–3 with 3 saves in 6 starts and 17 relief appearances, over the next three months, compiling a 2.63 ERA (125 ERA+) in 65.0 IP with a 1.015 WHIP and an outstanding 49/9 strikeout-to-walk ratio. Although he was the losing pitcher in the game that eliminated the Tigers from the pennant race on the final day of the 1967 season, his outstanding work had put him in the major leagues to stay.

As a 25-year-old lefty swing man, Hiller built on his excellent rookie season and was an important cog in the Tigers' World Series championship of 1968. In 12 starts and 27 relief appearances, he went 9–6 with 2 saves, a 2.39 ERA (126 ERA+), a 1.117 WHIP, and 1.9 WAR, over 128.0 IP. After pitching in relief for most of the first four months, he joined the rotation in early August and won several key games down the stretch. Highlights included a complete game shutout of the White Sox on August 20, throwing nine shutout innings in a 19-inning 3–3 tie against the Yankees on August 23, a complete game 8–2 win over the Angels on September 11, and a 9–1 complete game win over the Yankees on September 16.[4] But the pennant race was never really close, and McLain and Lolich were the two uncontested aces. Hiller made only two mop-up appearances in Detroit's 4–3 win over St. Louis in the World Series, and gave up 3 ER in 2.0 IP.

After a down season in 1969 (4–4, 2 saves, 3.99 ERA [94 ERA+], 1.419 WHIP, 0 WAR), Hiller bounced back to have his best season yet in 1970. Appearing mostly in relief, he went 6–6 with 3 saves, a 3.03 ERA (124 ERA+), a 1.231 WHIP, and 2.8 WAR in 104.0 IP. He was not the closer—that was Tom Timmerman with 27 saves—but in his four full seasons, Hiller had established himself as a valuable high-leverage reliever, who could step into a starting role when needed. However, he smoked 2–3 packs of cigarettes per day, and his 6'1" frame now carried 235 pounds.[5] Disaster lay just around the corner.

On a cold January morning in his northern Minnesota home, after he had spent the previous day clearing a blanket of snow from his property, Hiller lit up his first cigarette of the day and suddenly felt a crushing pain in his chest and running down his arms, accompanied by a light-headedness that forced him to lie down.[6] His doctor instructed his wife to get him to the hospital ASAP; tests confirmed that he had suffered a significant heart attack. He tried at first to hide his condition from the Tigers and the public, but after three weeks in the hospital and another extended period of bedrest, he had to notify the Tigers that he was too weak to report for spring training. By April, it was clear that more drastic measures were needed. Even in 1971, when the national death rate from heart attack was at its peak, heart attacks were unusual in 27-year-old men, except in those with an uncommon (one in 500) inherited disorder in cholesterol metabolism.[7] Today, a patient like Hiller would not only be advised to stop smoking and lose weight, but would be put on a daily dose of a statin and aspirin and undergo coronary angioplasty and placement of one or more stents to open his coronary arteries. But statins, angioplasty, and stents were not available in 1971. Instead, Hiller underwent intestinal bypass surgery to help control his weight and his cholesterol level. His chances for a successful recovery were decent, but his odds of returning to the mound were almost nil. It had never been done before.

Hiller stopped smoking and, after recovering from surgery, began a rigorous program of diet and exercise, and dropped 65 pounds.[8] After a year of working out religiously and learning to pitch again, he asked permission to report to spring training in 1972, but Tigers GM Jim Campbell was nervous about the risk to Hiller and the team. After consulting a cardiologist, Campbell agreed to allow Hiller to rejoin the Tigers as a pitching coach and batting practice pitcher. Finally, on July 7, Hiller was added to the active roster with the understanding that he would be used strictly in short relief stints. Over the last half of the 1972 season, Hiller pitched as well as he had before his heart attack, compiling a 2.03 ERA (158 ERA+) and 1.173 WHIP in 44.1 IP. He was also nearly perfect in the Tigers' unsuccessful playoff series against Oakland. He yielded only a hit and a walk and no ER in 3.1 IP, and was the winning pitcher in Game 4 to temporarily even the Series at 2–2. But Hiller's 1972 comeback was barely a taste of what was to come (Table 20).

Table 20: Selected Stats for John Hiller's Peak and Runner-Up Seasons and His Career*

Season	Age	BF	ERA	WHIP	ERA+	W-L	SV	SO	BB	WAR (P)
Peak 1973	34	498	1.44	1.021	283	10–5	**38**	124	39	7.9
per 1000 BF								249	78	15.9
Runner-Up 1974	32	633	2.64	1.260	143	17–14	13	134	62	4.1
per 1000 BF								212	98	6.5
Career (1965–80)		5206	2.83	1.268	134	87–76	125	1036	535	31.1
per 1000 BF								199	103	6.0

*League leading totals are shown in boldface type.

In 1973, Hiller pitched 125.1 innings and amassed a record-setting total of 38 saves plus 10 wins, thereby contributing to 56 percent of his team's 87 wins.[9] He compiled a minuscule 1.44 ERA (283 ERA+) and

1.021 WHIP, although 1973 was the year that AL introduced the designated hitter to boost run-scoring. His 7.9 WAR in 498 BF in 1973 translates to an eye-popping 15.9 WAR per 1000 BF—even better than Gossage's 14.1 WAR per 1000 BF in 1975. Hiller's unprecedented excellence in a relief role brought him fourth place finishes in both the AL MVP and Cy Young award voting, as well as Comeback of the Year honors.[10] He also received the American Heart Award and the Fred Hutchinson award for "fighting spirit and competitive desire."[11]

A more granular look at his 1973 season reveals that Hiller appeared in 65 games and finished 60. More than half of his appearances (35) were for more than one inning; 16 were for 3.0 innings or longer.[12] He held the opposition scoreless in 49 (75 percent) of his appearances. He gave up more than one ER only three times—3 ER in 0.2 IP in a loss to Kansas City on April 28, 2 ER in 5.1 IP in a loss to Milwaukee on May 13, and 2 ER in 2.2 IP in a win over the Angels on July 12. He converted 38 of his 42 save opportunities. He did not give up a run until his 21st save opportunity on July 10, and did not actually cough up a lead until July 12, when he allowed a game tying two-run HR to Angels catcher Bob Oliver in the eighth inning but stayed on to get the win. In his three other blown saves, he entered with a 3–2 lead and two men on base with no one out in the sixth inning and gave up a three-run HR to Milwaukee catcher Darrell Porter on August 2; he pitched 5.1 innings of one-run relief against the Yankees on August 4, but the run was a game-winning 14th-inning HR by Horace Clarke; and he relieved Woodie Fryman with a man on first and two out in the eighth inning, gave up a game-tying single to the Angels Mike Epstein, but went on to pitch 3.1 scoreless innings to pick up the 11-inning win. Only two of Hiller's 10 wins were "vultured" from blown save opportunities. Six wins came in games that were tied when he entered; he gave up a total of 3 ER in 14.3 IP in those games. He earned his other two wins by preserving leads in games in which the starter failed to last five innings, yielding only a single ER in a combined 9.3 IP.

One of Hiller's most impressive outings of the year was an extra inning loss to Texas on July 22, in which he relieved Joe Coleman in the second inning with the Tigers trailing 3–1 and held the Rangers scoreless with 10 strikeouts through the ninth inning while the Tigers tied the game, gave way to RP Bob Miller after putting two men on base with one out in the tenth inning, and took the loss when Miller yielded a game-winning single. He saved some of his best work for the best teams. In six appearances against AL East champion Baltimore, Hiller gave up 1 ER in 6.1 IP with 4 SV. In seven appearances against AL West champion Oakland, he gave up 1 ER in 12.1 IP with 2 W and 4 SV. He absolutely owned the 89-win Red Sox, yielding 2 ER in 17.0 IP and racking up 3 wins and 6 saves in 9 appearances. It was an altogether remarkable season for anyone, let alone a 30-year-old heart attack survivor.

Hiller continued to pitch well in 1974, although not at his 1973 level. The Tigers were a last place 72-win team that year, and save opportunities were infrequent, so Hiller often entered the game with the Tigers tied or behind. In 59 appearances totaling 150.0 IP, Hiller went 17–14 with only 13 saves, a 2.64 ERA (143 ERA+), a 1.260 WHIP, and 4.1 WAR. Although his 13 saves ranked only tenth in the major leagues, his 17 wins in relief fell just one short of the record 18 relief wins established by Pittsburgh's Roy Face in 1959. Although 1974 was a worthy encore to Hiller's 1973 achievements, his 4.1 WAR was little more than half of his 1973 WAR. However, he made his first and only All-Star team (but did not get into the game) and received a smattering of Cy Young and MVP votes at the end of the season.

Hiller continued to be a bullpen stalwart for the Tigers over the next four years and even made a start in 1976 and eight starts in 1977. He averaged 47 appearances, 102 IP, 8 wins, and 12 saves in 1975–78 with a composite 2.69 ERA (148 ERA+) and 1.294 WHIP, averaged 8.7 SO versus 4.4 BB per 9 IP, and added 11.9 WAR to his career total. However, the Tigers were terrible during three of those four seasons, and Hiller's consistent excellence went almost unnoticed.

Finally, in 1979–80, Hiller's performance declined precipitously. In his last two seasons, he averaged only 2 wins and 4 saves with an ERA of 4.99 (87 ERA+) and a WHIP of 1.727. His walks (5.6 per 9 IP) exceeded his strikeouts (5.2 per 9 IP), and his WAR was near zero. He decided to retire at age 37 and served as a roving pitching coach, but severe circulatory problems forced him to leave coaching in 1989.[13] He and his second wife Lynnette retired to Iron Mountain in Michigan's upper peninsula.

Why Was John Hiller a Shooting Star?

John Hiller was a fine pitcher for most of his 15-year career, but his 7.9-WAR 1973 season was something special—all the more so because it came after a near-fatal heart attack and major surgery (Figure 20).

It seems far-fetched to think of John Hiller—a pitcher with 87 career wins and 125 saves, who never attained postseason prominence and who received only 2.6 percent of the votes in his only time on the BBWAA HOF ballot—as a potential Hall of Famer, but the idea is not absurd. It is difficult to evaluate relief specialists because they pitch far fewer innings than top starting pitchers, and because the main metric

20. The Comeback Kid

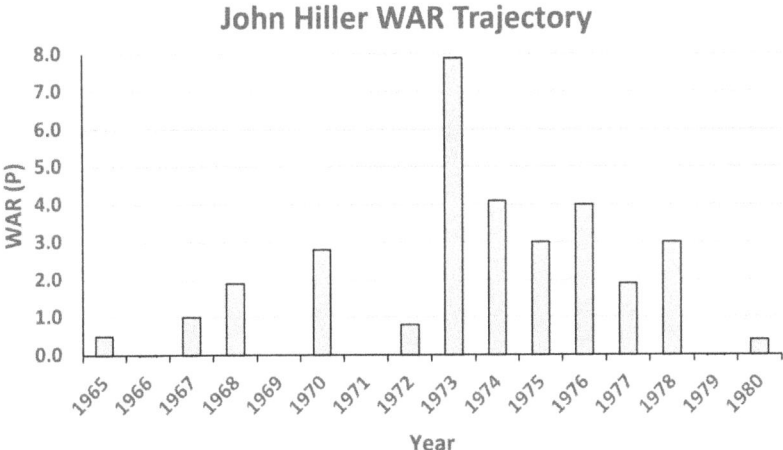

for evaluating them—the save—is an artificial construct invented by Chicago sportswriter Jerry Holtzman in the 1960s, which only began to gain traction in the early 1970s.[14] In the late 1980s, the tail began to wag the dog, as managers began to reserve their ace relief pitchers for ninth inning save opportunities, even if this usage did not maximize their value in winning games. In some ways, Hiller's usage in 1973, which was intended to minimize the risk to his heart, foreshadowed the evolution of the modern late inning closer, although 35 percent of Hiller's appearances came in non-save situations. As Tigers manager Billy Martin grew more confident that Hiller would not suffer a cardiac arrest on the mound, he was often allowed to pitch multiple innings—once as many as 8.1. But after 1973, Hiller was used more as an all-purpose reliever according to the conventions of his time and never again saved more than 15 games in a season.

But does Hiller's modest 125 career saves total really make him a lesser player than, say, Lee Smith, who amassed 474 career saves and was elected to the Hall of Fame by the Veterans Committee in 2021? Smith pitched 1289.1 innings over the course of his 18-year career—47.1 more than Hiller in his 15 years—and also faced 182 more batters.[15] However, Hiller had 16 more wins and 16 fewer losses than Smith and had a lower ERA (2.83 versus 3.03), a better ERA+ (134 versus 132), a slightly worse WHIP (1.268 versus 1.256), and a higher WAR (P) (31.1 versus 29.3). Smith held the advantage in strikeouts (8.7 versus 7.5) and walks (3.4 versus 3.9) per 9 IP but gave up more hits (7.9 versus 7.5) per 9 IP. Thus, despite their discrepant save totals, their fundamental stats were basically similar. The fact that Smith was deployed mostly in "save situations," while Hiller's managers used him whenever the team needed him most, does not make Smith the better pitcher. The tie-breaker, in my opinion, is Hiller's unique status as baseball's only heart attack survivor to return to the field and to pitch with constant uncertainty that his heart could withstand the stress of playing in the major leagues. I won't say that Hiller belongs in the Hall of Fame, but among relief specialists, considering both durability and peak value, my CVI metric ranks him behind only Mariano Rivera, Dennis Eckersley, Rich Gossage, and Hoyt Wilhelm—all Hall of Famers.[16]

◈ 21 ◈

The Bird Is the Word
Mark Steven "The Bird" Fidrych (1976)

"They're paying to see me, and they say *I'm* on drugs?"
—Mark Fidrych[1]

No shooting star had more fun and brought more fun to the fans than Mark Fidrych, the gangly curly-haired eccentric right-handed pitcher, who physically resembled Sesame Street's Big Bird and who came out of nowhere to take the AL by storm in 1976. An unheralded 21-year-old non-roster invitee, who did not make his first start until May 15, Fidrych quickly became the Tigers' ace and an All-Star. Moreover, his unique antics on the mound, like meticulously clearing the mound of debris like a strange bird collecting material for his nest while sustaining a constant profanity-laced monolog, accompanied by gesticulations, directed at the baseball and himself, made him a national phenomenon.[2] His exuberance and guilelessness earned him an avid following of fans who knew him simply as "The Bird." He drew crowds not only in Detroit but everywhere he went. The press loved him for his candor and unassuming personality. He was photographed by Annie Leibovitz and profiled in the Rolling Stone.[3] The Michigan state legislature passed a resolution to raise his salary. And yet barely a year later, the magic evaporated, and the adoring crowds grew still, as Fidrych suffered a series of injuries culminating in a career-ending torn rotator cuff in 1980. Fidrych, who won 19 games in 1976, won only 10 more over the remaining four years of his career.

Mark Steven Fidrych was born on August 14, 1954, in Worcester, MA, and grew up in the nearby town of Northborough, where his father was a public school teacher.[4] He was a poor student (Attention Deficit Hyperactivity Disorder, I would guess) and had to repeat the first and second grades. He played multiple sports in high school, but had to transfer to a private academy to play baseball as a senior because he had already turned 19. He received no scholarship offers, but Tigers scout Mark Cusic liked his fastball. So, the Tigers selected him in the tenth round of the 1974 amateur draft. He was assigned to Bristol of the Appalachian rookie league as a relief pitcher, where manager Jeff Hogan took one look at his 6'3" 175-pound frame and his mop of curly blonde hair and dubbed him "Big Bird" or just "The Bird."

After playing winter ball, Fidrych moved to the starting rotation and rapidly ascended the minor league ladder, compiling an 11–10 record with a 3.21 ERA and 1.257 WHIP in 171.0 IP at three levels. Although he was unknown to the public when he reported to spring training in 1976, the Tigers knew him well. They were coming off a horrendous 57–105 season in 1975 and had traded long-time ace Mickey Lolich, so the opportunity to fill a rotation spot was wide open.

Fidrych was used sparingly at first, making only two appearances—both in relief—in the first five weeks of the season.[5] In the first, on April 20, he faced only one batter (Don Baylor) and gave up a walk-off single to seal a 6–5 comeback victory by Oakland. His second appearance on May 5 was more successful, a scoreless ninth inning in an 8–2 loss to Minnesota. The third time was the charm. Given a spot start as a fill-in for Joe Coleman against Cleveland on May 15, Fidrych responded by pitching a two-hit complete game 2–1 victory. This earned

Left leg kicked high, tongue protruding, and blonde curls flying out from under his cap, it was impossible to take your eyes off Mark "The Bird" Fidrych of the 1976 Detroit Tigers as he wound up to deliver a pitch (National Baseball Hall of Fame Museum).

21. The Bird Is the Word

him another start ten days later—a tough 2–0 complete game loss in Fenway Park to the defending AL champion Red Sox, marred only by Carl Yastrzemski's two-run fourth inning HR. This performance earned Fidrych a permanent spot in the Tigers rotation.

Starting with an 11-inning complete game 5–4 win over Milwaukee on May 31, Fidrych rattled off eight consecutive wins—all complete games. In the last seven games of this streak, he gave up 2, 1, 2, 3, 3, 1, and 0 ER. As this streak progressed, Fidrych's antics on the mound began to attract national media attention. On June 5, a Sporting News article described his behavior as follows. "He talks to the ball.... He talks to himself.... He gestures toward the plate, pointing out the path he wants the pitch to take.... He struts in a circle around the mound after each out, applauding his teammates and asking for the ball.... And he's forever chewing gum and patting the dirt on the mound with his bare hand."[6] The June 28 game, a nationally televised 5–1 victory over the Yankees made him a celebrity. When a New York reported told him after the game that the Yankees' grumpy star catcher and captain Thurman Munson had called him an attention-seeking showboat, Fidrych merely asked, "Who is Thurman Munson?"[7] He was not being sarcastic; he really didn't know. He and Munson had a good laugh about it when they were the AL's starting All-Star battery two weeks later. By that time, Munson had realized that Fidrych was the genuine article.

Fidrych's winning streak ended in his last pre–All-Star game start with a complete game 1–0 loss to Kansas City on July 9. Then, perhaps feeling the jitters of his first All-Star appearance after a pre-game visit from President Gerald Ford, Fidrych yielded a single to Pete Rose and a triple to Steve Garvey before he could retire a batter.[8] But after allowing a run-scoring groundout, he got through two innings with no further damage. Still, he was tagged with the loss in a 7–1 NL victory. After the All-Star break, Fidrych picked up where he left off, hurling an 11-inning 1–0 shutout over Oakland on July 16. Fidrych slowed down a bit in his final 17 starts, winning nine (including two shutouts and six other complete games), losing seven (including five complete games), and taking one no-decision (a 4-ER-4.2-IP start versus Cleveland on August 3). Altogether, Fidrych gave up more than 4 ER in only 3 of 29 starts—7 in a 10-inning 7–3 complete game loss to Minnesota on August 21, 7 in 3.2 IP in an 11–2 loss to Milwaukee on September 3, and 6 ER in 2.2 IP in an 8–3 loss to Boston on September 13. On the plus side, he gave up 3 ER or fewer in 23 starts—*all complete games*, including four shutouts and two other games in which he yielded only a single unearned run. His main weakness was that he struck out only 3.5 per 9 IP; but on the other hand, he walked only 1.9 per 9 IP. At the end of the season, Fidrych led the AL in ERA, ERA+, CG, and WAR (P) finished third (behind Frank Tanana and Jim Palmer) in WHIP (Table 21). He finished second to Palmer in the AL Cy Young award voting, although he outpaced Palmer 9.6 to 6.5 in WAR, and eleventh in the AL MVP voting (won by Thurman Munson). Unlike Palmer (who won 22), he did not attain the magical twenty wins, and unlike Munson, he played for a losing team (74–87) that finished fifth out of six in the AL East.

Table 21: Selected Stats for Mark Fidrych's Peak and Runner-Up Seasons and His Career*

Season	Age	BF	ERA	WHIP	ERA+	W-L	CG	SHO	SO	BB	WAR (P)
Peak 1976	21	996	2.34	1.079	**159**	19–9	**24**	4	97	53	**9.6**
per 1000 BF							24	4	97	53	9.6
Runner-Up 1977	22	326	2.89	1.160	149	6–4	7	1	42	12	2.4
per 1000 BF							21	3	129	37	7.4
Career (1976–80)		1695	3.10	1.203	126	29–19	34	5	170	99	11.3
per 1000 BF							20	3	100	58	6.7

*League leading totals are shown in boldface type.

When Fidrych reported to spring training in 1977, he was a national celebrity with a new $55,000 contract, after playing for the major league minimum ($16,500) as a rookie. He was criticized for settling for such a modest sum, but he had presciently asked for and received guarantees of $90,000 in 1978 and $125,000 in 1979, as well as a retroactive pay raise to $30,000 for the 1976 season.[9] When he tore cartilage in his left knee while shagging flyballs in spring training, the subsequent surgery sidelined him until May 27. However, after losing his first two starts, 2–1 to Seattle and 6–4 to Cleveland, he ran off seven straight wins in June— all complete games—never giving up more than 3 ER.[10] One of his wins was a masterful 2–1 win over the AL Champion Yankees, in which he gave up only three hits, walked no one, and struck out a career high nine batsmen. He even made the All-Star team again. But that was as good at it would get. Fidrych was hit hard in his first two July starts by the Orioles and White Sox, yielding 6 ER in 5.2 IP in each game, and giving up a combined 21 hits and four walks. He complained of a "dead arm" but still made one more start against Toronto. He was removed after facing only three batters and was done for the season.

Fidrych came back to win his first two starts of 1978 (both complete games) 6–2 and 5–2. But his arm tightened again after yielding 2 ER on 6 H in his third start, and he left after four innings. He missed the remainder of the season. He tried to come back again in May 1979 but

21. The Bird Is the Word

struggled badly in four starts, giving up 17 ER in 14.2 IP and finishing 0–3. He agreed to report to Evansville (AAA) in 1980, but his good-guy image frayed a bit when he had a public spat with Tiger manager Sparky Anderson over Anderson's absence from his first minor league start.[11] Anderson told him he would not receive special treatment. He pitched well enough (6–7, 3.92 ERA) to earn a mid-season call-up to Detroit. But in nine starts for the Tigers, he could do no better than a 2–3 record with a 5.68 ERA and a 1.759 WHIP. He tried unsuccessfully to pitch his way back to Detroit again in 1981 and then tried to catch on in the Red Sox organization, making 27 starts in Pawtucket (AAA) in 1982 and 1983, but he never made another major league appearance. He was finished at age 28, the victim of a torn rotator cuff. The diagnosis and reparative surgery in 1985 came too late for another comeback attempt.

After his baseball career ended, Fidrych went back home to Northborough, MA, where he had bought a small farm with his modest baseball earnings in 1980. He married Ann Patazis in 1986, and they had a daughter, Jessica, shortly thereafter. When he sat for a "Where are they now?" interview for *Sports Illustrated* in 2001, he was working as an independent contractor, laying sewer pipe and doing road repairs, and coaching his daughter's soccer team in his spare time.[12] He was as exuberant and unpretentious as ever, as he reminisced about how awestruck he was to have pitched in the major leagues and to have gotten so much attention. He harbored no discernible bitterness over the injury that shortened his once promising career. Indeed, he was grateful for the hundreds of fan letters and autograph requests he continued to receive 25 years after the season that made him a household word (he compared himself to Mr. Clean). He continued to be an avid baseball fan and to do charity work. He allowed himself one wistful final comment, "It all goes by so fast, you know?" Fidrych's life would end less than eight years later. On April 13, 2009, his body was found under his beloved dump truck, which he appeared to have been working on at the time.[13] He was the victim of a freakish accident in which his clothes had become tangled in the truck's power takeoff shaft and suffocated him. He was 54 years old.

Why Was Mark Fidrych a Shooting Star?

A glance at Mark Fidrych's career trajectory confirms that he was a textbook one-year-wonder (Figure 21).

This career arc of a budding star struck down by injury just as his career was taking off is all too familiar. It is possible that Fidrych's arm

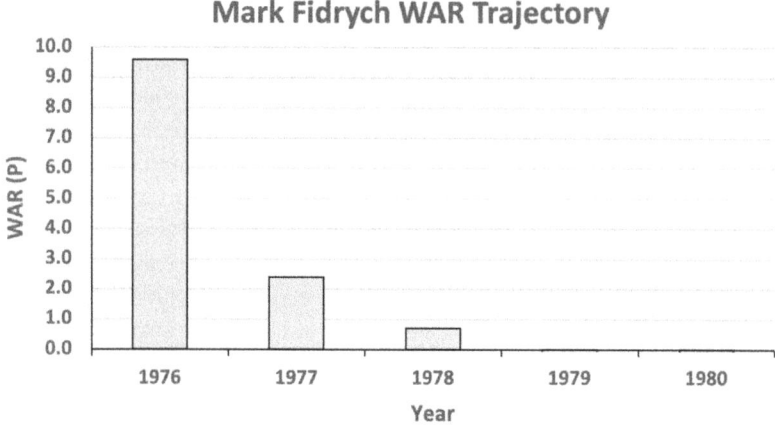

Mark Fidrych WAR Trajectory

woes can be attributed to coming back too soon from his 1977 knee surgery and altering his pitching motion, as happened to Dizzy Dean in 1937. Alternatively, one might hypothesize that throwing 250.1 innings and 24 complete games (five of them requiring extra innings) in four months was an excessive workload for a 21-year-old rookie—similar to what happened to Slim Jones (Chapter 7), who had an even better age 21 season back in 1934. However, Fidrych, who did not walk or strike out many batters, faced only 996 batters in 1976, not an unusually high workload.

What made Mark Fidrych's story unique—and especially poignant—was the national celebrity and adoration he had attained in a single year. His impact went far beyond his performance on the mound. Fidrych was a simple unsophisticated man, who had a special rapport with baseball fans in Detroit and beyond. He was humble and unaffected at the peak of his celebrity, and he bore his fate with grace and equanimity as fame and fortune slipped away. At a time when baseball fans had grown cynical that ballplayers cared only for money, Fidrych's sheer joy and apparent indifference to his meager rookie's salary offered a refreshing antidote. Of course, things were not really that simple. Team owners had been exploiting players for decades, and players were only beginning to get their due in 1976. The first million-dollar contract was still three years away. But perception is what mattered most, as fans across the country fell in love with "The Bird" and flocked to see his every start. In this sense, as Jim Leyland (Fidrych's manager at Evansville in 1980–81) commented after his death, "You can talk about Ty Cobb or anyone else, but for one year he was the biggest impact star in the history of the Tigers."[14] That may have been hyperbole, but Tony

Torchia, Fidrych's manager in Pawtucket, got it right when he told Fidrych on the occasion of his retirement in 1983, "You may not have been a great pitcher in terms of longevity, but for one year you had baseball in the palm of your hand."[15] What better description can there be of a shooting star?

◈ 22 ◈

Imperfect
Darrell Ray Porter (1979)

Darrell Porter was a perfectionist in a sport where even the best players fail in two-thirds of their at-bats. No matter what he accomplished, he always worried that his best wasn't good enough and that people wouldn't like or accept him. So he turned first to beer, then whiskey, then marijuana, then quaaludes and cocaine to escape his insecurities.[1] Despite it all, he still managed to put together an impactful MLB career, with his best season coming at a time (1979) when his substance abuse was at its worst. Nevertheless, his struggles with addiction, which he chronicled in his 1984 autobiography *Snap Me Perfect!: The Darrell Porter Story*, were profound and lifelong.[2]

Darrell Ray Porter was born in Joplin, MO, on January 17, 1952. The youngest of four children, Darrell grew up with a critical and demanding father, himself a disappointed former athlete, who drove his children to succeed where he had failed.[3] Darrell fit the part to a tee. Big and muscular with a powerful throwing arm and a smooth lefty swing, Porter was a multisport athlete at Southeast High School in Oklahoma City (where his family had moved), drawing comparisons to another famous Oklahoma catcher Johnny Bench.[4] He was the first winner of the Jim Thorpe Award for Oklahoma's best young athlete. Although he was offered a football scholarship to play quarterback at the University of Oklahoma, Darrell accepted a $70,000 bonus to sign with the Milwaukee Brewers, a recent expansion team, who had selected him with the fourth overall pick in the 1970 amateur draft. They assigned him to Class A Clinton.

The story of Porter's descent into alcoholism and addiction sounds like the premise for a corny movie: A naïve teetotaling 18 year-old kid visiting his first major league clubhouse is shocked and fascinated to find the players drinking beer and smoking.[5] When he struggles to hit, his teammates invite him out for beer. He hates beer at first, but before

22. Imperfect

long, he drinks four bottles and is hooked and soon progresses to the harder stuff, etc.

Porter hit only .200/.371/.324 in 237 PA that first season, but drinking helped him relax and made his failures more bearable. Porter returned to Class A ball in 1971, this time at Danville (IL) and did much better, hitting .271/.425/.557 with 24 HR, 70 RBI, and 75 R. His performance earned him a September call-up to the Brewers, where he received 80 PA but hit only.214/.300/.329 (80 OPS+). His failure to translate his minor league success to the big league stage put additional pressure on him. In the off-season, he drank and smoked marijuana regularly and discovered quaaludes, which became his drug of choice.[6] However, then and throughout his career, Porter reportedly confined his drug use to the off-season. Although he drank heavily during the season, he kept up a good front on the field.

Although Porter was only 20 years old and had no minor league experience above Class A, the Brewers, who were coming off a last-place finish in 1971, hoped that he was ready to claim at least a share of their catching duties in 1972. He was not. He played in 18 of their first 25 games but hit a dismal .125/.210/.196 (23 OPS+) in 63 PA. He was sent down to AAA Evansville for the rest of the season and hit a disappointing .216/.388/.412. Although he did hit 13 HR with 45 RBI, the season was a bust professionally. However, he fell in love with and married Teri Brown in May 1972.[7]

As a bad team with little to lose, the Brewers

In this photograph of Darrell Porter as a St. Louis Cardinals, circa 1981–85, he seemed to exude an air of quiet confidence, but he ultimately succumbed to the demons that lurked beneath the surface (National Baseball Hall of Fame Museum).

decided to install Porter as their starting catcher in 1973, come hell or high water. Although his batting average left something to be desired, he made up for it with a keen batting eye, moderate power, strong defense, and fiery competitiveness. In 1973–75, Porter hit a combined .242/.353/.415 (119 OPS+) and averaged 15 HR, 61 RBI, 58 R, 65 BB, and 3.5 WAR (including 0.9 dWAR) in 472 PA per season. In 1973, he finished third in the AL Rookie of the Year voting. In 1974, he was selected as a reserve on the AL All-Star team but did not play. In short, although his stats fell short of what the Brewers and Porter dreamed of, he was in fact one of the better catchers in the AL, with room to grow.

However, Porter took a big step backward in 1976. He struggled mightily on the field, hitting .208/.298/.288 (74 OPS+) in 449 PA with only 5 HR and 32 RBI. His 0.4 WAR was essentially at replacement level. Even his defense slipped (−0.4 dWAR). Off the field, Porter discovered cocaine and began using it regularly along with his drinking and other drugs. His wife could no longer tolerate the situation and divorced him.[8] Finally, on December 6, 1976, the Brewers, frustrated by what they viewed as the inconsistency and immaturity of their 24-year-old former star prospect, gave up on him and traded him to Kansas City for ten cents on the dollar.

The trade to Kansas City was a godsend for Porter's career. Not only did it provide a fresh start, he went from a losing team to a defending divisional champion with strong team chemistry and a cadre of stars, led by George Brett, Amos Otis, Hal McRae, and Frank White. It also connected him with a manager, Whitey Herzog, who appreciated his talents and became his mentor and cheerleader. Porter responded with a solid 2.5 WAR comeback season in 1977, hitting .275/.353/.452 (116 OPS+) with 16 HR, 60 RBI, and 61 R as the Royals repeated as AL West champs. Although Porter hit .333/.444/.333 in 18 PA in the ALCS, the Royals lost again to the Yankees 3–2. In 1978, Porter posted his best season to date, hitting .265/.358/.444 (123 OPS+) in 602 PA with 18 HR, 78 RBI, 77 R, and 4.2 WAR. He returned to the All-Star game as a reserve behind Carlton Fisk, and made the final out on a foul pop-up to end the game in his only AB.[9] Once more, Porter came through by hitting .357/.412/.429 in the ALCS, but the Yankees still prevailed 3–1 to win the AL pennant. At age 26, Porter had now established himself as one of the AL's top catchers, but he was still drinking heavily while somehow managing to keep it together on the field. After the season, his use of quaaludes and cocaine escalated.

Although his drinking continued unabated in 1979, Porter's extraordinary 7.6 WAR performance would far surpass anything he had done before or would do in the future (Table 22).

22. Imperfect

Table 22: Selected Stats for Darrell Porter's Peak and Runner-Up Seasons and His Career*

Season	Age	PA	AVG	OBP	SLG	OPS+	TB	HR	R	RBI	BB	WAR (H)	dWAR
Peak 1979	27	679	0.291	0.421	0.484	142	258	20	101	112	**121**	7.6	1.8
per 650 PA							247	19	97	107	116	7.3	1.7
Runner-Up 1978	26	602	0.265	0.358	0.444	123	231	18	77	78	75	4.2	1.1
per 650 PA							249	19	83	84	81	4.5	1.2
Career (1971–87)		6570	0.247	0.354	0.409	113	2266	188	765	826	905	40.8	10.6
per 650 PA							224	19	76	82	90	4.0	1.0

*League leading totals are shown in boldface type.

Porter achieved career highs in PA, AVG, OBP, SLG, H (155), TB, 3B (10), HR, BB, WAR and dWAR; his 121 BB led MLB. This combination of stats would constitute an excellent season for an OF or 1B but is rarified territory for a catcher. No previous catcher except Mickey Cochrane (in 1932) had ever posted more than 100 R, 100 RBI, and 100 BB in the same season, and none has done it since Porter.[10] Only four catchers—Bench (8.6 in 1972 and 7.9 in 1974), Piazza (8.7 in 1997), Carter (8.6 in 1982), and Mauer (7.8 in 2009) have ever surpassed Porter's 7.6 WAR in 1979; Posey also had 7.6 WAR in 2012.[11] Bench, Piazza, Mauer, and Carter are in the HOF, while Posey is likely to be elected when he is eligible.

Porter was productive in every month of the 1979 season.[12] His best months were April (.366/.483/.563), August (.315/.448/.598), and June (.308/.476/.528). His worst month was July (.261/.367/.386). His monthly output of RBI was quite steady, ranging from 15 in June to 23 in August. He received his first All-Star start and collected a single in 3 AB before giving way to Brian Downing.[13] However, 1979 was a disappointing year for the Royals, who won only 85 games and finished second to the Angels in the AL West. It was the only year in Porter's four-year stay in Kansas City that the Royals missed the postseason. Thus, Porter's nearly unprecedented season earned him only a ninth place finish in the 1979 AL MVP voting; the Angels' DH Don Baylor, who won the award, had only 3.7 WAR.

Although 1979 was Porter's best season on the field, it was agony off the field.[14] As the calendar turned to 1980 and there were no ballgames to provide any structure or distraction, his addictions were spinning out of control. His cocaine habit was costing him $1000 per day and taking over his life. Desperate, he approached ex–Dodger star and recovered alcoholic Don Newcombe in spring training and asked for help. Newcombe told him in no uncertain terms that he was unfit to play baseball and referred him to an Arizona rehab facility called The Meadows. With the approval of the Royals' front office, Porter spent the next six weeks in rehab. When he returned in late April, he told his story to teammates and reporters and hoped that they would forgive and accept him. He was nervous about how fans would react, especially when the Royals visited New York, and was touched and gratified when he received a standing ovation after he hit a home run off Yankee ace Ron Guidry.

If this were fiction, Porter, having shed the albatross of addiction, would have gone on to even bigger and better things. But reality is often cruel. He would never again approach his 7.6 WAR of 1979 or even his 4.2 WAR of 1978. But fate still had some good moments in store for him. His 1980 season was his worst since his pre–Kansas City days in 1976. After missing most of April, he hit only .249/.354/.342 (92 OPS+) with 2.4 WAR in 495 PA. His defense was still strong, but his power (7 HR) and run production (51 R and 51 RBI) fell off dramatically from his career highs of 1979. Whitey Herzog, who had been replaced by Jim Frey after failing to win the AL West in 1979, was no longer around to offer encouragement. However, Porter was again selected as an All-Star reserve. More importantly, the Royals finally got past the Yankees and won the AL pennant. Porter, who had performed well in previous post-season play, was of little help either in the ALCS (which they swept 3–0) or in the World Series (which they lost to the Phillies 4–2). He collected only three singles in 24 AB in the two series.

Porter became a free agent after the 1980 World Series. Although he liked Kansas City and the Royals tried to re-sign him, he and his new bride Deanna decided to accept a $3.5 million five-year deal from St. Louis, where Whitey Herzog was now the manager.[15] He was not greeted warmly by Cardinals fans, since his signing had pushed the popular incumbent catcher, Ted Simmons, out of St. Louis. Porter's unpopularity was compounded by the fact that he hit only .224/.364/.408 (117 OPS+) in 217 PA that year with 6 HR, 31 RBI, and 1.5 WAR. However, that stat line is somewhat misleading, since the middle two months of the 1981 season were wiped out by a work stoppage. Although this was hardly a good season for Porter or the Cardinals (who missed the post-season), Whitey Herzog was more than satisfied with Porter's defense and ability to handle a pitching staff.[16]

The 1982 season was a banner year for the Cardinals. Herzog had brought his "Whitey-ball" vision of speed, defense, and contact to full fruition, featuring Porter, 2B Tom Herr, SS Ozzie Smith, and CF Willie McGee at the key up-the-middle positions. The Cardinals won the NL East with a 92–70 record, swept the Atlanta Braves in the NLCS, and overcame the slugging Milwaukee Brewers in the World Series. Again, Porter's in-season stats were unimpressive. The 30-year-old veteran hit .231/.347/.402 (109 OPS+) in 445 PA with 12 HR, 48 RBI, 46 R, and 2.7 WAR. But he saved his best for the postseason, hitting .556/.714/.889 in the NLCS and .286/.310/.454 in the WS, and won MVP honors in both series. Porter's game-tying 2-run sixth inning double in Game 2 helped the Cardinals tie the World Series after losing 10–0 in Game 1.[17] Then, his two-run fourth-inning HR off future Hall of Famer Don Sutton in Game 6 staked the Cardinals to a 4–0 lead in the game that would tie the Series and set up the Cardinals decisive win in Game 7.

Porter's 1982 post-season heroics cemented his popularity in St. Louis and took some pressure off his shoulders. In 1983, Porter had his best year since 1979, hitting .262/.363/.431 (119 OPS+) in 519 PA with 15 HR, 66 RBI, 57 R, and 3.9 WAR (including 1.4 dWAR). The Cardinals, however, fell to 79–83 and finished fourth in a six-team division. But this was Porter's last hurrah. He hit only .232/.331/.363 (97 OPS+) in 493 PA with 11 HR, 68 RBI, 56 R, and 1.6 WAR in 1984. In 1985, Porter, now 33 years old, was platooned with C Tom Nieto and hit only .221/.335/.413 (108 OPS+) in 284 PA with 2.0 WAR. The 1985 Cardinals won the NL East pennant, their first since 1982, and upset the Dodgers in the 1985 NLCS which was memorable for Ozzie Smith's unlikely walk-off HR off Tom Niedenfuer in Game 6 to tie the Series. But they lost to Kansas City in the World Series, which featured umpire Don Denkinger's missed call at 1B in the ninth inning of Game 6 and Joakim Andujar's meltdown in Game 7. Porter was not a factor in either series. He finished his career with the Texas Rangers as a backup to Don Slaught in 1986–87, hitting a combined .253/.372/.484 (128 OPS+) in 341 PA with 1.4 WAR.

When Porter retired from baseball, he hosted a weekly sports radio show in Kansas City and dabbled in real estate development.[18] Now happily married and a father of three children and with his drug problems apparently behind him, he gave motivational speeches promoting his successful autobiography, which had been published in 1984, and speaking of how his Christian faith helped him overcome his addictions. But again the reality was more complicated. On August 5, 2002, Porter, whose weight had ballooned to nearly 300 pounds, was found dead next to his car, which had gone off the road and hit a tree stump alongside a highway. It was initially assumed that Porter had been overcome by the 97-degree heat or perhaps had a heart attack while trying to move his car.[19] However, an autopsy revealed blood levels of cocaine that, while not high enough to kill him outright, were consistent with a state of "excited delirium" which could have led to his erratic driving and contributed to his death.[20] He was only 50 years old.

Why Was Darrell Porter a Shooting Star?

Although Porter's 7.6 WAR 1979 season stands well above the rest (Figure 22), he was an excellent player, whose historical standing among catchers is higher than you might think.

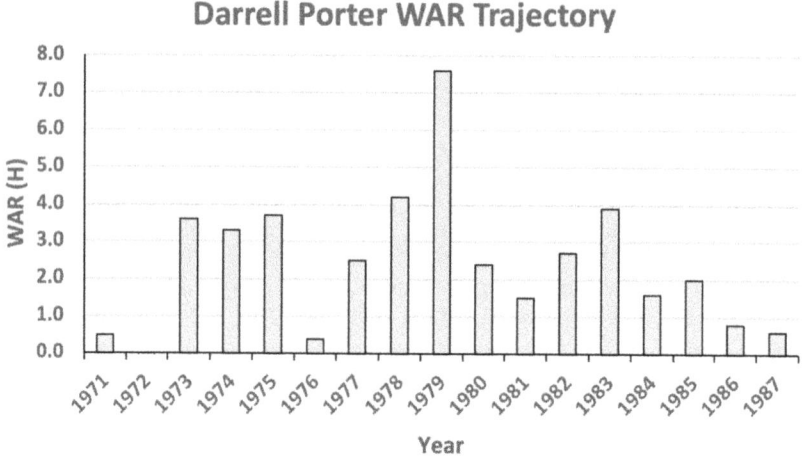

The 40.8 WAR Porter accrued in the course of his 17-year career ranks 23rd among catchers, not far below Hall of Famers Roger Bresnahan (42.1) and Roy Campanella (42.0) and above Ernie Lombardi (37.7), Ray Schalk (33.1), and Rick Farrell (30.8).[21] One is tempted to ask how good Porter might have been without the alcohol and drugs. The problem with that line of inquiry is that Porter performed significantly better in the nine years (1971–79) when he was drinking (.252/.356/.415, 116 OPS+, 25.5 WAR in 3776 PA) than in the eight years (1980–87) when he was sober (.241/.351/.401, 109 OPS+, 15.4 WAR in 2794 PA). Perhaps the more apt question is how good Porter might have been had he been confident and secure enough not to rely on alcohol and drugs all those years. The answer is unknowable.

Probably, Porter's greatest contribution to baseball was going public with his struggles with addiction. Baseball had a long tradition of winking at alcoholism and treating it largely as a laughing matter. Hall of Famers like Babe Ruth, Grover Alexander, Jimmie Foxx, Hack Wilson, Mickey Mantle, and Paul Waner were well-known for their affinity to the bottle, and their antics were tolerated—even celebrated—as long as they could perform on the field. For example, Casey Stengel once quipped that Waner, who always took a swig from a hip flask to relax

22. Imperfect

him before he stepped to the plate, "had to be a very graceful player because he could slide without breaking the bottle on his hip."[22] Grover Alexander's bravura scoreless relief appearance in Game 7 of the 1926 World Series, when he entered in the seventh inning, nursing a killer hangover, and struck out Tony Lazzeri with the bases loaded, is the stuff of legend—and a 1952 Hollywood movie starring Ronald Reagan and Doris Day.[23] Derrell Porter's courageous decision to pull back the curtain in a painfully public manner on his own addiction to alcohol and drugs and his early and tragic death have changed this narrative forever.

◈ 23 ◈

Doctor K
Dwight Eugene "Doc" Gooden (1985)

From baseball's crown prince at age 20 to banishment for multiple failed drug tests at age 30 to prison at age 40, Dwight Gooden's inexorable fall from light into darkness was of near biblical dimension. In 1985, the 20-year-old Mets righthander with a hard rising fastball and a devastating curveball that started high and inside to right-handed hitters, then dropped suddenly into the strike zone, was the brightest star in baseball's firmament. Sportswriters dubbed him Doctor K—or just Doc for short—and compared him favorably to Hall of Famers like Tom Seaver, Bob Feller, and Sandy Koufax.[1] And to top it off, he had an engaging smile and was unfailingly well-spoken and respectful. Yet, ten years later, following a series of alcohol and drug-related incidents, Gooden was sitting out a one-year suspension, his career in shambles. Although he managed a limited comeback with the Yankees in his early thirties, and even pitched a no-hitter, his downward spiral continued with multiple arrests, divorce, and financial ruin.

Dwight Eugene Gooden was born on November 16, 1964, in Tampa, FL, and grew up in Tampa's crime-ridden Hillsborough neighborhood.[2] He was the baby of the family; his two siblings were more than 13 years older than he was. He was only four years older than his nephew Gary Sheffield, who grew up in the same household. Dwight had a particularly close relationship with his father Dan, a hard drinking laborer with a third grade education, who coached youth baseball and nurtured his son's talent, teaching him his trademark overhand curveball at age seven. At age 9, Dwight was an integral member of a team that qualified for the Little League World Series, but he himself was too young to play in the tournament. After dominating the competition at Hillsborough High School, he was selected by the Mets with the fifth overall pick in the 1982 amateur draft. However, although his athletic prowess

23. Doctor K

sheltered him from the worst of it, he was exposed to alcoholism, adultery, and violence as a child, and was only five years old when his sister was shot five times by her husband while Dwight was playing in another room.

Gooden ascended rapidly through the Mets' system, starring in rookie ball and low Class A in 1982 and then going 19–4 with a 2.50 ERA at Lynchburg (high A) in 1983. He jumped straight to the major leagues at age 19 in 1984 and quickly became the Mets' undisputed ace, as they improved by 22 games over their last-place finish in 1983 to finish second behind Chicago in the NL East. He debuted on April 7, 1984, by pitching 5.0 innings of one-run three-hit baseball in a 3–2 win over Houston.[3] After getting knocked out in the fourth inning of an 11–2 rout by the Cubs six days later and being touched by Montreal for four unearned runs in a no-decision on April 19, he rattled off two consecutive one-run 10-strikeout seven inning outings in wins over Montreal and Chicago. Houston tagged him for 8 ER in 2.1 IP on May 6, but he rebounded with a four-hit, 11-strikeout shutout of Los Angeles on May 11. From then on, he was good more often than not, going 14–7 the rest of the way. He got better as the season went on, finishing 4–1 with a 1.29 ERA, an 0.810 WHIP, and 62 SO in five September starts. In one three-game stretch, from September 7–17, he pitched a one-hit, 11-strikeout 10–0 shutout over the first-place Cubs, and consecutive 16-strikeout

Would it be high heat or a knee-buckling curve? Either way, standing sixty feet away from New York Mets righthander Dwight Gooden, locked and loaded and ready to fire, was the last place any NL batter wanted to be in 1985 (National Baseball Hall of Fame Museum).

performances against the Pirates (a 2–0 win) and Phillies (a 2–1 defeat). Altogether, he made 31 starts, 20 of them "quality starts" and finished 17–9 with a 2.60 ERA (137 ERA+), a NL-leading 1.073 WHIP, 276 strikeouts (a rookie record), and 5.5 pitching WAR (6.26 WAR per 1000 BF) in 218.0 IP. He was selected to the All-Star team and pitched two scoreless innings with 3 SO.[4] Over the course of the season, he racked up three shutouts, eight complete games, and fifteen games with double-digit strikeouts. His total of 276 strikeouts led the NL and stands second to Amos Rusie's 341 (in 548.2 IP) among all 19-year-old pitchers.[5] His 11.4 strikeouts per 9 IP set an all-time record for 19-year old pitchers which still stands today; Gary Nolan's 7.2 SO per 9 IP in 1967 was the runner-up. Gooden was not only the near-unanimous choice for Rookie of the Year, but also finished second to Rick Sutcliffe for the NL Cy Young award and 15th in the NL MVP voting.

As brilliant as he was at age 19 in 1984, Gooden far surpassed himself at age 20 in 1985, putting together one of the best pitching seasons of all time for any pitcher of any age (Table 23). He led the NL in ERA, ERA+, SO, W, CG, and SHO and finished a close second to John Tudor in WHIP and to teammate Sid Fernandez in SO per 9 IP.

Table 23 Selected Stats for Dwight Gooden's Peak and Runner-Up Seasons and His Career*

Season	Age	BF	ERA	WHIP	ERA+	W-L	SO	SO/9 IP	CG	SHO	WAR (P)
Peak 1985	20	1065	**1.53**	0.965	**229**	**24–4**	**268**	8.7	**16**	**8**	12.2
per 1000 BF							252	8.2	15	8	11.5
Runner-Up 1984	19	879	2.60	**1.073**	137	17–9	**276**	11.4	7	3	5.3
per 1000 BF							314	13.0	8	3	6.0
Career (1984–2000)		11705	3.51	1.256	111	194–112	2293	7.4	68	24	48.1
per 1000 BF							196	7.4	6	2	4.1

*League-leading totals are shown in boldface type.

Gooden's 229 ERA+ was the best for any 20-year-old pitcher in MLB history.[6] His 12.2 WAR (P) in 1985 was (and remains) the highest for any pitcher of any age since Walter Johnson's 15.1 in 1913.[7] His pro-rated 11.46 WAR per 1000 BF is the sixth best of all time among qualifying starting pitchers, ranking only behind Pedro Martinez (14.32 in 2000 and 11.74 in 1999), Greg Maddux (12.36 in 1995), Walter Johnson (11.79 in 1913), and Aaron Nola (11.67 in 2018).

On a more granular level, Gooden made 35 starts, of which 33 qualified as quality starts (≥ 6.0 IP and ≤ 3 ER).[8] He yielded no ER in 13 starts (eight of which were complete game shutouts), 1 ER in 6 starts, 2 ER in nine starts (one of which he left in the third inning), 3 ER in six starts, and 5 ER in 5 IP in one start. (By contrast, Gooden had yielded 4 ER or more in eight of his 31 starts in 1984, and had failed to complete 6 IP in eight of those starts.) He was again selected for the NL All-Star team but did not pitch. He had ten or more strikeouts in eleven starts, topped by 16 against the Giants on August 20. His most dominant start was a 2-H 11-SO 9–0 shutout of the Phillies on September 15. The Mets improved by eight wins to 98–64 but still finished three games behind Whitey Herzog's St. Louis Cardinals, despite Gooden's best efforts. Still, Gooden was the unanimous choice for the NL Cy Young award—the youngest ever to win that award—and finished fourth behind Willie McGee in the NL MVP voting.

By the end of the 1985 season, Gooden had become the toast of baseball, receiving accolades from contemporaries and old-timers alike. Yankee lefty Ron Guidry, the 1978 AL Cy Young award winner, predicted that Gooden would strike out 4000.[9] Sandy Koufax added that "if nothing happens to him, he may set and break all the records realistically within reach."[10] Bob Gibson added that he saw no reason why Gooden couldn't become the best ever.[11] Whitey Ford and Don Drysdale basically concurred that Gooden was the best young pitcher they had ever seen.[12] Mickey Mantle stated that he could not have hit Gooden, but allowed that Ted Williams might have fared better.[13] If the rules had allowed it, the worshipful sports press might have voted him into the Hall of Fame right then without further ado. Of course, as we know now, something did happen to Gooden, and the nascent seeds of his downfall were already in place.

The 1986 season began well enough. The Mets had assembled a powerhouse team, one of the best of the 20th century, led by Gooden, Darryl Strawberry, Gary Carter, Keith Hernandez, and a host of top-notch supporting players. Gooden won his first five decisions with a sparkling 1.04 ERA as the Mets raced to a 20–4 record (en route to 108 wins and a World Series championship) and a five-game lead in the NL East by May 10. However, after finishing May 6–2 with a 1.96 ERA, Gooden's ERA rose gradually in June-July, reaching 2.97. Although he finished strongly in September, to wind up 17–6 with a 2.84 ERA (126 ERA+), a 1.108 WHIP, and 4.5 WAR, his strikeouts had fallen off to 200 (7.2 per 9 IP) with only five double-digit games; he was not quite the old Doctor K. He had only two shutouts and gave up 4 ER or more nine times.[14] He started in the All-Star Game but gave up a two-run HR to Lou Whitaker in 3 IP.[15] Gooden remained the nominal ace, but he finished only third on the Mets (behind Ron Darling and Bob Ojeda) in WAR (P). Although he pitched well in two NLCS losses to Houston, he was terrible in the World Series, yielding 8 ER and 17 H in 9.0 IP in

Game 1 and Game 5 losses to the Red Sox. Still, his overall performance earned him his third consecutive All-Star selection and a seventh place finish in the NL Cy Young award voting. Even the greatest players experience the occasional hiccup, and few thought anything more about it.

The first public sign that all was not right with the 21-year-old Mets ace, was when he overslept and missed the Mets World Series victory parade. In fact, he had been celebrating by using cocaine all night.[16] The baseball world learned that he and his 24-year-old teammate and drinking buddy Daryl Strawberry had regularly been using cocaine together. Then, in December in Tampa, Gooden and several friends got into a brawl with police officers who stopped them for driving erratically after attending a college basketball game. Racial epithets were exchanged, and it was not clear who initiated the violence, but it was fortunate that no one was shot.[17] Gooden got off with probation, but the episode made a big splash in the New York tabloids. Gooden repeatedly denied rumors of his spiraling drinking and cocaine habit, but his denials rang hollow after he tested positive for cocaine on March 30. Humiliated, he voluntarily checked in to the Smithers Alcoholism and Drug Treatment Center, pronounced himself rehabilitated after two months, and returned to the Mets on June 5. Nevertheless, within a month he was drinking again. Despite his late start and continued drinking, Gooden had a fine season, finishing 15–7 with a 3.21 ERA (119 ERA+), a 1.197 WHIP, 148 strikeouts, and 3.7 WAR (P). He even finished fifth in the Cy Young award voting. Still, the Mets won sixteen fewer games than they had in 1986 and finished three games behind the Cardinals. Many New York fans blamed Gooden's two-month absence for the team's failure to repeat as champions.

Gooden was able to keep his cocaine use more or less in check and to avoid further scandals for the next few years, although he still drank more than he should. In 1988, he went 18–8 with a 3.19 ERA (175 ERA+), a 1.204 WHIP, 175 strikeouts, and 3.4 WAR, as the Mets rebounded to win the NL East with 100 wins. He finished second on the Mets in pitching WAR (behind David Cone) and third in strikeouts (behind Cone and Sid Fernandez). Gooden was still a formidable pitcher, if not quite the Doctor K of 1985. Although the old Doctor K resurfaced in the NLCS against the Dodgers (2.95 ERA, 0.982 WHIP, and 19 SO in 18.1 IP), he received little offensive support and came away with no decisions in LA's 4–3 series win. Gooden never won a game in nine postseason starts and three relief appearances, although his ERA was a respectable 3.97. By the time he turned 24 (a month after the end of the 1988 season), Gooden was still on a Hall of Fame track. He had already won more games (91) than anyone that age since Bob Feller and had accrued more

23. Doctor K

WAR (29.2) than any twentieth-century pitcher except Feller, Blyleven, and Walter Johnson. He had also pitched 1172.2 innings in five years, a lot for a young arm. Nevertheless, with so many productive years seemingly still ahead for Gooden, it is no wonder that columnist Pete Coutros gave Seaver only a narrow edge over Doc as the greatest Mets pitcher of all time.[18]

Gooden got off to a terrific start in 1989. On June 19, after he notched his 100th career win, he was 9–2 with a 2.56 ERA, a 1.177 WHIP, and 90 strikeouts in 105.1 IP.[19] When he made his next start on June 26, the Mets led in the NL East with a 39–32 record. But Gooden felt a severe pain in his right shoulder and had to leave the game after giving up 5 ER in 4.0 IP. the Mets fell out of first place for good, eventually finishing six games behind the Cubs. After another abbreviated ineffective start on July 1, Gooden went on the disabled list. Still, he was able to rehab the damage to his rotator cuff without surgery and to make two effective relief appearances in September.

Gooden had a good and healthy season in 1990, finishing 19–7 in 34 starts, thanks in part to strong offensive support. His strikeout rate bumped up to 8.6 per 9 IP, but his 3.83 ERA (98 ERA+) and 1.283 WHIP in 232.2 IP were the worst they had ever been. His 2.5 WAR ranked only third on the Mets behind Frank Viola and David Cone, but he nevertheless finished fourth in the Cy Young award voting. The Mets again finished second in the NL East, four games behind the Pirates. At least, there was no unwelcome news off the field.

Gooden had another solid season in 1991, going 13–7 with a 3.60 ERA (102 ERA+), a 1.268 WHIP, 150 strikeouts (7.1 per 9 IP), and 3.3 WAR in 190 IP. However, without Darryl Strawberry and with many of their aging stars fading, the Mets fell to fifth place at 77–84. Gooden's season ended on September 7, when he was diagnosed with and underwent arthroscopic surgery for a torn labrum and a partial tear of his rotator cuff in his right shoulder.[20] He was expected to be ready for the 1992 season, but his fastball velocity would never be the same. Gooden again managed to stay out of the tabloids, but he continued to drink heavily and court trouble.

Personable as he was when he was sober, Gooden was a mean drunk. He was involved in an ugly incident in March 1991 in which he and two teammates (Vince Coleman and Daryl Boston) enticed a young woman they had met in a bar to Gooden's rented spring training house in Port Lucie where they were alleged to have raped her.[21] Despite the forensic proof that Gooden had had sex with her and the many prior rumors of lewd and loutish behavior by Gooden and his teammates on team flights and in bars, the incident received little publicity in the usually raucous tabloid press. Although the allegations against the three players were plausible, the charges were dropped a year later due to insufficient evidence regarding whether the sex was consensual. If the same thing happened today, they would likely have been charged and convicted.

Gooden came back from his shoulder surgery to post solid but unspectacular seasons in 1992–93 for abysmal Mets teams, which lost 90 and 107 games. He went a combined 22–28 with a 3.56 ERA (106 ERA+), 1.244 WHIP, 294 strikeouts (6.4 per 9 IP), and 5.8 WAR in 414.2 IP. Although his strikeout rate fell after his surgery and his W-L reflected the lowly status of his team, his other stats had remained near their 1990–91 levels.

Gooden's career went completely off the rails in 1994. He made only seven starts, going 3–4 with a 6.31 ERA (67 ERA+), a 1.476 WHIP, and -0.6 WAR. He began the season by giving up 3 HR to an obscure Cubs OF named Tuffy Rhodes and then breaking a toe when he kicked a bat rack as he was removed from the game. He was caught using cocaine while on rehab and was suspended by MLB.[22] He checked into the Betty Ford Center but relapsed as soon as he was released. He failed another drug test and was suspended for two months on June 28. He relapsed again after the strike began in mid–August and failed yet another drug test. Finally, MLB suspended him through the entire 1995 season. Reportedly, he even contemplated suicide in 1995, but his wife intervened to stop him.[23] Gooden would never pitch for the Mets again.

The Yankees threw Gooden a lifeline in 1996. He no longer threw hard and was no better than a league average pitcher and fifth starter for the eventual 1996 World Series champions, going 11–7 with a 5.01 ERA (100 ERA+), a 1.506 WHIP, 126 strikeouts, and 2.6 WAR in 170.2 IP. However, he pitched a no-hitter against Seattle on May 14—something that neither he nor any Mets pitcher had ever done before.[24] Although he did walk six batters and struck out only five, the no-hitter was all the more remarkable because Gooden had lost his first three starts while giving up 17 ER in 13.1 IP and still had a 5.67 ERA entering the game. Although he was a useful rotation piece, especially while ace David Cone was out with a shoulder aneurysm, Gooden wore down in September and was left off the postseason roster.

In 1997, Gooden's demons would soon sabotage his feel-good comeback story. After becoming intoxicated in a strip bar in May, Gooden got into a fight with a taxi driver after he refused to pay his taxi fare because the stripper with whom he was sharing the taxi rejected his repeated passes.[25] The story was all over the New York tabloids. Although Gooden pitched almost as well in 1997 as he did in 1996, he was used less frequently and wound up going 9–5 with a 4.91 ERA (92 ERA+), a 1.589 WHIP, 5.6 strikeouts per 9 IP, and 1.2 WAR in 106.1 IP. This time he made an effective post-season start in a losing cause against Cleveland in the ALDS. But the Yankees granted him free agency after the season.

Hope dies hard in baseball, and Gooden continued to receive opportunities from teams who remembered the young Doctor K. He pitched for Cleveland in 1998–99 and Houston, Tampa, and even the Yankees again in 2000. Although he did well enough in 29 starts for Cleveland in 1998 (8–6 with a 3.76 ERA), he was ineffective in two post-season starts (5 ER in 5 IP). However, his results in 1999–2000 were so ugly that Gooden had no choice but to retire at age 35.

Unfortunately, the sad trajectory of squandered opportunities and relapses into addiction in Gooden's baseball career has continued in retirement. His divorced his wife of 17 years in 2003, moved out of his New Jersey home, and allowed his family to be evicted for non-payment of household expenses.[26] He had several DUI convictions in 2005–06, culminating in an eight-month incarceration for violating his probation.[27] He was convicted for DUI and child endangerment in a 2010 automobile accident in which he was intoxicated and his five-year-old son was riding unstrapped in the back seat.[28] As recently as July 2019, he was arrested for DUI and cocaine possession and received a one-year probation.[29] To make matters worse, Gooden's shame has played out in public. His travails have been a New York tabloid staple for 35 years, along with impassioned pleas from friends, lovers, etc., berating him for his selfishness and irresponsibility and exhorting him to reform. For example, the *Post* published a compilation of letters from sixth graders titled "Doc, you're a real jerk" in 1987, and the *Daily News* published an angry accusatory open letter from his girlfriend entitled "Monster" in 2016.[30] Celebrity addiction is a special kind of hell.

Why Was Dwight Gooden a Shooting Star?

Gooden clearly fits the definition of a shooting star, since his historic 12.2 peak WAR (P) in 1985 was more than twice that of his 5.3 WAR (P) runner-up season and towers over the rest of his career (Figure 23).

Gooden is an outlier among the 30 shooting stars I have profiled, but the shooting star concept is about contrasts. The other 29 shooting stars generally range from one-year wonders to above-average players who performed briefly like superstars. For Gooden however, the contrast

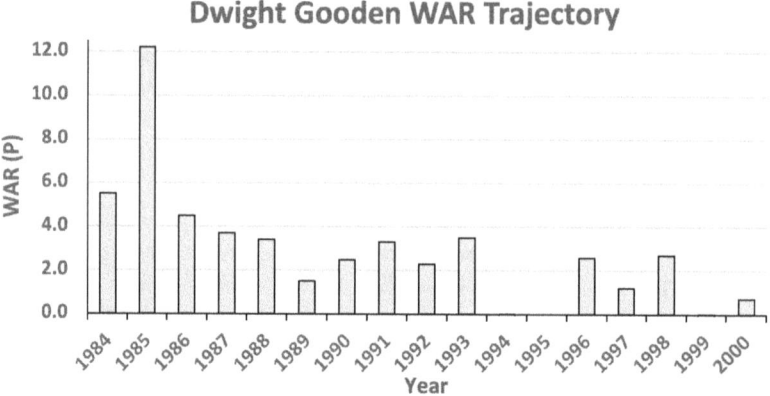

Dwight Gooden WAR Trajectory

is between an excellent but addiction-marred sixteen-year career in which he won 194 games and accrued 53.0 total WAR and a peak season that placed him on the short list of the best pitchers of all time at age 20. His 48.1 career WAR (P) ranks 114th of all time, falling between Bartolo Colon (48.2) and Ron Guidry and Mickey Lolich (47.9)—all excellent pitchers, but a far cry from the guys he was compared to in 1985 and well short of the usual HOF standard. Consequently, he received only 3.3 percent of the HOF votes in his lone appearance on the BBWAA ballot in 2006. That being said, Gooden's 48.1 WAR (P) is higher than 13 of the 66 non–Negro League players who have been elected to the HOF as starting pitchers—Addie Joss, Burleigh Grimes, Jim Kaat, Herb Pennock, Dizzy Dean, Jack Morris, Lefty Gomez, Chief Bender, Jack Chesbro, Bob Lemon, Catfish Hunter, Jesse Haines, and Rube Marquard. Furthermore, his 58.5 CVI, which considers his 4.8 WAR (H) and gives extra weight to peak value, places him 234th among all players as of October 2023—just below Hall of Famers Willie Stargell, Ted Simmons, and Hoyt Wilhelm, but above Vladimir Guerrero and Bill Terry.[31]

The story of Gooden's meteoric rise to stardom in 1985 and his subsequent fall is a classical Greek tragedy of a supremely gifted man who was doomed by his tragic flaw of addiction. The New York tabloids even provided the traditional Greek chorus. His struggle was epic, with ever diminishing periods of greatness undermined by self-destructive binges that landed him repeatedly in rehab centers and even prison and eventually cost him his marriage and his career. His battle with addiction has continued more for than two decades after his playing career ended; he is fortunate to have survived to age 59 (as of 2023). Gooden's talent was such that his statistical accomplishments are almost worthy of the Hall of Fame, despite his self-destructive addiction. Gooden achieved much in his career. He tops the Mets' all-time leaderboard in won-lost percentage, ranks second to Tom Seaver in wins, strikeouts, and WAR, third in games started, innings pitched, and complete games, and fourth in shutouts. But for a pitcher whose age 20 season is on the short list of the best pitching seasons in the history of MLB, one cannot help but feel that he should have accomplished so much more.

◈ 24 ◈

The Last 150-Inning Reliever
Mark Anthony Eichhorn (1986)

In 1986, when righthander Mark Eichhorn logged 157 IP exclusively in relief, no eyebrows were raised. Between 1920 (when relief specialists first became a thing) and 1985, 462 relievers (defined here as pitchers making at least 90 percent of their appearances in relief), led by Mike Marshall's (208.1 IP in 1974 and 181.1 IP in 1973) had logged at least 100 IP.[1] (Before 1920, complete games were the norm, and relief duties were handled mostly by starters on their days off.) Eichhorn's 157.0 IP tied Boston's Dick Radatz (1964) for 11th place on this list. Before 1986, 16 relievers had seasons with at least 150 IP, and 150 relievers—including Ted Abernathy (Chapter 17), John Hiller (Chapter 20), and Hall of Famers Rich Gossage, Hoyt Wilhelm, Rollie Fingers, and Bruce Sutter—had seasons with at least 120 IP. But when Tony La Russa and Dennis Eckersley "invented" the one-inning closer in 1987, the concept of a workhorse reliever quickly became obsolete. Since Eichhorn's 157 IP in 1986, only twelve relief pitchers—one of them Eichhorn himself in 1987—have logged at least 120 IP; the last was Greg Cadaret in 1991.[2]

Mark Anthony Eichhorn, who was born in San Jose, CA, on November 21, 1960, was an unlikely candidate to set any endurance records as a reliever, let alone to post a 7.3 WAR season. He was dragged reluctantly into pitching after being selected by Toronto in the January 1979 supplemental draft as a SS.[3] Although he had pitched occasionally at Watsonville High School (where he also starred in basketball) and at Cabrillo College, he far preferred to play every day. When the Blue Jays, who had assigned him to Medicine Hat, Alberta (Rookie League), decided they liked him better as a pitcher than a SS, Eichhorn persisted in taking Infield and batting practice, there and in the Florida

24. The Last 150-Inning Reliever

Instructional League that fall, until he was ordered off the field. Eichhorn then gradually worked his way up the minor league ladder as a starting pitcher—Class A in 1980, AA in 1981, and AAA in 1982—but did not particularly distinguish himself. After going 10–11 with a 4.54 ERA at AAA Syracuse, he made his major league debut on August 30, 1982. However, his shoulder was hurting, and he was hit hard in seven starts, going 0–3 with a 5.45 ERA and 1.421 WHIP in 38.0 IP. He spent most of the next three years in Syracuse and would not see major league action again until 1986.

Although Eichhorn's sore shoulder did not entirely prevent him from pitching, it undermined his command and effectiveness. He struggled badly at Syracuse as a starter in 1983, going 6–17 with a 5.06 ERA and 1.507 WHIP. It was more of the same in 1984, with Eichhorn pitching increasingly out of the bullpen. In August 1984, with his playing career on life support, Eichhorn received a call from Syracuse pitching coach Larry Hardy relaying a suggestion by Jays pitching coach Al Widmar that Eichhorn lower his arm slot to find an angle that didn't hurt his shoulder.[4] The first night he tried his new sidearm delivery he retired three batters in a row on infield grounders. Now reborn as a side-arming utility pitcher, Eichhorn was invited to spring training in 1985 and did not allow a run.[5] But he still did not make the major league club. He appeared in 34 games for Syracuse in 1985–17 as a starter and 17 in relief—and went 7–6 with a 3.46 ERA and 1.171 WHIP. He now had a future.

In 1986, Eichhorn joined a veteran Blue Jays staff, led by Jimmy Key, Dave Stieb, Jim Clancy, Doyle Alexander, and reliever Tom Henke, and quickly became their most valuable pitcher (Table 24).

Table 24: Selected Stats for Mark Eichhorn's Peak and Runner-Up Seasons and His Career

Season	Age	IP	BF	ERA	WHIP	ERA+	W-L	SV	SO	BB	WAR (P)
Peak 1986	25	157.0	612	1.72	0.955	246	14–6	10	166	45	7.3
per 1000 BF								16	271	74	11.9
Runner-Up 1991	30	81.7	311	1.98	0.931	208	3–3	1	49	13	2.9
per 1000 BF								3	158	42	9.3
Career (1982–96)		885.7	3702	3.00	1.236	142	48–43	32	640	270	19.2
per 1000 BF								9	173	73	5.2

Despite appearing exclusively in relief, Eichhorn's 7.3 WAR (P) led all Toronto pitchers (Jimmy Key was next with 4.8) and ranked third among all AL pitchers (behind only Teddy Higuera and Roger Clemens). He would have led the AL in ERA, WHIP and ERA+ had he not fallen short of the 162 IP required to qualify. He passed up an offer to start the season's final game to pick up the extra 5 IP he needed.[6] He also tied Key and Jim Clancy for most wins on his team. Eichhorn was great in every month except July, when he gave up 13 ER, 36 H, and 9 BB in 31.2 IP—a so-so 3.69 ERA and 1.421 WHIP.[7] In the other five months his ERA ranged from 0.48 in April to 1.67 in September-October, and his WHIP ranged from 0.429 in April to 1.185 in September-October. His 69 appearances averaged 2.28 IP; he held the opposition scoreless in 45 appearances, to 1 ER in 18 appearances, and to 2 ER in six appearances.[8] He never gave up more than 2 ER in any outing. Although Eichhorn was not selected to the AL All-Star team—an honor he never received during his career—he finished third behind Jose Canseco and Wally Joyner for AL Rookie of the Year and sixth in the AL Cy Young award voting (which was won by Roger Clemens). Eichhorn's only disappointment was that the Jays fell to 88 wins and failed to defend their AL East title. Nevertheless, it was a remarkable rookie season.

Eichhorn was again a valuable workhorse reliever for the 1987 Jays, with 127.2 IP in a league-leading 89 relief appearances, but the results were merely good, not outstanding. He went 10–6 with 4 saves, but his ERA rose to 3.17 (143 ERA+) and his WHIP rose to 1.269, while his strikeouts per 9 IP fell from 9.5 in 1986 to 6.8. His 2.7 WAR in 540 BF (5.0 WAR per 1000 BF) was solid but a far cry from his 11.9 WAR per 1000 BF in 1986. Although the Jays improved to 96 wins in 1987, they were overtaken by the Detroit Tigers, who swept a three game series over the Jays on the season's final weekend after the Jays had led by 3.5 games a week earlier. Eichhorn gave up a walk-off twelfth inning single to Alan Trammell in the penultimate game, which put the Tigers in first place for good.[9]

Eichhorn's performance took a sharp downward turn in 1988. After going 0–3 with a 4.19 ERA (94 ERA+) and 1.590 WHIP in 66.2 IP, he was unceremoniously demoted to AAA Syracuse after the All-Star break. The Jays had entered the break sitting at 42–46 and in sixth place, 11.5 games behind first place Detroit, and were looking to shake things up.[10] The Jays recovered to finish third at 88–74. Although he posted a nice 1.17 ERA in 38.1 IP at Syracuse, Eichhorn did not return to Toronto that year and was waived to last place Atlanta the following spring. Eichhorn's 1989 season was basically a reprise of 1988. He split the season between Atlanta and AAA Richmond, posting a brilliant 1.32 ERA in Richmond with 19 saves but struggling to a 4.35 ERA (84 ERA+) and 1.302 WHIP with no saves in Atlanta. Having accrued -0.5 WAR in 1988–89 and only 2.2 WAR since 1986, Eichhorn was looking increasingly like a one-year wonder.

24. The Last 150-Inning Reliever

However, Eichhorn revived his career with the California Angels in 1990 after signing with them as a free agent. Eichhorn credited Angels pitching coach Marcel Lacheman, who advised him to go back to relying on his splitter, which was a major factor in his earlier success.[11] In 1990–91 with the Angels, Eichhorn made 130 appearances, all in relief, and went 5–8 with 14 SV, a 2.54 ERA (156 ERA+), a 1.184 WHIP, and 4.2 WAR in 166.1 IP comprising 685 BF. In his 130 appearances, which averaged 1.28 IP, he held the opposition scoreless in 100, held them to 1 ER in 19, to 2 ER in seven, and gave up ≥ 3 ER in the other four.[12] His performance, spread out over two seasons and broken up into shorter outings, was not as dominant as in his 1986 peak season, but it was not that that far off.

Eichhorn continued to be effective with the Angels in 1992, posting a 2.38 ERA (167 ERA+) and 1.218 WHIP with 1.3 WAR over the first four months. But the Angels fell from contention and dealt Eichhorn to Toronto in a July 30 deadline trade. Toronto had a powerhouse team, featuring Hall of Famers Roberto Alomar, Dave Winfield, and Jack Morris, and other stars like Devon White, Joe Carter, David Cone, Jimmy Key, Juan Guzman, David Wells, Tom Henke, and Duane Ward. Eichhorn, now 31 years old, was just a depth addition and did not pitch particularly well in the last two months, finishing 4–4 with 2 SV, a 3.08 ERA (131 OPS+), a 1.266 WHIP, and 1.4 WAR in 87.2 IP for the season. However, Eichhorn got his first postseason opportunity, retiring all six batters he faced—three in the ALCS win over Oakland and three in the WS win over Atlanta. Eichhorn remained in Toronto in 1993 and went 3–1 with a 2.72 ERA (160 ERA+), a 1.349 WHIP, and 1.6 WAR in 72.2 IP. He again pitched effectively in the ACLS sweep of the Chicago White Sox, yielding just a single and a walk in 2.0 IP, but gave up a single and a walk (but no runs) in 0.1 IP in the 4–2 WS win over Philadelphia.

Eichhorn signed with Baltimore as a free agent in 1994 and was on his way to his best season since 1986 when the strike was called in August. He finished 6–5 with 1 SV, a 2.15 ERA (233 ERA+), a 1.141 WHIP, and 2.6 WAR in 71.0 IP in what amounted to two-thirds of a season. But that was his last hurrah. He needed rotator cuff surgery and missed the entire 1995 season. He returned to pitch 30.1 innings for the Angels in 1996, but was ineffective. He played briefly in Taiwan in 1997. He returned in 1998 to pitch 58 innings for AA Durham in the Tampa Bay system until he was sidelined by elbow tendonitis. He tried one last comeback in the Toronto system in 2000 and was in line for a September call-up with an 0.83 ERA in 21.2 IP, but with his wife pregnant with their fourth child, he abruptly decided to walk away.[13] He retired to Aptos, CA, where he and his wife Mariann have raised five sons. Eichhorn has kept his hand in baseball by coaching his sons in Little League and high school (as assistant baseball coach), and more recently by offering private coaching sessions.[14] One of his sons, Kevin, pitched for seven years in the Arizona Diamondbacks system.[15]

Why Was Mark Eichhorn a Shooting Star?

Mark Eichhorn's 7.3 WAR in 1986 was the third highest ever posted by a relief pitcher, trailing only Rich Gossage (8.2 in 1975) and John Hiller (7.9 in 1973).[16] Although he posted only 11.9 WAR in his other 10 seasons and no more than 2.9 WAR in any other single season, he was more than a mere one-year wonder (Figure 24).

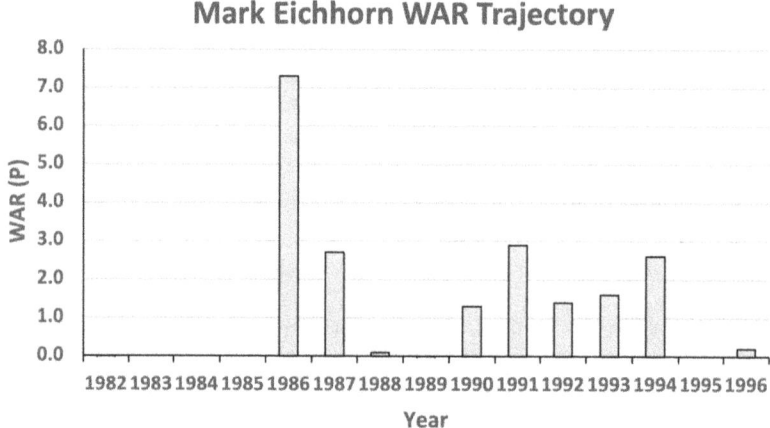

While arm problems and inconsistency certainly played a role in preventing Eichhorn from coming close to replicating his 1986 success, he actually had three other seasons—1991, 1993, and 1994—in which his ERA+ exceeded 160 in 71–82 innings. The apparent wide disparity in his performance between 1986 and these three later seasons was in part an optical illusion generated by the fact that managers were no longer allowing relievers to rack up 150 innings, 2–3 innings at a time, in the 1990s as Eichhorn had done in 1986. The fact that Mark Eichhorn, throwing sidearm to protect his damaged shoulder, was able to post 7.3 WAR in 157 IP is a truly remarkable feat, but it should not obscure the fact that he also had a pretty good career overall.

◆ 25 ◆

Skates
Lonnie Smith (1989)

In the bleak winter of 1987–88, there was little doubt that Lonnie Smith was washed up. The speedy but mistake-prone 32-year-old outfielder had enjoyed a brief run of success with the Phillies and Cardinals in the early 1980s, contributing to World Series championships in 1980 and 1982, but had not been an above average player since 1983, which is an eternity in the baseball universe. In 1987, the Kansas City Royals used him sporadically, sent him to the minors in mid-season, then released him at season's end. He grew so paranoid and depressed over the winter that he bought a gun and contemplated shooting the GM who had released him (John Schuerholz) and/or himself. No one could have foreseen that he was on the brink of a comeback that would lead to an 8.8-WAR season in 1989, which was not only the best season by far of his career but the highest one-season WAR of any left fielder in NL history except Barry Bonds.

Lonnie Smith never sought the spotlight but somehow, for better or worse, it always seemed to find him. Blessed with a keen batting eye and elite speed, he was also cursed with a propensity for taking pratfalls in the OF and on the bases. His teammate Larry Bowa gave him the unflattering nickname "Skates," which made him the butt of a hundred bad jokes.[1] His career had more twists and turns than a soap opera— The Sporting News Rookie of the Year at age 24, important contributor to three World Series champions in three different cities by age 29, relegated to the scrap heap at age 31, a comeback career year for a last place Braves team at age 33, yet another World Series appearance for a fourth different team at age 35. Unfortunately, it was his base running gaffe in Game 7 of the 1991 Series—his only World Series loss—for which he is best remembered. His career had enough highlights and lowlights to fill the backs of at least five baseball cards—like the time when he blind-side tackled the beloved Phillie Phanatic mascot to stop him from doing his "Skates" parody and nearly incited a riot and the time he delivered immunized testimony against other cocaine users in 1985. He was no Hall of Famer, but amidst all the drama, he managed to put together a memorable 38.5-WAR career.

Lonnie Smith was born in Chicago on December 22, 1955, and grew up in a gang-riddled neighborhood of Compton, CA. He focused on baseball and somehow managed to avoid gang involvement. The Phillies drafted him out of Compton's Centennial High School (the school that had produced Roy White in 1962 and Reggie Smith in 1963) with the #3 overall pick in the 1974 draft. He advanced to AAA in his third year, but stalled there for three years despite hitting .308/.390/.445, .277/.347/.373, and .315/.411/.421 with 26, 45, and 66 SB in 1976–78. He finally received his first call-up on September 2, 1978, appearing in 17 games, mostly as a pinch runner, but also garnering four hits in 8 AB. It was more of the same in 1979; he hit .330/.408/.475 with 52 SB in AAA, followed by five hits in 30 AB in Philadelphia.

Finally in 1980 (at age 24), Smith got his first real major league opportunity, accruing 331 PA as the fourth OF behind Greg Luzinski, Garry Maddox, and Bake McBride and hitting .339/.397/.483 (130 OPS+) with 33 SB in 46 attempts—good for 2.3 WAR. He saw only limited action in Philadelphia's 3–2 victory over Houston in the NLDS, going 3-for-5 with a stolen base and 2 R in three games. However, with the designated hitter rule in effect, Smith played in all six games of the Phillies' first ever World Series win over Kansas City, hitting

Lonnie Smith, shown here as a St. Louis Cardinal, circa 1982–84, had an eventful up-and-down career that embodied the turbulent 1980s (National Baseball Hall of Fame Museum).

25. Skates

.263/.300/.316. Although Smith finished only third in the official NL Rookie of the Year voting, the Sporting News honored him as NL Rookie Player of the Year. But despite his successful debut and the trade of Greg Luzinski to the White Sox, Smith remained stuck as the fourth OF in the strike-shortened 1981 season, hitting .324/.402/.472 (143 OPS+) in only 202 PA and stealing 21 bases in 31 attempts. Smith went 5-for-19 in the NLDS loss to Montreal. It was clear that Smith would have to go elsewhere to truly flourish.

A three-team off-season blockbuster trade to Whitey Herzog's St. Louis Cardinals in November 1981 was exactly what Smith needed. Smith was born to play the aggressive speed-centered "Whitey-ball" and immediately took over as the Cardinals' leadoff man and, after a brief trial in CF, as their left fielder. In 672 PA, he hit .307/.381/.434 (128 OPS+), scored a league-leading 120 runs, stole a career-high 68 bases in 94 attempts, and accrued 6.2 WAR. On September 4, he stole five bases in one game against the Giants.[2] He was also selected to his only All-Star team (he did not get a PA) and finished a close second to Dale Murphy in the NL MVP voting. After hitting a modest 273/.308/.273 in the three-game NLCS sweep of Atlanta, he absolutely tormented the AL champion Brewers to the tune of .321/.345/.536 with 2 SB and 6 R in 29 PA in the Cardinals' 4–3 World Series triumph.

However, an incident in Philadelphia on September 13, 1982, gave an early indication that something was amiss. Smith was used to being ribbed about his running and fielding misadventures and, when he played for the Phillies, did not object when mascot Dave Raymond (aka the Phillie Phanatic) spoofed him by performing a series of bellyflops. Now, as a visiting player, Smith had asked him not to do his "Skates" routine. So when the Phanatic ignored Smith's request and went into his routine before the game, Smith was furious and blindsided him with an NFL-style tackle, which left him dazed and in pain while Smith laughed and walked away.[3] The Philadelphia fans turned on Smith, booing him and showering him with debris in left field as the game progressed. Instead of backing down, Smith taunted the fans and gestured to them provocatively. Fearing a riot, Whitey Herzog ordered Smith to stop. What no one knew at the time was that Smith had already developed a serious cocaine habit and was high during the incident.

Although Smith continued to play well in 1983, by June his cocaine habit had progressed to a full-blown addiction that he feared would kill him if he did not get help.[4] On June 11, Whitey Herzog made a bombshell announcement that Smith would be placed on the disabled list to undergo rehabilitation for a serious drug problem.[5] Through 49 games, Smith had been hitting .311/.370/.429 in 219 PA with 28 R and 11 SB in

22 attempts.⁶ So, the shock and dismay of the Cardinals and their fandom is understandable. After a month of rehab at the Hyland Center in St. Louis, Smith returned to hit .328/.388/.470 with 55 R and 32 SB in 39 attempts over his final 72 games. He finished with .321/.321/.453 (130 OPS+) 3.5 WAR for the season. However, the Cardinals fell to 79–83 and missed the postseason—a first for a Lonnie Smith team.

Smith had a so-so 1.6 WAR season in 1984, hitting .250/.349/.341 (97 OPS+) in 590 PA albeit with 77 R and 50 SB in 63 attempts, as the Cardinals finished 84–78 and again missed the postseason. This was the first full season in which Smith failed to hit .300. When Smith started slowly in 1985, hitting .260/.377/.323 (98 OPS+) after 28 games, the Cardinals ran out of patience and traded him to Kansas City for minor league outfield prospect John Morris on May 17. Although Smith still slotted in as the Royals' everyday LF and batted in the second hole behind Willie Wilson, he was deeply dismayed because he considered himself an NL player and had loved St. Louis.⁷ He even considered retiring. He hit only .257/.321/.366 (89 OPS+) in 498 PA in Kansas City, but with 77 R and 40 SB in 47 attempts. His 1.7 WAR for the season was the worst of his career to date. The fact that Smith was called upon to testify (under immunity) against other players in a September drug trial—which cannot have done much for his popularity in the clubhouse—added to the sensitive Smith's inner turmoil.⁸ Still, Smith contributed significantly to Kansas City's successful run to 91 wins and first place in the AL West Division and to their first ever World Series championship. His .333/.400/.444 performance against his ex-teammates in the Royals' come-from-behind 4–3 victory in the 1985 World Series had to be gratifying.

Although Smith had a solid bounce-back season in 1986, hitting .287/.357/.411 (108 OPS+) in 568 PA and accruing 2.3 WAR, he had begun to slow down (26 SB) as he passed his 30th birthday. Moreover, the aging Royals had fallen off to 76–86 in 1986 and had a gifted young left fielder named Bo Jackson waiting in the wings. Smith, who attained free agency after the 1986 season, had trouble finding a new team in that winter of collusion by MLB owners. So, he had little choice but to re-sign a one-year deal with the Royals, where he remained unhappy and no longer had an everyday role. The players would ultimately receive a $280 million settlement in their class action collusion suit against MLB in 1990.⁹ Smith hit only .251/.355/.359 (89 OPS+) for the Royals in part-time play (197 PA) in 1987 and spent more than a month (40 games) in the minors. When he had trouble finding a job after the Royals released him on December 14, he grew depressed and relapsed into drug use. In his distress, Smith became deluded that Kansas City GM

John Schuerholz had blackballed him and was trying to drive him out of baseball. Smith even bought a gun with the intent of shooting Schuerholz, but fortunately he did not follow through.[10] The sad and simple truth is that there was no market for a player whom most MLB executives viewed as a paranoid, out-of-shape 32-year-old has-been with a drug problem.

However, Lonnie Smith's career had a second act. He swallowed his pride, called general managers around the league, and finally accepted Atlanta GM Bobby Cox's offer of a minor league contract with the lowly Braves on March 12, 1988. Although the Braves were the worst team in baseball (54–106) in 1988 and fielded a mediocre outfield of Dion James, Terry Blocker, and the fading Dale Murphy, Lonnie Smith remained stuck in the minors until late July. Finally, after hitting .300/.438/.472 with 26 SB in 93 AAA games, Smith got his opportunity to join the Braves. However, he played sparingly and hit only .237/.296/.342 with 4 SB in 125 PA. Nothing about his performance suggested a player on the verge of the best season of his career.

After playing winter ball in Puerto Rico, Smith easily won the Braves' starting LF job in spring training in 1989. He went only 1/10 in the opening series against Houston but then broke out with a three-hit game against Fernando Valenzuela and the Dodgers and never looked back. By May 19, when he went on the disabled list after injuring his ankle while colliding with the left field wall, he was hitting .324/.431/.582 with 6 HR, 30 R, 18 RBI and 13 SB.[11] His AVG, OBP, R, and SB were in line with his best prior seasons, but his .582 slugging percentage was more than 100 points higher than his previous benchmark (.453 in 1983), due mainly to homering six times in only 40 games. When Smith returned to action about three weeks later, he picked up right where he left off, hitting .328/.388/.624 in June and .344/.448/.594 in July. His unaccustomed power continued with 10 HR in June-July—more in two months than he had ever hit in a full season—but his tender ankle limited him to 5 SB. Although he cooled off a bit in August and September, he finished with career highs in HR, SLG, OPS+, and WAR, while leading the league in OBP. Smith was a markedly different player in 1989 from his previous heyday seven years earlier (Table 25).

The Lonnie Smith of the early 1980s was purely a speed merchant with good on-base skills but little power. The Lonnie Smith of 1989 had lost several steps but showed 20-HR power and even better on-base skills. Even his fielding was uncharacteristically strong (2.1 dWAR) in 1989; he made only two errors all year. Smith finished eleventh in the 1989 NL MVP voting, despite the fact that the Braves lost 97 games and again finished in the NL West cellar. After the season, Smith was named

Comeback Player of the Year.[12] But this was more than a comeback; it was a resurrection.

Table 25: Selected Stats for Lonnie Smith's Peak and Runner-Up Seasons and His Career*

Season	Age	PA	AVG	OBP	SLG	OPS+	TB	HR	R	RBI	SB	WAR (H)	dWAR
Peak 1989	33	577	0.315	**0.415**	0.533	168	257	21	89	79	25	**8.8**	2.1
per 650 PA							290	24	100	89	28	9.9	2.4
Runner-Up 1982	26	672	0.307	0.381	0.434	128	257	8	**120**	69	68	6.2	0.3
per 650 PA							249	8	116	67	66	6.0	0.3
Career (1978–84)		5952	0.288	0.371	0.420	118	2171	98	909	533	370	38.5	-2.3
per 650 PA							237	11	99	58	40	4.2	-0.3

*League leading totals are shown in boldface type.

The resurrection of the moribund Atlanta Braves franchise would come next. Now a fixture in left field, Smith had another strong season in 1990. Although he could not replicate his 1989 stats, he still managed to hit .305/.384/.459 (127 OPS+) in 537 PA and again reached double digits (barely) with 10 HR. His 4.6 WAR was the third best of his career, but his elite speed was gone; he only stole 10 bases while scoring 72 runs. Although the Braves once again lost 97 games and finished last, young players like Tom Glavine, John Smoltz, Steve Avery, David Justice, Ron Gant, Jeff Blauser, and Mark Lemke—all under 25—were beginning to emerge. The seeds of the worst-to-first 1991 team which would go on to put a stranglehold on the NL East for more than a decade were in place. Lonnie Smith was the bridge to that dynasty. Even the appointment of Smith's erstwhile "nemesis" John Schuerholz as the Braves' GM (while Bobby Cox became the field manager) could not upset Smith's newfound serenity.

Smith was 35 years old in 1991 and no longer a fulltime player, ceding playing time to Deion Sanders and Otis Nixon. However he still played 122 games, made 416 PA, hit a more than respectable .275/.377/.394 (113 OPS+), and scored 58 runs, mostly out of the leadoff spot. When the Braves clinched the NL West Division pennant, he mended fences with Schuerholz by embracing him in the post-game locker room celebration. In the postseason, with Sanders playing in the NFL and Nixon serving a drug suspension, Smith was in the lineup every day. His NLCS performance was not memorable, but he had several good moments in the World Series. His home runs in Games 3 and 4 provided the winning margin in two one-run victories that evened the Series at 2–2.[13] He delivered another HR in the seventh inning of Game 5 that extended the Braves' lead to 6–3 in a game they eventually won

14–5, putting them on the brink of winning the World Series. But it is his "Skates moment" in Game 7 than everyone remembers.

To refresh your memory, Game 7 of the 1991 World Series was an all-time classic, as Jack Morris and John Smoltz dueled through seven tense scoreless innings.[14] Then, Smith led off the eighth inning with a single and took off for 2B as Morris delivered to Terry Pendleton, who hit a line drive into the left-center field gap. Smith, who had lost sight of the ball and feared that LF Dan Gladden might make the catch, hesitated near second base; by the time he started running again, it was too late for him to advance beyond 3B. With men on second and third base and no one out, Ron Gant grounded weakly to 1B, and the runners could not advance. Then after Morris intentionally walked David Justice, Sid Bream grounded into an inning-ending double play. The game continued scoreless until the 10th inning, when Gene Larkin won it with a bases-loaded one-out single off of reliever Alejandro Pena. While Smith's misread helped cost the Braves a scoring opportunity, Ron Gant and Sid Bream deserve a bigger measure of blame for failing to deliver with less than two outs when a hit or even a well-hit fly ball could have scored the winning run. Given that Smith had lost much of his foot speed by 1991, one might also second-guess Atlanta management for not carrying a speedy bench player on their post-season roster who could have been deployed as a pinch runner in this situation. The "Skates" narrative just made Smith the convenient scapegoat for a team failure. Although attributing the Braves' ultimate defeat to Smith's baserunning miscue was grossly unfair, this remains the popular perception.[15]

The 1991 World Series was Smith's last turn as a regular. As the Braves' fifth outfielder in 1992 (behind Justice, Gant, Nixon, and Sanders), he hit only .247/.324/.437 (108 OPS+) in 182 PA and stole only four bases. He signed with Pittsburgh as a free agent in 1993 and hit .286/.422/.442 (134 OPS+) in part time play (252 PA) then went to Baltimore in a September trade to provide an extra bat off the bench for the Orioles, who were then embroiled in a tight three-team race with the Blue Jays and Yankees. Smith got only five hits (two of them HR) in 24 AB, as Baltimore faded to finish 10 games behind the Jays. He re-signed with Baltimore in 1994, but made only 72 PA before a strike ended the season in August. At age 38, Smith's 17-year career was over—this time for good.

Lonnie Smith stepped away from baseball and retired to Spartanburg, SC, his offseason home since 1984 and, when he was interviewed in 2003 and 2006, was living a quiet life with his second wife Dorothy and their three children. He had not ingested an illegal drug since 1988.[16]

Why Was Lonnie Smith a Shooting Star?

Although Smith was not a great player, he was a very good one, with 38.5 career WAR. Unlike some players in this book, Smith's unexpected career year in 1989 was not an island of greatness in a sea of mediocrity (Figure 25).

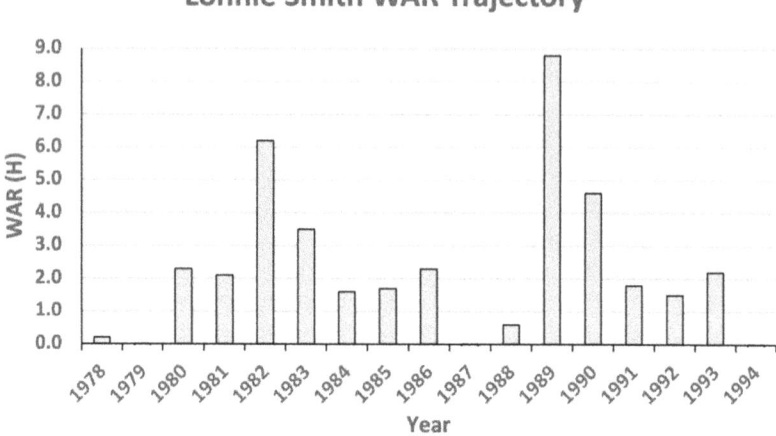

It was nonetheless totally unexpected in light of his prolonged decline in 1984–88 and of the fact that he had to fight his way back through the minors with a last-place team after plummeting to the depths of despair and being left for dead.

Apart from his compelling comeback story, one can think of Lonnie Smith as the quintessential baseball player of the 1980s, when the prevalence of African Americans like Smith in MLB ranged from 16–19 percent—its all-time high.[17] His career touched upon the major historical highlights of MLB in that turbulent decade—the renewed emphasis on OBP, speed, and aggressive small-ball tactics over power, the surge of cocaine as MLB's drug of choice before the Steroid Era, and MLB's collusive attempt to freeze the movement of free agents in 1986–87. He was also a key player on three iconic World Series champions, including two first-time champs—the 1980 Phillies and the 1985 Royals—and he was there at the onset of the rise of the Braves as the NL team of the 1990s.

When we think of Lonny Smith's many stumbles, physical and spiritual, we are poignantly reminded of the frailty and vulnerability of our sports heroes. But let us remember not just the stumbles but all the times he got up, dusted himself off, and played on. His wondrous comeback from the depths at age 33 in 1989 gives eloquent testimony to the resilience of the player who was disparagingly known as "Skates."

◆ 26 ◆

Journeyman
Richard David "Rick" Wilkins (1993)

What can you say about a player who hit 30 HR in one season, and averaged 5 HR over the remaining 10 years of his career? "One-year wonder" is the term that comes quickly to mind. For most of his eleven-year career, Rick Wilkens was nothing more than a journeyman backup catcher, who played for eight teams and finished with only 14.0 WAR. But in 1993, the slugging lefty-hitting catcher came out of nowhere to post the highest WAR ever (6.6) by a Cubs catcher and to join Hall of Famer Gabby Hartnett as the only Cubs catchers ever to hit 30 HR in a season.

Richard David Wilkins was born in Jacksonville, FL, on June 4, 1967. His father, who played baseball at South Georgia State College, worked for CSX Transportation. Wilkins grew up a Yankees fan, idolizing Yogi Berra and Thurman Munson.[1] He was an all-state star in baseball and wrestling at Bolles high school, the same school that later gave us Chipper Jones, where his number is now retired. The Bolles baseball team made it to the Florida state final four in 1985 and 1986. Wilkins went to Furman University with the intent to play football (as a linebacker) and baseball but transferred to Florida Community College at Jacksonville when the Furman coach asked him to give up baseball to focus only on football. After his team was eliminated in the semifinals of the 1987 NJCAA World Series in May 1987, Wilkins signed with the Cubs, who had selected him out of high school in the 23rd round of the June 1986 amateur draft.

Wilkins gradually ascended through the Cubs system in 1987–1990, excelling defensively but never hitting more than .251, albeit with decent power (.227/.300/.385 with 17 HR and 71 RBI in AA in 1990). When he began the 1991 AAA season hitting .271/.339/.458 in 123 PA, he earned his first promotion to the Cubs on June 6. In Chicago, he hit

26. Journeyman

only .222/.307/.355 (83 OPS+) with 6 HR, 22 RBI, and 1.3 WAR in 235 PA while sharing catching duties with Hector Villanueva, Damon Berryhill, and Joe Girardi. However, he did provide strong defense and threw out 39 percent of baserunners trying to steal. Still, after receiving only 10 AB in the first three weeks of the 1992 season, he was sent back to AAA.[2] Initially devastated by the demotion, he recovered to hit .277/.362/.471 in 47 games and earned his recall to Chicago on June 19. He hit .270/.344/.414 (112 OPS+) with 8 HR, 22 RBI, and 1.9 WAR in 274 PA the rest of the way and by the end of the season had established himself as the Cubs' #1 catcher.

In 1993, everything just fell into place for Wilkins, who played in 136 games and was the uncontested starting catcher after the Cubs lost Joe Girardi to Colorado in the expansion draft. The Cubs' pitching from their 78-win 1992 team had taken a big hit from the departure of Greg Maddux to Atlanta as a free agent, but their already strong lineup (which included the still-potent Ryne Sandberg and Mark Grace) was bolstered by Wilkins and the ascent of Sammy Sosa to replace the fading Andre Dawson in RF. Although Wilkins did not lead the NL in any categories, he finished second to Mike Piazza among NL catchers in WAR, HR, AVG, H (135), and OPS+, and TB, second to Darren Daulton in OBP, and third behind Daulton and Piazza in R (Table 26). Furthermore his 2.3 dWAR ranked second among all major league catchers, behind only Fred Manwaring (2.4), and he threw out 46 percent of all aspiring base stealers.

Table 26: Selected Stats for Rick Wilkins's Peak and Runner-Up Seasons and His Career

Season	Age	PA	AVG	OBP	SLG	OPS+	TB	HR	2B	R	RBI	WAR (H)	dWAR
Peak 1993	26	500	0.303	0.376	0.561	151	250	30	23	78	73	6.6	2.3
per 650 PA							325	39	30	101	95	8.6	3.0
Runner-Up 1992	25	274	0.270	0.344	0.414	112	101	8	9	20	22	1.9	0.9
per 650 PA							240	19	21	47	52	4.5	2.1
Career (1991–2001)		2435	0.244	0.332	0.410	100	867	81	95	280	278	14.0	7.9
per 650 PA							231	22	25	75	74	3.7	2.1

Wilkins got off to a sluggish start in 1993, hitting an anemic .122/.234/.195 with 1 HR, 5 R, and 2 RBI in 47 PA in April.[3] Then he quickly made up ground as the weather warmed up, hitting .299/.357/.546 with 5 HR, 12 R, and 6 RBI in May and a torrid .414/.485/.793 with 8 HR, 19 R, and 20 RBI in June. But despite his .312/.387/.580 slash line with 14 HR, 36 R, and 28 RBI entering July, Wilkins was snubbed for All-Star honors, losing out to Daulton and Piazza.[4] Wilkins continued to rake in the second half, hitting .295/.367/.545 with 16 HR, 42 R, and 45 RBI. After all was said and done, Wilkins's 6.6 WAR ranked third in the NL behind Barry Bonds (9.9) and Mike Piazza (7.0). Still, with the 84-win Cubs finishing a distant fourth in the NL East, Wilkins was shut out in the MVP voting.

The following winter, Wilkins's agent Scott Boras approached the Cubs seeking a long-term contract comparable to Piazza's three year $4.2 million deal with the Dodgers.[5] But Wilkins, who (like Piazza) had less than the three years of service time required for arbitration eligibility, had no negotiating leverage. The Cubs unilaterally renewed his contract for $350,000, leaving Wilkins seriously disgruntled entering the 1994 season.[6] The 1994 season was a disaster; Wilkins hit only .227/.317/.387 (83 OPS+) with 7 HR, 39 RBI, and 0.9 WAR in 358 PA (100 games) before the strike ended his (and everyone's) season on August 11. The Cubs fell to 49–64 (fifth place), and Wilkins fell out of favor.

The delayed 1995 season was even worse. After hitting only .191/.340/.315 (77 OPS+), Wilkins was unceremoniously dispatched to Houston in exchange for OF Luis Gonzalez and C Scott Servais—a trade that would have worked out very well for the Cubs if they had held on to Gonzalez for long enough to enjoy his 57-HR season in 2001. In any case, the change of scenery did nothing for Wilkins, who appeared in only 15 games for the Astros after requiring neck surgery following his second game. The Astros complained that the Cubs had concealed the injury, but to no avail. Wilkins fared only slightly better for the Astros in 1996 and was traded to San Francisco on July 27.

This was just the beginning of a long meandering journey for Wilkins, who went to Seattle in 1997, the New York Mets in 1998, Los Angeles in 1999, St. Louis in 2000, and San Diego in 2001, with five minor league stops along the way. He was strictly a backup wherever he went, never receiving more than 224 PA in any season. After leaving the Cubs, he enjoyed the most success in San Francisco, where he hit .239/.308/.403 (88 OPS+) with 14 HR, 59 RBI, and 1.8 WAR over parts of the 1996 and 1997 seasons. GMs have long memories, and they kept trying to tap into the vein of gold the Cubs mined in 1993.[7] But Wilkins could never recapture the magic. He was released by San Diego on October 11, 2001, played one year of independent baseball, then retired and returned to Jacksonville.

In 2009, Rick Wilkins, inspired by his sister's lengthy battle with cerebral palsy, established the Wilkins Family Foundation and the Wilkins Academy of Baseball to raise money for institutions that provided recreational opportunities for adults with disabilities.[8] The foundation also worked with the University of North Florida to help fund their baseball program and stadium and to provide scholarships in the department of health. He and his wife Vandy have a son and a daughter. His son Mac played baseball at Florida State College (formerly Florida Community College) at Jacksonville, Rick's alma mater.

Why Was Rick Wilkins a Shooting Star?

Except for 1993, Rick Wilkins had a negligible journeyman's career, mostly as a backup catcher. His post–1993 WAR never exceeded 1.9 (Figure 26).

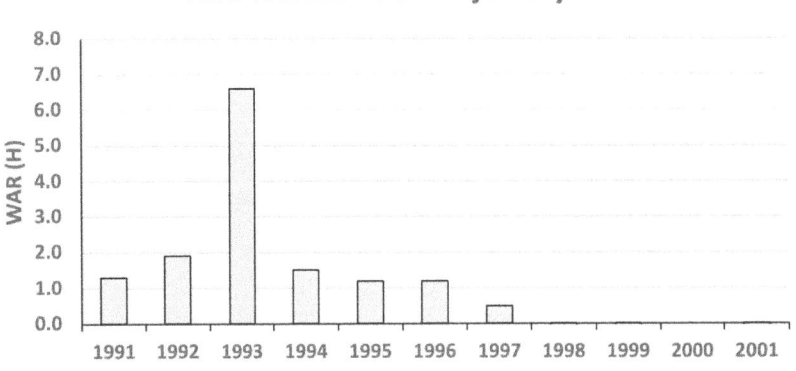

Wilkins accrued 27 percent of his career RBI total, 28 percent of his R, 37 percent of his HR, and 47 percent of his career WAR in his one shooting star season! There was no easy explanation for Wilkins' precipitous descent into mediocrity after such a promising beginning. One could not attribute his precipitous decline to injury, substance abuse, or any personal failing. It just happened. He was not lacking in ability. Although his .303 AVG in 1993 was clearly a fluke, he remained a fine defensive catcher with good power. But after two strike-shortened seasons and a very public salary dispute, he may simply have gotten typecast into the good-field-no-hit backup catcher role. His mixture of defense, power, and low AVG might have played better in today's era of advanced analytics, as it has for players like Martin Maldonado. Perhaps, in that sense he was unlucky not to have been born 20 years later.

In any case, Rick Wilkins's career arc illustrates the fragile and ephemeral nature of hope. Fans of teams like the Cubs, recognizing this sad fact of life, have learned to temper their hope so as to render their ultimate and inevitable disappointment less painful.

◆ 27 ◆

Bad Boy
Esteban Antonio Loaiza (2003)

As a longtime "owner" of two Fantasy Baseball teams, I can tell you that 31-year-old journeyman pitchers who come out of nowhere to become Cy Young award contenders are either loved or hated in Fantasy Baseball circles. I loved Esteban Loaiza in 2003, because I picked him up at no cost in our league's free agent pool after he went undrafted that spring, and he rewarded me with a totally unanticipated 7.2 WAR season that helped win me a league championship. Then, I loved him again in 2004 when one of my rivals wasted his #4 draft pick on Loaiza's disappointing follow-up season and finished ninth. Needless to say, my rivals who missed out on Loaiza in 2003 and the one who drafted him in 2004 did not share my fondness for Mr. Loaiza, but that's how it goes.

Esteban Antonio Loaiza was born in Tijuana, Mexico on December 31, 1971, and grew up in poverty living mostly in Imperial City on the California side of the Mexican border. There he attended Mar Vista High School. He was 19 years old and pitching for the Mexico City Red Devils in 1991, when the Pittsburgh Pirates discovered him and signed him to a contract.[1] He impressed the Pirates with his ability to throw strikes and quickly climbed the ladder from Rookie ball in 1991, to Class A Augusta (ME) in 1992, to high A Salem (MA) in 1993 and AA Carolina in 1993–94. His 10–5 record and 3.79 ERA in 24 starts in 1994 earned him a promotion to the Pittsburgh starting rotation in 1995.[2] But after he went only 8–9 with a 5.16 ERA (83 ERA+) and 1.506 WHIP in 172.2 IP, covering 31 starts and one relief appearance, he split the 1996 season between Pittsburgh and AAA Calgary, not pitching particularly well at either level. He reached the major leagues for good at age 25 in 1997.

For the next six years, Esteban Loaiza was neither more nor less than a slightly below average bottom-of-the-rotation starter for

Pittsburgh (1997–98), Texas (1998–2000), and Toronto (2000–2002). The 6'2" Mexican righty averaged 171 IP (750 BF) per season and compiled a 59–61 record with a 4.83 ERA (97 ERA+) and 1.442 WHIP. He struck out 5.6 and walked 2.5 batters per 9 IP and averaged 1.8 WAR per season. He never won fewer than 9 or more than 11 games per season. His best performance in this period was his 3.7 WAR 1997 season in Pittsburgh, when he started 32 games and went 11–11 with a 4.13 ERA (105 ERA+) and a 1.375 WHIP in 196.1 IP. His worst performance was his 0.1 WAR 2002 season in Toronto when he started 25 games and went 9–10 with a 5.71 ERA (81 ERA+) and 1.520 WHIP in 151.1 IP.

However, Loaiza was anything but boring, especially during his two-year tenure with Texas, which was marred by repeated displays of immaturity and bad judgment. He loved a party and never saw a fast car or met a fast woman that he could resist. He was once spotted washing his Ferrari in the team parking in mid-game. He spent freely on expensive gifts for his favorite friends and cousins. More significantly, perhaps, Loaiza had very public extramarital affair with Ivan Rodriguez's 19-year-old nanny Ashley Esposito.[3] Pudge took it in stride and hired another nanny, but Loaiza's wife Cristina did not and filed for divorce. Accusations surrounding the messy divorce and Loaiza's subsequent marriage to Ashley spilled into the tabloids. As if this weren't enough drama, the Rangers' MVP outfielder Juan Gonzalez angrily accused Loaiza of stealing his expensive leather coat.[4] Finally, the Rangers had seen enough of Loaiza and his drama and traded him to Toronto for two minor leaguers.[5] The Rangers made out like bandits, since one of the minor leaguers they received was Michael Young, who went on to become a franchise stalwart at SS, 2B, and 3B from 2001 to 2012.

On the field, Loaiza had made little progress as he aged from a raw 23-year-old problem child into an established 30-year-old mediocrity, who was probably more trouble than he was worth. So, at the end of the 2002 season, the Blue Jays cut their losses and made no effort to stop Loaiza from becoming a free agent. When he signed with the White Sox on January 24, 2003, there was barely a ripple in the baseball universe.

When Loaiza arrived in Spring training camp, White Sox pitching coach Dan Cooper confronted him: "Your stuff is too good to give up this many hits. How the hell are you doing it?"[6] Loaiza was defensive at first, but he worked closely with Cooper to improve his pitch selection and command. The result was a career year. Loaiza started 34 games, logging 226.1 IP, and won 21 games for the second-place White Sox, who improved by 5 G over 2002. He led the AL in strikeouts and ranked second in ERA and ERA+, tied for second in W, third in WAR (P), and fifth in WHIP (Table 27). His 7.2 WAR in 922 BF translated to 7.8 WAP per 1000 BF.

Table 27: Selected Stats for Esteban Loaiza's Peak
and Runner-Up Seasons and His Career*

Season	Age	BF	ERA	WHIP	ERA+	W-L	SO	BB	CG	SHO	WAR (P)
Peak 2003	31	922	2.90	1.113	159	21–9	**207**	56	1	0	7.2
per 1000 BF							225	61	1	0	7.8
Runner-Up 2000	28	871	4.56	1.430	111	10–13	137	57	1	1	3.8
per 1000 BF							157	65	1	1	4.4
Career (1995–2008)		9106	4.65	1.408	98	126–114	1382	604	14	6	22.9
per 1000 BF							152	66	2	1	2.5

*League leading totals are shown in boldface type.

A more granular look at his 2003 season shows that Loaiza got off to a red hot start, going 5–0 in April with a 1.25 ERA and 0.667 WHIP.[7] His ERA remained below 3.00 in each of the next three months—2.65 in May, 2.57 in June, and 2.55 in July. Loaiza was selected to start for the AL in the All-Star game and pitched two scoreless innings, marred only by a first-inning single by Jim Edmonds.[8] Although Loaiza's ERA inched up to 3.15 in August, he won five of his six decisions that month. and was 18–6 entering September. September was the only month in which he pitched like the old Esteban Loaiza—3–3 with a 5.30 ERA and a 1.346 WHIP.

Overall, Loaiza pitched six or more innings in 30 of his 34 starts, including 27 "quality starts," in which he yielded three or fewer ER.[9] Curiously, he had only one complete game—a 1–0 loss to Detroit on an unearned run on July 10. His best games were a one-hit seven-inning nine-strikeout scoreless outing in a 13–2 win at Yankee Stadium, a two-hit eight-inning scoreless outing against Detroit in a 5–0 victory over Detroit on April 11, and a one-run six-hit, eleven-strikeout performance in an 8–2 win over Kansas City on April 17. His shortest and least effective outing was against Minnesota on September 16, when he was removed after yielding 4 ER in 2.1 IP. Loaiza's performance propelled the White Sox to 86 wins and a second place finish in the AL Central, four games behind the Twins. But he finished a distant second to Roy Halladay in the voting for the AL Cy Young award.

Unfortunately, Loaiza went back to business as usual in 2004. Although he got off to a 4–0 start in April, his 3.71 ERA suggested that some luck was involved.[10] He slid to 2–3 with a 3.68 ERA in May, 2–0 with a 5.35 ERA in June, and 1–2 with a bloated 6.89 ERA in July. The downhill trajectory was obvious. In a July 31 deadline deal, the White Sox and Yankees exchanged disappointing pitchers.[11] Jose Contreras would become an important piece of Chicago's first World Series championship team since 1917 in 2005. Esteban Loaiza, on the other hand, quickly pitched himself out of New York. He had a bloated 8.50 ERA in 42.1 IP in his two months with the Yankees and finished the 2004 season with a 10–7 W-L record, a 5.70 ERA (117 ERA+), a 1.574 WHIP, and -0.1 WAR. Loaiza tried to restore the Yankees' faith in him in the postseason. After pitching effectively in a 2.0 IP relief appearance against Minnesota in the 2004 ALDS, Loaiza was brought into the tenth inning of Game 5 of the ALCS against Boston with the game tied 4–4. Loaiza held the Red Sox scoreless through the twelfth inning but was beaten by David Ortiz's walk-off single in the thirteenth inning.[12] Although Loaiza added another three scoreless innings in the Yankees 10–3 Game 7 defeat, it was not enough to offset the sour taste of his regular season failures. The Yankees made no effort to retain him.

In 2005, Loaiza signed with the Nationals, who had just moved to Washington from Montreal. Although Loaiza pitched better than in any year except 2003, he was more innings-eater than ace. He finished 12–10 for the scrappy Nationals with a respectable 3.77 ERA (108 ERA+) and 1.300 WHIP in 217.0 IP with 3.8 WAR. But that wasn't enough to keep the Nationals from allowing him to move on to Oakland in 2006. Although Loaiza pitched respectably again in 2006, going 11–9 with a 4.89 ERA (91 ERA+), a 1.416 WHIP, and 0.7 WAR, the biggest headline he generated was off the field. In mid–June he was arrested for drunk driving after being caught driving his Ferrari over 100 MPH on Interstate 580.[13] He was sentenced to three years' probation. Chastened by the experience, he vowed never again to drive after drinking.[14] Loaiza made two post-season starts for Oakland in 2006. He gave up 2 ER in 5.0 IP in an ALDS win over Minnesota (getting no decision) and giving up 7 ER in 6.0 IP in an ALCS loss to Detroit. His total post season record was 0–3 with a 4.44 ERA and 1.367 WHIP in 26.1 IP.

Loaiza bounced from Oakland to Los Angeles and back to the White Sox in 2007–08. He compiled a 3–6 W-L record in ten starts and seven relief appearances, with a 5.60 ERA (79 ERA+), a 1.368 WHIP, and -0.1 WAR in 64.1 IP. At age 36, his major league career was over. But he continued to enjoy the high life and quickly found the spotlight again. He married Mexican pop star Jenni Rivera in 2010 after they met at one of her concerts. They became a major celebrity couple in Mexico, and each got a star on the Las Vegas Walk of Fame.[15] However, two years later their marriage was on the rocks. Rivera filed for divorce in October 2012. On December 9, before the divorce became final, Ms. Rivera was killed in a private plane crash under suspicious circumstances.[16] Foul play was suspected—*not on Loaiza's part*—but never proven.

Loaiza, who would certainly have been on that plane were it not for the pending divorce, continued to run with the wild celebrity crowd he had met during his marriage, and had several very public affairs (including a rumored affair with his adult step-daughter).[17] His world finally came crashing down on February 12, 2018, when he was caught with 20 kilos of cocaine in the trunk of his Mercedes during a traffic stop in San Diego County after he had crossed the Mexican border from Tijuana.[18] In March 2019, he was sentenced to three years in federal prison. He was deported to Mexico in August 2021 after serving his sentence minus time off for good behavior.[19]

Why Was Esteban Loaiza a Shooting Star?

Although his 126 career wins place him second to Fernando Valenzuela among Mexican-born MLB pitchers, Esteban Loaiza was a classic underachiever for most of his 14 year career (Figure 27).[20]

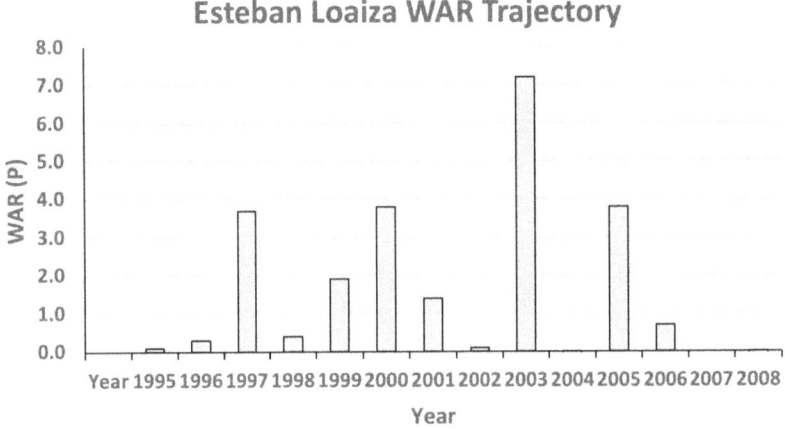

In 2003, he briefly showed what he could do when he was focused, but more often his mind was elsewhere. It wasn't that he was a bad guy—just immature and irresponsible. His teammates described him as open-hearted and generous to a fault. But his was a classic story of a child of poverty who came into more money than he ever dreamed of and never learned to manage his riches or fame. After burning through his $40 million in baseball earnings to buy houses, cars, and other expensive goodies for himself and his entourage of friends, girlfriends, and extended family, he had no legitimate source of income when his baseball career ended. When his celebrity marriage went up in smoke, his life went totally off the rails, leading ultimately to his arrest and conviction for cocaine trafficking. He was more of a knucklehead (as Oakland broadcaster Vince Cantroneo once called him) than a hard-core criminal.[21] But in the end, he will be remembered mainly as a guy who squandered his talent and good name.

28

Brian's Little Brother
Marcus William Giles (2003)

As the younger brother of hard-hitting and underrated OF Brian Giles, who compiled an impressive 51.1 WAR in his 15-year career with Cleveland, Pittsburgh, and San Diego, 5'8" Marcus Giles had big shoes to fill. For a short time, in 2003, it appeared he might do just that and perhaps even surpass Brian, who was seven year older and 3" taller. His 7.9 WAR in 2003 was more than double the 3.4 WAR of his big brother that year. But due in part to some poorly timed injuries, Marcus declined quickly and did not appear in the major leagues after 2007, when Brian was still going strong.

Marcus William Giles was born in El Cajon, CA (a middle-class suburb of San Diego), on May 18, 1978. The entire Giles family—Brian, Marcus, their father Bill, their mother Monica, and their sisters Kami and Brandi loved baseball.[1] Bill coached both Brian and Marcus in Little League. Like Brian, Marcus played baseball at Granite Hills High School in El Cajon, but he was not the multisport star athlete that Brian was. While Brian was drafted by Cleveland in the 17th round of the 1989 amateur draft right out of high school, Marcus spent a year at Grossmont College before the Braves selected him at age 19 in the 53rd round of the 1996 amateur draft.

The righty-hitting Giles was not initially viewed as a top prospect. The Braves, who had a stranglehold on the NL East pennant at that time, could afford to bring him along slowly. He made his way gradually up the chain from rookie ball (Danville) in 1997 to Class A Macon in 1998 to High A Myrtle Beach in 1999 to AA Greenville in 2000 to AAA Richmond in 2001, hitting at least .326/.387.472 at every level, except for a .290 AVG at Greenville in 2000. He hit 37 HR with 111 R and 108 RBI in Macon in 1998, but his typical output for a full season was more like 15 HR and 70–80 R and RBI. After hitting .290/.388/.472 with 17 HR, 73

R, 62 RBI and 25 SB in Greenville in 2000, Giles opened the 2001 season in Atlanta. He appeared in only nine games in April-May, getting four hits in 13 PA, before the Braves optioned him to AAA Richmond.[2] His .333/.387/.488 slash line in 273 PA in Richmond earned him a return trip to Atlanta in July to become the Braves' starting second baseman. He hit .262/.338/.430 (95 OPS+) in 273 PA in Atlanta with 9 HR, 36 R, 31 RBI, but only 2 SB. This translated to 0.6 WAR. Giles played in all eight games of Atlanta's three-game sweep of Houston in the NLDL and their five game loss to Arizona in the NLCS and collected a HR, two doubles, and four singles in 35 PA.

Giles started the 2002 season well enough, going .279/.382/.454 in 102 PA in April, but slumped in May and was hitting only .237/.320/.388 when he severely sprained his ankle turning a double play in the sixth inning of a May 28 game against Montreal.[3] Shortly after he went on the disabled list, his wife Tracy, who was six months pregnant, gave birth prematurely; his daughter lived only 16 days.[4] When Giles was ready to play again, he was once again optioned to Richmond. He hit .322/.385/.452 in 130 PA to earn a recall to Atlanta on August 11. However, he did not play every day and finished the star-crossed season hitting only .230/.315/.399 (86 OPS+) with 0.4 WAR in 242 PA with the Braves. Giles collected one single in 2 PA in Atlanta's three-game loss to San Francisco in the NLDS.

The stars finally aligned for Marcus Giles in 2003. Fully healthy and with an uncontested hold on the Braves' starting 2B job and the #2 slot in the batting order, Giles posted a career-best 7.9 WAR season, including 2.3 dWAR (Table 28).

Table 28: Selected Stats for Marcus Giles's Peak and Runner-Up Seasons and His Career*

Season	Age	PA	AVG	OBP	SLG	OPS+	TB	HR	2B	SB	R	WAR (H)	dWAR
Peak 2003	25	635	0.316	0.390	0.526	136	290	21	49	14	101	7.9	2.3
per 650 PA							297	21	50	14	103	8.1	2.4
Runner-Up 2005	27	654	0.291	0.365	0.461	114	266	15	45	16	104	4.0	0.5
per 650 PA							264	15	45	16	103	4.0	0.5
Career (2001–07)		3340	0.277	0.353	0.429	103	1260	76	187	70	468	16.7	3.5
per 650 PA							245	15	36	14	91	3.3	0.7

Giles started fast and never looked back. He hit a torrid .360/.431/.618 in 106 PA with 4 HR, 22 R, and 15 RBI in April and a solid .280/.358/.473 in 111 PA with 3 HR, 15 R and 16 RBI in May.[5] Although Giles slumped to .234/.308/.351 in 104 PA in June, he was elected to the All-Star Game at 2B for the NL. Unfortunately, Giles suffered a

28. Brian's Little Brother

concussion in a collision with Mark Prior on July 11 and was held out of the game.[6] He would not get another chance to play in an All-Star game. Despite the temporary setback, Giles surged to .404/.456/.628 in July, .321/.410/.623 in August, and .293/.377/.440 in September-October. Although Atlanta led the NL with 101 wins and Giles ranked third in the NL in WAR, trailing only Barry Bonds and Albert Pujols, he placed only 18th in the NL MVP voting, far behind Bonds, Pujols and 15 others.

After meeting with little post-season success in 2001–02, Giles came up big in the NLDS against the Cubs in 2003, hitting .357/.412/.571 in 17 PA with 1 HR, 3 R, and 3 RBI. His five hits included a fourth-inning HR against Kerry Wood that scored the first run of the series and a pinch-hit RBI single that put the Braves up 3–2 in the sixth inning of the 5–3 Braves victory in Game 2.[7] But it was not enough, as the Cubs prevailed 3–2 and advanced into the NLCS to face the Marlins.

Giles was 26 years old and presumably entering his prime as the 2004 season got underway. He again got off to a hot start and was hitting .339/.381/.475 on May 15, when he suffered a broken collar bone and concussion in a collision with Andruw Jones while trying to field a shallow fly ball.[8] He missed the next two months. When he returned on July 15, he picked up where he left off and finished the season at .311/.378/.443 (111 OPS+) in 434 PA with 8 HR, 61 R, 48 RBI, 17 SB, and 3.3 WAR. It was a fine follow-up season, but because of the missed time and falloff in power, it did not measure up to 2003. Although the Braves extended their string of NL East pennants to 13 (not counting the strike-shortened 1994 season), they again fell 3–2 in the NLDS—this time to Houston. Giles was of no help; Houston pitchers held him to three singles and no walks in 24 PA.

Giles enjoyed a healthy season in 2005 and hit .291/.365/.461 (114 OPS+) in 654 PA with 15 HR, 104 R, 63 RBI, 16 SB, and 4.0 WAR. It was his second best season, but his WAR total was barely half as large as it had been in 2003. Not only was his OPS+ only 14 percent above the league average (versus 36 percent in 2003), but his defensive value declined from 2.3 dWAR in 2003 to 0.5 dWAR in 2005. The Braves were no longer dominant but managed to eke out one last NL East pennant at 90–72. However, eventual NL champion Houston quickly dispatched them in the NLDS. Giles was again a non-factor, hitting .200/.304/.250 in 23 PA in the 3–1 NLDS defeat.

Despite the fact that he was healthy and seemingly in his prime at age 28, Giles declined markedly in 2006, hitting only .262/.341/.387 (87 OPS+) in 626 PA with 11 HR, 87 R, 60 RBI, 10 SB, and 0.7 WAR. This was by far the worst of any full season in Giles's career and was totally unexpected. Giles had hit a composite .292/.366/.465 (114 OPS+) in 2001–05 with the Braves and had hit even better at every minor league level before that. Meanwhile, the Braves lost more games (83) than they won (79) in 2006 for the first time since 1990 and were looking to rebuild. So, the Braves non-tendered Giles after the season. Giles decided to join his brother Brian close to home and signed a $3.75 million one-year contract with the San Diego Padres, the reigning NL West champion.[9]

At age 29 and with a successful season as recently as 2005, Giles seemed to be a strong comeback candidate. Certainly, the raucous interplay of the two brothers would enliven the Padres' clubhouse.[10] However, an incident at San Diego's Qualcomm Stadium in January 16, in which Giles was arrested after getting into a fight after a Chargers playoff game, may have been a bad omen.[11] Giles got off to his usual hot start for his new team in 2007, hitting .327/376/.459 in 111 PA in April.[12] However, he then fell into a deep slump and never recovered. He hit only .214/.301/.294 in 227 PA in May-June. When he began to lose playing time to 34-year-old utility player Geoff Blum, Giles's struggles only worsened. He hit only .162/.222/.242 in 111 PA in July-August. He improved slightly to .227/.370/.227 in only 27 PA in September, but by then, the frustrated and disgruntled Giles had lost his job to Blum. The Padres finished tied for second at 89–73 in an extremely tight NL West Division, one game behind Arizona, but lost a one-game playoff 9–8 to eventual NL champion Colorado on October 1.[13] Marcus Giles did not get into the game. When the Padres declined the one-year option on Giles's contract after the season, he was once again a free agent.

Giles never played another major league game. He signed a minor league contract with Colorado in 2008 but was cut in spring training.[14] He got another minor league contract offer from the Dodgers, but ultimately decided to sit out the season and perhaps retire permanently.[15] He tried a comeback with the Phillies in 2009, but again was released at the end of spring training.[16]

Retirement did not go well. In the fall of 2009, he assaulted his wife Tracy, the mother of his three children, after an argument and was subsequently sentenced to three years' probation plus anger management counseling.[17] They subsequently divorced.

Why Was Marcus Giles a Shooting Star?

Marcus Giles came to the majors leagues at age 23 with a strong familial pedigree and a successful minor league track record and produced a 7.9-WAR season at age 25. But his performance fell off rapidly thereafter (Figure 28).

28. Brian's Little Brother

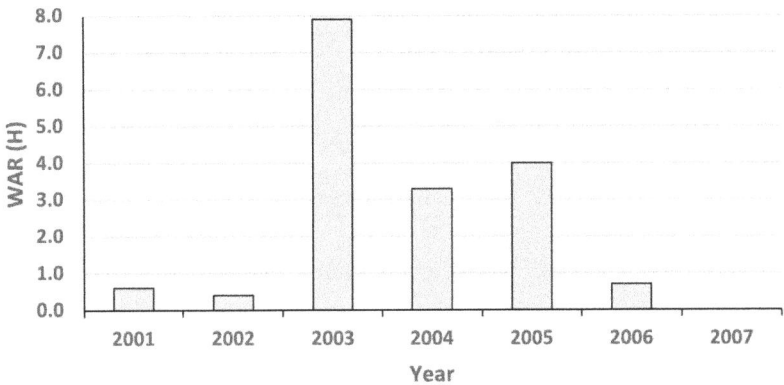

While injuries played a role in slowing his ascension to stardom in 2002 and preventing him from consolidating his stardom in 2004, his early decline in 2006 and total collapse in 2007, all before he was 30, are inexplicable. Perhaps the emotional issues that came to a head in 2009 played a role in his early decline, but that is mere speculation. We are left In the end with another shooting star who burned out far too soon.

◈ 29 ◈

The Perfect Pitching Prospect
Mark William Prior (2003)

It is often said that there is no such thing as a surefire pitching prospect; Mark Prior is a case in point. When the Cubs selected Mark Prior with the second overall pick in the 2001 amateur draft, they saw him as just the guy to lead them to the promised land after 94 years wandering in the wilderness.[1] Hailed as the next Tom Seaver (another Southern California alumnus) after winning the Golden Spikes Award as the nation's top amateur player as a junior, Prior was as close as you can get to a can't-miss prospect.[2] Unlike the Cubs' other young ace righthander Kerry Wood, who was always an accident waiting to happen, Prior had impeccable mechanics. He was also considered major-league ready. The Cubs could barely believe their good fortune when cash-strapped Minnesota passed on Prior and selected the more "signable" local high school star Joe Mauer.[3] (How did that one work out?) Unfortunately, Mark Prior's career illustrates the fragility of pitching prospects.

Mark William Prior was born in San Diego, CA, on September 7, 1980, and grew up there. He decided to be a ballplayer when he was 11, but didn't take up pitching until high school, where he starred in basketball as well as baseball. He finally focused exclusively on baseball as a senior.[4] He became a high school All-American and San Diego County Player of the Year at San Diego's University High School. He was selected by the Yankees as the 43rd overall pick in the 1998 amateur draft, but turned them down to accept a scholarship at Vanderbilt. He then transferred to the University of Southern California as a sophomore and enlisted pitching guru Tom House as his tutor. The Cubs drafted him with the second overall pick in 2001 after he posted a 15–1

29. The Perfect Pitching Prospect

record and 1.69 ERA with 202 strikeouts versus 18 walks in 138.2 IP as a junior and led the Trojans to the College World Series.

The minor leagues were a mere formality for Prior. The 2002 Cubs were a lackluster 67-win team and were eager to see what they had in their prize rookie. After only nine starts and 51.0 IP at AA West Tennessee and AAA Iowa, where he went 5–2 with a 2.29 ERA and 79 strikeouts, Prior made his major debut on May 22 in Wrigley Field against Pittsburgh. He gave up only 2 ER, 4 hits, and 2 walks in 6.0 IP, while striking out 10 batters, to get the win.[5] He performed similarly in Pittsburgh five days later, yielding only 1 ER, 3 hits, and 2 walks with 7 strikeouts in 6.0 IP, but this time came out with no decision in a game won by the Pirates 3–2. Houston got to Prior early in his third start—7 ER, 7 H and 3 BB in 3.2 IP, but he came back strong against Seattle six days later, giving up no runs, 4 hits, and a walk in 7.0 IP, while striking out 11 to pick up his second win. Of Prior's 19 starts that year, 13 were quality starts (3 or fewer ER in 6 or more IP). He gave up two or fewer runs in 15 of his 19 starts. For the season, he went 6–6 with a 3.32 ERA (122 ERA+), 1.166 WHIP, 147 strikeouts, and 3.0 WAR in 116.2 IP for a losing team. It was a promising beginning.

Prior gave the Cubs exactly the young ace they were looking for in 2003, going 18–6 with a 2.43 ERA (179 ERA+), a 1.103 WHIP, 245 strikeouts in 211.1 IP, despite missing four weeks on the disabled list (Table 29).

Table 29: Selected Stats for Mark Prior's Peak and Runner-Up Seasons and His Career*

Season	Age	BF	ERA	WHIP	ERA+	W-L	SO	BB	CG	SHO	WAR (P)
Peak 2003	22	863	2.43	1.103	179	18–6	**245**	50	3	1	**7.4**
per 1000 BF							284	58	3	1	8.6
Runner-Up 2005	24	701	3.67	1.212	120	11–7	188	59	1	0	3.6
per 1000 BF							268	84	1	0	5.1
Career (2002–06)		2771	3.51	1.225	124	42–29	757	223	5	1	15.7
per 1000 BF							273	80	2	0	5.7

*League leading totals are shown in boldface type.

His 7.4 WAR (P) led the NL, and he ranked second in ERA+ (behind Jason Schmidt) and in SO (behind Kerry Wood), tied with Woody Williams for second in W (behind Russ Ortiz), third in ERA (behind Schmidt and Kevin Brown), and third in WHIP (behind Schmidt and Curt Schilling). His excellence plus the emergence of 22-year-old Carlos Zambrano combined with young veterans Kerry Wood and Matt

Clement to give the Cubs a formidable starting rotation. With the help of improved (but still only league-average) run production, anchored by still potent Sammy Sosa and strong seasons from Moises Alou and Alex Gonzalez and bolstered by a mid-season trade for Aramis Ramirez and Kenny Lofton, the Cubs won 88 games (a 21-game improvement over 2002) under new manager Dusty Baker and narrowly won the NL Central Division by one game over Houston and three games over St. Louis.[6]

Prior was terrific from the start. He opened with wins in his first two games, giving up 1 ER and 4 H in 6.0 IP against the Mets in New York and pitching his first and only complete game shutout against the Expos in Wrigley Field, striking out 7 and 12 batters, respectively.[7] He logged at least 6.0 IP in 27 of his 30 outings, 23 of which were quality starts (≤ 3 ER), and 5.2 IP in two other starts (in which he gave up a combined 3 ER). His only truly ineffective outing—6 ER in 4.2 IP—came against Atlanta on July 11—but he had an excuse. He injured his shoulder in a third-inning collision with Atlanta 2B Marcus Giles; Giles left the game immediately, but Prior stayed in to give up 2 ER in the fourth and 2 more in the fifth before finally exiting. He immediately went on the disabled list and did not return until August 5. Prior's 10.4 strikeouts per 9 IP also ranked second in MLB, behind only teammate Kerry Wood. He logged 10 or more strikeouts in eight of his starts, topped by 16 in 8.0 IP in a 5–3 loss to Milwaukee, in which Prior got no decision after yielding only 2 ER and 4 H.. Looked at another way, Prior struck out 28.4 percent of the 863 batters he faced in 2003.

The Cubs, of course, were distinct underdogs going into the post-season against the 101-win Braves, the 100-win Giants, and even the 91-win Wild Card Marlins. But anything is possible when you have two ace starting pitchers like Prior and Wood.[8] The Cubs upset the Braves in the NLDS 3–2 behind strong outings from Wood in Games 1 and 5 and Prior in Game 3. It was the Cubs' first post-season series win since 1908. Prior was masterful in his Game 3 match-up against Greg Maddux, pitching a complete game and yielding only a 1 ER and 2 H (but 4 BB) while striking out seven, to protect a 2–0 first inning lead and emerge with a 3–1 win. With the Marlins surprising Barry Bonds and the defending NL champion Giants 3–1 in their NLDS and Prior and Wood available to make two starts apiece in the NLCS, the Cubs seemed to have a realistic shot at their first NL pennant since 1945.

After the Marlins outlasted the Cubs 9–8 in a Game 1 slugfest, Prior righted the ship in Game 2, an easy 12–3 Cub win. Prior give up 2 ER, 8 H, and 2 BB in 7.0 IP, while striking out five. When the Cubs won two of the three games in Miami to take a 3–2 series lead back to Wrigley Field, things looked bright for the Cubs, who needed only one more win from either of their two aces to wrap up a spot in the World Series against the Yankees. The Cubs' prospects brightened still further when Prior sailed through seven scoreless three-hit innings and took a 3–0 lead into the eighth inning of Game 6. Then it all fell apart.[9] After a one-out double by Juan Pierre, Luis Castillo worked the count to 1–2 and hit a lazy fly ball down the left field line. As it drifted into foul territory, the ball seemed destined for Moises Alou's glove until am unthinking Cubs fan reached out over the wall and deflected it away from the irate left fielder.[10] Although Prior was visibly upset and had thrown 113 pitches, he remained in the game. Given another chance, Castillo eventually drew a walk on a 3–2 wild pitch that advanced Pierre to 3B. Ivan Rodriguez followed with a run-scoring single, but the Cubs had a chance to escape with a 3–1 lead when slow-footed rookie Miguel Cabrera hit a tailor-made double play groundball to normally sure-handed SS Alex Gonzalez. He booted it to load the bases. Then, Derrek Lee delivered a 2-run double to tie the game and knock out Prior. The bullpen, the Cubs' Achilles heel all season, then threw gasoline on the fire, and when the smoke cleared, the Marlins had an 8–3 lead. The Marlins' momentum carried into Game 7, when they scored three first inning runs off Kerry Wood, weathered a five-run comeback which gave the Cubs a short-lived 5–3 lead, and eventually prevailed 9–6. The hapless fan who interfered with the Castillo flyball is often blamed for the Cubs collapse, but Alex Gonzalez (who fumbled the subsequent double play opportunity) and Dusty Baker, who left the rattled and tiring Prior in the game to face at least three batters too many, are guiltier. It is often said that you can't afford to give a good team four outs. What can you expect when you give them five?

Despite the disappointing ending to 2003, the Cubs and their 22-year-old ace looked forward to many future post-season opportunities. Those opportunities never came. The 2004 season began inauspiciously, as Prior suffered from Achilles tendonitis in spring training and spent the first two months of the season on the disabled list. Prior and the Cubs vehemently denied rumors of elbow issues and imminent Tommy John surgery.[11] The rumors were false, but they sowed seeds of distrust between the secretive Prior and the Cubs fan base. Prior finally started his first game on June 4 and made 21 starts, but was used more lightly than he was in 2003 and did not pitch as well. He went only 6–4 with an unimpressive 4.02 ERA (110 ERA+), 1.348 WIP, and 2.6 WAR in only 118.2 IP. However, his strikeout rate (10.5 per 9 IP) was as good as ever. With the return of Greg Maddux and the emergence of Carlos Zambrano as staff ace—each won 16 games—the Cubs actually won one more game in 2004 than they had in 2003, despite Prior's diminished contribution. However, they were no match for the 105-win St. Louis Cardinals in the NL Central and finished three games behind Houston for the Wild Card spot..

Prior suffered another significant injury in 2005, when his right elbow was fractured by a line drive off the bat of Colorado OF Brad Hawpe on May 27.[12] Although he was expected to be sidelined until after the All-Star game, Prior returned on June 26 and shut out the White Sox on one hit through 6.0 IP in a 2–0 Cubs win. Despite the scary injury, Prior's numbers improved to 11–7 with a 3.67 ERA (120 ERA+), a 1.212 WHIP, and 3.6 WAR in 166.2 IP in 2005. However, Baker now treaded carefully and sometimes removed Prior after 5 IP, even when he pitched well. Twenty of Prior's 27 starts in 2005 were quality starts, and he only had three truly bad starts—8 ER in 5.0 IP against Houston on May 1, 6 ER in 4.2 IP against Atlanta on July 7, and 6 ER in 4.1 IP against Philadelphia on August 4.[13] However, although Prior still maintained a 10.2 strikeout rate per 9 IP, he did not otherwise resemble the ace of 2003. Without Sammy Sosa (traded to Baltimore) and with Maddux also fading, the Cubs slipped to 79 wins, fourth in the NL Central division in 2005.

By the end of the 2005 season, Prior had become a fragile pitcher, but one who was still effective when he was healthy enough to pitch. But the latter was no longer the case in 2006. As in 2004, he spent the first two months of the season on the disabled list—but this time with a more ominous strained right shoulder.[14] The Cubs and Prior took considerable criticism for trying to hide, then minimize the injury.[15] Prior's 2006 debut against Detroit on June 18 was a debacle. The Tigers pounded him for six runs in the first inning and sent him packing in the fourth. After going 0–4 with a 7.71 ERA in four starts, Prior returned to the disabled list with a strained left oblique on July 14. He was again ineffective when he returned and went on the disabled list for good on August 12. He finished the season 1–6 with a 7.21 ERA (65 ERA+), a 1.695 WHIP, and -0.9 WAR in only 43.2 IP spread over nine starts. The Cubs finished 66–96, last in the NL Central. Neither Prior nor the Cubs knew it then, but at age 25, he had pitched his last major league game.

Prior was optioned to AAA Iowa in March 2007 but underwent exploratory surgery in April after only one start in extended spring training.[16] The procedure revealed severe structural damage, including tears in his labrum, anterior capsule and rotator cuff. He was out for the season and was non-tendered by the Cubs after the season. He tried to come back with San Diego in 2008–09, Texas in 2010, the Yankees in 2011, Boston in 2012, and Cincinnati in 2013 but without success. Finally he called it quits. He accepted a job as the San Diego Padres minor league pitching coordinator In 2015. Prior was hired as the Dodgers bullpen coach under Dave Roberts in 2018 and was promoted to pitching coach in 2020.[17] He was elected to the University of Southern California Hall of Fame in 2014.[18]

Why Was Mark Prior a Shooting Star?

Mark Prior finished with only 15.7 career WAR, almost half of them in that single memorable 2003 season (Figure 29).

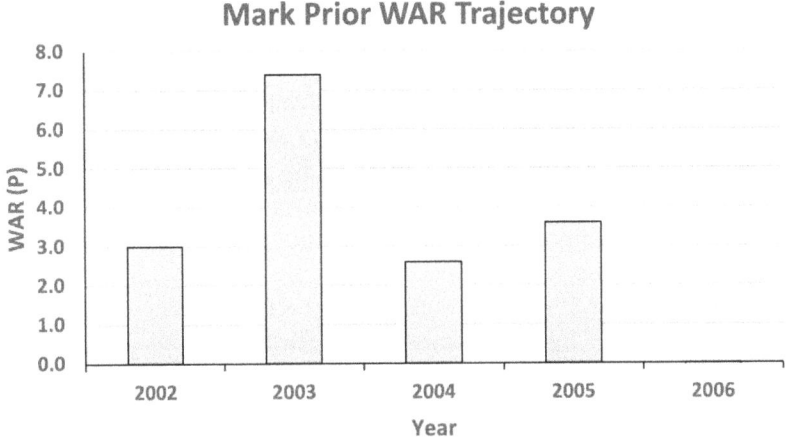

Like Slim Jones (Chapter 7) and Mark Fidrych (Chapter 21) before him, Prior represents yet another cautionary tale of a supremely gifted pitching prospect whose career flamed out due to injury. Prior was perhaps the most gifted of all, going by his accomplishments as an amateur, although we have too little information to say much about Slim Jones. Dusty Baker has often been criticized after the fact for overusing Prior, who led the NL with 124 pitches per game in 2003, but his usage was not unusual at that time.[19] Indeed, what happened to Prior undoubtedly helped drive the paradigm shift of the subsequent two decades, in which young pitchers today are *never* allowed to throw > 100 pitches, even in a no-hitter. If the 2023 version of Dusty Baker could go back in time to manage the 2003 Cubs, Prior would not have even started the seventh inning Game 6 of the 2003 NLCS, let alone pitched into the eighth. Of course, given the quality of the 2003 Cubs' bullpen, they probably would have lost anyway. But perhaps Prior would not have flamed out by age 25.

◈ 30 ◈

The Natural
Joshua Holt (Josh) Hamilton (2010)

Josh Hamilton was a superstar caliber talent with a fatal weakness for alcohol and drugs, whose athleticism and lefty power tantalized the teams that employed him but who disappointed them in the end. He was the first overall selection (by Tampa Bay) in the 1999 amateur draft as an 18-year-old high school senior, but drinking and drugs nearly ended his career before it began. Hamilton never played for Tampa Bay and did not even make his major league debut until 2007, with Cincinnati, at age 26. Once in the major leagues, he soon became one of MLB's top sluggers and an All-Star, but his career was marred by recurring relapses into substance abuse and eventually ended by injury.

Josh Hamilton was born in Raleigh, NC, on May 21, 1981. He grew up in a sheltered middle-class church-going family and was never exposed to alcohol or drugs as a teenager.[1] At Athens Drive high school, he was viewed as a once-in-a-generation five-tool talent—a natural. He not only hit with tape-measure power, but he also pitched, easily touching 96 mph with his smooth southpaw delivery. The Tampa Bay Devil Rays, then a one-year-old expansion team with the number one pick in the 1999 draft, chose Hamilton over Josh Becket, citing his "makeup" as well as his talent. Hamilton received a $3.96 M signing bonus—enough for his parents to quit their jobs to watch over him in his minor league travels until he was old enough to be independent. An unnamed Tampa Bay scout opined, "You read so many bad things about professional athletes, but I don't think you ever will about Josh."[2]

Hamilton's first two years in the lower minors went well enough. He hit .312/.340/.510 with 10 HR and 55 RBI in 327 PA in rookie ball and low Class A in 1999 and .302/.348/.476 with 13 HR and 61 RBI in 423 PA in Class A in 2000. He began the 2001 season in AA, but suffered a significant lower back injury during spring training when his mother's car (in which he was a passenger) was hit by a dump truck that ran a red light.³ When his parents returned to Raleigh to rehabilitate her injuries, Hamilton was on his own for the first time in his life. Unsupervised and with too much time on his hands, Hamilton hung out at the local tattoo parlor and began to experiment with alcohol and drugs. A series of injuries and failed drug tests limited him to 108 PA in Orlando (AA) and Charleston (A) in 2001 and 235 PA in Bakersfield (A) in 2002. He did not play at all in 2003–05 after the Rays placed him on the restricted list in 2003 and MLB suspended him for failing to show up for a mandatory drug test in August 2004. Finally, Hamilton was allowed to return in June 2006 after remaining clean and sober for eight months. He hit only .260/.327/.360 with no HR in 55 PA with the Hudson Valley Renegades (low A). He was removed from the Rays' 40-man roster, allowing any team to claim him for a pittance.

Hamilton finally made his major league debut in 2007, after Cincinnati arranged to purchase his contact from the Cubs, who selected Hamilton on their behalf in the Rule 5 Draft the previous December. Cincinnati's gamble paid off immediately as Hamilton appeared in 90 games, mostly in a CF platoon with Ryan Freel, and hit .292/.368/.554 (131 OPS+) with 19 HR, 47 RBI, and 2.5 WAR in 337 PA. He received no votes for Rookie of the Year (won by Ryan Braun), but he had put himself on the radar of the Texas Rangers. The Rangers were an aging 75-win team that needed a center fielder and would have put in a waiver claim for Hamilton a year earlier but for his drug history. The Reds, who had finished 72–90 in 2007 and needed pitching, were willing to trade Hamilton but demanded young ace Edinson Volquez in return. After vetting Hamilton thoroughly, Texas agreed to the trade on December 21. To protect their investment, the Rangers assigned assistant hitting coach Johnny Narron to keep tabs on him and required Hamilton to submit a urine sample for drug testing three times a week.

Hamilton started the 2008 season like a house afire, hitting .330/.379/.591 with 6 HR and 32 RBI in April and .322/.360/.617 with 8 HR and 29 RBI in May.⁴ Although he cooled off to .278/.349/.464 in June, he entered the All-Star break hitting .310/.367/.552 with 21 HR and a league-leading 95 RBI (25 more than Carlos Quentin, his closest rival).⁵ He was selected to start the All-Star Game in CF and got a single in 3 AB in a 4–3 AL win.⁶ However, Hamilton's All-Star week highlight came a day earlier when he hit 28 HR in the first round of the Home Run Derby, a tour de force performance which established a record that would last for 13 years until Salvatore Perez hit 29 in 2021.⁷ Hamilton eventually finished the season hitting .304/.371/.530 (135 OPS+) with 32 HR, 98 R, a league-leading 130 RBI, and 5.5 WAR in 704 PA, won a Silver

Slugger award, and finished seventh in the AL MVP voting (despite the Rangers' mediocre 79–83 record). It was a memorable season that definitively established Hamilton as a rising star at age 27.

Unfortunately, Hamilton had a miserable injury-marred 2009 season, hitting only .268/.315/.426 (90 OPS+) with 10 HR and 54 RBI in 365 PA. Two lengthy stints on the disabled list on June 1–July 4 (torn abdominal muscle) and September 3–24 (cracked ribs) after wall-crashing catches limited him to 90 games and diminished his performance after he returned.[8] Still, based largely (I suppose) on his 2008 Home Run Derby performance, he was selected as the All-Star starter in CF, despite the fact that he was hitting only .243/.298/.428 at the break.[9] He again went 1-for-3, this time with a first-inning RBI in another 4–3 AL victory.[10] Then, in August, embarrassing photos of Hamilton cavorting drunkenly in a strip bar the previous January emerged, forcing Hamilton to publicly apologize.[11] However, despite Hamilton's many woes the Rangers improved to 87–75, thanks to outstanding seasons from Ian Kinsler, Nelson Cruz, and Michael Young and strong pitching from Kevin Millwood and Scott Feldman.

In 2010, Josh Hamilton put the disappointment of 2009 behind him with the season that everyone envisioned for him a decade earlier when he was the most coveted amateur prospect in baseball, leading the Rangers to 90 wins and their first ever AL pennant (Table 30).

Table 30: Selected Stats for Josh Hamilton's Peak and Runner-Up Seasons and His Career*

Season	Age	PA	AVG	OBP	SLG	OPS+	TB	HR	2B	RBI	R	WAR (H)	dWAR
Peak 2010	29	571	**0.359**	0.411	**0.633**	170	328	32	40	100	95	**8.7**	0.8
per 650 PA							373	36	46	114	108	9.9	0.9
Runner-Up 2008	27	704	0.304	0.371	0.530	135	331	32	35	**130**	98	5.5	-0.6
per 650 PA							306	30	32	120	90	5.1	-0.6
Career (2007–15)		4350	0.290	0.349	0.516	129	2016	200	234	701	609	28.2	-2.8
per 650 PA							301	30	35	105	91	4.2	-0.4

*League leading totals are shown in boldface type.

His .359 AVG, .633 SLG, and 8.7 WAR easily led MLB, and he trailed only Joey Votto (.424), Miguel Cabrera (.420), and Albert Pujols (.414) in OBP. He was an easy choice as AL MVP and MLB Player of the Year. Hamilton had actually started the 2010 season relatively slowly, hitting .265/.351/.494 with 3 HR and 11 RBI in April and improving to .294/.322/.505 with 6 HR and 16 RBI in May.[12] But he caught fire in June, hitting an astounding .454/.483/.815 with 9 HR and 31 RBI, and nearly maintained that torrid pace through the rest of the summer. He hit .418/.468/.704 with 5 HR and 17 RBI in July and .356/.433/.644 with 8 HR and 22 RBI in August. Only a collision with a wall while attempting a catch at Minnesota's Target Field on September 4, which sidelined him until October 1, finally put a stop to his onslaught against AL pitching and prevented him from adding further to his stats.[13] Hamilton, of course, made his third consecutive All-Star start and again collected one hit in 3 AB as the AL lost 3–1.[14]

Hamilton was good to go for the postseason. His bat was quiet in the Rangers' 3–2 NLDS win over Tampa Bay, in which he collected only two hits and two walks in 20 PA. But he single-handedly destroyed the heavily favored defending World Series champion Yankees in the ALCS. He hit .350/.536/1.000 in 28 PA with 4 HR, 6 R, 7 RBI, 8 BB, and 3 SB, as the Rangers prevailed 4–2.[15] After hitting a 3-R HR in 4 AB in a 6–5 Game 1 loss and being pitched around (4 BB) in Game 2, Hamilton tagged Andy Pettitte for a 2-run first inning HR in Game 3, which were the only runs scored until the Rangers blew the game open with a 6-run ninth. He hit two more HR to spearhead a 10–3 Texas rout in Game 4. He contributed a hit and three more walks to the Rangers' clinching victory in Game 6. He was named ALCS MVP for his efforts. However, neither Hamilton nor his team brought their A game to the World Series, which the Giants won in five games. In 21 World Series PA, Hamilton collected only two hits, including a meaningless fifth inning solo HR off Jonathan Sanchez in the 4–2 Game 3 loss.

If Hamilton hoped to build on his 2010 success in 2011, that hope ended quickly on April 12, when he broke his right upper arm (humerus) while attempting to dive head first into home plate after tagging up on a foul popup in what he himself deemed a stupid play.[16] He did not return until May 23. Still Hamilton hit a more than solid .298/.346/.536 (130 OPS+) with 25 HR, 80 R, 94 RBI, and 3.8 WAR as the Rangers improved to 96–66 and easily repeated as AL West Division champion. Hamilton was again chosen to start the All-Star Game, this time in LF, and went 1-for-2 in a 5–1 AL defeat.[17] He finished 22nd in the AL MVP voting. The Rangers won their second consecutive AL pennant, with solid contributions from Hamilton in their 3–1 ALDS win over Tampa Bay (.267/.313/.333) and in their 4–2 ALCS win over Detroit (.308/.310/.462). However, Hamilton's bat was silent (3-for-19 with 2 RBI) in Games 1–5 of the World Series as the Rangers took a 3–2 lead over the Cardinals.[18] They headed back to St. Louis, needing just one win to bring home their first World Series championship. Hamilton's bat suddenly came alive with a run-scoring single in the first inning of Game 6 to put the Rangers ahead. He scored another run in the fifth inning on a double by Michael Young to break a 3–3 tie after reaching 1B on an error. Then after Texas coughed up a 7–5 lead on a 2-out 2-run triple by David Freese, Hamilton put them on top again in the 10th inning with a two-run HR—his first of the postseason. But the Cardinals came back to tie the game in the bottom of the tenth, and won on a walk-off eleventh inning HR by Freese. Hamilton again gave the Rangers an early lead in Game 7 with a run-scoring one-out double in the first inning, then came around to score on a double by Michael Young. But then the Rangers' bats fell silent as Chris Carpenter and three relievers cruised to a 6–2 win. Hamilton hit .241/.258/.414 in 31 PA with 1 HR, 4 R, and 6 RBI for the Series.

After his "accountability partner," Johnny Narron, accepted a coaching job with the Milwaukee Brewers, Hamilton had a brief alcoholic relapse in February, but was not disciplined.[19] The Rangers hired Shayne Kelley, a former college assistant coach, to replace Narron.[20] Hamilton rebounded to have another big year in 2012, hitting .285/.354/.577 (141 OPS+) in 636 PA and achieving career highs in HR (43) and R (103), along with 128 RBI, His 4.0 WAR was the third highest of his career. He finished fifth in the AL MVP voting and received his third Silver Slugger award. But unlike his 2008 and 2010 seasons, Hamilton's performance was inconsistent.[21] He hit a torrid .368/.420/.764 with 21 HR and 57 RBI in 207 PA through May 31, including a 4-HR-8-RBI game on May 8—a 10–3 win over Baltimore.[22] However, he slumped badly to .223/.318/.436 with 4 HR and 16 RBI in June and to .177/.253/.354 with 4 HR and 11 RBI in July. Some (including Nolan Ryan) attributed his slump to his sudden decision to quit using smokeless tobacco.[23] He was elected to start his fifth (and last) consecutive All-Star Game, but was hitless in 2 AB as the AL lost 8–0.[24] Although he bounced back to hit .310/.368/.575 in August with 7 HR and 28 RBI and .245/.330/.543 with 7 HR and 16 RBI in September, he missed five late September games with blurred vision due to ocular keratitis.[25] He also made a critical error in the final game of the season, dropping a routine flyball to extend the 6-run Oakland rally that enabled the A's to overcome a 5–1 deficit and win the AL West Division championship by a single game, thereby relegating Texas to a Wild Card berth.[26] The Rangers lost the first-ever AL Wild Card game 5–1 to Baltimore, as Hamilton went hitless with two strikeouts in 4 AB.

Josh Hamilton became a free agent following the 2012 season and signed a $125 million 5-year contract to join Mike Trout and Albert Pujols with the Angels. The abruptness of his departure engendered some bitterness in the Texas front office, which had supported him through his many travails and had believed that Hamilton would grant them first refusal before signing with another team.[27] Hamilton rubbed salt in the wound by disparaging the Texas fanbase in spring training as not being true baseball fans. It turned out that the Rangers dodged a bullet. Despite being healthy all year, Hamilton declined to .250/.307/.432 (108 OPS+) with 21 HR, 73 R, 79 RBI, and 1.3 WAR in 636 PA. It was a respectable performance—but not what the Angels thought they were buying. The Angels finished fourth at 78–84.

Hamilton appeared primed for a comeback in 2014, as he started the season red hot, hitting .500/.600/.833 with 2 HR and 6 RBI through April 7 and winning Player of the Week Honors. But on April 8 he tore a ligament in his left thumb while sliding head-first into 1B and missed the next two months.[28] He was never right all year, hitting .263/.331/.414 (115 OPS+) with only 10 HR, 43 R, 44 RBI, and 1.4 WAR in 381 PA. The Angels compiled the best record in the AL (98–64) despite Hamilton's miseries but were swept in the ALDS by wild card Kansas City. Hamilton was a non-factor in the ALDS defeat, going hitless in 13 AB. He underwent shoulder surgery after the season ended.

While Hamilton was recuperating, he began drinking and using cocaine again. To make matters worse, his 10-year marriage to Katie ended in divorce due to his repeated infidelities and abusive behavior; he had lost his major source of emotional support.[29] A court order forbade him to see his four daughters without supervision.[30] Infuriated by MLB's (arbitrator-guided) decision not to suspend Hamilton (which would have gotten them off the hook for his $23 million salary), Angels owner Artie Moreno traded him to Texas on April 21 for the proverbial bag of baseballs, while eating 80 percent of the $75 million remaining on his contract.[31] But the return to a more supportive setting and the scene of his glory days was not the elixir that Hamilton and the Rangers had hoped for. Injuries limited him to 182 PA, and he hit only .253/.291/.441 (94 OPS+) with 8 HR and 25 RBI. He wasn't able to play at all until May 25 and a strained hamstring limited him to only one game in June.[32] He played regularly in July and the first half of August but was increasingly bothered by swelling in his left knee due to damaged cartilage. After three weeks on the disabled list, he finally had arthroscopic surgery on September 11 and returned to the lineup a week later to prepare for the postseason. He got only three unproductive hits and a walk in 19 PA in the Rangers' 3–2 ALDS loss to Toronto. That was the end of his major league career.

Hamilton tried to come back in 2016, but his knee was swollen when he reported to spring training and the Rangers signed Ian Desmond to replace him in left field.[33] On May 23, Hamilton underwent season-ending surgery. The Rangers released him on August 23, but later re-signed him to a minor league deal. However, when he reported to spring training in 2017, his left knee still wasn't right and required another arthroscopic repair, which would sideline him for eight more weeks. Finally, he injured his right knee while rehabbing his left knee. The Rangers released him for good on April 21.

Hamilton retired to a ranch near College Station, TX, but is still fighting his demons. In April 2020, he was indicted on a felony charge for striking and injuring his 14-year-old daughter in a 2019 altercation.[34] It is not clear whether alcohol was involved. In February 2022, he pleaded guilty to a misdemeanor and received a suspended sentence. Conditions of probation included abstinence from alcohol, regular urine tests, anger management classes, and community service.[35]

Why Was Josh Hamilton a Shooting Star?

An overview of the trajectory of Josh Hamilton's career shows that he had a five-year run (2008–12), interrupted by an off-season in 2009, as one of the top players in the AL (Figure 30). But in only one of those seasons did he fully realize the potential that everyone saw in him when Tampa Bay selected him with the #1 pick in the 1999 amateur draft.

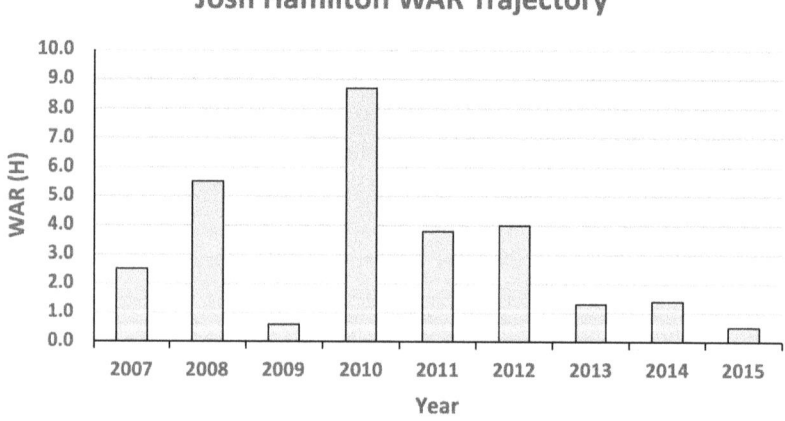

His 2010 season might have been even better if an injury hadn't forced him to the sidelines for most of September. His 8.7 WAR that year projects to 9.904 over a full 650-PA season. To put that in context, Hamilton's pro-rated WAR in 2010 slightly exceeded Aaron Judge's 9.899 WAR per 650 PA in his record-breaking 10.6 WAR 2022 season. It was not a surprise that Hamilton eventually achieved such a season, but it was a surprise that it took him a decade to get there.

30. The Natural

Like Dwight Gooden (Chapter 23), Josh Hamilton stands out as a clear example of a shooting star with Hall of Fame talent who did not become the player he was expected to be. Alcoholism and drug addiction obliterated the front end of his career, and injuries, compounded by the occasional relapse into substance abuse, curtailed the back end of his career. He did not even play the minimum 10 years required for HOF eligibility (although he did make it to the Rangers HOF).[36] Somehow, the fact that he was a five-time All-Star who was a serious MVP contender in 2008 and 2012 as well as the 2010 winner, doesn't seem quite enough.

Unlike Gooden who was left to cope on his own with the temptations of the big city and the voracious New York tabloid press, Hamilton had the good fortune to spend his prime years with the Texas Rangers, who did their best to support him and protect him from his demons— even hiring glorified babysitters to watch over him—and to minimize his exposure to adverse publicity. Even so, Hamilton's problems are not over. He has lost his family and barely avoided a prison sentence in the 2019 altercation with his teenage daughter. In discussing his many tattoos in a 2010 interview, Hamilton addressed his state of mind when he got devil faces tattooed on his arms and when he had Christ's face tattooed on his calf. He metaphorically described his body as a battlefield with God and Satan vying for control.[37] That battle will be lifelong.

◈ 31 ◈

The Next Dave Winfield

Matthew Ryan "Matt" Kemp (2011)

It is never fair to compare an unproven young player to a Hall of Famer, but the physical resemblance of emerging star Matt Kemp in the 2000s to Dave Winfield, another righty-hitting African American slugger of the 1970s, was hard to deny. At 6'4" and 225 he was two inches shorter and slightly heavier than Winfield had been, but both had the chiseled muscular build of an NFL tight end. Furthermore, Kemp's raw power was at least as impressive as Winfield's, and he was faster. But Winfield developed a remarkably thick skin in his nine-plus years of working for and feuding with George Steinbrenner, while Kemp was famously thin-skinned and mercurial. Nonetheless, Kemp had a respectable 15-year 21.4-WAR career, including one near–MVP season and three other pretty good ones. Sure, he was no Dave Winfield—but who is? The fact that Kemp's career is widely viewed as disappointing speaks at least as much to the unrealistic expectations placed on him as to his own shortcomings.

Matthew Ryan Kemp was born in Midwest City, OK, on September 23, 1984. His mother Judy Henderson, a registered nurse, and his grandmother raised him, but his father Carl Kemp saw him regularly.[1] Matt attended Midwest City High School, where he was a standout in basketball as well as baseball. In basketball, he averaged twenty points per game led his team to two consecutive state championships and was chosen for the All-City team. However, seeing baseball as his best opportunity for long-term financial success, Kemp turned down a basketball scholarship from the University of Oklahoma to sign with the Dodgers, who selected him in the sixth round of the 2003 amateur draft.

Kemp gradually worked his way up through the Dodgers' minor

league system, starting with 43 PA in the Gulf Coast Rookie League in 2003, and progressing to Class A Columbus and high A Vero Beach in 2004–05. Despite the increasing level of competition, he improved each year, hitting .293/.337/.504 with 18 HR, 72 R, 75 RBI, and 10 SB in 500 PA in 2004, then .306/.349/.569 with 27 HR, 76 R, 90 RBI, and 23 SB in 454 PA in 2005. His combination of power and speed led Baseball America to rank him as the #5 prospect in the Florida State League after the season.[2] A hot start at AA Jacksonville in 2006 earned Kemp his first promotion to Los Angeles on May 28, but he was sent down to AAA Las Vegas after hitting only .253/.289/.448 in 154 PA. He finished his 2006 minor league season hitting .346/.414/.543. Baseball America ranked him the #6 prospect in the Pacific Coast League.[3] The Dodgers, a veteran team who had finished 88–74 but missed the postseason in 2006, were eager to see what younger players like Kemp, Andre Ethier, and James Loney could do in 2007.

Kemp began the 2007 season in Los Angeles but was sent down to AAA Las Vegas after getting into only five games, despite hitting .429/.438/.500 in 16 PA.[4] He returned to LA to stay in June and hit .342/.373/.521 in 311 PA with 10 HR, 47 R, 42 RBI, 10 SB, and 1.6 WAR in LA. The 23-year-old Kemp had established himself as a regular and a big part of the Dodgers' future. However, the Dodgers finished only 82–80, and dissension between the veterans and younger players led to the replacement of manager Grady Little with Joe Torre after the season.[5]

In 2008, his first full major league season, Kemp embarked on a four-year almost Ripken-esque stretch, in which he played in 637 (98 percent) of the Dodgers' 647 games, mostly in CF, and accrued 15.6 of his 21.4 career WAR. He hit .290/.340/.459 (110 OPS+) in 657 PA with 18 HR, 93 R, 76 RBI, 35 SB, and 3.9 WAR (including 0.8 dWAR) in 2008. The Dodgers improved slightly to 84–78, enough to win the NL West pennant by two games over Arizona. Kemp managed only two doubles in 13 PA in the Dodgers 3–0 sweep of the Cubs in the NLDS, but hit .333/.474/.400 in the 4–1 loss to the Phillies in the NLCS.

Kemp built on this success in 2009, hitting .297/.352/.490 (125 OPS+) with 26 HR, 97 R, 101 RBI, 34 SB, and 4.9 WAR in 667 PA. Although this was not sufficient to gain All-Star recognition, he did win Gold Glove and Silver Slugger awards and finished 10th in the voting for NL MVP. Thanks in large part to the performances of Kemp and 21-year-old Clayton Kershaw, who led the team with 4.9 and 4.7 WAR, respectively, the Dodgers won 95 games and edged Colorado (who won 92) for the NL West pennant. But the Dodgers were once again eliminated 4–1 by the Phillies in the NLCS after sweeping the Cardinals in the NLDS. Kemp hit a 2-R HR in the first inning to provide what turned out to be the winning margin in Game 1 of the NLDS, but got only one hit—a single—in his remaining 13 AB.[6] He hit another HR in the NLCS and hit .250/.286/.400 overall, but was not really a factor in the outcome of any game.

Big things were expected for Matt Kemp in 2010. Instead, his season was a hot mess. This was the year when Kemp dated pop star Rihanna and "went Hollywood."[7] He hit only .249/.310.450 (106 OPS+) in 668 PA. Although he played in every game and did manage to accrue 28 HR, 82 R, and 89 RBI, the value of his 19 SB was more than negated by his 15 times caught stealing. Worse still, his defense was godawful. His -3.5 dWAR (which drove his WAR down to -1.1—below replacement level) was more than just bad; it was the absolute worst of the 5388 defensive seasons in the entire history of MLB from 1871 to 2023 among those who played at least 60 percent of their games in CF.[8] If a major league center fielder ever had a worse defensive season than Kemp, he must either have been shifted to another position or to the bench before his dWAR could reach -3.5. Kemp was so bad that the Dodgers coaches and GM Ned Colletti publicly called him out for lack of effort.[9] While it is perhaps too facile to attribute Kemp's lackluster performance to the distractions of celebrity, like the overheated tabloid coverage of sightings of Kemp with Rihanna at LA's hottest night spots, there was certainly a perception among sportswriters, fans, and teammates that baseball was not Kemp's highest priority that year. Meanwhile, the Dodgers fell to fourth place at 80–82. Through it all, Kemp developed a reputation for moodiness and high-handedness with the press, which would prove difficult to overcome.

With the sour taste and dashed expectations of 2010 still lingering and his relationship with Rihanna now over, Kemp entered the 2011 season with a fresh determination to focus and improve.[10] The result was a Winfield-like season (circa 1979), in which he posted a NL-leading 8.0 WAR (Table 31).

Table 31: Selected Stats for Matt Kemp's Peak and Runner-Up Seasons and His Career*

Season	Age	PA	AVG	OBP	SLG	OPS+	TB	HR	R	RBI	SB	WAR (H)	dWAR
Peak 2011	26	689	0.324	0.399	0.586	**172**	**353**	39	**115**	**126**	40	**8.0**	-0.4
per 650 PA							333	37	108	119	38	7.5	-0.4
Runner-Up 2009	24	667	0.297	0.352	0.490	125	297	26	97	101	34	4.9	0.0
per 650 PA							289	25	95	98	33	4.8	0.0
Career (2006–220)		6983	0.284	0.337	0.484	121	3081	287	950	1031	184	21.4	-17.3
per 650 PA							287	27	88	96	17	2.0	-1.6

*League leading totals are shown in boldface type.

31. The Next Dave Winfield

Kemp played every game and led the NL in TB, HR, R, and RBI, as well as WAR, and threw in 40 SB (tied for third in the NL) for good measure. He also finished second to Ryan Braun in SLG and fourth in OBP. His best months were June (.375/.472/.796 with 9 HR, 18 R, and 23 RBI), September-October (.343/.419/.667 with 8 HR 28 R, and 24 RBI), April (.368/.446/.613 with 6 HR, 20 R, and 19 RBI), and August (.330/.400/.518 with 5 HR, 23 R, and 20 RBI).[11] But even in May and July, when he hit .253/.327/.495 and .274/.324/.453, respectively, he contributed a combined 11 HR, 26 R, and 40 RBI. He was elected for the first time to start in CF for the NL All-Stars and collected a hit and a walk in 3 PA and scored on a three-run fourth-inning HR, which gave the NL a 3–1 lead that they never relinquished.[12] At the end of the season, he received a Silver Slugger award and the Hank Aaron award as the top hitter in the NL.[13] He was also honored by his teammates with the Roy Campanella award, as the Dodgers' most inspirational player—which shows how far he had come in one year in the eyes of his teammates.[14] However, he finished a close second to Ryan Braun (388–332 points) in the MVP voting, perhaps because the Brewers had won the NL Central Division pennant while the Dodgers finished a weak third in the NL West.[15] This outcome became extremely controversial when Braun tested positive for PED after the vote had been taken.[16] An informal poll of 20 BBWAA voting members suggested that Kemp would have won the award easily if they could have held another vote after Braun's PED use became public.[17] Although Kemp did receive an undeserved Gold Glove award despite his -0.4 dWAR (perhaps because he had improved so much over the 2010 season), this was poor compensation for missing out on a well-deserved MVP award.[18] But Kemp did get compensated in November 2011 with a record-setting eight-year $160 M contract that he hoped would make him a Dodger for life.[19]

Entering his age 27 season, Kemp picked up right where he had left off in 2011. He hit a scorching .417/.490/.893 in 98 PA in April with 12 HR, 24 R, and 25 RBI—at least as good as any month of the 2011 season—and was unanimously elected NL Player of the Month.[20] However, he tailed off sharply during the first two weeks of May before a pulled hamstring ended his streak of 399 consecutive games on May 14. He spent the next two weeks on the disabled list, then aggravated the injury in the second game after his return, sending him to the disabled list for another eight weeks. He was again elected to start in the All-Star Game but could not play. He returned shortly after the All-Star break and finished with solid numbers, hitting .303/.367/.538 (147 OPS+) with 23 HR, 74 R, 69 RBI, 9 SB, and 2.8 WAR (which included -0.8 dWAR). It was a fine season, considering that he had missed 10 weeks, but the decline in

SB and dWAR suggested that he had lost some mobility. The Dodgers improved to 86–76, second in the NL West, but missed the postseason. Kemp had surgery on his left shoulder after the season.[21]

After so many seasons in which he hardly missed a game, Kemp experienced his second consecutive injury-plagued season in 2013. He missed most of June with a strained hamstring, another two weeks in July with a shoulder problem reportedly unrelated to his off-season surgery, and another six weeks in August-September after he injured his ankle on July 21 in a collision at home plate.[22] Although he returned from the ankle injury on September 16, he was used sparingly in the final two weeks of the season and missed the postseason when the ankle worsened and required surgery.[23] However, with the arrival of 22-year-old Cuban sensation Yasiel Puig on June 3, the Dodgers were beginning to wean themselves away from Kemp and won the NL West without him. Unlike 2012, when Kemp's prorated stats were quite strong, Kemp was ineffective when he was able to play. He hit .270/.328/.395 (104 OPS+) in 290 PA with only 6 HR, 35 R, 33 RBI, 9 SB, and 0.7 WAR. This was a far cry from what the Dodgers expected when Kemp signed his huge contract two years earlier—and they were still committed to six more years.

Kemp was healthy in 2014, and the offensive results were much better. He hit .287/.346/.506 (140 OPS+) with 25 HR, 77 R, 52 RBI, and 8 SB, but only 1.2 WAR. The problem was that his defense (-3.1 dWAR) deteriorated nearly to his 2010 level and made him an intolerable liability in CF. As the season went on, Yasiel Puig gradually took over in CF while Kemp was used mostly in the corner OF spots (59 G in RF, 44 G in LF, and 41 G in CF). On the brighter side, Kemp's 2014 postseason in 2014 was the best of his career, albeit in a losing cause. He hit .353/.353/.529 in 17 PA in the Dodgers' 3–1 NLDS loss to St. Louis. His eighth inning HR against Pat Neshek to break a 2–2 tie gave the Dodgers their only victory of the series.[24] Nevertheless, with Carl Crawford, Andre Ethier, Puig, and Joc Pederson on the roster, Matt Kemp, who was no longer the durable speedy centerfielder of 2008–11, had become expensive excess baggage. So, in what was intended primarily as a salary dump but turned out to be a very good trade, the Dodgers sent Kemp, Tim Federowicz, and $31 million to the Padres, for Yasmani Grandal, Zach Eflin, and Joe Wieland.[25]

Although he was still only 30 years old, Matt Kemp would never again come close to being the player he was in 2011. However, he remained a near-everyday player and a potent offensive force in 2015–2018, playing in 571 (88 percent) out of 648 possible games for three different teams, hitting .274/316/.472 (111 OPS+), and averaging 573 PA, 24 HR, 70 R, 89 RBI, 34 BB, 129 SO, 3 SB, and 0.1 WAR (including -2.1 dWAR) per season.

Although he still had excellent power, he rarely walked, he struck out often, and his speed and defense were gone. In a league that did not have the DH rule, Kemp was essentially a DH forced to play RF. He was traded twice during that time—to Atlanta in a July 2016 deadline deal and back to the Dodgers after the 2017 season. The first trade was an outright salary dump in which the Padres received Hector Olivera, who had been on the restricted list for domestic violence. Olivera was released immediately after the trade and never played another major league game.[26] Padres executive chairman Ron Fowler blasted Kemp publicly after the trade as selfish, lazy, and uninterested in improving.[27] The second trade was a more complicated exchange of two bad contracts—Kemp and Adrian Gonzalez.[28] Since the Dodgers won the NL West in 2018 and made it all the way to the World Series, Kemp got the opportunity to play in his fourth and final postseason. He was used sparingly and got only four hits, a walk, and a sacrifice fly in 25 PA. However one of his hits was a solo HR off Chris Sale at Fenway Park in Game 1 of the World Series.[29] The Red Sox won the game 8–4 and the Series 4–1.

After the 2018 season, the Dodgers traded Kemp to Cincinnati along with Puig, Kyle Farmer, Alex Wood, and cash for Homer Bailey and minor league prospects Josiah Gray and Jeter Downs. Kemp started slowly in 2019, fractured a rib in a collision with the wall, and was released in May after only 20 games. He signed a minor league contract with the Mets but was released in July after eight games without ever making it to New York. He signed with Colorado as a free agent for the pandemic-shortened 2020 season but hit only .239/.326/.419 (89 OPS+) in 132 PA, good for 0.1 WAR. That was the end of the line for Matt Kemp.

Why Was Matt Kemp a Shooting Star?

Matt Kemp is sometimes caricatured as a selfish player who was dazzled by the bright lights of Hollywood, got a big head, and squandered his considerable athletic gifts except for a single MVP-caliber season in 2011. While that description contains a grain of truth—at least regarding his lost 2010 season—it does not fairly describe the totality of his 15-year major league career (Figure 31).

If you give him a mulligan for 2010, he rapidly progressed from a promising 21-year-old rookie to a major star at age 26. Even in the worst of these five years, he rarely missed a game. It was the injuries he suffered to his hamstring, shoulder, and ankle in 2012–13—not bad character or laziness—that derailed him and permanently diminished

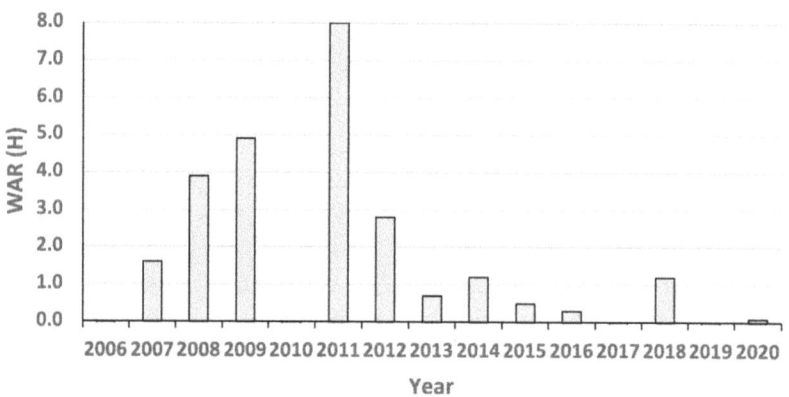

his natural speed and athleticism. Even then, he still managed to provide power and run production, despite no longer being able to run well or play even passable OF defense. Also, the portrayal of Kemp as self-centered is belied by stories of how he visited a young cancer victim in the stands or donated $1000 per home run to support victims of the tornadoes in Oklahoma in May 2013.[30]

Obviously, Kemp's career did not measure up to Winfield's, but their career arcs did have a few things in common. Like Kemp, Winfield began as an extremely athletic player with power, speed, and strong defense, although unlike Kemp, he never hit more than 37 HR or stole more than 26 bases in a season. Like Kemp, Winfield received a massive long term contract following his peak season (1979), and subsequently had to endure the public vitriol of a disappointed team owner, George Steinbrenner, who dubbed him "Mr. May" for not replicating Reggie Jackson's post-season heroics. Both players suffered steep defensive declines during the last half of their careers. Although Winfield never had < -2.6 dWAR in any season, his career dWAR (-22.2) was even worse than Kemp's (-17.3). But Winfield (who played a less demanding corner OF position) escaped criticism because he moved to DH in his last four seasons after his bad back immobilized him. Unfortunately for Kemp, injuries cut into his effectiveness far earlier in his career, and his defensive flaws could not be hidden at DH. Of course, Kemp had no one but himself to blame for his lackluster play in 2010, a season in the heart of his physical prime. But human beings are complicated and imperfect. We should, I think, be more forgiving of our athletic heroes when they disappoint our outsized expectations.

❖ 32 ❖

Wrap-Up

In the preceding thirty chapters, I have described the careers of a virtual all-star team of "shooting stars," whose stardom was concentrated in a single career year, in which (with a single exception) their WAR and/or their WAR per 650 PA (hitters) or 1000 BF (pitchers) exceeded 7.2. Typically, these players had solid but unspectacular careers (10–25 WAR) apart from their signature years. However, eight shooting stars—Cash (42.8), Porter (33.2), Brecheen (32.6), Smith (29.7), Dunlap (29.1), Petrocelli (29.1), Leonard (27.8), and Holmes (27.4)—had more than 25 WAR over the remainder of their long careers, albeit with no single season approaching their peak season. Eight others—Grabarkewitz (-0.7), Jones (0.6), Fidrych (1.7), Versalles (5.4), Wilkins (7.4), Prior (8.3), Giles (8.8), and Moore (9.3)—had < 10 WAR over the remainder of their careers and might be termed "one-year wonders."

Injuries often played a key role in the transience of the stardom of these thirty players. One does not have to search hard to find examples of pitchers who achieved stardom before age 25, only to suffer an early career-ending injury. Slim Jones, Mark Fidrych, and Mark Prior all fit this profile. There are far too many others like them to include in this book. For hitters—Grabarkewitz, Hamilton, Kemp, Rosen, Stone—the erosion of their skills after injuries was usually more gradual. Other shooting stars overcame early physical ailments to achieve stardom in their late 20s and 30s. Abernathy, Brecheen, Hiller, Moore, and Seymour (who converted from sore-armed pitcher to outfielder at age 28 and posted his career year at age 32) are the most notable examples. Bobby Shantz and Mark Eichhorn were hybrids; both overcame early arm troubles early on to achieve stardom as a starter and a multi-inning reliever, respectively, at age 25, then re-injured their arms and reinvented themselves as successful short relievers in their 30s.

Addiction to alcohol and/or drugs (especially cocaine) is another factor that curtailed the careers of some of our shooting stars. Josh

Hamilton, whose addictions delayed his arrival in the major leagues until age 26 and continued to plague him throughout his brief career until injuries eventually brought him down, and Dwight Gooden, who attained superstar status at age 20 but then turned to alcohol and cocaine, are the most prominent examples in this book. Addiction also played a prominent role in the career arcs of Slim Jones, Darrell Porter, and Lonnie Smith.

A prolonged minor league apprenticeship significantly shortened the careers of Harry Brecheen, Tommy Holmes, Al Rosen, Jim Gentile, and Hank Aguirre, who wasted many productive years in the minor leagues before receiving opportunities with their parent clubs. The extensive farm systems of 1935–60, which enabled teams like the Cardinals, Yankees, and Dodgers to hoard quality players in the minor leagues, and the limited number of major league opportunities before expansion—especially after integration enlarged the pool of available talent—kept players like these down and limited the length of their careers. Although Billy Grabarkewitz, who began his career after expansion but before free agency became an option, made it to the major leagues for good at age 24, the Dodgers' surplus of infield talent kept him in a utility role when he could have been starting at 2B for many other major league teams.

Of course, some shooting stars were not brought down by injuries, addiction, or lack of opportunity. Some—like Dunlap, Leonard, Ellsworth, Versalles, and Loaiza—did not seem emotionally equipped for the demands of stardom. And others—like Rick Wilkins and Marcus Giles—just fizzled for no apparent reason. Every shooting star had his own story.

You may wonder about many players who have not been included in this book. The following players each had a memorable "signature season" but do not qualify as shooting stars:

- Roger Maris's 61 HR in 1961 (6.9 WAR): His WAR was even better (7.5) in his 1960 MVP season.
- Jose Canseco's 42 HR and 40 SB in 1988 (7.3 WAR): His 7.3 WAR in 1998 was only 35 percent higher than his 5.4 WAR in 1990 and only 38 percent better than his 5.3 WAR in 1991.
- Denny McLain's 31 wins in 1968 (7.4 WAR): Although he won "only" 24 in 1969, his 8.1 WAR was even better than in 1968.
- Herb Score's 7.3 WAR 166 ERA+ season at age 23 in 1955: He had been almost as good—5.7 WAR and 141 ERA+ at age 22 in 1954. Then, in 1956, a Gil McDougald line drive struck him in the eye and ruined his career.

32. Wrap-Up

- Brady Anderson's 50 HR and 110 RBI in 1996 (6.9 WAR): Although his HR and RBI totals were clear outliers, Anderson had a long productive career, which included a 5.9 WAR season in 1999 and 5.2 WAR season in 1992.
- Chris Davis's 53 HR and 138 RBI in 2013 (7.1 WAR): His 7.1 WAR (6.9 per 650 PA) was a little light and only 45 percent better than his 4.9 WAR in 2015.
- Smokey Joe Wood's 34 wins and 10.1 WAR in 2012: Although he technically qualifies as a shooting star, he had just gone 23–17 with 5.3 WAR in 1911. Later, his pro-rated 8.5 WAR per 1000 BF (5.1 WAR in 600 BF) in 1915 was even better than his 7.6 pro-rated WAR per 1000 BF in his 1912 "peak" season.
- Dolf Luque's 27–8 season for Cincinnati in 1923 (10.7 WAR): His a 6.3-WAR 1925 season disqualifies him. Besides, Luque, who was MLB's first Hispanic superstar, was just too good for too long (including his pitching exploits in Cuba) to be called a shooting star.
- "Fernando-mania" in 1981 (4.8 WAR in 758 BF → 6.3 WAR per 1000 BF): Valenzuela's WAR, even when prorated to account for the strike-shortened 1981 season, was not high enough. Valenzuela had 5.4 WAR in 1985 and 1986.
- Ed Williamson's record-setting 27 HR in 1884 (6.3 WAR in 459 PA → 8.9 WAR per 650 PA): Williamson's HR record lasted for 35 years before Ruth broke it in 1919. The longevity of Williamson's record *exceeded* that of Ruth's 60 HR in 1927 by one year and fell only two years shy of Maris's 61 in 1961. However, Williamson's record was a mirage, created by a ground rule change that allowed pop flies over the 200 foot LF and RF fences of Chicago's tiny Lake Front Park, which would have been ground rule doubles in 1883, to count as home runs in 1884.[1] Without this assist from the change in ground rules, Williamson's 1884 season was not really much better than his 4.3 WAR in 375 PA (7.5 WAR per 650 PA) in 1882.

I was unable to include every qualified shooting star in this book. A non-exhaustive list (below) of shooting stars I left out is provided below. Players who were strongly suspected of PED use are marked by an asterisk (*).

- C: Art Wilson (1914), Tim McCarver (1967), Chris Hoiles (1993), Javy Lopez (2003)*
- 1B: Ted Kluszewski (1954), Cecil Fielder (1990)
- 2B: Randy Velarde (1999), Bret Boone (2001)*

- SS: Terry Turner (1906), Eddie Lake (1945), Ron Hansen (1964), John Valentin (1995), Rich Aurilia (2001)*
- 3B: Ezra Sutton (1884), Art Devlin (1906), Tommy Harper (1970), Ken Caminiti (1996),* Chone Figgins (2009)
- OF: Mike Greenwell (1988), Bernard Gilkey (1996), Nick Markakis (2008), Carlos Gomez (2013)
- SP: Billy Rhines (1890), Ed Reulbach (1905), George McQuillan (1908), Jack Coombs (1910), Reb Russell (1913), Fred Toney (1915), Guy Morton (1915), Cy Blanton (1935), Warren Hacker (1952), Bill Hands (1969), Larry Dierker (1969), Wayne Twitchell (1971), Mike Caldwell (1978), Britt Burns (1980), Justin Thompson (1997), Ben Sheets (2004), Dontrelle Willis (2005), Jair Jurrjens (2009), Ryan Minor (2019)
- RP: Jim Konstanty (1950), Jim Kern (1979), Willie Hernandez (1984)

The designation "shooting star" is inescapably subjective. Although I have laid out objective criteria, our degree of surprise at a player's sudden ascent to short-term stardom and our disappointment about their unanticipated sharp decline are shaped by the expectations we bring to the table as much as by what actually happened. Whatever heights a player achieved, we know that all stardom is transitory. Whether we are talking about Billy Grabarkewitz or Babe Ruth, everyone's star burns out in the end. In that sense, we are all shooting stars.

Glossary of Terms and Abbreviations

Term—Definition

1B—1. First Base. 2. A 1-base hit (or single).

2B—1. Second Base. 2. A 2-base hit (or double).

3B—1. Third Base. 2. A 3-base hit (or triple).

AA—1. American Association (1882–91). 2. Class Double-A in modern minor leagues.

AAA—Class Triple-A in modern minor leagues

AB—At-bats

AL—American League (1901–present)

ALCS—American League Championship Series

ALDS—American League Division Series

ANL—American Negro League (1929)

ASG—All-Star game. Held annually starting in 1933—two per year in 1959–62

AVG—Batting average (H/AB)

BB—Bases on balls (or walks)

BBWAA—Baseball Writers Association of America—votes on postseason awards and Hall of Fame

BF—Batters faced (by a pitcher)

C—Catcher

CF—1. Center field. 2. Defensive player positioned in center field.

CG—Complete games—team uses a single pitcher for entire game

CVI—Career Value Index—Metric used to rank player value

CYA—Cy Young Award (1956–present)—award recognizing best pitcher in each league

Glossary of Terms and Abbreviations

DH—Designated hitter (AL, 1973 to present)—batsman designated to hit in the pitcher's place

ECL—Eastern Colored League (1923–28)

ER—Earned run—run scored without the help of a fielding error

ERA—Earned run average = 9*ER/IP

ERA+—100 times the ratio of the league ERA to a pitcher's ballpark-adjusted ERA

EWL—East-West (Negro) League (1932)

FL—Federal League (1914–15)

GS—Games started

H—Base hits

H9—Hits allowed per 9 IP

HBP—Hit by pitch—batter awarded 1B

HGH—Human growth hormone

HOF—Baseball's National Hall of Fame in Cooperstown, NY

HR—Home runs

IBB—Intentional Bases on Balls

IP—Innings pitched (numbers 1 and 2 after decimal point refer to thirds of an inning)

L—Loss attributed to pitcher

LF—Left field

LG—League

MLB—Major League Baseball

MVP—Most Valuable Player in each league (1922–present)

NA—National Association (1871–75)—first professional baseball league

NAL—Negro American League (1937–48)

NL—National League (1876–present)

NLCS—National League Championship Series

NLDS—National League Division Series

NNL—Original Negro National League (1920–31)

NN2—Negro National League (1933–48)

NSL—Negro Southern League (1932)

OBP—On-base percentage—sum of H + BB + HBP divided by PA–SH

OF—Outfield

OPS—OBP + SLG

OPS+—100 times the ratio of the ballpark-adjusted OPS to the league average OPS

Glossary of Terms and Abbreviations

PA—Plate appearances

PED—Performance Enhancing Drugs (includes HGH as well as androgenic steroids)

PL—Players League (1890)

Pos—Primary position played

PTBN—Player to be named at a later date to complete a trade

QS—Quality Start, in which the starter pitches at least 6.0 innings and yields no more than 3 ER

R—Runs scored

RBI—Runs batted in

RF—Right field

RP—Relief pitcher

SABR—Society for American Baseball Research

SB—Stolen base

SH—Sacrifice hits

SHO—Shutouts—CG in which the opponent scores no runs

Slash Line—AVG/OBP/SLG

SLG—Slugging percentage—total bases divided by AB

SO—Strikeouts

SO9—Strikeouts per 9 IP

SP—Starting pitcher

SS—Shortstop

SV—Saves—counting stat for RP who close out winning games

TB—Total bases (= H + 2B + 3B * 2 + HR * 3)

UA—Union Association (1884)

VC—Veterans Committee (and various iterations)

W—Win attributed to pitcher.

WAR—Wins above replacement

WAR (H)—WAR as a non-pitcher (includes offense and defense, but is not simply oWAR + dWAR)

WAR (P)—WAR as a pitcher

dWAR—WAR as a defender

oWAR—WAR as a hitter

WHIP—The sum of H + BB given up by a pitcher divided by his IP

W-L—Won-Lost record attributed to a pitcher

WP—Wild pitch

WS—World Series

Chapter Notes

Chapter 1

1. Baseball-Reference.com, WAR Explained, https://www.baseball-reference.com/about/war_explained.shtml.
2. SABR Baseball Biography Project, https://sabr.org/bioproject.
3. BR Bullpen, Front Page Category: Player, https://www.baseball-reference.com/bullpen/Category:Player.
4. Baseball Player Profiles, http://baseball.playerprofiles.com/sampleSearch.asp.
5. Hall of Fame Library and Research Center, https://baseballhall.org/discover-more/education/research.
6. Baseball-Reference.com, https://www.baseball-reference.com/#site_menu_link. Stathead Baseball, https://stathead.com/baseball/.

Chapter 2

1. Fred Dunlap Death Certificate, Philadelphia, PA, No. 2956, December 1, 1902 (Clipping from Fred Dunlap's player file at the Baseball Hall of Fame Library). Note that the age (41) on Dunlap's death certificate is erroneous; he was born on May 21, 1859, making him 43 years old when he died.
2. Centers for Disease Control, Leading Causes of Death, 1900–1998, https://www.cdc.gov/nchs/data/dvs/lead1900_98.pdf. Life expectancy in the USA, 1900–98, https://u.demog.berkeley.edu/~andrew/1918/figure2.html.
3. Sam Crane, "The Fifty Greatest Players in History, No. 23: Fred Dunlap," *New York Journal*, January 30, 1912 (Clipping from Fred Dunlap's player file at the Baseball Hall of Fame Library). Robert Smith, "Of Kings and Commoners," in John Thorn, *The Complete Armchair Book of Baseball* (New York: Sterling, 1997), 762–764. Dennis Goldstein and Richard A. Puff, "Frederick C. Dunlap," in Joseph M. Overfield, Paul Adomites, Richard Puff, and L. Robert Davids, *Nineteenth Century Stars* (Phoenix: Society for American Baseball Research, 2012), 82–83 (Clipping from Fred Dunlap's player file at the Baseball Hall of Fame Library). Wikipedia, Fred Dunlap, https://en.wikipedia.org/wiki/Fred_Dunlap#cite_note-DFP4-17. Unattributed, "Fred Dunlap: Biography," https://fampeople.com/cat-fred-dunlap_4.
4. Baseball-Reference.com, Union Association, https://www.baseball-reference.com/bullpen/Union_Association.
5. Wikipedia, Union Association, https://en.wikipedia.org/wiki/Union_Association.
6. Baseball Almanac, Hit for the Cycle, https://www.baseball-almanac.com/hitting/Major_League_Baseball_Players_to_hit_for_the_cycle.shtml (Clipping from Fred Dunlap's player file at the Baseball Hall of Fame Library).
7. "Dunlap for Detroit: The Famous Player Secured by President Marsh," *Detroit Free Press*, August 7, 1886.
8. "Dunlap on His Mettle," *New York Times*, November 17, 1987.
9. "Dunlap Released by Pittsburg,"

Detroit Free Press (quoting from article in *Pittsburg Dispatch*), May 17, 1890.

10. Bill James, *The New Bill James Historical Baseball Abstract* (New York: Free Press, 2001), 21–34.

11. James, *The New Bill James Historical Baseball Abstract*, 530.

12. "The Union Association—Is It a Major League?" Mighty Casey Baseball, April 1, 2018, https://mightycaseybaseball.com/2018/04/01/the-union-association-is-it-a-major-league/.

13. Goldstein and Puff, "Frederick C. Dunlap," 82–83.

Chapter 3

1. Bill Kirwin, "Cy Seymour," https://sabr.org/bioproj/person/Cy-Seymour/. Adapted from a chapter in Tom Simon, *Deadball Stars of the National League* (Cleveland: Society for American Baseball Research, 2004), 239–242.

2. Kirwin, "Cy Seymour."

3. David J. Gordon, "The Rise and Fall of the Deadball Era," *Baseball Research Journal* 47, no. 2 (Fall 2018): 92–102.

4. "Cy Seymour's Iron Man," Unattributed interview with John McGraw, circa 1917–19, (Clipping from Cy Seymour's player file at the Baseball Hall of Fame Library).

5. Kirwin, "Cy Seymour."

6. Stathead Baseball, Player Batting Season and Career Stats Finder 1903–1909, https://stathead.com/baseball/player-batting-season-finder.cgi?request=1&order_by=b_rbi&year_min=1903&year_max=1909.

7. Baseball-Reference.com, Yearly League Leaders & Records for Batting Average, https://www.baseball-reference.com/leaders/batting_avg_leagues.shtml.

8. Stathead Baseball, Cy Seymour Player Batter Split Finder, 1905 Season by Month, https://stathead.com/baseball/split_finder.cgi?request=1&order_by_asc=1&order_by=Name&player_id=seymocy01&year_min=1905&year_max=1905&split_1=dates%3Amonth&class=player&type=b.

9. Kirwin, "Cy Seymour."

10. Kirwin, "Cy Seymour."

11. Kirwin, "Cy Seymour."

12. David J. Gordon, "Using Career Value Index (CVI) to Evaluate Hall of Fame Credentials of Negro League Players," *Baseball Research Journal* 51, no. 2 (Fall 2022): 112–21.

Chapter 4

1. Baseball-Reference.com, Yearly League Leaders & Records for Batting Average, https://www.baseball-reference.com/leaders/batting_avg_leagues.shtml.

2. John McMurray, "George Stone," https://sabr.org/bioproj/person/George-Stone-2/. Adapted from a chapter in David Jones, *Deadball Stars of the American League* (Cleveland: Society for American Baseball Research, 2004), 786–87.

3. Baseball-Reference.com, George Stone, https://www.baseball-reference.com/players/s/stonege01.shtml, *Clinton Herald*, January 6, 1945, Deaths—George Stone (Letter from George Stone's player file at the Baseball Hall of Fame Library).

4. McMurray, "George Stone."

5. Frank Parker, "Crouches at Bat," *St. Louis Globe-Dispatch*, November 3, 1906 (Clipping from George Stone's player file at the Baseball Hall of Fame Library).

6. McMurray, "George Stone."

7. Stathead Baseball, George Stone Player Batting Split Finder 1906, https://stathead.com/baseball/split_finder.cgi?request=1&order_by_asc=1&order_by=Name&player_id=stonege01&year_min=1906&year_max=1906&split_1=dates%3Amonth&class=player&type=b.

8. "Stone's Belief Is That a Player Should Retire While Still Young," *The Sporting Life*, October 6, 1906 (Clipping from George Stone's player file at the Baseball Hall of Fame Library).

9. Stathead Baseball, Player Batting Season & Career Stats Finder AL of 1907, sorted by WAR, https://stathead.com/baseball/player-batting-season-finder.cgi?request=1&order_by=b_war&year_min=1907&year_max=1907&positions%5B%5D=13&games_prop=50&comp_id%5B%5D=AL.

10. McMurray, "George Stone."

11. Stathead Baseball, Player Game Stats Finder, George Stone 1909, https://stathead.com/baseball/player-batting-game-finder.cgi?request=1&order_by_asc=1&order_by=date&player_id=-

stone-003geo&year_min=1909&year_max=1909.
12. McMurray, "George Stone."

Chapter 5

1. David Jones, "Dutch Leonard," https://sabr.org/bioproj/person/Dutch-Leonard/.
2. Baseball-Reference.com, 1914 American League Statistics, https://www.baseball-reference.com/leagues/AL/1914.shtml.
3. Stathead Baseball, Dutch Leonard 1914 Player Pitching Game Stats Finder, https://stathead.com/baseball/player-pitching-game-finder.cgi?request=1&match=player_game&order_by_asc=1&order_by=date&player_id_hint=Dutch+Leonard&player_id_select=Dutch+Leonard&player_id=leonar001hub&year_min=1914&year_max=1914&comp_type=reg&team_game_min=1&team_game_max=165&player_game_min=1&player_game_max=9999&is_pitcher=1&role=GS&days_rest_comp=%3D&location=pob&locationMatch=is&min_temperature=0&max_temperature=120&min_wind_speed=0&max_wind_speed=90.
4. Jones, "Dutch Leonard."
5. Baseball-Reference.com, 1915 World Series Game 3, Phillies at Red Sox, October 11, https://www.baseball-reference.com/boxes/BOS/BOS191510110.shtml.
6. Baseball-Reference.com, St. Louis Browns vs Boston Red Sox Box Score, August 30, 1916, https://www.baseball-reference.com/boxes/BOS/BOS191608300.shtml.
7. Baseball-Reference.com, 1916 World Series Game 4, Red Sox at Robins, October 11, https://www.baseball-reference.com/boxes/BRO/BRO191610110.shtml.
8. Wikipedia, Spitball, https://en.wikipedia.org/wiki/Spitball.
9. Jones, "Dutch Leonard."
10. Jones, "Dutch Leonard."
11. Bob Broeg, "Solace for Hall in Cobb Case," *The Sporting News*, May 12, 1973 (Clipping from Dutch Leonard's player file at the Baseball Hall of Fame Library).

12. AKC Mitchell, "The Sensational Outburst of Pitcher Hubert Leonard Elicits a Prompt, Complete and Crushing Answer from President Lannin," June 5, 1915 (Clipping from Dutch Leonard's player file at the Baseball Hall of Fame Library). Jones, "Dutch Leonard." Ian S. Kahanowitz, *Baseball Gods in Scandal: Ty Cobb, Tris Speaker, and the Dutch Leonard Affair* (South Orange, NJ: Summer Game Books, 2019). Broeg, "Solace for Hall in Cobb Case." Jerome Holtzman, "Cobb and Speaker got themselves into a real fix," *Chicago Tribune*, May 21, 1989, https://www.chicagotribune.com/news/ct-xpm-1989-05-21-8902030567-story.html. Lowell L. Blaisdell, "The Cobb-Speaker Scandal: Exonerated but Probably Guilty," *NINE: A Journal of Baseball History and Culture* 13, no. 2, February 21, 2005, https://www.deepdyve.com/lp/university-of-nebraska-press/the-cobb-speaker-scandal-exonerated-but-probably-guilty-m0S1E5GG6s.
13. "H.B. Leonard, Ex-Baseball Great, is Dead," July 11, 1952 (Clipping from Dutch Leonard's player file at the Baseball Hall of Fame Library).
14. Baseball-Reference.com, 1914 Boston Red Sox Statistics, https://www.baseball-reference.com/teams/BOS/1914.shtml.
15. Joseph Simenic, December 13, 1968 (Letter from Dutch Leonard's player file at the Baseball Hall of Fame Library).

Chapter 6

1. Fred Gluckstein, "Wilcy Moore," https://sabr.org/bioproj/person/Wilcy-Moore/.
2. Leo Trachtenberg, "Moore Blazed the Trail for Yankee Firemen," *Yankees Magazine*, September 3, 1987, 37–39 (Clipping from Wilcy Moore's player file at the Baseball Hall of Fame Library). Gluckstein, "Wilcy Moore."
3. Stathead Baseball, Wilcy Moore Player Split Finder by Role 1927, https://stathead.com/baseball/split_finder.cgi?request=1&order_by_asc=0&order_by=SO&player_id=moorewi01&year_min=1927&year_max=1927&split_1=ro

le%3Asprel&class=player&type=p&sr_pitching_splits_output=view_pitching.

4. Stathead Baseball, Wilcy Moore Pitching Game Stats Finder 1927 Role = Starter, https://stathead.com/baseball/player-pitching-game-finder.cgi?request=1&player_id=moore-022wil&year_min=1927&year_max=1927&role=GS.

5. Stathead Baseball, Wilcy Moore Player Split Finder by Role 1927, https://stathead.com/baseball/player-pitching-game-finder.cgi?request=1&player_id=moore-022wil&year_min=1927&year_max=1927.

6. Stathead Baseball, Wilcy Moore Pitching Game Stats Finder 1927 Role = Reliever, https://stathead.com/baseball/player-pitching-game-finder.cgi?request=1&player_id=moore-022wil&year_min=1927&year_max=1927&role=noGS.

7. Baseball-Reference.com, 1927 World Series New York Yankees over Pittsburgh Pirates (4–0), https://www.baseball-reference.com/postseason/1927_WS.shtml.

8. Trachtenberg, "Moore Blazed the Trail for Yankee Firemen."

9. Ken Tingley, "Wilcy Moore: The Missing Link of the 1927 Yankees," *Oreonta Daily Star*, September 21, 1985 (Clipping from Wilcy Moore's player file at the Baseball Hall of Fame Library).

10. "Famed Yank Reliever of '27, Dies at 65," *New York Times*, April 1, 1963 (Clipping from Wilcy Moore's player file at the Baseball Hall of Fame Library).

11. Baseball-Reference.com, 1932 World Series Game 4, Yankees at Cubs, October 2, https://www.baseball-reference.com/boxes/CHN/CHN193210020.shtml.

12. Tyler Kepner, "Holtzman, Creator of the Save Rule, Dies at 82," *New York Times*, July 21, 2008. Baseball-Refernce.com, 1927 American League Team Statistics, https://www.baseball-reference.com/leagues/AL/1928.shtml.

Chapter 7

1. Frederick C. Bush, "Slim Jones," (https://sabr.org/bioproj/person/slim-jones/. I have followed Bush in spelling his name Stewart, rather than Stuart. Johnny Goodtimes, "The Tragedy of Slim Jones," *Philly Sports History*, May 13, 2011, https://phillysportshistory.com/2011/05/13/the-tragedy-of-slim-jones/.

2. John Holway, "Slim Strasburg," May 2010 (Clipping from Slim Jones's player file at the Baseball Hall of Fame Library).

3. Baseball-Reference.com, 1934 Negro National League II Team Statistics, https://www.baseball-reference.com/leagues/NN2/1934.shtml. The numbers in the standings don't match the numbers of wins and losses in the team pitching totals. For example, the standings show the Philadelphia Stars with 39 wins, 18 losses and 10 ties in 67 games. The pitching totals on the team page show 46 wins and 22 losses (68 games). First- and second-half standings are not provided. No box scores or team schedules are provided as primary sources.

4. Frederick C. Bush, "Stewart 'Slim' Jones," Chapter 17 in Frederick C. Bush and Bill Nowlin, *The Stars Shone on Philadelphia: The 1934 Negro National League Champions* (Phoenix: Society for American Baseball Research, 2023), 101–108.

5. Bush, "Stewart 'Slim' Jones."

6. Lawrence H. Hogan, *Shades of Glory* (Washington, D.C.: National Geographic, 2006), 267–268. James Overmyer, "September 9, 1934, Satchel Paige and Slim Jones Throw Head-to-Head Pitching Gems," Chapter 32 of Frederick C. Bush and Bill Nowlin, *The Stars Shone on Philadelphia: The 1934 Negro National League Champions* (Phoenix: Society for American Baseball Research, 2023), 218–220.

7. Jim Croce, "You Don't Mess Around with Jim," https://www.azlyrics.com/lyrics/jimcroce/youdontmessaroundwithjim.html.

8. Goodtimes, "The Tragedy of Slim Jones."

9. Holway, "Slim Strasburg."

10. Bush, "Slim Jones."

11. *Pittsburgh Courier* Poll of Greatest Black Players, 1952, http://johndonaldson.bravehost.com/a.html.

Chapter 8

1. Saul Wisnia, "Tommy Holmes," https://sabr.org/bioproj/person/Tommy-Holmes/.
2. Wisnia, "Tommy Holmes."
3. Jack McCarthy, "How They Loved Tommy," *Boston Herald*, July 30, 1978 (Clipping from Tommy Holmes's player file at the Baseball Hall of Fame Library).
4. Hy Hurwitz, "Holmes Another Foxx in Miniature," *Boston Sunday Globe*, January 11, 1942 (Clipping from Tommy Holmes's player file at the Baseball Hall of Fame Library).
5. Wisnia, "Tommy Holmes."
6. Wisnia, "Tommy Holmes."
7. Wisnia, "Tommy Holmes."
8. Stathead Baseball, Tommy Holmes Player Batting Split Finder 1945 by Month, https://stathead.com/baseball/split_finder.cgi?request=1&order_by_asc=1&order_by=Name&player_id=holmeto01&year_min=1945&year_max=1945&split_1=dates%3Amonth&class=player&type=b.
9. Baseball-Reference.com, Career Leaders & Records for AB per SO, https://www.baseball-reference.com/leaders/at_bats_per_strikeout_career.shtml.
10. David J. Gordon, "Using Career Value Index (CVI) to Evaluate Hall of Fame Credentials of Negro League Players," *Baseball Research Journal* 51, no. 2 (Fall 2022): 112–21.
11. Baseball-Reference.com, Single-Season Leaders & Records for AB per SO, https://www.baseball-reference.com/leaders/at_bats_per_strikeout_season.shtml.
12. Baseball-Reference.com, 1948 All Star Game Box Score, July 13, https://www.baseball-reference.com/allstar/1948-allstar-game.shtml.
13. Baseball-Reference.com, 1948 World Series Game 1, Indians at Braves, October 6, https://www.baseball-reference.com/boxes/BSN/BSN194810060.shtml.
14. Wisnia, "Tommy Holmes."
15. Edward Burns, "Southworth Quits Boston; Name Holmes," *Chicago Tribune*, June 20, 1951 (Clipping from Tommy Holmes's player file at the Baseball Hall of Fame Library).
16. "Grimm Back in Majors; Replaces Holmes as Braves' Pilot Today," *Chicago Tribune* (Associated Press), June 1, 1952 (Clipping from Tommy Holmes's player file at the Baseball Hall of Fame Library).
17. Wisnia, "Tommy Holmes."
18. Richard Goldstein, "Tommy Holmes, 91, Who Set NL Hitting Mark, Is Dead," *New York Times*, April 15, 2008 (Clipping from Tommy Holmes's player file at the Baseball Hall of Fame Library). Laura Albanese, "Tommy Holmes, 91, Held NL Hit Streak Record," *Newsday*, April 15, 2008 (Clipping from Tommy Holmes's player file at the Baseball Hall of Fame Library).

Chapter 9

1. Baseball-Reference.com, 1940 Minor League Affiliates, https://www.baseball-reference.com/register/affiliate.cgi?year=1940.
2. Gregory H. Wolf, "Harry Brecheen," https://sabr.org/bioproj/person/harry-brecheen/.
3. Bob Broeg, "Keep Your Eye on the Cat," *Sport Magazine*, October 1947.
4. J. Roy Stockton, "Lefty Brecheen Meshes into Cardinals Machine," *The Sporting News*, July 1, 1943 (Clipping from Harry Brecheen's player file at the Baseball Hall of Fame Library).
5. Broeg, "Keep Your Eye on the Cat."
6. Red Smith, "Views of Sport: The Cat of the Cardinals," *New York Herald Tribune*, May 1948 (Clipping from Harry Brecheen's player file at the Baseball Hall of Fame Library).
7. Baseball-Reference.com, 1946 World Series Game 7, Red Sox at Cardinals, October 15, https://www.baseball-reference.com/boxes/SLN/SLN194610150.shtml.
8. Wolf, "Harry Brecheen."
9. Stathead Baseball, Harry Brecheen 1948 Player Pitching Game Stats Finder, https://stathead.com/baseball/player-pitching-game-finder.cgi?request=1&match=player_game&order_by_asc=1&order_by=date&player_id_hint=Harry+Brecheen&player_id_select=Harry+Brecheen&player_id=breche001har&year_min=1948&year_max=1948&comp_type=reg&team_game_min=1&team_game_max=165&player_game_

min=1&player_game_max=9999&is_pitcher=1&role=GS&days_rest_comp=%3D&location=pob&locationMatch=is&min_temperature=0&max_temperature=120&min_wind_speed=0&max_wind_speed=90.

10. Stathead Baseball, Harry Brecheen 1948 Player Pitching Game Stats Finder.

11. Ray Gillespie, "The Cat in Middle of St. Louis Rhubarb," *The Sporting News*, November 5, 1952 (Clipping from Harry Brecheen's player file at the Baseball Hall of Fame Library).

12. John Steadman, "Brecheen Big Brother to Orioles Hurlers," *The Sporting News*, October 26, 1961 (Clipping from Harry Brecheen's player file at the Baseball Hall of Fame Library).

13. Richard Goldstein, "Harry Brecheen, 89, Pitcher with 3 Victories in '46 Series," *New York Times*, January 20, 2004 (Clipping from Harry Brecheen's player file at the Baseball Hall of Fame Library).

Chapter 10

1. Mel Marmer, "Bobby Shantz," https://sabr.org/bioproj/person/Bobby-Shantz/. John M. Ross, "Mighty Mite of the A's," 1952 (Clipping from Bobby Shantz's player file at the Baseball Hall of Fame Library).

2. Marmer, "Bobby Shantz."

3. Marmer, "Bobby Shantz."

4. Dirk Lammers, "May 6, 1949: Bobby Shantz Tosses 9 No-Hit Innings in Relief for A's," SABR, https://sabr.org/gamesproj/game/may-6-1949-bobby-shantz-tosses-9-no-hit-innings-in-relief-for-as/.

5. Baseball-Reference.com, 1952 All-Star Game Box Score, July 8, https://www.baseball-reference.com/allstar/1952-allstar-game.shtml.

6. Baseball-Reference.com, 1952 Awards Voting, https://www.baseball-reference.com/awards/awards_1952.shtml#all_AL_MVP_voting.

7. Stathead Baseball, Player Pitching Stats Game Finder Bobby Shantz Starts 1952, https://stathead.com/baseball/player-pitching-game-finder.cgi?request=1&order_by_asc=1&order_by=date&player_id=shantz001rob&year_min=1952&year_max=1952&role=GS.

8. Stathead Baseball, Bobby Shantz Player Pitching Split Finder 1952 by Month, https://stathead.com/baseball/split_finder.cgi?request=1&order_by_asc=0&order_by=SO&player_id=shantbo01&year_min=1952&year_max=1952&split_1=dates%3Amonth&class=player&type=p&sr_pitching_splits_output=view_pitching.

9. Stathead Baseball, Bobby Shantz Player Pitching Split Finder 1953 by Month, https://stathead.com/baseball/split_finder.cgi?request=1&order_by_asc=0&order_by=year_game&player_id=shantbo01&year_min=1953&year_max=1953&split_1=dates%3Amonth&class=player&type=p&sr_pitching_splits_output=view_pitching.

10. Marmer, "Bobby Shantz."

11. Stathead Baseball, Bobby Shantz Player Pitching Split Finder 1957 by Month, https://stathead.com/baseball/split_finder.cgi?request=1&order_by_asc=0&order_by=year_game&player_id=shantbo01&year_min=1957&year_max=1957&split_1=dates%3Amonth&class=player&type=p&sr_pitching_splits_output=view_pitching.

12. Baseball-Reference, 1957 World Series Milwaukee Braves Over New York Yankees (4–3), https://www.baseball-reference.com/postseason/1957_WS.shtml.

13. Baseball-Reference, 1960 World Series Game 7, https://www.baseball-reference.com/boxes/PIT/PIT196010130.shtml.

14. Yankee Scorebook, 1977, "Where Are They Today? Bobby Shantz" (Clipping from Bobby Shantz's player file at the Baseball Hall of Fame Library).

Chapter 11

1. Stathead Baseball, Player Batting Season & Career Finder, 3B Sorted by Descending WAR, https://stathead.com/baseball/player-batting-season-finder.cgi?request=1&order_by=b_war&positions%5B%5D=5&games_prop=50,

2. Ralph Berger, "Al Rosen," https://sabr.org/bioproj/person/Al-Rosen/.

3. Berger, "Al Rosen."

4. Baseball-Reference.com, Cleveland Indians vs Boston Red Sox Box Score:

August 19, 1952, https://www.baseball-reference.com/boxes/BOS/BOS195208190.shtml.

5. Hal Lebovitz, "Majeski on Third," *Cleveland Plain Dealer*, August 20, 1952 (Clipping from Al Rosen's player file at the Baseball Hall of Fame Library).

6. Baseball-Reference.com, 1953 Awards Voting, https://www.baseball-reference.com/awards/awards_1953.shtml#all_AL_MVP_voting.

7. Richard Goldstein, "Al Rosen, Who Missed Triple Crown by a Step, Dies at 91," *New York Times*, March 14, 2015 (Clipping from Al Rosen's player file at the Baseball Hall of Fame Library).

8. Stathead Baseball, Player Batting Split Finder Al Rosen 1953 by Month, https://stathead.com/baseball/split_finder.cgi?request=1&order_by_asc=1&order_by=Name&player_id=rosenal01&year_min=1953&year_max=1953&split_1=dates%3Amonth&class=player&type=b,

9. Stathead Baseball, Player Batting Split Finder Al Rosen 1954 by Month, https://stathead.com/baseball/split_finder.cgi?request=1&order_by_asc=1&order_by=HR&player_id=rosenal01&year_min=1954&year_max=1954&split_1=dates%3Amonth&class=player&type=b.

10. Stathead Baseball, Player Batting Game Finder Al Rosen 1954, https://stathead.com/baseball/player-batting-game-finder.cgi?request=1&order_by_asc=1&order_by=date&player_id=-rosen-001alb&year_min=1954&year_max=1954. Goldstein, "Al Rosen, Who Missed Triple Crown by a Step, Dies at 91."

11. Baseball-Reference.com, 1954 All-Star Game Box Score, July 13, https://www.baseball-reference.com/allstar/1954-allstar-game.shtml.

12. Baseball-Reference.com, 1954 World Series New York Giants over Cleveland Indians (4–3), https://www.baseball-reference.com/postseason/1954_WS.shtml.

13. "Rosen of Indians Quits Baseball; 'I Can't Do Job Anymore,'" United Press International, January 31, 1957 (Clipping from Al Rosen's player file at the Baseball Hall of Fame Library).

14. Berger, "Al Rosen."

15. "Plunges to Death," Associated Press, March 6, 1971 (Clipping from Al Rosen's player file at the Baseball Hall of Fame Library).

16. Stephanie Storm, "Competitive Streak Still Burning in Al Rosen," *Akron Beacon-Journal*, February 29, 2004 (Clipping from Al Rosen's player file at the Baseball Hall of Fame Library).

17. Berger, "Al Rosen."

18. Berger, "Al Rosen."

19. Jimmy Keenan, "Billy Martin," https://sabr.org/bioproj/person/Billy-Martin/.

20. Baseball-Reference.com, 1978 New York Yankees Schedule, https://www.baseball-reference.com/teams/NYY/1978-schedule-scores.shtml.

21. Jane Gross, "Al Rosen Resigns Post with Yanks," *New York Times*, September 20, 1979 (Clipping from Al Rosen's player file at the Baseball Hall of Fame Library).

22. "Rosen Authorized Bad Credit in Loss by Four Casinos," Associated Press, November 1980 (Clipping from Al Rosen's player file at the Baseball Hall of Fame Library).

23. Goldstein, "Al Rosen, Who Missed Triple Crown by a Step, Dies at 91."

24. "Rosen Promises Giant Overhaul," *Albany Times Union* (Associated Press), September 19, 1985 (Clipping from Al Rosen's player file at the Baseball Hall of Fame Library).

25. Bill Lubinger, "Indians' Great Al Rosen on Anti-Semitism: 'I Had Broad Shoulders,'" *Cleveland Plain Dealer*, October 11, 2010 (Clipping from Al Rosen's player file at the Baseball Hall of Fame Library).

Chapter 12

1. Corey Stolzenbach, "Jim Gentile," SABR Biography, https://sabr.org/bioproj/person/Jim-Gentile/.

2. Stolzenbach, "Jim Gentile."

3. Stolzenbach, "Jim Gentile."

4. Stolzenbach, "Jim Gentile."

5. Stathead Baseball, Jim Gentile Player Batting Split Finder 1960 by Month, https://stathead.com/baseball/split_finder.cgi?request=1&order_by_asc=1&order_by=Name&player_id=gentiji01&year_min=1960&year_max

=1960&split_1=dates%3Amonth&class=player&type=b.

6. "Gentile Hits Two Grand Slam Homers in Row!" *Chicago Tribune*, May 10, 1961 (Clipping from Jim Gentile's player file at the Baseball Hall of Fame Library). "Jim Gentile Tees Off and Joins Babe Ruth," *Orioles Journal*, July 8, 1961 (Clipping from Jim Gentile's player file at the Baseball Hall of Fame Library).

7. Stathead Baseball, Jim Gentile Player Batting Split Finder 1961 by Month, https://stathead.com/baseball/split_finder.cgi?request=1&order_by_asc=1&order_by=Name&player_id=gentiji01&year_min=1961&year_max=1961&split_1=dates%3Amonth&class=player&type=b.

8. Baseball-Reference.com, 1961 All-Star Game Box Score, July 11, https://www.baseball-reference.com/allstar/1961-allstar-game-1.shtml.

9. Stolzenbach, "Jim Gentile."

10. Larry Klein, "How Good Can Jim Gentile Get?" *Sport Magazine*, 1961 (Clipping from Jim Gentile's player file at the Baseball Hall of Fame Library).

11. Baseball-Reference.com, 1962 All-Star Game Box Score, July 10, https://www.baseball-reference.com/allstar/1962-allstar-game-1.shtml.

12. Stolzenbach, "Jim Gentile."

13. Doug Brown, "Orioles Expect Siebern to Add Hustle and Spark," *Baltimore Sun*, December 7, 1963 (Clipping from Jim Gentile's player file at the Baseball Hall of Fame Library).

14. Joe McGuff, "'Now A's Have Best 1–2 Punch in Gentile, Rocky,' Says Friday," *Kansas City Star*, December 7, 1963 (Clipping from Jim Gentile's player file at the Baseball Hall of Fame Library).

15. John Wilson, "Bat-Tosser Gentile Headed for Minors, Fights Back Tears," *Houston*, June 25, 1966 (Clipping from Jim Gentile's player file at the Baseball Hall of Fame Library).

16. Stolzenbach, "Jim Gentile."

17. Dennis Lustig, "Whatever Happened to Jim Gentile?" August 12, 1970 (Clipping from Jim Gentile's player file at the Baseball Hall of Fame Library). Stolzenbach, "Jim Gentile."

Chapter 13

1. Maxwell Kates, "Norm Cash," SABR Biography, https://sabr.org/bioproj/person/norm-cash/.

2. Kates, "Norm Cash." Note: Baseball-Reference.com lists his birth year as 1933, but the Kates biography and the articles in Cash's player file at the Baseball Hall of Fame Library list it as 1934.

3. Joe Falls, "Detroit's Ready Cash," *Saturday Evening Post*, May 19, 1962 (Clipping from Norm Cash's player file at the Baseball Hall of Fame Library).

4. Baseball-Reference.com, 1961 Detroit Tigers Schedule, https://www.baseball-reference.com/teams/DET/1961-schedule-scores.shtml.

5. Baseball-Reference.com, Norm Cash 1961 Game Log, https://www.baseball-reference.com/players/gl.fcgi?t=b&id=cashno01&year=1961&__hstc=205977932.3724889d1bee9dd31d9ca321db6a8db4.1647277489371.1657395798122.1657485590178.34&__hssc=205977932.3.1657485590178&__hsfp=1191625704#-248-251-sum.

6. Baseball-Reference.com, 1961 Detroit Tigers Schedule.

7. Baseball-Reference.com, 1962 Detroit Tigers Schedule, https://www.baseball-reference.com/teams/DET/1962-schedule-scores.shtml.

8. Kates, "Norm Cash."

9. Baseball-Reference.com, 1968 Detroit Tigers Schedule, https://www.baseball-reference.com/teams/DET/1968-schedule-scores.shtml. See box scores for July 24–29.

10. Stathead Baseball, Norm Cash Player Batting Split Finder—1968 Monthly Stats, https://stathead.com/baseball/split_finder.cgi?request=1&match=season&order_by_asc=1&order_by=batting_avg&player_id_hint=Norm+Cash&player_id_select=Norm+Cash&player_id=cashno01&year_min=1968&year_max=1968&split_1=dates%3Amonth&split_total_comp=gt&class=player&type=b&age_min=0&age_max=99&season_start=1&season_end=-1&location=pob&locationMatch=is.

11. Baseball-Reference.com, 1968 World Series, Detroit Tigers Over St. Louis Cardinals (4–3), https://www.

baseball-reference.com/postseason/ 1968_WS.shtml.

12. Baseball-Reference.com, 1972 ALCS, Oakland Athletics Over Detroit Tigers (3–2), https://www.baseball-reference.com/postseason/1972_ALCS.shtml.

13. Detroit Tigers press release, July 28, 1973 (Clipping from Norm Cash's player file at the Baseball Hall of Fame Library).

14. Jim Hawkins, "Devalued Cash Rejects Over-Hill Tag," *Detroit Free Press*, April 13, 1974 (Clipping from Norm Cash's player file at the Baseball Hall of Fame Library).

15. Kates, "Norm Cash."

16. This Day in Baseball, Norm Cash Stats and Facts, https://thisdayinbaseball.com/norm-cash-page/.

17. Jim Hawkins, "Cash Undergoes Tests After Suffering a Stroke," *Detroit Free Press*, July 17, 1979 (Clipping from Norm Cash's player file at the Baseball Hall of Fame Library).

18. Kates, "Norm Cash."

19. Norm Cash Obituary, *Newark Star-Ledger*, October 13, 1986 (Clipping from Norm Cash's player file at the Baseball Hall of Fame Library).

20. Baseball-Reference.com, 1B JAWS Leaders, https://www.baseball-reference.com/leaders/jaws_1B.shtml.

21. David J Gordon, "Using Career Value Index (CVI) to Evaluate Hall of Fame Credentials of Negro League Players," *Baseball Research Journal* 51, no. 2 (Fall 2022): 112–121.

22. Stathead Baseball, Player Batting Season and Career Stats Finder, 1961–69, https://stathead.com/baseball/player-batting-season-finder.cgi?request=1&match=player_season_combined&order_by_asc=0&order_by=b_hr&year_min=1961&year_max=1969&comp_type=reg&exactness=anymarked&games_min_max=min&minpasVal=502&mingamesVal=100&ccomp%5B1%5D=gt&cval%5B1%5D=180&cstat%5B1%5D=b_hr&season_start=1&season_end=-1&weight_min=0&weight_max=500&location=pob&location Match=is&date_type=dob&date_comp=%3D&month_val=0&day_val=0&year_val=0&num_franchises_comp=gt&all_stars_comp=g.t

23. Dan Holmes, "Did the Corked Bat Help Norm Cash?" *VintageDetroit*, December 4, 2019, https://www.vintagedetroit.com/did-the-corked-bat-help-norm-cash/.

24. Norm Cash Obituary, *Newark Star-Ledger*.

Chapter 14

1. Joe Falls, "Aguirre Always Delivered in Life," *USA Today Baseball Weekly*, September 12, 1994 (Clipping from Hank Aguirre's player file at the Baseball Hall of Fame Library).

2. Joe Falls, "Aguirre Always Delivered Happiness," *The Detroit News*, September 6, 1994 (Clipping from Hank Aguirre's player file at the Baseball Hall of Fame Library).

3. Joe Falls, "Aguirre Always Delivered Happiness."

4. Baseball-Reference.com, Detroit Tigers Team History & Encyclopedia, https://www.baseball-reference.com/teams/DET/.

5. Baseball-Reference.com, 1962 Detroit Tigers Schedule, https://www.baseball-reference.com/teams/DET/1962-schedule-scores.shtml.

6. Stathead Baseball, Player Pitching Game Stats Finder, Hank Aguirre 1962, https://stathead.com/baseball/player-pitching-game-finder.cgi?request=1&order_by_asc=1&order_by=date&player_id=aguirr001hen&year_min=1962&year_max=1962.

7. Stathead Baseball, Player Pitching Split Finder, Hank Aguirre 1962, by Month, https://stathead.com/baseball/split_finder.cgi?request=1&order_by_asc=0&order_by=Name&player_id=aguirha01&year_min=1962&year_max=1962&split_1=dates%3Amonth&class=player&type=p&sr_pitching_splits_output=view_all.

8. Stathead Baseball, Player Pitching Split Finder Hank Aguirre 1962, First vs Second Half, https://stathead.com/baseball/split_finder.cgi?request=1&order_by_asc=0&order_by=Name&player_id=aguirha01&year_min=1962&year_max=1962&split_1=dates%3Ahalf&class=player&type=p&sr_pitching_splits_output=view_all.

9. Baseball-Reference.com, 1962 New York Yankees vs Detroit Tigers Box Score, June 22, 1962, https://www.baseball-reference.com/boxes/DET/DET196206220.shtml.
10. Baseball-Reference.com, 1962 All-Star Game, July 30, 1962, https://www.baseball-reference.com/allstar/1962-allstar-game-2.shtml.
11. Baseball-Reference.com, 1962 Awards Voting, https://www.baseball-reference.com/awards/awards_1962.shtml#all_AL_MVP_voting.
12. Watson Spoelstra, "New-Style Hank Big Roar in Tiger Tank," *The Sporting News*, March 1966 (Clipping from Hank Aguirre's player file at the Baseball Hall of Fame Library).
13. Charlie Vincent, "Hank Aguirre 1931–1994: He Put His Money Where His Heart Was," *Detroit Free Press*, September 5, 1994 (Clipping from Hank Aguirre's player file at the Baseball Hall of Fame Library). Sharony Andrews Green, "Former Tiger Threw Talent, Energy into Hispanic Firm," *Detroit Free Press*, September 5, 1994 (Clipping from Hank Aguirre's player file at the Baseball Hall of Fame Library).
14. Joe Falls, "Aguirre Always Delivered Happiness."

Chapter 15

1. David E. Skelton, "Dick Ellsworth," https://sabr.org/bioproj/person/Dick-Ellsworth/.
2. Tom Meehan, "Fresno renowned as the cradle of mound stars," *The Sporting News*, September 28, 1963 (Clipping from Dick Ellsworth's player file at the Baseball Hall of Fame Library).
3. Wikipedia, Bonus Rule, https://en.wikipedia.org/wiki/Bonus_rule.
4. Baseball-Reference.com, Chicago Cubs vs Cincinnati Redlegs Box Score: June 22, 1958, https://www.baseball-reference.com/boxes/CIN/CIN195806221.shtml.
5. Wikipedia, College of Coaches, https://en.wikipedia.org/wiki/College_of_Coaches.
6. Stathead Baseball, Dick Ellsworth 1963 Player Pitching Game Stats Finder, https://stathead.com/baseball/player-pitching-game-finder.cgi?request=1&match=player_game&order_by_asc=1&order_by=date&player_id_hint=Dick+Ellsworth&player_id_select=Dick+Ellsworth&player_id=ellswo001ric&year_min=1963&year_max=1963&comp_type=reg&is_pitcher=1&role=anyGS&days_rest_comp=%3D&location=pob&locationMatch=is&min_temperature=0&max_temperature=120&min_wind_speed=0&max_wind_speed=90.
7. Stathead Baseball, Dick Ellsworth 1963 Player Pitching Game Stats Finder.
8. Baseball-Reference.com, Chicago Cubs vs Philadelphia Phillies Box Score, June 1, 1963, https://www.baseball-reference.com/boxes/PHI/PHI196306010.shtml.
9. Richard Dozer, "Ellsworth wins comeback award," *Chicago Tribune*, October 15, 1963 (Clipping from Dick Ellsworth's player file at the Baseball Hall of Fame Library).
10. James Enright, "20 Defeats Shaped Ellsworth into Ace," *The Sporting News*, August 17, 1963 (Clipping from Dick Ellsworth's player file at the Baseball Hall of Fame Library). George Vecsey, "How Ellsworth Did It," *Sport Magazine*, December 1963 (Clipping from Dick Ellsworth's player file at the Baseball Hall of Fame Library). Red Foley, "Cub Ace Dick First in 28 Years to Lose 20, then Log 20 Wins," *The Sporting News*, September 28, 1963 (Clipping from Dick Ellsworth's player file at the Baseball Hall of Fame Library). Barney Kremenko, "Ellsworth: Dream Pitcher," *New York Journal American*, August 18, 1963 (Clipping from Dick Ellsworth's player file at the Baseball Hall of Fame Library).
11. Baseball-Reference.com, Pittsburgh Pirates vs Chicago Cubs Box Score: June 14, 1964, https://www.baseball-reference.com/boxes/CHN/CHN196406140.shtml.
12. Baseball-Reference.com, 1964 Chicago Cubs Schedule, https://www.baseball-reference.com/teams/CHC/1964-schedule-scores.shtml.
13. Stathead Baseball, Dick Ellsworth 1964 Player Pitching Split Finder, https://stathead.com/baseball/split_finder.cgi?request=1&match=season&order_by_asc=1&order_by=year_game&player_

id_hint=Dick+Ellsworth&player_id_select=Dick+Ellsworth&player_id=ellswdi01&year_min=1964&year_max=1964&split_1=dates%3Amonth&split_total_comp=gt&class=player&type=p&sr_pitching_splits_output=view_all&age_min=0&age_max=99&season_start=1&season_end=-1&location=pob&locationMatch=is.

14. Sandy O'Grady, "Trade well worth it—to Ellsworth," *Philadelphia Bulletin*, March 7, 1967 (Clipping from Dick Ellsworth's player file at the Baseball Hall of Fame Library).

15. Stathead Baseball, Dick Ellsworth 1967 Player Pitching Split Finder, https://stathead.com/baseball/split_finder.cgi?request=1&order_by_asc=1&order_by=year_game&player_id=ellswdi01&year_min=1967&year_max=1967&split_1=dates%3Amonth&class=player&type=p&sr_pitching_splits_output=view_all.

16. Skelton, "Dick Ellsworth."

17. Baseball-Reference.com, 1968 American League Team Statistics, https://www.baseball-reference.com/leagues/AL/1968.shtml.

18. Al Yellon, "Former Cubs Lefthander Dick Ellsworth Has Died," bleedcubbieblue.com, October 12, 2022. https://www.bleedcubbieblue.com/2022/10/12/23399001/former-cubs-lefthander-dick-ellsworth-died.

Chapter 16

1. Wikipedia, Zorro, https://en.wikipedia.org/wiki/Zorro.

2. Peter C. Bjarkman, "Zoilo Versalles," https://sabr.org/bioproj/person/Zoilo-Versalles/.

3. Milton Gross, "Palace of Versalles," *New York Post*, October 5, 1965 (Clipping from Zoilo Versalles's player file at the Baseball Hall of Fame Library). Jerry Izenberg, "Izenberg at Large," *Syracuse Post-Standard*, July 17, 1973 (Clipping from Zoilo Versalles's player file at the Baseball Hall of Fame Library).

4. Bjarkman, "Zoilo Versalles."

5. Tom Briere, "Fizzle or Flash—Flighty Zoilo Prime Puzzle for Twins Brass," *The Sporting News*, May 23, 1962

(Clipping from Zoilo Versalles's player file at the Baseball Hall of Fame Library).

6. Baseball-Reference.com, 1963 All-Star Game Box Score, July 9, https://www.baseball-reference.com/allstar/1963-allstar-game.shtml.

7. Baseball-Reference.com, Minnesota Twins vs Baltimore Orioles Box Score: July 5, 1963 (Game 1), https://www.baseball-reference.com/boxes/BAL/BAL196307051.shtml. Arno Goethel, "Boots and Beauts Marked Zoilo's Play," *The Sporting News*, December, 28, 1963 (Clipping from Zoilo Versalles's player file at the Baseball Hall of Fame Library).

8. Max Nichols, "Cal Weary of Twin Beefs, Backs Mele's Crackdown on Versalles," *The Sporting News*, April 17, 1965 (Clipping from Zoilo Versalles's player file at the Baseball Hall of Fame Library). Ed Rumili, "Twins' Versalles the 'Little Meter,'" *The Christian Science Monitor*, October 8, 1965 (Clipping from Zoilo Versalles's player file at the Baseball Hall of Fame Library).

9. Bjarkman, "Zoilo Versalles."

10. Stathead Baseball, Zoilo Versalles 1965 Player Batting Split Finder by Month, https://stathead.com/baseball/split_finder.cgi?request=1&order_by_asc=1&order_by=Name&player_id=versazo01&year_min=1965&year_max=1965&split_1=dates%3Amonth&class=player&type=b.

11. Baseball Reference, 1965 Minnesota Twins Schedule, https://www.baseball-reference.com/teams/MIN/1965-schedule-scores.shtml.

12. Baseball-Reference.com, 1965 All-Star Game Box Score, July 13, https://www.baseball-reference.com/allstar/1965-allstar-game.shtml.

13. Julio Ojeda-Zapata and Charley Walters, "Versalles Dies at 55," *St. Paul Pioneer Press*, June 10, 1995 (Clipping from Zoilo Versalles's player file at the Baseball Hall of Fame Library).

14. Bjarkman, "Zoilo Versalles."

15. Baseball-Reference, 1965 World Series Los Angeles Dodgers Over Minnesota Twins (4–3), https://www.baseball-reference.com/postseason/1965_WS.shtml.

16. Baseball-Reference.com, Minnesota Twins vs Chicago White Sox Box Score: June 11, 1966, https://www.

baseball-reference.com/boxes/CHA/CHA196606110.shtml?__hstc=205977932.b08e7af248b5e4ce1b1e624af7b2c48a.1661105685144.1692989596569.1693067056467.362&__hssc=205977932.6.1693067056467&__hsfp=551255700

17. Baseball-Reference.com, 1966 Minnesota Twins Schedule, https://www.baseball-reference.com/teams/MIN/1966-schedule-scores.shtml.

18. Max Nichols, "Joyful News from Zoilo: Arm's Sore," *The Sporting News*, April 1, 1967 (Clipping from Zoilo Versalles's player file at the Baseball Hall of Fame Library).

19. Baseball-Reference.com, 1967 Major League Value (hitters, sorted by ascending WAR), https://www.baseball-reference.com/leagues/majors/1967-value-batting.shtml.

20. Charles Maher, "Versalles, Grant Traded by Minnesota to Dodgers," *Los Angeles Times*, November 29, 1967 (Clipping from Zoilo Versalles's player file at the Baseball Hall of Fame Library).

21. Milton Richman, "Ermer Cost Twins Flag—Zoilo," *The Knickerbocker News*, February 21, 1968 (Clipping from Zoilo Versalles's player file at the Baseball Hall of Fame Library).

22. Bill Madden, "Versalles Battles Post-Career Pains, Problems," *The Sporting News*, May 28, 1984 (Clipping from Zoilo Versalles's player file at the Baseball Hall of Fame Library).

23. Madden, "Versalles Battles Post-Career Pains, Problems."

24. World Series Time Capsules, "Zolio Versalles," *The Sporting News*, October 31, 1981 (Clipping from Zoilo Versalles's player file at the Baseball Hall of Fame Library).

25. Patrick Reusse, "Versalles Was Our Early Hero," *Minneapolis Star-Tribune*, June 10, 1995 (Clipping from Zoilo Versalles's player file at the Baseball Hall of Fame Library).

Chapter 17

1. Jerome Holtzman, "Hurler Abernathy Proves Lifesaver as Ace Reliever," *The Sporting News*, June 12, 1965 (Clipping from Ted Abernathy's player file at the Baseball Hall of Fame Library).

2. Holtzman, "Hurler Abernathy Proves Lifesaver as Ace Reliever."

3. Stathead Baseball, Ted Abernathy, Player Pitching Split Finder, 1965, https://stathead.com/baseball/split_finder.cgi?request=1&match=season&order_by_asc=0&order_by=SV&player_id_hint=Ted+Abernathy&player_id_select=Ted+Abernathy&player_id=abernte02&year_min=1965&year_max=1965&split_1=dates%3Amonth&split_total_comp=gt&class=player&type=p&sr_pitching_splits_output=view_pitching&age_min=0&age_max=99&season_start=1&season_end=-1&location=pob&locationMatch=is.

4. Jerome Holtzman, "Iron-Man Abernathy Cops Fireman Prize—Fisher AL King," *The Sporting News*, October 16, 1965 (Clipping from Ted Abernathy's player file at the Baseball Hall of Fame Library).

5. Stathead Baseball, Ted Abernathy, Player Pitching Stats Finder, 1966, hpps://Stathead.com/baseball/player-pitching-stats-finder.cgi?request=1&match=player_game&order_by_asc=1&order_by=date&player_id_hint=Ted+Abernathy&player_id_select=Ted+Abernathy&player_id=aberna001the&year_min=1966&year_max=1966&comp_type=reg&team_game_min=1&team_game_max=165&player_game_min=1&player_game_max=9999&is_pitcher=1&role=anyGS&days_rest_comp=%3D&location=pob&locationMatch=is&min_temperature=0&max_temperature=120&min_wind_speed=0&max_wind_speed=90.

6. Baseball-Reference.com, 1966 National League Standard Pitching, https://www.baseball-reference.com/leagues/NL/1966-standard-pitching.shtml.

7. Stathead Baseball, Player Pitching Stats & Career Finder (Leaders in One-Season WAR by Pitchers with at Least 75% of Appearances in Relief), https://stathead.com/baseball/player-pitching-season-finder.cgi?request=1&order_by=p_war&games_started=60&role=reliever&games_relieved=75.

8. Stathead Baseball, Ted Abernathy, Player Pitching Stats Finder, 1967, hpps://Stathead.com/baseball/

player-pitching-stats-finder.cgi?request=1&match=player_game&order_by_asc=1&order_by=date&player_id_hint=Ted+Abernathy&player_id_select=Ted+Abernathy&player_id=aberna001the&year_min=1967&year_max=1967&comp_type=reg&team_game_min=1&team_game_max=165&player_game_min=1&player_game_max=9999&is_pitcher=1&role=anyGS&days_rest_comp=%3D&location=pob&locationMatch=is&min_temperature=0&max_temperature=120&min_wind_speed=0&max_wind_speed=90.

9. Baseball-Reference.com, Cincinnati Reds vs Los Angeles Dodgers Box Score, April 18, 1967, https://www.baseball-reference.com/boxes/LAN/LAN196704180.shtml.

10. Sid Bordman, "Dear Abby: Royals Think You're Super," *The Sporting News*, July 25, 1970 (Clipping from Ted Abernathy's player file at the Baseball Hall of Fame Library).

11. Baseball Reference Bullpen, Ted Abernathy, https://www.baseballreference.com/bullpen/Ted_Abernathy_(abernte02).

Chapter 18

1. Ron Marshall, "Rico Petrocelli," https://sabr.org/bioproj/person/Rico-Petrocelli/.

2. Marshall, "Rico Petrocelli."

3. Baseball-Reference.com, 1964 American League Team Statistics, https://www.baseball-reference.com/leagues/AL/1964.shtml.

4. Baseball-Reference.com, 1965 American League Team Statistics, https://www.baseball-reference.com/teams/BOS/1965.shtml.

5. Marshall, "Rico Petrocelli."

6. Larry Claflin, "Rico's Sensational ... Sometimes; What Ails the Bosox Flash?," *Boston Globe*, August 27, 1966 (Clipping from Rico Petrocelli's player file at the Baseball Hall of Fame Library).

7. Baseball-Reference.com, 1967 All-Star Game Box Score, July 11, https://www.baseball-reference.com/allstar/1967-allstar-game.shtml.

8. Baseball-Reference.com, 1967 World Series Game 6, Cardinals at Red Sox, October 11, https://www.baseball-reference.com/boxes/BOS/BOS196710110.shtml.

9. Stathead Baseball, Player Batting Season & Career Stats Finder, SS sorted by WAR, https://stathead.com/baseball/player-batting-season-finder.cgi?request=1&order_by=b_war&positions%5B%5D=6&games_prop=50.

10. Baseball-Reference.com, 1969 All-Star Game Box Score, July 23, https://www.baseball-reference.com/allstar/1969-allstar-game.shtml.12

11. Stathead Baseball, Rico Petrocelli 1969 Player Batting Split Finder by Month, https://stathead.com/baseball/split_finder.cgi?request=1&match=season&order_by_asc=0&order_by=sOPS&player_id_hint=Rico+Petrocelli&player_id_select=Rico+Petrocelli&player_id=petrori01&year_min=1969&year_max=1969&split_1=dates%3Amonth&split_total_comp=gt&class=player&type=b&age_min=0&age_max=99&season_start=1&season_end=-1&location=pob&locationMatch=is.

12. Stathead Baseball, Rico Petrocelli 1969 Player Batting Split Finder by Opponent, https://stathead.com/baseball/split_finder.cgi?request=1&match=season&order_by_asc=0&order_by=HR&player_id_hint=Rico+Petrocelli&player_id_select=Rico+Petrocelli&player_id=petrori01&year_min=1969&year_max=1969&split_1=oppon%3Aoppon&split_total_comp=gt&class=player&type=b&age_min=0&age_max=99&season_start=1&season_end=-1&location=pob&locationMatch=is.

13. Stathead Baseball, Rico Petrocelli 1969 Player Batting Game Stats Finder, https://stathead.com/baseball/player-batting-game-finder.cgi?request=1&match=player_game&order_by_asc=1&order_by=date&player_id_hint=Rico+Petrocelli&player_id_select=Rico+Petrocelli&player_id=petroc001ame&year_min=1969&year_max=1969&comp_type=reg&team_game_min=1&team_game_max=165&player_game_min=1&player_game_max=9999&exactness=anymarked&GF=anyGF&location=pob&locationMatch=is&min_temperature=0&max_

temperature=120&min_wind_speed=0&max_wind_speed=90.

14. Marshall, "Rico Petrocelli."

15. Alfred Albelli and Henry Lee, "Calls Shortstop Foul Ball: Blonde Says Rico Made Wrong Play," *New York Daily News*, March 12, 1971 (Clipping from Rico Petrocelli's player file at the Baseball Hall of Fame Library).

16. Bill Braucher, "Sympathizes with Kekich, Peterson: Petrocelli Had His Shock Too," *The Miami Herald*, March 9, 1973 (Clipping from Rico Petrocelli's player file at the Baseball Hall of Fame Library).

17. Baseball-Reference.com, 1975 American League Championship Series (ALCS) Game 2 Athletics at Red Sox, https://www.baseball-reference.com/boxes/BOS/BOS197510050.shtml.

18. Marshall, "Rico Petrocelli."

19. Stathead Baseball, Rico Petrocelli Player Batting Split Finder, Home versus Away, https://stathead.com/baseball/split_finder.cgi?request=1&match=seasons&order_by_asc=0&order_by=sOPS&player_id_hint=Rico+Petrocelli&player_id_select=Rico+Petrocelli&player_id=petrori01&year_min=1963&year_max=1976&split_1=locat%3Ahmvis&split_total_comp=gt&class=player&type=b&age_min=0&age_max=99&season_start=1&season_end=-1&location=pob&locationMatch=is.

20. Stathead Baseball, Rico Petrocelli 1969 Player Batting Split Finder, Home versus Away, https://stathead.com/baseball/split_finder.cgi?request=1&match=seasons&order_by_asc=0&order_by=sOPS&player_id_hint=Rico+Petrocelli&player_id_select=Rico+Petrocelli&player_id=petrori01&year_min=1969&year_max=1969&split_1=locat%3Ahmvis&split_total_comp=gt&class=player&type=b&age_min=0&age_max=99&season_start=1&season_end=-1&location=pob&locationMatch=is.

21. Baseball-Reference.com, 1969 Boston Red Sox statistics, https://www.baseball-reference.com/teams/BOS/1969.shtml.

Chapter 19

1. David E. Skelton, "Billy Grabarkewitz," https://sabr.org/bioproj/person/Billy-Grabarkewitz/.

2. Skelton, "Billy Grabarkewitz."

3. Skelton, "Billy Grabarkewitz."

4. Skelton, "Billy Grabarkewitz."

5. Fred Claire, Los Angeles Dodgers press release, November 1968 (Clipping from Billy Grabarkewitz's player file at the Baseball Hall of Fame Library). Skelton, "Billy Grabarkewitz."

6. Baseball-Reference.com, Cincinnati Reds vs Los Angeles Dodgers Box Score: April 7, 1970, https://www.baseball-reference.com/boxes/LAN/LAN197004070.shtml.

7. Baseball-Reference.com, San Diego Padres vs Los Angeles Dodgers Box Score: April 12, 1970, https://www.baseball-reference.com/boxes/LAN/LAN197004120.shtml.

8. Stathead Baseball, Billy Grabarkewitz Player Batting Split Finder 1970 by Month, https://stathead.com/baseball/split_finder.cgi?request=1&order_by_asc=1&order_by=Name&player_id=grababi01&year_min=1970&year_max=1970&split_1=dates%3Amonth&class=player&type=b.

9. Bob Hunter, "Billy G. Is Just Great, Dodgers Crow," *The Sporting News*, August 1, 1970 (Clipping from Billy Grabarkewitz's player file at the Baseball Hall of Fame Library).

10. Baseball-Reference.com, 1970 All-Star Game Box Score, July 14, https://www.baseball-reference.com/allstar/1970-allstar-game.shtml.

11. Baseball-Reference.com, Top Year-by-Year Top-Tens Leaders & Records for Strikeouts, https://www.baseball-reference.com/leaders/SO_top_ten.shtml.

12. Skelton, "Billy Grabarkewitz."

13. Skelton, "Billy Grabarkewitz."

14. Skelton, "Billy Grabarkewitz."

15. Ron Rapaport, "Dodgers Trade Robinson to Angels," *Los Angeles Times*, November 27, 1972 (Clipping from Billy Grabarkewitz's player file at the Baseball Hall of Fame Library).

16. Skelton, "Billy Grabarkewitz."

Chapter 20

1. Stathead Baseball, Player Pitching Stats & Career Finder (Leaders in One-Season WAR by Pitchers with at Least 75% of Appearances in Relief), https://stathead.com/baseball/player-pitching-season-finder.cgi?request=1&order_by=p_war&games_started=60&role=reliever&games_relieved=75.

2. Stathead Baseball, Player Pitching and Career Stats Finder, Leaders in Career WAR by Pitchers with at Least 75% of Appearances in Relief), https://stathead.com/baseball/player-pitching-season-finder.cgi?request=1&match=player_season_combined&order_by=p_war&games_started=60&role=reliever&games_relieved=75.

3. Rob Hilliard and Larry Hilliard, "John Hiller," https://sabr.org/bioproj/person/John-Hiller/.

4. Stathead Baseball, Player Pitching and Career Stats Finder John Hiller 1968, https://stathead.com/baseball/player-pitching-game-finder.cgi?request=1&order_by_asc=1&order_by=date&player_id=hiller001joh&year_min=1968&year_max=1968.

5. "Admiration for Hiller Replaces Sympathy," *Syracuse Herald-American* (Associated Press), June 17, 1973 (Clipping from John Hiller's player file at the Baseball Hall of Fame Library).

6. John Hiller, "What It Takes to Begin Again," *Guideposts*, May 1974 (Clipping from John Hiller's player file at the Baseball Hall of Fame Library). William Leggett, "Pitching a No-Quitter," *Sports Illustrated*, June 11, 1973 (Clipping from John Hiller's player file at the Baseball Hall of Fame Library).

7. David Gordon, *The American Cardiovascular Pandemic: A 100-Year History* (Jefferson: McFarland, 2021).

8. "Admiration for Hiller Replaces Sympathy."

9. Chris Rowe, "Hiller, Marshall Set Relief Marks," *The Sporting News*, October 27, 1973 (Clipping from John Hiller's player file at the Baseball Hall of Fame Library).

10. Ben Henkey, "Hiller, Dave Johnson Win Comeback Crowns," *The Sporting News*, December 1, 1973 (Clipping from John Hiller's player file at the Baseball Hall of Fame Library).

11. James Enright, "Hutch Award Thrills Tigers' Hiller," *Chicago Today*, January 21, 1974 (Clipping from John Hiller's player file at the Baseball Hall of Fame Library).

12. Stathead Baseball, John Hiller 1973 Pitching Game Stats Finder, https://stathead.com/baseball/player-pitching-game-finder.cgi?request=1&match=player_game&order_by_asc=1&order_by=date&player_id_hint=John+Hiller&player_id_select=John+Hiller&player_id=hiller001joh&year_min=1973&year_max=1973&comp_type=reg&team_game_min=1&team_game_max=165&player_game_min=1&player_game_max=9999&is_pitcher=1&role=anyGS&days_rest_comp=%3D&location=pob&locationMatch=is&min_temperature=0&max_temperature=120&min_wind_speed=0&max_wind_speed=90.

13. Jerry Green, "Hiller a Specialist in Fine Art of Survival," *Detroit Free Press*, January 5, 1997 (Clipping from John Hiller's player file at the Baseball Hall of Fame Library).

14. Tyler Kepner, "Holtzman, Creator of the Save Rule, Dies at 82," *New York Times*, July 21, 2008.

15. Baseball-Refereence.com, John Hiller vs. Lee Smith: Head-to-Head Stats Comparison, https://stathead.com/baseball/versus-finder.cgi?player_id2=smith-001lee&player_id1=hiller001joh&request=1&utm_campaign=2023_01_wdgt_player_comparison&utm_source=br&utm_medium=sr_xsite&utm_id=hillejo01.

16. David J. Gordon, "Using Career Value Index (CVI) to Evaluate Hall of Fame Credentials of Negro League Players," *Baseball Research Journal* 51, no. 2 (Fall 2022): 112–121.

Chapter 21

1. Dave Marsh, "The Tale of the Bird," *Rolling Stone*, May 5, 1977 (Clipping from Mark Fidrych's player file at the Baseball Hall of Fame Library).

2. Barry Furlong, "Will Success Spoil the Bird?" *New York Times Magazine*, August 22, 1976 (Clipping from Mark Fidrych's player file at the Baseball Hall of Fame Library).

3. Dave Marsh, "The Tale of the Bird."
4. Rich Puerzer, "Mark Fidrych," https://sabr.org/bioproj/person/Mark-Fidrych/.
5. Stathead Baseball, Mark Fidrych 1976 Player Pitching Game Stats Finder, https://stathead.com/baseball/player-pitching-game-finder.cgi?request=1&match=player_game&order_by_asc=1&order_by=date&player_id_hint=Mark+Fidrych&player_id_select=Mark+Fidrych&player_id=fidryc001mar&year_min=1976&year_max=1976&comp_type=reg&is_pitcher=1&role=anyGS&days_rest_comp=%3D&location=pob&locationMatch=is&min_temperature=0&max_temperature=120&min_wind_speed=0&max_wind_speed=90.
6. Dave Marsh ("The Tale of the Bird") quoting from Jim Hawkins, "The Bird Amuses Tigers, Befuddles Enemy Swingers," *The Sporting News*, June 5, 1976 (Clipping from Mark Fidrych's player file at the Baseball Hall of Fame Library).
7. Steve Rushin, "The Bird Is Back," *Sports Illustrated*, July 2, 2001 (Clipping from Mark Fidrych's player file at the Baseball Hall of Fame Library).
8. "'The Bird' Visited by Ford," *The Columbus Dispatch* (Associated Press), July 14, 1976 (Clipping from Mark Fidrych's player file at the Baseball Hall of Fame Library).
9. Jim Hawkins, "Two Years Later, The Bird's a Wise Old Owl," *The Sporting News*, January 27, 1979 (Clipping from Mark Fidrych's player file at the Baseball Hall of Fame Library).
10. Stathead Baseball, Mark Fidrych 1977 Player Pitching Game Stats Finder, https://stathead.com/baseball/player-pitching-game-finder.cgi?request=1&match=player_game&order_by_asc=1&order_by=date&player_id_hint=Mark+Fidrych&player_id_select=Mark+Fidrych&player_id=fidryc001mar&year_min=1977&year_max=1977&comp_type=reg&team_game_min=1&team_game_max=165&player_game_min=1&player_game_max=9999&is_pitcher=1&role=anyGS&days_rest_comp=%3D&location=pob&locationMatch=is&min_temperature=0&max_temperature=120&min_wind_speed=0&max_wind_speed=90
11. "Sparky Tells 'Bird' to Put Up or Shut Up," Associated Press, April 6, 1980 (Clipping from Mark Fidrych's player file at the Baseball Hall of Fame Library).
12. Steve Rushin, "The Bird Is Back."
13. Micheline Maynard, "Fidrych, Baseball's Beloved 'Bird,' Dies at 54," *New York Times*, April 14, 2009 (Clipping from Mark Fidrych's player file at the Baseball Hall of Fame Library).
14. Doug Wilson, *The Bird: The Life and Legacy of Mark Fidrych* (New York: Thomas Dunne/St. Martin's, 2013).
15. "Bird's Struggle for Life in Baseball is Over," United Press International, June 30, 1983 (Clipping from Mark Fidrych's player file at the Baseball Hall of Fame Library).

Chapter 22

1. Darrell Porter, "The Comeback," *Guideposts*, November 1981, pp 27–30 (Clipping from Darrell Porter's player file at the Baseball Hall of Fame Library).
2. Darrell Porter and William Deerfield, *Snap Me Perfect! The Darrell Porter Story* (Nashville: Thomas Newson, 1984).
3. Glen Sparks, "Darrell Porter," https://sabr.org/bioproj/person/Darrell-Porter/.
4. Robert T. Nelson, "Darrell Porter: Cards New Catcher Has Two Sides—The All-Star Athlete and the Insecure Young Man Who Sought Refuge in Alcohol," *St. Louis Post Dispatch*, circa January 1981 (Clipping from Darrell Porter's player file at the Baseball Hall of Fame Library).
5. Porter, "Darrell Porter."
6. Sparks, "Darrell Porter."
7. Sparks, "Darrell Porter."
8. Sparks, "Darrell Porter."
9. Baseball-Reference.com, 1978 All-Star Game Box Score, https://www.baseball-reference.com/allstar/1978-allstar-game.shtml.
10. Stathead Baseball, Player Batting and Career Stats Finder Catchers, ≥100 R, ≥100 RBI, ≥100 BB, https://stathead.com/baseball/player-batting-season-finder.cgi?request=1&order_by_asc=1&order_by=year_id&positions%5B%5D=2&games_prop=50&ccomp%5B1%5D=gt&cval%5B1%5D=100&cstat%5B1%5D=b_r&ccomp%5B2%5D=gt&cval%5B2%5D=100&cstat%5B2%5D=b_rbi&ccomp%5B5

B3%5D=gt&cval%5B3%5D=100&cstat%5B3%5D=b_bb.

11. Stathead Baseball, Player Batting and Career Stats Finder Catchers, Sorted by Descending WAR, https://stathead.com/baseball/player-batting-season-finder.cgi?request=1&order_by=b_war&positions%5B%5D=2&games_prop=50.

12. Stathead Baseball, Darrell Porter Player Batting Split Finder 1979, https://stathead.com/baseball/split_finder.cgi?request=1&order_by_asc=1&order_by=Name&player_id=porteda02&year_min=1979&year_max=1979&split_1=dates%3Amonth&class=player&type=b.

13. Baseball-Reference.com, 1979 All-Star Game Box Score, https://www.baseball-reference.com/allstar/1979-allstar-game.shtml,

14. Porter, *Snap Me Perfect!*.

15. Sparks, "Darrell Porter."

16. Arnold Irish, "Porter Has Rare Talent for Handling Pitchers," *St. Louis Post-Dispatch*, May 9, 1983 (Clipping from Darrell Porter's player file at the Baseball Hall of Fame Library).

17. Baseball-Reference.com, 1982 World Series, St. Louis Cardinals over Milwaukee Brewers (4–3), https://www.baseball-reference.com/postseason/1982_WS.shtml.

18. Sparks, "Darrell Porter."

19. Dick Kaegel, "Former Royal Porter Played to Win," *Kansas City Star*, August 7, 2002 (Clipping from Darrell Porter's player file at the Baseball Hall of Fame Library). Bob Dutton, "Former Royal Overcame Addiction, Touched Hundreds of Lives," *Kansas City Star*, August 7, 2002 (Clipping from Darrell Porter's player file at the Baseball Hall of Fame Library).

20. "Doctor Says Porter Did Not Die of an Overdose," ESPN Baseball, August 13, 2002 (Clipping from Darrell Porter's player file at the Baseball Hall of Fame Library).

21. Baseball-Reference.com, Catcher JAWS Leaders, https://www.baseball-reference.com/leaders/jaws_C.shtml.

22. Steven Goldman, "You could look it up: The importance of being Paul Waner," *Baseball Prospectus*, May 12, 2009, https://www.baseballprospectus.com/news/article/8863/you-could-look-it-up-the-importance-of-being-paul-waner/.

23. *The Winning Team*, IMDb, 1952, https://www.imdb.com/title/tt0045332/.

Chapter 23

1. Lee Kluck, "Dwight Gooden," https://sabr.org/bioproj/person/Dwight-Gooden/.

2. Kluck, "Dwight Gooden." Ken Verducci, "The High Price of Hard Living," *Sports Illustrated*, February 27, 1995 (Clipping from Dwight Gooden's player file at the Baseball Hall of Fame Library).

3. Stathead Baseball, Dwight Gooden Player Pitching Game Finder 1984, https://stathead.com/baseball/player-pitching-game-finder.cgi?request=1&match=player_game&order_by_asc=1&order_by=date&player_id_hint=Dwight+Gooden&player_id_select=Dwight+Gooden&player_id=gooden001dwi&year_min=1984&year_max=1984&comp_type=reg&team_game_min=1&team_game_max=165&player_game_min=1&player_game_max=9999&is_pitcher=1&role=anyGS&days_rest_comp=%3D&location=pob&locationMatch=is&min_temperature=0&max_temperature=120&min_wind_speed=0&max_wind_speed=90.

4. Baseball-Reference.com, 1984 All-Star Game Box Score, July 10, https://www.baseball-reference.com/allstar/1984-allstar-game.shtml.

5. Baseball-Reference.com, Pitching Leaders Seasons Age 19, https://www.baseball-reference.com/leaders/leaders_20_pitch_season.shtml.

6. Baseball-Reference.com, Single-Season Leaders & Records for WAR for Pitchers, https://www.baseball-reference.com/leaders/WAR_pitch_season.shtml.

7. Baseball-Reference.com, Pitching Leaders Seasons Age 20, https://www.baseball-reference.com/leaders/leaders_20_pitch_season.shtml.

8. Stathead Baseball, Dwight Gooden Player Pitching Game Finder 1985, https://stathead.com/baseball/player-pitching-game-finder.cgi?request=1&match=player_game&order_by_asc=1&order_by=date&player_id_

hint=Dwight+Gooden&player_id_select=Dwight+Gooden&player_id=gooden001dwi&year_min=1985&year_max=1985&comp_type=reg&team_game_min=1&team_game_max=165&player_game_min=1&player_game_max=9999&is_pitcher=1&role=anyGS&days_rest_comp=%3D&location=pob&locationMatch=is&min_temperature=0&max_temperature=120&min_wind_speed=0&max_wind_speed=90.

9. Mike McAlary, "Guidry on Gooden: He'll strike out 4000," *New York Post*, July 5, 1985 (Clipping from Dwight Gooden's player file at the Baseball Hall of Fame Library).

10. Michael Kay, "Greats Agree: Gooden's the Best," *New York Post*, November 14, 1985 (Clipping from Dwight Gooden's player file at the Baseball Hall of Fame Library).

11. Michael Kay, "Greats Agree: Gooden's the Best."

12. Michael Kay, "Greats Agree: Gooden's the Best."

13. Maury Allen, "Mantle: I Couldn't Have Hit Gooden," *New York Post*, December 21, 1985 (Clipping from Dwight Gooden's player file at the Baseball Hall of Fame Library).

14. Stathead Baseball, Dwight Gooden Player Pitching Game Finder 1986, https://stathead.com/baseball/player-pitching-game-finder.cgi?request=1&match=player_game&order_by_asc=1&order_by=date&player_id_hint=Dwight+Gooden&player_id_select=Dwight+Gooden&player_id=gooden001dwi&year_min=1986&year_max=1986&comp_type=reg&team_game_min=1&team_game_max=165&player_game_min=1&player_game_max=9999&is_pitcher=1&role=anyGS&days_rest_comp=%3D&location=pob&locationMatch=is&min_temperature=0&max_temperature=120&min_wind_speed=0&max_wind_speed=90.

15. Baseball-Reference.com, 1986 All-Star Game Box Score, July 16, https://www.baseball-reference.com/allstar/1986-allstar-game.shtml

16. "Secret Shame of Met Star Doc," *New York Post*, May 19, 2013 (Clipping from Dwight Gooden's player file at the Baseball Hall of Fame Library). Excerpt from Dwight Gooden and Ellis Henican, *Doc: A Memoir* (New York: New Harvest, 2003).

17. Tim McDarrah and Amy Pagnozzi, "'Doc' Throws Dwight Hook in Brawl-game with Cops," *New York Post*, December 15, 1986 (Clipping from Dwight Gooden's player file at the Baseball Hall of Fame Library). Bob Drury, "Home, Bittersweet Home," *Newsday*, December 19, 1986 (Clipping from Dwight Gooden's player file at the Baseball Hall of Fame Library).

18. Pete Coutros, "The Great Debate: Seaver vs Gooden," *New York Daily News*, July 22, 1988 (Clipping from Dwight Gooden's player file at the Baseball Hall of Fame Library).

19. Stathead Baseball, Dwight Gooden Player Pitching Split Finder 1989, https://stathead.com/baseball/split_finder.cgi?request=1&match=season&order_by_asc=0&order_by=win_loss_perc&player_id_hint=Dwight+Gooden&player_id_select=Dwight+Gooden&player_id=goodedw01&year_min=1989&year_max=1989&split_1=dates%3Amonth&split_total_comp=gt&class=player&type=p&sr_pitching_splits_output=view_all&age_min=0&age_max=99&season_start=1&season_end=-1&location=pob&locationMatch=is.

20. Joe Sexton, "Can Gooden Work Off the Cuff?" *New York Times*, January 19, 1992 (Clipping from Dwight Gooden's player file at the Baseball Hall of Fame Library).

21. Daniel Engber, "You Guys Are Scaring Me," *Slate*, January 12, 2020, https://slate.com/culture/2020/01/mets-rape-accusation-spring-training-1991.html.

22. Jennifer Frye, "Another Strike Against Gooden in Drug Violations," *New York Times*, September 16, 1994 (Clipping from Dwight Gooden's player file at the Baseball Hall of Fame Library). Lee Kluck, "Dwight Gooden."

23. Mel Antonen, "Gooden Says Only Miracle Kept Him Alive," *USA Today*, March 5, 1999 (Clipping from Dwight Gooden's player file at the Baseball Hall of Fame Library).

24. Jack Curry, "Dr. No: A Revived Gooden No-Hits the Mariners," *New York Times*, May 15, 1996 (Clipping from Dwight Gooden's player file at the Baseball Hall of Fame Library).
25. George King, "Yanks Doubt Doc's Story," *New York Post*, May 24, 1997 (Clipping from Dwight Gooden's player file at the Baseball Hall of Fame Library).
26. Jeff Testerman, "Where Did Gooden's Millions Go?" *St. Petersburg Times*, November 16, 2003 (Clipping from Dwight Gooden's player file at the Baseball Hall of Fame Library).
27. Joe Henderson, "Unfortunately Gooden May Never Learn," *TBO Sports*, April 6, 2006, http://www.tbo.com/sports/mgbtt3qkole.html (Clipping from Dwight Gooden's player file at the Baseball Hall of Fame Library).
28. Kimberly Martin, "Gooden Facing Slew of Charges," *Newsday*, March 25, 2010 (Clipping from Dwight Gooden's player file at the Baseball Hall of Fame Library).
29. "Dwight Gooden Gets Probation for 2019 Drug Arrest," Associated Press, November 13, 2020 (Clipping from Dwight Gooden's player file at the Baseball Hall of Fame Library).
30. Chris Oliver, "Doc, you're a real jerk …," *New York Post*, April 4, 1987 (Clipping from Dwight Gooden's player file at the Baseball Hall of Fame Library). "Monster," *New York Daily News*, August 22, 2016 (Clipping from Dwight Gooden's player file at the Baseball Hall of Fame Library).
31. David J. Gordon, "Using Career Value Index (CVI) to Evaluate Hall of Fame Credentials of Negro League Players," *Baseball Research Journal* 51, no. 2 (Fall 2022): 112–121.

Chapter 24

1. Stathead Baseball, Player Pitching Season and Career Finder Relievers with ≥ 100 IP, 1871–1985, https://stathead.com/baseball/player-pitching-season-finder.cgi?request=1&order_by=p_ip&year_min=1871&year_max=1985&games_started=60&role=reliever&games_relieved=90&ccomp%5B1%5D=gt&cval%5B1%5D=100&cstat%5B1%5D=p_ip.

2. Stathead Baseball, Player Pitching Season and Career Finder Relievers with ≥ 100 IP, 1987–2023, https://stathead.com/baseball/player-pitching-season-finder.cgi?request=1&order_by=p_ip&year_min=1987&year_max=2023&games_started=60&role=reliever&games_relieved=90&ccomp%5B1%5D=gt&cval%5B1%5D=100&cstat%5B1%5D=p_ip.
3. Tim Sitar, "Mark Eichhorn," https://sabr.org/bioproj/person/mark-eichhorn/.
4. Sitar, "Mark Eichhorn." David Bush, "New Delivery Route Saved Blue Jays' Eichhorn," *Toronto Chronicle*, May 23, 1987 (Clipping from Mark Eichhorn's player file at the Baseball Hall of Fame Library).
5. Sitar, "Mark Eichhorn."
6. Sitar, "Mark Eichhorn."
7. Stathead Baseball, Player Pitching Split Finder Mark Eichhorn 1986 by Month, https://stathead.com/baseball/split_finder.cgi?request=1&order_by_asc=1&order_by=Name&player_id=eichhma01&year_min=1986&year_max=1986&split_1=dates%3Amonth&class=player&type=p&sr_pitching_splits_output=view_all.
8. Stathead Baseball, Player Pitching Game Stats Finder Mark Eichhorn 1986, https://stathead.com/baseball/player-pitching-game-finder.cgi?request=1&order_by_asc=1&order_by=date&player_id=eichho001mar&year_min=1986&year_max=1986.
9. Baseball-Reference.com, Toronto Blue Jays vs Detroit Tigers Box Score: October 3, 1987, https://www.baseball-reference.com/boxes/DET/DET198710030.shtml.
10. Baseball-Reference.com, MLB Scores and Standingsb Sunday, July 10, 1988, https://www.baseball-reference.com/teams/TOR/1988-schedule-scores.shtml.
11. Sitar, "Mark Eichhorn."
12. Stathead Baseball, Player Pitching Game Stats Finder Mark Eichhorn 1990–91, https://stathead.com/baseball/player-pitching-game-finder.cgi?request=1&order_by_asc=1&order_by=date&player_id=eichho001mar&year_min=1990&year_max=1991.
13. Marty York, "Jays Disappointed as Eichhorn Ends Comeback Attempt,"

Toronto Globe, August 22, 2000 (Clipping from Mark Eichhorn's player file at the Baseball Hall of Fame Library).
 14. Sitar, "Mark Eichhorn."
 15. Sitar, "Mark Eichhorn."
 16. Stathead Baseball, Player Pitching Season & Career Stats Finder Relievers Sorted by Descending WAR, https://stathead.com/baseball/player-pitching-season-finder.cgi?request=1&order_by=p_war&games_started=60&role=reliever&games_relieved=90.

Chapter 25

 1. Carroll Rogers, "Lonnie Smith Is Safe at Home," *Atlanta Journal Constitution*, July 12, 2003 (Clipping from Lonnie Smith's player file at the Baseball Hall of Fame Library).
 2. Baseball-Reference.com, St. Louis Cardinals vs San Francisco Giants Box Score: September 4, 1982, https://www.baseball-reference.com/boxes/SFN/SFN198209040.shtml.
 3. Stan Hochman, "Lonnie's Act is Anything but Funny," *Philadelphia Daily News*, September 14, 1982 (Clipping from Lonnie Smith's player file at the Baseball Hall of Fame Library). George Vecsey, "Smith, Cards on Thin Ice," *New York Times*, October 18, 1982 (Clipping from Lonnie Smith's player file at the Baseball Hall of Fame Library).
 4. Hal Bodley, "Cards' Lonnie Smith Reflects on Sober Life," *USA Today*, September 14 1983 (Clipping from Lonnie Smith's player file at the Baseball Hall of Fame Library).
 5. Jack Herman, "Cardinals 'Shocked, Surprised' by Smith's Disclosure," *St. Louis Globe-Democrat*, June 13, 1983 (Clipping from Lonnie Smith's player file at the Baseball Hall of Fame Library).
 6. Stathead Baseball, Lonnie Smith Player Batting Split Finder 1983, https://stathead.com/baseball/split_finder.cgi?request=1&match=season&order_by_asc=0&order_by=onbase_plus_slugging&player_id_hint=Lonnie+Smith&player_id_select=Lonnie+Smith&player_id=smithlo01&year_min=1983&year_max=1983&split_1=dates%3Ahalf&split_total_comp=gt&class=player&type=b&age_min=0&age_max=99&season_start=1&season_end=-1&location=pob&locationMatch=is.
 7. Bernie Miklasz, "Lonnie Smith Is Blue, but Not Yet Royal," *St. Louis Post-Dispatch*, June 24, 1885 (Clipping from Lonnie Smith's player file at the Baseball Hall of Fame Library).
 8. Mark Di Ionno, "Keith Takes a Beating During Pittsburgh Drug Trial," *New York Post*, September 6, 1985 (Clipping from Lonnie Smith's player file at the Baseball Hall of Fame Library).
 9. Wikipedia, Major League Baseball Collusion, https://en.wikipedia.org/wiki/Major_League_Baseball_collusion.
 10. Mike Fish, "Lonnie Smith Gives Up on Baseball," *Kansas City Star*, September 30, 1987 (Clipping from Lonnie Smith's player file at the Baseball Hall of Fame Library). Rogers, "Lonnie Smith is Safe at Home." Kent Babb, "Lonnie Smith (Nearly) Driven to Murder John Schuerholz," *Baseball Fever*, November 7, 2006, https://www.baseball-fever.com/forum/general-baseball/current-events/17310-lonnie-smith-nearly-driven-to-murder-john-schuerholz.
 11. Stathead Baseball, Lonnie Smith Player Batting Split Finder 1989, https://stathead.com/baseball/split_finder.cgi?request=1&match=season&order_by_asc=0&order_by=onbase_plus_slugging&player_id_hint=Lonnie+Smith&player_id_select=Lonnie+Smith&player_id=smithlo01&year_min=1989&year_max=1989&split_1=dates%3Amonth&split_total_comp=gt&class=player&type=b&age_min=0&age_max=99&season_start=1&season_end=-1&location=pob&locationMatch=is.
 12. Terrence Moore, "Baseball Renaissance: Given Up for Dead—Except by Braves—Smith Revives Career," *The Sporting News*, August 7, 1989 (Clipping from Lonnie Smith's player file at the Baseball Hall of Fame Library).
 13. Baseball-Reference.com, 1991 World Series, Minnesota Twins Over Atlanta Braves (4–3), https://www.baseball-reference.com/postseason/1991_WS.shtml.
 14. Baseball-Reference.com, 1991 World Series Game 7, Braves at Twins, October 27, https://www.baseball-

reference.com/boxes/MIN/MIN 199110270.shtml.

15. "Lonnie Takes the Blame," *The Sporting News*, February 16, 1992 (Clipping from Lonnie Smith's player file at the Baseball Hall of Fame Library). Rogers "Lonnie Smith Is Safe at Home."

16. Rogers "Lonnie Smith Is Safe at Home."

17. Mark Armour and Daniel R. Levitt, "Baseball Demographics, 1947–2016," http://sabr.org/bioproj/topic/baseball-demographics-1947-2012.

Chapter 26

1. Jonas Thoms, "Rick Wilkins," https://sabr.org/bioproj/person/rick-wilkins/.

2. Joseph A. Reaves, "Wilkins Learns from His Demotion," *Chicago Tribune*, February, 28, 1994 (Clipping from Rick Wilkins's player file at the Baseball Hall of Fame Library).

3. Stathead Baseball, Rick Wilkins Player Batting Split Finder, https://stathead.com/baseball/split_finder.cgi?request=1&match=season&order_by_asc=0&order_by=onbase_plus_slugging&player_id_hint=Rick+Wilkins&player_id_select=Rick+Wilkins&player_id=wilkiri01&year_min=1993&year_max=1993&split_1=dates%3Amonth&split_total_comp=gt&class=player&type=b&age_min=0&age_max=99&season_start=1&season_end=-1&location=pob&locationMatch=is.

4. Baseball-Reference.com, 1993 All-Star Game Box Score, https://www.baseball-reference.com/allstar/1993-allstar-game.shtml.

5. Thoms, "Rick Wilkins."

6. "Wilkins Angered by Ridiculous Contract," *USA Today Baseball Weekly*, March 1, 1994 (Clipping from Rick Wilkins's player file at the Baseball Hall of Fame Library).

7. Thomas Hill, "Mets' Trade a Nice Catch," *New York Daily News*, May 13, 1998 (Clipping from Rick Wilkins's player file at the Baseball Hall of Fame Library).

8. Thoms, "Rick Wilkins."

Chapter 27

1. Scott Miller, "Esteban Loaiza's Wrong Turn," *Bleacher Report*, May 28, 2020, https://bleacherreport.com/articles/2890521-esteban-loaizas-wrong-turn.

2. Wikipedia, Esteban Loaiza, https://en.wikipedia.org/wiki/Esteban_Loaiza.

3. Miller, "Esteban Loaiza's Wrong Turn."

4. Miller, "Esteban Loaiza's Wrong Turn."

5. "Blue Jays Get Pitching Help," *Albany Times Union* (Associated Press), July 20, 2000 (Clipping from Esteban Loaiza's player file at the Baseball Hall of Fame Library).

6. Miller, "Esteban Loaiza's Wrong Turn."

7. Stathead Baseball, Esteban Loaiza Player Pitching Split Finder 2003 by Month, https://stathead.com/baseball/split_finder.cgi?request=1&order_by_asc=1&order_by=Name&player_id=loaizes01&year_min=2003&year_max=2003&split_1=dates%3Amonth&class=player&type=p&sr_pitching_splits_output=view_all.

8. Baseball-Reference.com, 2003 All-Star Game Box Score, July 15, https://www.baseball-reference.com/allstar/2003-allstar-game.shtml.

9. Player Pitching Game Stats Finder Esteban Loaiza, 2003, https://stathead.com/baseball/player-pitching-game-finder.cgi?request=1&order_by_asc=1&order_by=date&player_id=loaiza001est&year_min=2003&year_max=2003.

10. Stathead Baseball, Esteban Loaiza Player Pitching Split Finder 2004 by Month, https://stathead.com/baseball/split_finder.cgi?request=1&order_by_asc=1&order_by=Name&player_id=loaizes01&year_min=2004&year_max=2004&split_1=dates%3Amonth&class=player&type=p&sr_pitching_splits_output=view_all.

11. Arthur McCarron, "Jose Getting Thrown Away," *New York Daily News*, August 1, 2004 (Clipping from Esteban Loaiza's player file at the Baseball Hall of Fame Library).

12. Baseball-Reference, 2004 American League Championship Series (ALCS)

Game 5, Yankees at Red Sox, October 18, https://www.baseball-reference.com/boxes/BOS/BOS200410180.shtml.

13. Miller, "Esteban Loaiza's Wrong Turn."

14. Susan Slusser, "Loaiza a Changed Man Since last Year's DUI," SFGate.com, May 4, 2007 (Clipping from Esteban Loaiza's player file at the Baseball Hall of Fame Library).

15. Miller, "Esteban Loaiza's Wrong Turn."

16. Craig Calcaterra, "Esteban Loaiza's Wife, Music Star Jenni Rivera, Dies in a Plane Crash," NBCSports.com, December 11, 2012 (Clipping from Esteban Loaiza's player file at the Baseball Hall of Fame Library).

17. Miller, "Esteban Loaiza's Wrong Turn."

18. "Former MLB Pitcher Esteban Loaiza Denies Smuggling, Dealing Cocaine," ESPN.com (Associated Press), February 14, 2018 (Clipping from Esteban Loaiza's player file at the Baseball Hall of Fame Library).

19. Adry Torres, "Former MLB All-Star Esteban Loaiza Is Set to Be Released from Prison and Deported to Mexico after Serving Two Years for Trafficking 20 Kilos of Cocaine," Daily-Mail.com, August 5, 2021, https://www.dailymail.co.uk/news/article-9865681/Former-MLB-Star-Esteban-Loaiza-released-prison-cocaine-trafficking-conviction.html.

20. Stathead Baseball, Player Pitching Season & Career Stats Finder Mexican-Born Players with ≥ 50 Wins, https://stathead.com/baseball/player-pitching-season-finder.cgi?request=1&match=player_season_combined&order_by=p_w&ccomp%5B1%5D=gt&cval%5B1%5D=50&cstat%5B1%5D=p_w&location=pob&pob=MEX.

21. Miller, "Esteban Loaiza's Wrong Turn."

Chapter 28

1. Mark Hodermarsky, "Brian Giles," https://sabr.org/bioproj/person/brian-giles-2/.

2. Stathead Baseball, Marcus Giles Player Batting Split Finder 2001 by Month, https://stathead.com/baseball/split_finder.cgi?request=1&order_by_asc=1&order_by=Name&player_id=gilesma01&year_max=2001&split_1=dates%3Amonth&class=player&type=b.

3. Stathead Baseball, Player Batting Game Stats Finder Marcus Giles 2002, https://stathead.com/baseball/player-batting-game-finder.cgi?request=1&order_by_asc=1&order_by=date&player_id=giles-001mar&year_min=2002&year_max=2002. Wikipedia, Marcus Giles, https://en.wikipedia.org/wiki/Marcus_Giles. Baseball-Reference.com, Montreal Expos vs Atlanta Braves Box Score: May 28, 2002, https://www.baseball-reference.com/boxes/ATL/ATL200205280.shtml?__hstc=205977932.b08e7af248b5e4ce1b1e624af7b2c48a.1661105685144.1694013806073.1694027587117.380&__hssc=205977932.13.1694027587117&__hsfp=551255700.

4. Andy Martino, "Personal Loss Drives the Phillies' Giles," *The Philadelphia Enquirer*, March 9, 2009 (Clipping from Marcus Giles's player file at the Baseball Hall of Fame Library).

5. Stathead Baseball, Marcus Giles Player Batting Split Finder 2003 by Month, https://stathead.com/baseball/split_finder.cgi?request=1&order_by_asc=1&order_by=Name&player_id=gilesma01&year_min=2003&year_max=2003&split_1=dates%3Amonth&class=player&type=b.

6. David O'Brien, "Giles Suffers a Concussion, Might Miss All-Stars," AJC.com, July 11, 2003 (Clipping from Marcus Giles's player file at the Baseball Hall of Fame Library).

7. Baseball-Reference.com, 2003 NL Division Series Chicago Cubs Over Atlanta Braves (3–2), https://www.baseball-reference.com/postseason/2003_NLDS2.shtml.

8. Baseball-Reference.com, Atlanta Braves vs Milwaukee Brewers Box Score: May 15, 2004, https://www.baseball-reference.com/boxes/MIL/MIL200405150.shtml?__hstc=205977932.b08e7af248b5e4ce1b1e624af7b2c48a.1661105685144.1694027587117.16941021 35938.381&__hssc=205977932.2.169410 2135938&__hsfp=551255700#explain. Wikipedia, Marcus Giles.

9. Bill Center, "Oh, brother! Padres

Getting Marcus Giles for Second Base," *San Diego Union*, December 19, 2006 (Clipping from Marcus Giles's player file at the Baseball Hall of Fame Library).

10. Bill Center, "Giles Brothers Put 'Play' in Ballplayers," *San Diego Union*, December 21, 2006 (Clipping from Marcus Giles's player file at the Baseball Hall of Fame Library).

11. Ben Schroetenboer, "Marcus Giles Detained After Fight at Qualcomm," *Union-Tribune*, January 17, 2007 (Clipping from Marcus Giles's player file at the Baseball Hall of Fame Library).

12. Stathead Baseball, Marcus Giles Player Batting Split Finder 2007 by Month, https://stathead.com/baseball/split_finder.cgi?request=1&order_by_asc=1&order_by=Name&player_id=gilesma01&year_min=2007&split_1=dates%3Amonth&class=player&type=b.

13. Baseball-Reference.com, San Diego Padres vs Colorado Rockies Box Score: October 1, 2007, https://www.baseball-reference.com/boxes/COL/COL200710010.shtml.

14. David O'Brien, "Braves Make No Offers to Giles, Reitsma," AJC.com, December 13, 2006, http://www.ajc.com/braves/content/sports/braves/stories/2006/12/12/1213gilesgone.html.

15. Tim Dierkes, "Dodgers Almost Sign Marcus Giles," MLBTradeRumors.com, April 3, 2008, https://www.mlbtraderumors.com/2008/04/dodgers-almost.html.

16. Martino, "Personal Loss Drives the Phillies' Giles."

17. Doug Miller, "Former Infielder Sentenced to Three Years' Probation," MLB.com, April 1, 2010 https://www.mlbtraderumors.com/2008/04/dodgers-almost.html.

Chapter 29

1. Tim Kirkjian, "Prior Destined for Greatness," ESPN.com, March 29, 2003 (Clipping from Mark Prior's player file at the Baseball Hall of Fame Library).

2. Carrie Muscat, "Father and Son Fueled by Baseball," MLB.com Cubs News, June 23. 2003 (Clipping from Mark Prior's player file at the Baseball Hall of Fame Library).

3. Don Connolly, "Mauer, Twins' Calculated Risk, Pays Off," *Baltimore Sun*, June 18, 2006 (Clipping from Mark Prior's player file at the Baseball Hall of Fame Library).

4. Doug Miller, "Mark Prior in the Present Tense," MLB.com, February 8, 2013 (Clipping from Mark Prior's player file at the Baseball Hall of Fame Library).

5. ESPN Baseball Game Day Recap, "Prior Strikes Out 10 in Big League Debut," May 22, 2002 (Clipping from Mark Prior's player file at the Baseball Hall of Fame Library). Bob Nightingale, "Southern California's Prior Has the Wrigley Faithful Riding a New High," *USA Today Baseball Weekly*, May 29–June 4, 2002 (Clipping from Mark Prior's player file at the Baseball Hall of Fame Library). Stathead Baseball, Mark Prior 2002 Player Pitching Game Stats Finder, https://stathead.com/baseball/player-pitching-game-finder.cgi?request=1&match=player_game&order_by_asc=1&order_by=date&player_id_hint=Mark+Prior&player_id_select=Mark+Prior&player_id=prior-001mar&year_min=2002&year_max=2002&comp_type=reg&team_game_min=1&team_game_max=165&player_game_min=1&player_game_max=9999&is_pitcher=1&role=anyGS&days_rest_comp=%3D&location=pob&locationMatch=is&min_temperature=0&max_temperature=120&min_wind_speed=0&max_wind_speed=90.

6. Baseball-Reference.com, 2003 National League Statistics, https://www.baseball-reference.com/leagues/NL/2003.shtml.

7. Stathead Baseball, Mark Prior 2003 Player Pitching Game Stats Finder, https://stathead.com/baseball/player-pitching-game-finder.cgi?request=1&match=player_game&order_by_asc=1&order_by=date&player_id_hint=Mark+Prior&player_id_select=Mark+Prior&player_id=prior-001mar&year_min=2003&year_max=2003&comp_type=reg&team_game_min=1&team_game_max=165&player_game_min=1&player_game_max=9999&is_pitcher=1&role=anyGS&days_rest_comp=%3D&location=pob&locationMatch=

is&min_temperature=0&max_temperature=120&min_wind_speed=0&max_wind_speed=90.

8. Daniel G. Habib, "Double Whammy: The Surprising Cubs Are Banking on Mark Prior and Kerry Wood to End Their Championship Drought," *Sports Illustrated*, July 7, 2003 (Clipping from Mark Prior's player file at the Baseball Hall of Fame Library). Greg Couch, "Top Guns Have Rare Shot at Baseball History," *Chicago Sun-Times*, August 26, 2003 (Clipping from Mark Prior's player file at the Baseball Hall of Fame Library).

9. Baseball-Reference.com, 2003 National League Championship Series (NLCS) Game 6, Marlins at Cubs, October 14, https://www.baseball-reference.com/boxes/CHN/CHN200310140.shtml.

10. Doug Miller, "Mark Prior in the Present Tense."

11. Paul Sullivan, "Baker: Prior Report 'Crazy'—Disputes Claim of 'Bleak Prognosis,'" *Chicago Tribune*, April 12, 2004 (Clipping from Mark Prior's player file at the Baseball Hall of Fame Library).

12. Dave van Dyck, "Prior Breaks Elbow; Out two Months," *Chicago Tribune*, May 28, 2005 (Clipping from Mark Prior's player file at the Baseball Hall of Fame Library).

13. Stathead Baseball, Mark Prior 2005 Player Pitching Game Stats Finder, https://stathead.com/baseball/player-pitching-game-finder.cgi?request=1&order_by_asc=1&order_by=date&player_id=prior-001mar&year_min=2005&year_max=2005.

14. Phil Rogers, "Pitch for Success Can Be Costly; Cubs Now Paying for Pushing Prior, Wood," *Chicago Tribune*, March 15, 2006 (Clipping from Mark Prior's player file at the Baseball Hall of Fame Library).

15. Paul Sullivan, "Cubs Running Out of Excuses," *Chicago Tribune*, March 15, 2006 (Clipping from Mark Prior's player file at the Baseball Hall of Fame Library).

16. Paul Sullivan, "Employee Prior Accepts Demotion," *Chicago Tribune*, March 29, 2007 (Clipping from Mark Prior's player file at the Baseball Hall of Fame Library). "Prior to Have Surgery on His Shoulder; Miller Put on DL," Associated Press, April 24, 2007 (Clipping from Mark Prior's player file at the Baseball Hall of Fame Library).

17. Doug Miller, "Mark Prior in the Present Tense."

18. David Minie, "Former Cub Mark Prior Selected to the USC Hall of Fame," CubbiesCrib, July 7, 2014, https://cubbiescrib.com/2014/07/07/former-cub-mark-prior-selected-usc-hall-fame/#:~:text=Former%20Cub%20Mark%20Prior%20selected%20to%20USC%20Hall,and%20current%20Seattle%20Seahawks%20head%20coach%20Pete%20Carroll.

19. Cary Osborne, "Been Through It All, Mark Prior Leads a New Team of Pitching Coaches," *Dodger Insider*, February 3, 2020, https://dodgers.mlblogs.com/been-through-it-all-mark-prior-leads-a-new-pitching-coach-team-e21db292535.

Chapter 30

1. Albert Chen, "The Super Natural," *Sports Illustrated*, June 2, 2008 (Clipping from Josh Hamilton's player file at the Baseball Hall of Fame Library).

2. Chen, "The Super Natural."

3. Chen, "The Super Natural."

4. Stathead Baseball, Josh Hamilton 2008 Player Batting Split Finder by Month, https://stathead.com/baseball/split_finder.cgi?request=1&match=season&order_by_asc=0&order_by=onbase_plus_slugging&player_id_hint=Josh+Hamilton&player_id_select=Josh+Hamilton&player_id=hamiljo03&year_min=2008&year_max=2008&split_1=dates%3Amonth&split_total_comp=gt&class=player&type=b&age_min=0&age_max=99&season_start=1&season_end=-1&location=pob&locationMatch=is.

5. Stathead Baseball, Josh Hamilton 2008 Player Batting Split Finder First vs Second Half, https://stathead.com/baseball/split_finder.cgi?request=1&order_by_asc=0&order_by=onbase_plus_slugging&player_id=hamiljo03&year_min=2008&year_max=2008&split_1=dates%3Ahalf&class=player&type=b.

6. Baseball Reference, 2008 All-Star Game Box Score, July 15, https://www.baseball-reference.com/allstar/2008-allstar-game.shtml.

7. Jayson Stark, "Hamilton's Power Display Defies Explanation," ESPN.com, July 15, 2008 (Clipping from Josh Hamilton's player file at the Baseball Hall of Fame Library). Ethan Sears, "The Insane Story Behind Josh Hamilton's Legendary Home Run Derby," *New York Post*, January 16, 2018, https://nypost.com/2018/07/16/the-insane-story-behind-josh-hamiltons-legendary-home-run-derby/.

8. Richard Durrett, "Hurt Josh Hamilton Out 6–8 Weeks," ESPN.com Baseball, April 13, 2011 (Clipping from Josh Hamilton's player file at the Baseball Hall of Fame Library).

9. Stathead Baseball, Josh Hamilton 2009 Player Batting Split Finder First vs Second Half, https://stathead.com/baseball/split_finder.cgi?request=1&order_by_asc=0&order_by=onbase_plus_slugging&player_id=hamiljo03&year_min=2009&year_max=2009&split_1=dates%3Ahalf&class=player&type=b.

10. Baseball Reference, 2009 All-Star Game Box Score, July 14, https://www.baseball-reference.com/allstar/2009-allstar-game.shtml.

11. "Rangers Slugger Hamilton Admits Alcohol Relapse," FoxSports.com (Associated Press), August 10, 2009 (Clipping from Josh Hamilton's player file at the Baseball Hall of Fame Library).

12. Stathead Baseball, Josh Hamilton 2010 Player Batting Split Finder, https://stathead.com/baseball/split_finder.cgi?request=1&match=season&order_by_asc=0&order_by=onbase_plus_slugging&player_id_hint=Josh+Hamilton&player_id_select=Josh+Hamilton&player_id=hamiljo03&year_min=2009&year_max=2009&split_1=dates%3Amonth&split_total_comp=gt&class=player&type=b&age_min=0&age_max=99&season_start=1&season_end=-1&location=pob&locationMatch=is.

13. Durrett, "Hurt Josh Hamilton Out 6–8 Weeks."

14. Baseball Reference, 2010 All-Star Game Box Score, July 13, https://www.baseball-reference.com/allstar/2010-allstar-game.shtml.

15. Baseball-Reference.com, 2010 ALCS, https://www.baseball-reference.com/postseason/2010_ALCS.shtml.

16. Durrett, "Hurt Josh Hamilton Out 6–8 Weeks."

17. Baseball-Reference.com, 2011 All-Star Game Box Score, July 12, https://www.baseball-reference.com/allstar/2011-allstar-game.shtml.

18. Baseball-Reference.com, 2011 World Series, https://www.baseball-reference.com/postseason/2011_WS.shtml.

19. ESPN.com/Dallas, "Josh Hamilton Addresses Relapse," ESPN.com: Baseball, February 3, 2012 (Clipping from Josh Hamilton's player file at the Baseball Hall of Fame Library).

20. Baseball-Reference.com Bullpen: Josh Hamilton, https://www.baseball-reference.com/bullpen/Josh_Hamilton.

21. Stathead Baseball, Josh Hamilton 2012 Player Batting Split Finder, https://stathead.com/baseball/split_finder.cgi?request=1&match=season&order_by_asc=0&order_by=onbase_plus_slugging&player_id_hint=Josh+Hamilton&player_id_select=Josh+Hamilton&player_id=hamiljo03&year_min=2012&year_max=2012&split_1=dates%3Amonth&split_total_comp=gt&class=player&type=b&age_min=0&age_max=99&season_start=1&season_end=-1&location=pob&locationMatch=is.

22. "Rangers' Hamilton Hits 4 Homers vs. O's," FoxSports.com/MLB (Associated Press), May 9, 2012 (Clipping from Josh Hamilton's player file at the Baseball Hall of Fame Library).

23. Richard Durrett, "Nolan Ryan Questions Josh Hamilton," ESPN.com: Baseball, October 11, 2012 (Clipping from Josh Hamilton's player file at the Baseball Hall of Fame Library).

24. Baseball-Reference.com, 2012 All-Star Game Box Score, July 10, https://www.baseball-reference.com/allstar/2012-allstar-game.shtml.

25. Baseball-Reference.com Bullpen, Josh Hamilton, https://www.baseball-reference.com/bullpen/Josh_Hamilton.

26. Baseball-Reference.com, Texas Rangers vs. Oakland Athletics Box Score: October 3, 2012, https://www.baseball-reference.com/boxes/OAK/OAK201210030.shtml.

27. Jerry Crasnick, "Josh Hamilton's Messy Texas Exit," ESPN.com: Baseball,

December 14, 2012 (Clipping from Josh Hamilton's player file at the Baseball Hall of Fame Library).
   28. "Josh Hamilton to Miss 6–8 Weeks," ESPN.com: Baseball (Associated Press), April 9, 2014 (Clipping from Josh Hamilton's player file at the Baseball Hall of Fame Library).
   29. ESPN.com News Service, "Josh Hamilton Files for Divorce from Wife Katie," ESPN.com, April 20, 2015 (Clipping from Josh Hamilton's player file at the Baseball Hall of Fame Library).
   30. Emma Baccelieri, "Katie Hamilton Will Speak for Herself, Thank You," *Sports Illustrated*, July 8, 2021 (Clipping from Josh Hamilton's player file at the Baseball Hall of Fame Library).
   31. Mike Digiovanna, "Josh Hamilton Will Not Be Suspended for Substance-Abuse Relapse," *Sports Now*, April 3, 2015 (Clipping from Josh Hamilton's player file at the Baseball Hall of Fame Library). Mike Digiovanna, "Josh Hamilton Officially Traded by Angels to Texas Rangers," *Sports Now*, April 27, 2015 (Clipping from Josh Hamilton's player file at the Baseball Hall of Fame Library).
   32. Baseball-Reference.com Bullpen, Josh Hamilton.
   33. Baseball-Reference.com Bullpen, Josh Hamilton.
   34. Jeff Wilson, "Josh Hamilton Indicted, Accused of Injuring His Oldest Daughter," *Tampa Bay Times*, April 8, 2020 (Clipping from Josh Hamilton's player file at the Baseball Hall of Fame Library). Emma Baccelieri, "Katie Hamilton Will Speak for Herself, Thank You."
   35. Dayn Perry, "Former MLB Star Josh Hamilton Pleads Guilty to Misdemeanor in Assault Case Involving Daughter, per Report," CBS.com: MLB, February 23, 2022, https://www.cbssports.com/mlb/news/former-mlb-star-josh-hamilton-pleads-guilty-to-misdemeanor-in-assault-case-involving-daughter-per-report/.
   36. "Josh Hamilton Bound for Rangers Hall of Fame," ESPN.com: Baseball (Associated Press), May 20, 2019 (Clipping from Josh Hamilton's player file at the Baseball Hall of Fame Library).
   37. "Conversation: Josh Hamilton," *The Sporting News*, September 27, 2010 (Clipping from Josh Hamilton's player file at the Baseball Hall of Fame Library).

Chapter 31

   1. BaseballPlayerProfiles.com, "Matt Kemp," http://baseball.playerprofiles.com/sampleplayerprofile.asp?playerID=7622.
   2. BR Bullpen, Matt Kemp Biographical Information, https://www.baseball-reference.com/bullpen/Matt_Kemp.
   3. BR Bullpen, Matt Kemp.
   4. Stathead Baseball, Matt Kemp Player Batting Split Finder 2007 by Month, https://stathead.com/baseball/split_finder.cgi?request=1&order_by_asc=1&order_by=Name&player_id=kempma01&year_min=2007&year_max=2007&split_1=dates%3Amonth&class=player&type=b.
   5. BR Bullpen, Matt Kemp.
   6. Baseball-Reference.com, 2009 National League Division Series (NLDS) Game 1, Cardinals at Dodgers, October 7, https://www.baseball-reference.com/boxes/LAN/LAN200910070.shtml.
   7. Dylan Hernandez, "Fame Finds Dodgers' Matt Kemp," *Los Angeles Times*, February 25, 2010 (Clipping from Matt Kemp's player file at the Baseball Hall of Fame Library).
   8. Stathead Baseball, Player Batting Season & Career Stat Finder: Players with ≥60% of Their Games in CF, Sorted by Ascending dWAR, https://stathead.com/baseball/player-batting-season-finder.cgi?request=1&order_by_asc=1&order_by=b_war_def&positions%5B%5D=8&games_prop=60.
   9. Jerry Crasnick, "Kemp Ready to Turn Page," ESPN.com, March 1, 2011 (Clipping from Matt Kemp's player file at the Baseball Hall of Fame Library).
   10. Crasnick, "Kemp Ready to Turn Page."
   11. Stathead Baseball, Matt Kemp Player Batting Split Finder 2011 by Month, https://stathead.com/baseball/split_finder.cgi?request=1&order_by_asc=1&order_by=Name&player_id=kempma01&year_min=2011&year_max=2011&split_1=dates%3Amonth&class=player&type=b.
   12. Baseball-Reference.com, 2011

All-Star Game Box Score, July 12, https://www.baseball-reference.com/allstar/2011-allstar-game.shtml.

13. ESPN.com News Services, "Silver Slugger Awards Announced," ESPN.com, November 2, 2011 (Clipping from Matt Kemp's player file at the Baseball Hall of Fame Library). MLB press release memo, "Jose Bautista, Matt Kemp Win the 2011 Hank Aaron Award," October 24, 2011 (Clipping from Matt Kemp's player file at the Baseball Hall of Fame Library).

14. Dylan Hernandez, "Kemp Is Voted Most Inspirational by Dodgers Teammates," *Los Angeles Times*, September 21, 2011 (Clipping from Matt Kemp's player file at the Baseball Hall of Fame Library).

15. Baseball-Reference.com, 2011 Awards Voting, https://www.baseball-reference.com/awards/awards_2011.shtml#all_NL_MVP_voting.

16. "Kemp: Ryan Braun Should Lose MVP," Associated Press, July 23, 2013 (Clipping from Matt Kemp's player file at the Baseball Hall of Fame Library).

17. Dylan Hernandez, "Dodgers' Matt Kemp Would Win MVP Award Over Ryan Braun in a New Vote," LATimes.com, December 20, 2011 (Clipping from Matt Kemp's player file at the Baseball Hall of Fame Library).

18. "Dodgers, Red Sox Boast 6 Gold Glovers," ESPN.com (Associated Press), November 1, 2011 (Clipping from Matt Kemp's player file at the Baseball Hall of Fame Library).

19. Ramona Shelbourne, "Dodgers, Matt Kemp Finalize Contract," ESPN.com, November 18, 2011 (Clipping from Matt Kemp's player file at the Baseball Hall of Fame Library).

20. Stathead Baseball, Matt Kemp Player Batting Split Finder 2012 by Month, https://stathead.com/baseball/split_finder.cgi?request=1&order_by_asc=1&order_by=Name&player_id=kempma01&year_min=2012&year_max=2012&split_1=dates%3Amonth&class=player&type=b. BR Bullpen, Matt Kemp.

21. BR Bullpen, Matt Kemp.

22. BR Bullpen, Matt Kemp.

23. Mark Saxon, "Kemp Has Surgery on Ankle," ESPN.com, October 21, 2013 (Clipping from Matt Kemp's player file at the Baseball Hall of Fame Library).

24. Baseball-Reference.com, 2014 National League Division Series (NLDS) Game 2, Cardinals at Dodgers, October 4, https://www.baseball-reference.com/boxes/LAN/LAN201410040.shtml.

25. ESPN.com News Services, "Dodgers Agree to Trade Matt Kemp," ESPN.com, December 11, 2014 (Clipping from Matt Kemp's player file at the Baseball Hall of Fame Library).

26. "Braves Acquire Matt Kemp, Send Hector Olivera to San Diego," Boston-Herald.com (Associated Press), July 31, 2016 (Clipping from Matt Kemp's player file at the Baseball Hall of Fame Library).

27. Gordon Dixon, "Padre Exec Rips Players Padres Traded Away," Larry Brown Sports, November 19, 2016 (Clipping from Matt Kemp's player file at the Baseball Hall of Fame Library).

28. ESPN News Services, "Dodgers Part Ways with Adrian Gonzalez in Five-Player Deal with Braves," ESPN.com, December 17, 2017 (Clipping from Matt Kemp's player file at the Baseball Hall of Fame Library).

29. Baseball-Reference.com, 2018 World Series (NLDS) Game 1, Dodgers at Red Sox, October 23, https://www.baseball-reference.com/boxes/BOS/BOS201810230.shtml.

30. Tim Brown, "Viral Video of Matt Kemp's Touching Gesture to Young Fan Catches Dodger Off Guard," Yahoo Sports, May 7, 2013 (Clipping from Matt Kemp's player file at the Baseball Hall of Fame Library). Fox Sports West Staff, "Matt Kemp to Donate $1000 to Tornado Relief for Every HR," Fox Sports, May 20, 2013 (Clipping from Matt Kemp's player file at the Baseball Hall of Fame Library).

Chapter 32

1. John C. Tattersall, "Clarifying an early home run record." *Baseball Research Journal* 1 (1972), https://sabr.org/journal/article/clarifying-an-early-home-run-record/.

Bibliography

SABR Baseball Biography Project (https://sabr.org/bioproject)

Berger, Ralph. "Al Rosen."
Bjarkman, Peter C. "Zoilo Versalles."
Bush, Frederick C. "Slim Jones."
Gluckstein, Fred. "Wilcy Moore."
Hilliard, Rob, and Larry Hilliard. "John Hiller."
Hodermarsky, Mark. "Brian Giles."
Jones, Mark. "Dutch Leonard."
Kates, Maxwell. "Norm Cash."
Keenan, Jimmy. "Billy Martin."
Kirwin, Bill. "Cy Seymour." Adapted from a chapter in Simon, Tom. *Deadball Stars of the National League.* Cleveland: Society for American Baseball Research, 2004, 239–242.
Kluck, Lee. "Dwight Gooden."
Marmer, Mel. "Bobby Shantz."
Marshall, Ron "Rico Petrocelli."
McMurray, John. "George Stone" Adapted from a chapter in Jones, David. *Deadball Stars of the American League.* Cleveland: Society for American Baseball Research, 2004, 786–787.
Puerzer, Rich. "Mark Fidrych."
Sitar, Tim. "Mark Eichhorn."
Skelton, David E. "Billy Grabarkewitz."
Skelton, David E. "Dick Ellsworth."
Sparks, Glen. "Darrell Porter."
Stolzenbach, Corey. "Jim Gentile."
Thoms, Jonas. "Rick Wilkins."
Wisnia, Saul "Tommy Holmes."
Wolf, Gregory H. "Harry Brecheen."

Articles

"Admiration for Hiller Replaces Sympathy." *Syracuse Herald-American* (Associated Press), June 17, 1973.
Albanese, Laura. "Tommy Holmes, 91, Held NL Hit Streak Record." *Newsday*, April 15, 2008.
Albelli, Alfred, and Henry Lee. "Calls Shortstop Foul Ball: Blonde Says Rico Made Wrong Play." *New York Daily News*, March 12, 1971.
Allen, Maury. "Mantle: I Couldn't Have Hit Gooden." *New York Post*, December 21, 1985.
Antonen, Mel. "Gooden Says Only Miracle Kept Him Alive." *USA Today*, March 5, 1999.
Armour, Mark, and Dan R. Levitt. "Baseball Demographics, 1947–2016." http://sabr.org/bioproj/topic/baseball-demographics-1947-2012
Babb, Kent. "Lonnie Smith (Nearly) Driven to Murder John Schuerholz." *Baseball Fever*, November 7, 2006. https://www.baseball-fever.com/forum/general-baseball/current-events/17310-lonnie-smith-nearly-driven-to-murder-john-schuerholz.
Bacceliari, Emma. "Katie Hamilton Will Speak for Herself, Thank You." *Sports Illustrated*, July 8, 2021.
"'The Bird' Visited by Ford." *Columbus Dispatch* (Associated Press), July 14, 1976.
"Bird's Struggle for Life in Baseball Is Over." United Press International, June 30, 1983.
Blaisdell, Lowell L. "The Cobb-Speaker Scandal: Exonerated but Probably Guilty."

NINE: A Journal of Baseball History and Culture 13, no. 2 (February 21, 2005). https://www.deepdyve.com/lp/university-of-nebraska-press/the-cobb-speaker-scandal-exonerated-but-probably-guilty-m0S1E5GG6s.
"Blue Jays Get Pitching Help." *Albany Times Union* (Associated Press), July 20, 2000.
Bodley, Hal. "Cards' Lonnie Smith Reflects on Sober Life." *USA Today*, September 14, 1983.
Bordman, Sid. "Dear Abby: Royals Think You're Super." *The Sporting News*, July 25, 1970.
Braucher, Bill. "Sympathizes with Kekich, Peterson: Petrocelli Had His Shock Too." *Miami Herald*, March 9, 1973.
"Braves Acquire Matt Kemp, Send Hector Olivera to San Diego." BostonHerald.com (Associated Press), July 31, 2016.
Briere, Tom. "Fizzle or Flash—Flighty Zoilo Prime Puzzle for Twins Brass." *The Sporting News*, May 23, 1962.
Broeg, Bob. "Keep Your Eye on the Cat." *Sport Magazine*, October 1947.
Broeg, Bob. "Solace for Hall in Cobb Case." *The Sporting News*, May 12, 1973.
Brown, Doug. "Orioles Expect Siebern to Add Hustle and Spark." *Baltimore Sun*, December 7, 1963.
Brown, Tim. "Viral Video of Matt Kemp's Touching Gesture to Young Fan Catches Dodger Off Guard." Yahoo Sports, May 7, 2013.
Burns, Edward. "Southworth Quits Boston; Name Holmes." *Chicago Tribune*, June 20, 1951.
Bush, David. "New Delivery Route Saved Blue Jays' Eichhorn." *Toronto Chronicle*, May 23, 1987.
"Cal Weary of Twin Beefs, Backs Mele's Crackdown on Versalles." *The Sporting News*, April 17, 1965.
Calcaterra, Craig. "Esteban Loaiza's Wife, Music Star Jenni Rivera, Dies in a Plane Crash." NBCSports.com, December 11, 2012.
Center, Bill. "Giles Brothers Put 'Play' in Ballplayers." *San Diego Union*, December 21, 2006.
Center, Bill. "Oh, Brother! Padres Getting Marcus Giles for Second Base." *San Diego Union*, December 19, 2006.
Chen, Albert. "The Super Natural." *Sports Illustrated*, June 2, 2008.
Claflin, Larry. "Rico's Sensational ... Sometimes; What Ails the Bosox Flash?" *Boston Globe*, August 27, 1966.
Claire, Fred. Los Angeles Dodgers press release. November 1968.
Connolly, Don. "Mauer, Twins' Calculated Risk, Pays Off." *Baltimore Sun*, June 18, 2006.
"Conversation: Josh Hamilton." *The Sporting News*, September 27, 2010.
Couch, Greg. "Top Guns Have Rare Shot at Baseball History." *Chicago Sun-Times*, August 26, 2003.
Coutros, Pete. "The Great Debate: Seaver vs Gooden." *New York Daily News*, July 22, 1988.
Crane, Sam. "The Fifty Greatest Players in *History*, No. 23: Fred Dunlap." *New York Journal*, January 30, 1912.
Crasnick, Jerry. "Josh Hamilton's Messy Texas Exit." ESPN.com: Baseball, December 14, 2012.
Crasnick, Jerry. "Kemp Ready to Turn Page." ESPN.com, March 1, 2011.
Curry, Jack. "Dr. No: A Revived Gooden No-Hits the Mariners." *New York Times*, May 15, 1996.
"Cy Seymour's Iron Man." Unattributed interview with John McGraw, circa 1917–19.
Detroit Tigers press release. July 28, 1973.
Dierkes, Tim. "Dodgers Almost Sign Marcus Giles." MLBTradeRumors.com, April 3, 2008, https://www.mlbtraderumors.com/2008/04/dodgers-almost.html.
Digiovanna, Mike. "Josh Hamilton Officially Traded by Angels to Texas Rangers." *Sports Now*, April 27, 2015.
Digiovanna, Mike. "Josh Hamilton Will Not Be Suspended for Substance-Abuse Relapse." *Sports Now*, April 3, 2015.

Bibliography

Di Ionno, Mark. "Keith Takes a Beating During Pittsburgh Drug Trial." *New York Post*, September 6, 1985.
Dixon, Gordon. "Padre Exec Rips Players Padres Traded Away." Larry Brown Sports, November 19, 2016.
"Dodgers, Red Sox Boast 6 Gold Glovers." ESPN.com (Associated Press), November 1, 2011.
Dozer, Richard. "Ellsworth wins comeback award." *Chicago Tribune*, October 15, 1963.
Drury, Bob. "Home, Bittersweet Home." *Newsday*, December 19, 1986.
"Dunlap for Detroit: The Famous Player Secured by President Marsh." *Detroit Free Press*, August 7, 1886.
"Dunlap on His Mettle." *New York Times*, November 17, 1987.
"Dunlap Released by Pittsburg." *Detroit Free Press*, May 17, 1890.
Durrett, Richard. "Nolan Ryan Questions Josh Hamilton." ESPN.com: Baseball, October 11, 2012.
Dutton, Bob. "Former Royal Overcame Addiction, Touched Hundreds of Lives." *Kansas City Star*, August 7, 2002.
"Dwight Gooden Gets Probation for 2019 Drug Arrest." Associated Press, November 13, 2020.
Engber, Daniel. "You Guys Are Scaring Me." Slate, January 12, 2020. https://slate.com/culture/2020/01/mets-rape-accusation-spring-training-1991.html.
Enright, James. "Hutch Award Thrills Tigers' Hiller." *Chicago Today*, January 21, 1974.
Enright, James. "20 Defeats Shaped Ellsworth into Ace." *The Sporting News*, August 17, 1963.
ESPN Baseball. "Doctor Says Porter Did Not Die of an Overdose." August 13, 2002.
ESPN Baseball Game Day Recap. "Prior Strikes Out 10 in Big League Debut." May 22, 2002.
ESPN.com/Dallas. "Josh Hamilton Addresses Relapse." ESPN.com: Baseball, February 3, 2012.
ESPN.com News Services. "Dodgers Agree to Trade Matt Kemp." ESPN.com, December 11, 2014.
ESPN.com News Services. "Dodgers Part Ways with Adrian Gonzalez in Five-Player Deal with Braves." ESPN.com, December 17, 2017.
ESPN.com News Services. "Josh Hamilton Files for Divorce from Wife Katie." ESPN.com, April 20, 2015.
ESPN.com News Services. "Silver Slugger Awards Announced." ESPN.com, November 2, 2011.
Falls, Joe. "Aguirre Always Delivered Happiness." *Detroit News*, September 6, 1994.
Falls, Joe. "Aguirre Always Delivered in Life." *USA Today Baseball Weekly*, September 12, 1994.
Falls, Joe. "Detroit's Ready Cash." *Saturday Evening Post*, May 19, 1962.
Fish, Mike. "Lonnie Smith Gives Up on Baseball." *Kansas City Star*, September 30, 1987.
Foley, Red. "Cub Ace Dick First in 28 Years to Lose 20, Then Log 20 Wins." *The Sporting News*, September 28, 1963.
"Former MLB Pitcher Esteban Loaiza Denies Smuggling, Dealing Cocaine." ESPN.com (Associated Press), February 14, 2018.
Fox Sports West Staff. "Matt Kemp to Donate $1000 to Tornado Relief for Every HR." Fox Sports, May 20, 2013.
Fred Dunlap Death Certificate, Philadelphia, PA, No. 2956, December 1, 1902.
Frye, Jennifer. "Another Strike Against Gooden in Drug Violations." *New York Times*, September 16, 1994.
Furlong, Barry. "Will Success Spoil The Bird?" *New York Times Magazine*, August 22, 1976.
"Gentile Hits Two Grand Slam Homers in Row!" *Chicago Tribune*, May 10, 1961.
"George Stone." *Clinton Herald*, January 6, 1945.
Gillespie, Ray. "The Cat in Middle of St. Louis Rhubarb." *The Sporting News*, November 5, 1952.

Goethel, Arno. "Boots and Beauts Marked Zoilo's Play." *The Sporting News,* December, 28, 1963.

Goldman, Steven. "You Could Look It Up: The Importance of Being Paul Waner." *Baseball Prospectus,* May 12, 2009. https://www.baseballprospectus.com/news/article/8863/you-could-look-it-up-the-importance-of-being-paul-waner/.

Goldstein, Dennis, and Richard A Puff. "Frederick C. Dunlap." In Overfield, Joseph M., Paul Adomites, Richard Puff, and L. Robert Davids, *Nineteenth Century Stars.* Phoenix: Society for American Baseball Research, 2012, 82–83.

Goldstein, Richard. "Al Rosen, Who Missed Triple Crown by a Step, Dies at 91." *New York Times,* March 14, 2015.

Goldstein, Richard. "Harry Brecheen, 89, Pitcher With 3 Victories in '46 Series." *New York Times,* January 20, 2004.

Goldstein, Richard. "Tommy Holmes, 91, Who Set NL Hitting Mark, Is Dead." *New York Times,* April 15, 2008.

Gooden, Dwight, and Ellis Henican, *Doc: A Memoir.* New York: New Harvest, 2003.

Goodtimes, Johnny. "The Tragedy of Sim Jones." *Philly Sports History,* May 13, 2011, https://phillysportshistory.com/2011/05/13/the-tragedy-of-slim-jones/.

Gordon, David J. "Using Career Value Index (CVI) to Evaluate Hall of Fame Credentials of Negro League Players." *Baseball Research Journal* 51, no. 2 (Fall 2022): 112–21.

Green, Jerry. "Hiller a Specialist in Fine Art of Survival." *Detroit Free Press,* January 5, 1997.

Green, Sharony Andrews. "Former Tiger Threw Talent, Energy into Hispanic Firm." *Detroit Free Press,* September 5, 1994.

"Grimm Back in Majors; Replaces Holmes as Braves' Pilot Today." *Chicago Tribune* (Associated Press), June 1, 1952.

Gross, Jane. "Al Rosen Resigns Post with Yanks." *New York Times,* September 20, 1979.

Gross, Milton. "Palace of Versailles." *New York Post,* October 5, 1965.

Habib, Daniel G. "Double Whammy: The Surprising Cubs Are Banking on Mark Prior and Kerry Wood to End Their Championship Drought." *Sports Illustrated,* July 7, 2003.

Hawkins, Jim. "Cash Undergoes Tests After Suffering a Stroke." *Detroit Free Press,* July 17, 1979.

Hawkins, Jim. "Devalued Cash Rejects Over-Hill Tag." *Detroit Free Press,* April 13, 1974.

Hawkins, Jim. "Two Years Later, The Bird's a Wise Old Owl." *The Sporting News,* January 27, 1979.

"H.B. Leonard, Ex-Baseball Great, Is Dead." July 11, 1952.

Henderson, Joe. "Unfortunately Gooden May Never Learn." TBO Sports, April 6, 2006, http://www.tbo.com/sports/mgbtt3qkole.html.

Henkey, Ben. "Hiller, Dave Johnson Win Comeback Crowns." *The Sporting News,* December 1, 1973.

Herman, Jack. "Cardinals 'Shocked, Surprised' by Smith's Disclosure." *St. Louis Globe-Democrat,* June 13, 1983.

Hernandez, Dylan. "Dodgers' Matt Kemp Would Win MVP Award Over Ryan Braun in a New Vote." LATimes.com, December 20, 2011.

Hernandez, Dylan. "Fame Finds Dodgers' Matt Kemp." *Los Angeles Times,* February 25, 2010.

Hernandez, Dylan. "Kemp Is Voted Most Inspirational by Dodgers Teammates." *Los Angeles Times,* September 21, 2011.

Hill, Thomas. "Mets' Trade A Nice Catch." *New York Daily News,* May 13, 1998.

Hiller, John. "What It Takes to Begin Again." *Guideposts,* May 1974.

Hochman, Stan. "Lonnie's Act Is Anything but Funny." *Philadelphia Daily News,* September 14, 1982.

Holmes, Dan. "Did the Corked Bat Help Norm Cash?" VintageDetroit, December 4, 2019, https://www.vintagedetroit.com/did-the-corked-bat-help-norm-cash/.

Holtzman, Jerome. "Cobb and Speaker got themselves into a real fix." *Chicago Tribune,*

Bibliography

May 21, 1989, https://www.chicagotribune.com/news/ct-xpm-1989-05-21-8902030567-story.html.
Holtzman, Jerome. "Hurler Abernathy Proves Lifesaver as Ace Reliever." *The Sporting News*, June 12. 1965.
Holtzman, Jerome. "Iron-Man Abernathy Cops Fireman Prize—Fisher AL King." *The Sporting News*, October 16, 1965.
Holway, John. "Slim Strasburg." May 2010.
Hunter, Bob. "Billy G. Is Just Great, Dodgers Crow." *The Sporting News*, August 1, 1970.
"Hurt Josh Hamilton Out 6–8 Weeks." ESPN.com Baseball, April 13, 2011.
Hurwitz, Hy. "Holmes Another Foxx in Miniature." *Boston Sunday Globe*, January 11, 1942.
Irish, Arnold. "Porter Has Rare Talent for Handling Pitchers." *St. Louis Post-Dispatch*, May 9, 1983.
Izenberg, Jerry. "Izenberg at Large." *Syracuse Post-Standard*, July 17, 1973.
"Jim Gentile Tees Off and Joins Babe Ruth." *Orioles Journal*, July 8, 1961.
"Josh Hamilton Bound for Rangers Hall of Fame." ESPN.com: Baseball (Associated Press), May 20, 2019.
"Josh Hamilton to Miss 6–8 Weeks." ESPN.com: Baseball (Associated Press), April 9, 2014.
Kaegel, Dick. "Former Royal Porter Played to Win." *Kansas City Star*, August 7, 2002.
Kay, Michael. "Greats Agree: Gooden's the Best." *New York Post*, November 14, 1985.
"Kemp: Ryan Braun Should Lose MVP." Associated Press, July 23, 2013.
Kepner, Tyler. "Holtzman, Creator of the Save Rule, Dies at 82." *New York Times*, July 21, 2008.
King, George. "Yanks Doubt Doc's Story." *New York Post*, May 24, 1997.
Kirkjian, Tim. "Prior Destined for Greatness." ESPN.com, March 29, 2003.
Klein, Larry. "How Good Can Jim Gentile Get?" *Sport Magazine*, 1961.
Kremenko, Barney. "Ellsworth: Dream Pitcher." *New York Journal American*, August 18, 1963..
Lammers, Dirk. "May 6, 1949: Bobby Shantz Tosses 9 No-Hit Innings in Relief for A's." SABR Games Project, https://sabr.org/gamesproj/game/may-6-1949-bobby-shantz-tosses-9-no-hit-innings-in-relief-for-as/.
Lebovitz, Hal. "Majeski on Third." *Cleveland Plain Dealer*, August 20, 1952.
Leggett, William. "Pitching a No-Quitter." *Sports Illustrated*, June 11, 1973.
"Lonnie Takes the Blame." *The Sporting News*, February 16, 1992.
Lubinger, Bill. "Indians' Great Al Rosen on Anti-Semitism: 'I Had Broad Shoulders,'" *Cleveland Plain Dealer*, October 11, 2010.
Lustig, Dennis. "Whatever Happened to Jim Gentile?" August 12, 1970.
Madden, Bill. "Versalles Battles Post-Career Pains, Problems." *The Sporting News*, May 28, 1984.
Maher, Charles. "Versalles, Grant Traded by Minnesota to Dodgers." *Los Angeles Times*, November 29, 1967.
Marsh, Dave. "The Tale of the Bird." *Rolling Stone*, May 5, 1977.
Martin, Kimberly. "Gooden Facing Slew of Charges." *Newsday*, March 25, 2010.
Martino, Andy. "Personal Loss Drives the Phillies' Giles." *Philadelphia Enquirer*, March 9, 2009.
Maynard, Micheline. "Fidrych, Baseball's Beloved 'Bird,' Dies at 54." *New York Times*, April 14, 2009.
McAlary, Mike. "Guidry on Gooden: He'll Strike Out 4000." *New York Post*, July 5, 1985.
McCarron, Arthur. "Jose Getting Thrown Away." *New York Daily News*, August 1, 2004.
McCarthy, Jack. "How They Loved Tommy." *Boston Herald*, July 30, 1978.
McDarrah, Tim, and Amy Pagnozzi. "'Doc' Throws Dwight Hook in Brawlgame with Cops." *New York Post*, December 15, 1986.
McGuff, Joe. "'Now A's Have Best 1–2 Punch in Gentile, Rocky,' Says Friday." *Kansas City Star*, December 7, 1963.

Meehan, Tom. "Fresno renowned as the cradle of mound stars." *The Sporting News*, September 28, 1963.
Miklasz, Bernie. "Lonnie Smith Is Blue, but Not Yet Royal." *St. Louis Post-Dispatch*, June 24, 1885.
Miller, Doug. "Former Infielder Sentenced to Three Years' Probation." MLB.com, April 1, 2010. https://www.mlbtraderumors.com/2008/04/dodgers-almost.html.
Miller, Doug. "Mark Prior in the Present Tense." MLB.com, February 8, 2013.
Miller, Scott. "Esteban Loaiza's Wrong Turn." *Bleacher Report*, May 28, 2020, https://bleacherreport.com/articles/2890521-esteban-loaizas-wrong-turn.
Minie, David. "Former Cub Mark Prior Selected to the USC Hall of Fame." Cubbies-Crib, July 7, 2014, https://cubbiescrib.com/2014/07/07/former-cub-mark-prior-selected-usc-hall-fame/#:~:text=Former%20Cub%20Mark%20Prior%20selected%20to%20USC%20Hall,and%20current%20Seattle%20Seahawks%20head%20coach%20Pete%20Carroll
Mitchell, AKC. "The Sensational Outburst of Pitcher Hubert Leonard Elicits a Prompt, Complete and Crushing Answer from President Lannin." June 5, 1915.
MLB press release memo. "Jose Bautista, Matt Kemp Win the 2011 Hank Aaron Award." October 24, 2011.
"Monster." *New York Daily News*, August 22, 2016.
Moore, Terrence. "Baseball Renaissance: Given Up for Dead—Except by Braves—Smith Revives Career." *The Sporting News*, August 7, 1989.
Muscat, Carrie. "Father and Son Fueled by Baseball." MLB.com Cubs News, June 23. 2003.
Nelson, Robert T.. "Darrell Porter: Cards New Catcher Has Two Sides—The All-Star Athlete and the Insecure Young Man Who Sought Refuge in Alcohol." *St. Louis Post Dispatch*, circa January 1981.
Nichols, Max. "Joyful News from Zoilo: Arm's Sore." *The Sporting News*, April 1, 1967.
Nightingale, Bob. "Southern California's Prior Has the Wrigley Faithful Riding a New High." *USA Today Baseball Weekly*, May 29-June 4, 2002.
Norm Cash Obituary. *Newark Star-Ledger*, October 13, 1986.
O'Brien, David. "Braves Make No Offers to Giles, Reitsma." AJC.com, December 13, 2006, http://www.ajc.com/braves/content/sports/braves/stories/2006/12/12/1213gilesgone.html.
O'Brien, David. "Giles Suffers a Concussion, Might Miss All-Stars." AJC.com, July 11, 2003.
O'Grady, Sandy. "Trade Well Worth It—to Ellsworth." *Philadelphia Bulletin*, March 7, 1967.
Ojeda-Zapata, Julio, and Charley Walters. "Versalles Dies at 55." *St. Paul Pioneer Press*, June 10, 1995.
Oliver, Chris. "Doc, You're a Real Jerk ...." *New York Post*, April 4, 1987.
Osborne, Cary. "Been Through It All, Mark Prior Leads a New Team of Pitching Coaches." *Dodger Insider*, February 3, 2020, https://dodgers.mlblogs.com/been-through-it-all-mark-prior-leads-a-new-pitching-coach-team-e21db292535.
Parker, Frank. "Crouches at Bat." *St. Louis Globe-Dispatch*, November 3, 1906.
Perry, Dayn. "Former MLB Star Josh Hamilton Pleads Guilty to Misdemeanor in Assault Case Involving Daughter, per Report." CBS.com: MLB, February 23, 2022, https://www.cbssports.com/mlb/news/former-mlb-star-josh-hamilton-pleads-guilty-to-misdemeanor-in-assault-case-involving-daughter-per-report/.
"Plunges to Death." Associated Press, March 6, 1971.
Porter, Darrell. "The Comeback." *Guideposts*, November 1981, pp 27–30.
"Prior to Have Surgery on His Shoulder; Miller Put on DL." Associated Press, April 24, 2007.
"Rangers' Hamilton Hits 4 Homers vs. O's." FoxSports.com/MLB (Associated Press), May 9, 2012.
"Rangers Slugger Hamilton Admits Alcohol Relapse." FoxSports.com (Associated Press), August 10, 2009.

Rapaport, Ron. "Dodgers Trade Robinson to Angels." *Los Angeles Times,* November 27, 1972.
Reaves, Joseph A. "Wilkins Learns From His Demotion." *Chicago Tribune,* February 28, 1994.
Reusse, Patrick. "Versalles Was Our Early Hero." *Minneapolis Star-Tribune,* June 10, 1995.
Richman, Milton. "Ermer Cost Twins Flag—Zoilo." *Knickerbocker News,* February 21, 1968.
"The Rise and Fall of the Deadball Era." *Baseball Research Journal* 47, no. 2 (Fall 2018): 92–102.
Rogers, Carroll. "Lonnie Smith Is Safe at Home." *Atlanta Journal Constitution,* July 12, 2003.
Rogers, Phil. "Pitch for Success Can B Costly; Cubs Now Paying for Pushing Prior, Wood." *Chicago Tribune,* March 15, 2006.
"Rosen Authorized bad Credit in Loss by Four Casinos." Associated Press, November 1980.
"Rosen of Indians Quits Baseball; 'I Can't Do Job Anymore.'" United Press International, January 31, 1957.
"Rosen Promises Giant Overhaul." *Albany Times Union* (Associated Press), September 19, 1985.
Ross, John M. "Mighty Mite of the A's." 1952.
Rowe, Chris. "Hiller, Marshall Set Relief Marks." *The Sporting News,* October 27, 1973.
Rumili, Ed. "Twins' Versalles the 'Little Meter.'" *Christian Science Monitor,* October 8, 1965.
Rushin, Steve. "The Bird is Back." *Sports Illustrated,* July 2, 2001
Saxon, Mark. "Matt Kemp Has Surgery on Ankle." ESPN.com, October 21, 2013.
Schroetenboer, Ben. "Marcus Giles Detained After Fight at Qualcomm." *Union-Tribune,* January 17, 2007.
Sears, Ethan. "The Insane Story Behind Josh Hamilton's Legendary Home Run Derby." *New York Post,* January 16, 2018, https://nypost.com/2018/07/16/the-insane-story-behind-josh-hamiltons-legendary-home-run-derby/.
"Secret Shame of Met Star Doc." *New York Post,* May 19, 2013.
Sexton, Joe. "Can Gooden Work Off the Cuff?" *New York Times,* January 19, 1992.
Shelbourne, Ramona. "Dodgers, Matt Kemp Finalize Contract." ESPN.com, November 18, 2011.
Simenic, Joseph. Letter, December 13, 1968.
Slusser, Susan. "Loaiza A Changed Man Since last Year's DUI." SFGate.com, May 4, 2007.
Smith, Red. "Views of Sport: The Cat of the Cardinals." *New York Herald Tribune,* May 1948.
"Sparky Tells 'Bird' to Put Up or Shut Up." Associated Press, April 6, 1980.
Spoelstra, Watson. "New-Style Hank Big Roar in Tiger Tank." *The Sporting News*, March 1966.
Stark, Jayson. "Hamilton's Power Display Defies Explanation." ESPN.com, July 15, 2008.
Steadman, John. "Brecheen Big Brother to Orioles Hurlers." *The Sporting News,* October 26, 1961.
Stockton, J. Roy. "Lefty Brecheen Meshes into Cardinals Machine." *The Sporting News,* July 1. 1943.
"Stone's Belief Is That a Player Should Retire While Still Young." *Sporting Life,* October 6, 1906.
Storm, Stephanie. "Competitive Streak Still Burning in Al Rosen." *Akron Beacon-Journal,* February 29, 2004.
Sullivan, Paul. "Baker: Prior Report 'Crazy'—Disputes Claim of 'Bleak Prognosis.'" *Chicago Tribune,* April 12, 2004.
Sullivan, Paul. "Cubs Running Out of Excuses." *Chicago Tribune,* March 15, 2006.
Sullivan, Paul. "Employee Prior Accepts Demotion." *Chicago Tribune,* March 29, 2007.

Tattersall, John C.. "Clarifying an Early Home Run Record." *Baseball Research Journal* 1 (1972). https://sabr.org/journal/article/clarifying-an-early-home-run-record/.
Testerman, Jeff. "Where Did Gooden's Millions Go?" *St. Petersburg Times*, November 16, 2003.
Tingley, Ken. "Wilcy Moore: The Missing Link of the 1927 Yankees." *Oneonta Daily Star*, September 21, 1985.
Torres, Adry. "Former MLB All-Star Esteban Loaiza Is Set to be Released from Prison and Deported to Mexico after Serving Two Years for Trafficking 20 Kilos of Cocaine." DailyMail.com, August 5, 2021, https://www.dailymail.co.uk/news/article-9865681/Former-MLB-Star-Esteban-Loaiza-released-prison-cocaine-trafficking-conviction.html.
Trachtenberg, Leo. "Moore Blazed the Trail for Yankee Firemen." *Yankees Magazine*, September 3, 1987, 37–39.
"The Union Association—Is It a Major League?" Mighty Casey Baseball, April 1, 2018. https://mightycaseybaseball.com/2018/04/01/the-union-association-is-it-a-major-league/.
van Dyck, Dave. "Prior Breaks Elbow; Out two Months." *Chicago Tribune*, May 28, 2005.
Vecsey, George. "How Ellsworth Did It." *Sport Magazine*, December 1963.
Vecsey, George. "Smith, Cards on Thin Ice." *New York Times*, October 18, 1982.
Verducci, Ken. "The High Price of Hard Living." *Sports Illustrated*, February 27, 1995.
Vincent, Charlie. "Hank Aguirre 1931–1994: He Put His Money Where His Heart Was." *Detroit Free Press*, September 5, 1994.
"Where Are They Today? Bobby Shantz." Yankee Scorebook, 1977.
"Wilcy Moore, Famed Yank Reliever of '27, Dies at 65." *New York Times*, April 1, 1963.
"Wilkins Angered by Ridiculous Contract." *USA Today Baseball Weekly*, March 1, 1994.
Wilson, Jeff. "Josh Hamilton Indicted, Accused of Injuring His Oldest Daughter." *Tampa Bay Times*, April 8, 2020.
Wilson, John. "Bat-Tosser Gentile Headed for Minors, Fights Back Tears." *Houston*, June 25, 1966.
Yellon, Al. "Former Cubs Lefthander Dick Ellsworth Has Died." bleedcubbieblue.com, October 12, 2022. https://www.bleedcubbieblue.com/2022/10/12/23399001/former-cubs-lefthander-dick-ellsworth-died.
York, Marty. "Jays Disappointed as Eichhorn Ends Comeback Attempt." *Toronto Globe*, August 22, 2000.
"Zolio Versalles." *The Sporting News*, October 31, 1981.

Books

Bush, Frederick C., and Bill Nowlin. *The Stars Shone on Philadelphia: The 1934 Negro National League Champions*. Phoenix: Society for American Baseball Research, 2023.
Gooden, Dwight, and Ellis Henican. *Doc: A Memoir*. New York: New Harvest, 2003.
Gordon, David. *The American Cardiovascular Pandemic: A 100-Year History*. Jefferson: McFarland, 2021.
Hogan, Lawrence H. *Shades of Glory*. Washington, D.C.: National Geographic, 2006.
James, Bill. *The New Bill James Historical Baseball Abstract*. New York: Free Press, 2001.
Jones, David. *Deadball Stars of the American League*. Cleveland: Society for American Baseball Research, 2004.
Kahanowitz, Ian S. *Baseball Gods in Scandal: Ty Cobb, Tris Speaker, and the Dutch Leonard Affair*. South Orange, NJ: Summer Game Books, 2019.
Overfield, Joseph M., Paul Adomites, Richard Puff, and L. Robert Davids. *Nineteenth Century Stars*. Phoenix: Society for American Baseball Research, 2012.
Porter, Darrell, and William Deerfield. *Snap Me Perfect! The Darrell Porter Story*. Nashville: Thomas Newson, 1984.

Bibliography

Simon, Tom. *Deadball Stars of the National League.* Cleveland: Society for American Baseball Research, 2004.
Thorn, John. *The Complete Armchair Book of Baseball.* New York: Sterling, 1997.
Wilson, Doug. *The Bird: The Life and Legacy of Mark Fidrych.* New York: Thomas Dunne, 2013.

Index

Aaron, Henry 80, 85
Abernathy, Ted 6–8, 105–110, 124, 156, 207
Agee, Tommy 120
Aguirre, Hank 6–8, 39, 87–91, 98, 208
Alexander, Doyle 157
Alexander, Grover 144–145
Allen, Dick 121
Allen, Johnny 39
Allison, Bob 99–100
Alomar, Roberto 159
Alou, Moises 188–189
Anderson, Brady 209
Anderson, George "Sparky" 135
Andujar, Joaquin 143
Ankiel, Rick 19
Anson, Adrian " Cap" 12, 15
Aparicio, Luis 115
Aurilia, Rich 5, 210
Avery, Steve 166
Avila, Bobby 71

Bagwell, Jeff 12
Bailey, Homer 205
Baker, Frank "Home Run" 68
Baker, Johnnie "Dusty" 188–191
Banks, Ernie 1, 92
Barber, Steve 59
Barrow, Ed 38
Battey, Earl 99–100
Bauer, Hank 59
Baylor, Don 132, 141
Beazley, Johnny 56
Beckett, Josh 192
Beckley, Jake 15
Bell, Cool Papa 44
Bell, William 44
Beltre, Adrian 68
Bench, Johnny 141
Bender, Charles "Chief" 154

Bennett, Charlie 14
Berra, Lawrence "Yogi" 64, 170
Berryhill, Damon 171
Betts, Mookie 12
Blanton, Darrell "Cy" 210
Blauser, Jeff 166
Blocker, Terry 165
Blum, Geoff 184
Blyleven, Bert 151
Boggs, Wade 68
Bolden, Ed 46
Bond, Tommy 17
Bonds, Barry 10, 12, 161, 172, 183, 188
Bonds, Bobby 120
Boone, Bret 5, 209
Boras, Scott 172
Boston, Daryl 151
Bottomley, Jim 85
Boudreau, Lou 114
Bowa, Larry 161
Boyd, Bob 75
Boyer, Clete 65
Boyer, Ken 80
Braun, Ryan 193, 203
Bream, Sid 167
Brecheen, Harry 6–8, 54–60, 75, 98, 207–208
Bresnahan, Roger 22, 144
Brett, George 12, 68, 140
Briles, Nelson 84
Bristol, Dave 108
Brock, Lou 24, 66, 92, 95
Broglio, Ernie 95
Brouthers, Dan 12, 14
Brown, Kevin 187
Brown, Mordecai 17
Buhl, Bob 92–93, 95
Bunker, Wally 59
Bunning, Jim 81, 88, 96
Burdette, Lew 65

253

Burkett, Jesse 19, 26
Burns, Britt 210

Cabrera, Miguel 80, 189, 194
Cadaret, Greg 156
Caldwell, Mike 210
Cambria, Joe 98
Caminiti, Ken 210
Campanella, Roy 42, 144
Campaneris, Bert 78
Campanis, Al 121
Campbell, Jim 86, 126
Canseco, Jose 158, 208
Cantroneo, Vince 178
Carpenter, Chris 196
Carrigan, Bill 34
Carter, Gary 141, 149
Carter, Joe 159
Caruthers, Bob 24
Cash, Norm 5, 7, 77, 80–86, 97, 207
Cash, Ron 84
Castillo, Luis 189
Cavaretta, Phil 50
Cepeda, Orlando 85
Cey, Ron 119, 121
Chance, Frank 85
Charleston, Oscar 44
Chesbro, Jack 154
Clancy, Jim 157–158
Clark, Will 73
Clarke, Horace 125
Clemens, Roger 30, 43, 157–158
Clement, Matt 187–188
Clemente, Roberto 66, 82
Cobb, Ty 12, 25, 27, 33–36, 136
Cochrane, Gordon "Mickey" 141
Colavito, Rocky 78, 80–81, 83
Colbert, Nate 120
Coleman, Joe 125, 132
Coleman, Ken 116
Coleman, Vince 151
Colletti, Ned 202
Collins, Jimmy 26
Colon, Bartolo 154
Combs, Earle 37
Combs, Jack 210
Comiskey, Charles 21
Cone, David 150–152, 159
Conigliaro, Tony 112
Contreras, Jose 177
Contros, Pete 151
Cooney, Johnny 49
Cooper, Dan 176
Cooper, Mort 56
Corrales, Pat 92
Covington, Wes 94

Cox, Bobby 165–166
Craig, Roger 72
Crawford, Carl 204
Crawford, Sam 27
Cross, Lave 51
Cruz, Nelson 194
Culp, Ray 96
Cusic, Mark 132

Daniels, Bennie 66
Darling, Ron 149
Daulton, Darren 171
Davis, Chris 209
Dawson, Andre 12, 171
Day, Doris 145
Dean, Jay "Dizzy" 136, 154
deGrom, Jacob 43
Demeter, Steve 81
Denkinger, Don 143
Dent, Russell "Bucky" 72
Derringer, Paul 94
Desmond, Ian 197
Devlin, Art 210
Dierker, Larry 210
Dihigo, Martin 19
DiMaggio, Dom 57
DiMaggio, Joe 1, 50
Ditmar, Art 65
Doby, Larry 42, 71
Downing, Brian 141
Downs, Jeter 205
Doyle, Denny 121
Drabowski, Moe 59
Dressen, Chuck 89, 124
Drott, Dick 93
Drysdale, Don 59, 101, 149
Dunlap, Fred 5, 7, 10–18, 23, 28, 54, 207–208
Durocher, Leo 89–90, 93, 96, 107
Dykes, Jimmy 59

Eckersley, Dennis 156
Edmonds, Jim 177
Eflin, Zach 204
Eichhorn, Mark 6–7, 40, 108, 156–160, 207
Ellsworth, Dick 2, 6–7, 30, 92–97, 208
Ellsworth, Steve 97
Epstein, Mike 125
Ermer, Cal 102
Esposito, Ashley 176
Estrada, Chuck 59
Ethier, Andre 204
Evans, Billy 33
Evans, Dwight 115
Evers, Johnnie 17

Face, Roy 126
Fairbanks, Douglas 98
Fairly, Ron 75
Farmer, Kyle 205
Farrell, Richard "Turk" 94
Federowicz, Tim 204
Feldman, Scott 194
Feller, Bob 52, 146, 150–151
Fernandez, Sid 148, 150
Ferrell, Rick 144
Fetzer, John 90
Fidrych, Mark 4, 6–7, 97, 118, 131–137, 191, 207
Fielder, Cecil 209
Figgins, Chone 210
Fingers, Rollie 24, 115, 156
Fisher, Jack 59
Fisk, Carlton 140
Flick, Elmer 25, 27
Flood, Curt 14
Ford, Edward "Whitey" 65, 149
Ford, Gerald 133
Fosse, Ray 120
Foster, Bill 43–44
Foster, George "Rube" 31–32
Fowler, Dick 62
Fowler, Ron 205
Fox, Nellie 51
Fox, Terry 88
Foxx, Jimmie 77, 144
Foy, Joe 112
Foytack, Paul 88
Frasee, Harry 34
Freedman, Andrew 21
Freehan, Bill 84
Freel, Ryan 193
Freese, David 196
Frey, Jim 142
Frick, Ford 59
Fryman, Woodie 125

Gallaher, Marv 121
Galvin, James "Pud" 15
Gant, Ron 166–167
Garcia, Mike 71
Garvey, Steve 119–121, 133
Gehrig, Lou 1, 37, 50
Gentile, Jim 5–7, 75–80, 82, 98, 208
Gibson, Bob 113, 149
Gibson, Josh 10, 42, 45
Giles, Brian 181, 184
Giles, Marcus 5, 7, 181–185, 188, 207–208
Gilkey, Bernard 210
Gilks, Bob 38
Girardi, Joe 171

Gladden, Dan 167
Glasscock, Jack 11–12, 17
Glavine, Tom 166
Gomez, Carlos 210
Gomez, Vernon "Lefty" 154
Gonzalez, Adrian 205
Gonzalez, Alex 188–189
Gonzalez, Juan 176
Gonzalez, Luis 172
Gooden, Dwight 6–8, 30, 43, 80, 146–155, 199, 208
Gordon, Tom 124
Gossage, Rich 4, 108, 124, 127, 156, 160
Grabarkewitz, Billy 5–7, 118–123, 207–208, 210
Grace, Mark 171
Grandal, Yasmani 204
Grant, Jim "Mudcat" 101
Gray, Josiah 205
Gray, Pete 17
Greenberg, Hank 69, 77, 80
Greenwell, Mike 210
Greinke, Zack 43
Griffith, Cal 103
Grimes, Burleigh 154
Grimm, Charlie 52
Grove, Robert "Lefty" 43
Guerrero, Vladimir 154
Guidry, Ron 142, 149, 154
Guzman, Juan 159

Hacker, Warren 93, 210
Haines, Jesse 154
Hall, Jimmy 100
Halladay, Roy 177
Hamilton, Billy 13
Hamilton, Josh 5, 7, 192–199, 207–208
Hands, Bill 210
Hanlon, Ned 14
Hansen, Ron 76, 210
Hardy, Larry 157
Harper, Tommy 210
Harrelson, Ken 78
Harris, Gail 81
Harris, Victor 44
Hartnett, Gabby 170
Hawpe, Brad 190
Hedges, Robert 27
Hegan, Jim 88
Henderson, Rickey 12
Henke, Tom 157, 159
Henrichs, Tommy 50
Herman, Billy 112
Hernandez, Keith 149
Hernandez, Willie 210
Herr, Tom 142

Herzog, Dorrel "Whitey" 140, 142, 149, 163
Higuera, Teddy 157
Hiller, John 6–8, 40, 108, 124–130, 156, 160, 207
Hitchcock, Billy 59, 78
Hoak, Don 65
Hobbie, Glen 93, 95
Hobson, Clell "Butch" 115
Hodges, Gil 75, 85
Hogan, Jeff 132
Hoiles, Chris 209
Hollocher, Charlie 51
Holmes, Tommie 5, 7, 17, 49–54, 75, 98, 207–208
Holtzman, Jerry 127
Hornsby, Rogers 12, 51, 114
Horton, Willie 83
House, Tom 186
Howard, Frank 85
Hoyt, Waite 37, 39
Hubbell, Carl 55
Hubbs, Ken 92
Huggins, Miller 38
Hunter, Jim "Catfish" 24, 78, 114, 154

Irvin, Monte 42, 45

Jackson, Larry 92–93, 95–96
Jackson, Reggie 206
Jackson, Vincent "Bo" 164
James, Bill 16–17
James, Dion 165
Johnson, Randy 87
Johnson, Walter 30, 43, 148
Johnson, William "Judy" 44
Jones, Andruw 183
Jones, Larry "Chipper" 170
Jones, Stewart "Slim" 4, 6–8, 42–48, 54, 64, 118, 136, 191, 207–208
Joss, Addie 154
Joyner, Wally 158
Judge, Aaron 198
Jurrjens, Jair 210
Justice, David 166–167

Kaat, Jim 99, 102, 154
Kaline, Al 80–83
Kauff, Benny 17
Keefe, Tim 30
Keeler, Willie 51
Keller, Charlie 50
Kelley, Shayne 196
Kelly, George "High Pockets" 85
Kelly, Michael "King" 10
Keltner, Ken 69

Kemp, Matt 5, 7, 200–207
Kennedy, Bob 93, 95
Kern, Jim 210
Kershaw, Clayton 4, 201
Key, Jimmy 157–159
Killebrew, Harmon 73, 82, 85, 92, 99–100
Kinsler, Ian 194
Klein, Lou 95
Kluszewski, Ted 81, 209
Konstanty, Jim 210
Koufax, Sandy 59, 92, 94, 101, 146, 149
Krichell, Paul 50
Kruk, John 87
Krukow, Mike 73

Lacheman, Marcel 159
Lacy, Lee 121
Lajoie, Bill 76
Lajoie, Nap 18, 25–26
Lake, Eddie 210
Landis, Kenesaw Mountain 35
Lane, Frank 88
Lanier, Max 56
Lannin, Joseph 34
Larkin, Gene 167
LaRussa, Tony 156
Lary, Frank 80–83, 88
Law, Vern 65
Lazerri, Tony 37, 145
Lee, Derrek 189
Lefebvre, Jim 119, 121
Leibovitz, Annie 131
Lemke, Mark 166
Lemon, Bob 24, 71, 154
Leonard, Emil "Dutch" 30
Leonard, Hubert "Dutch" 6–8, 30–36, 43, 54, 64, 207–208
Lewis, George "Duffy" 34
Leyland, Jim 136
Little, Grady 201
Loaiza, Esteban 6, 7, 175–180, 208
Lockman, Carroll "Whitey" 64, 90
Lofton, Kenny 188
Lolich, Mickey 83, 114, 125, 132, 154
Lombardi, Ernie 144
Lonborg, Jim 112
Lopes, Davey 121
Lopez, Al 70
Lopez, Javy 5, 209
Lucas, Henry 12–14
Luque, Dolf 209
Luzinsky, Greg 162–163
Lynn, Fred 115
Lyons, Ted 38

Index

Mack, Connie 32, 34, 62
Mackey, James "Biz" 44
Macon, Max 76
Maddox, Garry 162
Maddux, Greg 30, 43, 148, 171, 188–190
Majeski, Hank 70
Maldonado, Martin 173
Maloney, Jim 30, 92
Mantle, Mickey 1, 12, 64, 77, 80, 82, 144, 149
Manwaring, Fred 171
Maranville, Walter "Rabbit" 24
Marberry, Frederick "Firpo" 40
Marchildon, Phil 62
Marichal, Juan 94
Maris, Roger 77, 80, 82, 208–209
Markakis, Nick 210
Marquard, Richard "Rube" 32, 154
Marshall, Mike 156
Martin, Alfred "Billy" 72, 100–101, 129
Martin, Fred 93, 95
Martinez, Pedro 30, 43, 148
Masterman, Walt 64
Mathews, Eddie 52, 68
Mathewson, Christy 23
Mauch, Gene 96
Mauer, Joe 141, 186
Mays, Carl 31, 32
Mays, Willie 12, 71, 80, 85
Mazeroski, Bill 66
McAuliffe, Dick 83
McBride, Arnold "Bake" 162
McCarthy, Joe 50
McCarthy, Tommy 17
McCarver, Tim 209
McCormick, Jim 17
McCovey, Willie 85
McDaniel, Lindy 92, 107
McDougald, Gil 208
McGee, Willie 142, 149
McGinnity, Joe 20
McGraw, John 22
McGriff, Fred 85
McInnis, John "Stuffy" 51
McKinnon, Alex 13
McLain, Denny 83, 125, 208
McMullen, Ken 121
McMullin, John 72
McNally, Dave 59, 84
McPhee, John "Bid" 18
McQuillan, George 210
McRae, Hal 140
Mele, Sam 100
Melton, Bill 84
Merkel, Fred 22
Messersmith, Andy 121

Miller, Bob 102, 127
Millwood, Kevin 194
Minor, Ryan 210
Minoso, Saturnino "Minnie" 42, 81
Miranda, Willie 76, 98
Moore, Wilcy 6–7, 37–41, 54, 108, 124, 207
Moreno, Artie 197
Morgan, Joe 12
Morris, Jack 154, 167
Morris, John 164
Morton, Guy 210
Moseby, Lloyd 3
Moses, Wally 57
Mossi, Don 88
Muesel, Bob 37
Munson, Thurman 133–134, 170
Murphy, Dale 163, 165
Musial, Stan 17–18, 53, 64

Narron, Johnny 193
Neshek, Pat 204
Newcombe, Don 141
Niedenfuer, Tom 143
Nieto, Tom 143
Nixon, Otis 166–167
Nola, Aaron 43, 148
Nolan, Gary 148
Northrup, Jim 83–84

O'Donnell, Harry 62
Ohtani, Shohei 24
Ojeda, Bob 149
Oliva, Tony 100–101
Oliver, Bob 125
Olivera, Hector 205
O'Neil, John "Buck" 42
O'Neill, James "Tip" 12
Ordway, Glenn 116
Ortiz, David 177
Ortiz, Russ 187
Otis, Amos 140

Paige, Leroy "Satchel" 42-46, 50
Palmer, Jim 59, 134
Pappas, Milt 59
Parker, Wes 119
Pascual, Camilo 99
Pederson, Joc 204
Pena, Alejandro 167
Pendleton, Terry 167
Pennock, Herb 37, 154
Perez, Salvadore 193
Perez, Tony 120
Perranoski, Ron 102
Pesky, Johnny 57

Index

Petrocelli, Rico 5, 7, 111–117, 207
Pettitte, Andy 195
Piazza, Mike 141, 171–172
Pierre, Juan 189
Pinson, Vada 80
Plank, Eddie 17
Popowski, Eddie 112
Porter, Darrell 5, 7, 127, 138–145, 207–208
Porter, Jay 88
Posey, Gerald "Buster" 141
Powell, John "Boog" 78
Power, Tyrone 98
Prior, Mark 2, 6–8, 183, 186–191
Puig, Yasiel 204
Pujols, Albert 183, 194, 196

Quentin, Carlos 193
Quilici, Frank 101

Radatz, Dick 156
Radbourn, Charles "Old Hoss" 4
Ramirez, Aramis 188
Ramos, Pedro 99
Raymond, Dave 163
Reagan, Ronald 145
Reese, Harold "PeeWee" 118
Reniff, Hal 88
Reulbach, Ed 210
Reynolds, Allie 64
Rhines, Billy 210
Rhodes, James "Dusty" 71
Rhodes, Karl "Tuffy" 152
Rice, Jim 115
Rice, Sam 19
Richards, Paul 59, 76
Richardson, Hardy 14
Rickey, Branch 56
Rihanna 202
Ripken, Cal, Jr. 113, 116, 201
Rivera, Jenni 178
Rivera, Mariano 124
Roberts, Robin 59, 63, 76
Robinson, Brooks 68
Robinson, Frank 59, 80, 85, 121
Robinson, Jackie 64
Rodriguez, Alex "A-Rod" 68
Rodriguez, Ivan 176
Rogan, Charles "Bullet" 19, 43
Rosar, Warren "Buddy" 53
Rose, Pete 49, 120, 133
Roseboro, John 102
Rosen, Al 3, 5, 7, 54, 68–75, 98, 207–208
Roush, Edd 17, 51
Rowe, Jack 14
Runnels, Pete 112

Rusie, Amos 20, 148
Russell, Bill 119, 121
Russell, Ewell "Reb" 210
Ruth, George "Babe" 1, 10, 12, 17, 19, 31–32, 37, 39, 63, 77, 144, 209–210
Ryan, Mike 96
Ryan, Nolan 20, 80, 85, 196

Sanchez, Jonathan 195
Sandberg, Ryne 171
Sanders, Deion 166–167
Santo, Ron 68, 92
Schalk, Ray 144
Scheffing, Bob 82
Scheuerholz, John 161, 165–166
Schieb, Carl 62–63
Schilling, Curt 187
Schmidt, Jason 187
Schmidt, Mike 12, 68, 74
Score, Herb 208
Scott, George 112
Seaver, Tom 30, 92, 146, 151, 155, 186
Servais, Scott 172
Sewell, Joe 51
Seymour, James "Cy" 5, 7, 19–25, 28, 54, 207
Shafer, George "Orator" 17
Shantz, Billy 61
Shantz, Bobby 6–7, 61–67, 207
Shawkey, Bob 32
Sheets, Ben 210
Shocker, Urban 37–38
Shore, Ernie 31–32, 34, 63
Short, Chris 96
Siebern, Norm 78
Simmons, Curt 62
Simmons, Ted 142, 154
Singer, Bill 121
Sisler, Geroge 19
Sizemore, Ted 119–120
Slaton, Jim 115
Slaught, Don 143
Slaughter, Enos 57
Smith, Hal 66
Smith, Lee 129–130
Smith, Lonnie 5–8, 161–169, 207–208
Smith, Ozzie 142–143
Smith, Reggie 112, 162
Smith, Tal 72
Smith, Walter "Red" 57
Smoltz, John 166–167
Sosa, Sammy 171, 188, 190
Speaker, Tris 25, 34–36
Spink, Al 18
Stanley, Mickey 83
Stargell, Willie 154

Start, Joe 51
Stearns, Norman "Turkey" 44
Steinbrenner, George 72, 206
Stengel, Charles "Casey" 50, 144
Stieb, Dave 157
Stone, George R. 5, 7, 25–29, 54, 207
Strahler, Mike 121
Strawberry, Darryl 149–151
Stuart, Dick 112
Sturdivant, Tom 65
Sudakis, Bill 119
Sutcliffe, Rick 148
Sutter, Bruce 24, 108, 156
Suttles, Gerge "Mule" 44
Sutton, Don 143
Sutton, Ezra 210
Swift, Bob 63

Tanana, Frank 134
Terry, Bill 154
Terry, Ralph 66
Thomas, Lee 107
Thomas, Tommy 38
Thompson, Justin 210
Thompson, Robbie 73
Thompson, Sam 14–15
Tiant, Luis 114–115
Timmerman, Tom 125
Tinker, Joe 17, 23
Toney, Fred 210
Torchia, Tony 136–137
Torgeson, Earl 81
Torre, Joe 201
Trammell, Alan 158
Traynor, Harold "Pie" 24, 51
Triandos, Gus 76
Trout, Mike 196
Turner, Terry 26, 210
Twitchell, Wayne 210

Valdevielso, Jose 99
Valentin, John 210
Valentine, Bobby 119, 121
Valenzuela, Fernando 165, 179, 209
Vargo, Ed 78
Vaughan, Joseph "Arky" 114
Velarde, Randy 209
Vernon, Mickey 70
Versailles, Zoilo 5, 7, 98–104, 119, 207–208
Villanueva, Hector 171
Viola, Frank 151

Volquez, Edinson 193
Votto, Joey 194

Wagner, John "Honus" 12, 22, 25, 113–114
Wallace, Bobby 19
Waner, Lloyd 51
Waner, Paul 50, 52, 144
Ward, Duane 159
Ward, John Montgomery 19
Wells, David 159
Wells, Willie 44
Wertz, Vic 63
Whitaker, Lou 149
White, Devon 159
White, Frank 140
White, James "Deacon" 14, 15
White, Roy 162
Whitfield, Fred 78
Widmar, Al 157
Wieland, Joe 204
Wilhelm, Hoyt 119, 124, 154, 156
Wilkins, Rick 2, 5–7, 170–174, 207–208
Williams, Billy 85, 92
Williams, Dick 112
Williams, Fred "Cy" 124
Williams, Gregory "Woody" 187
Williams, Guy 98
Williams, Ted 17–18, 57, 149
Williamson, Ed 209
Willis, Dontrelle 210
Wills, Maury 119–121
Wilson, Art 209
Wilson, Earl 83
Wilson, Lewis "Hack" 144
Wilson, Willie 164
Winfield, Dave 159, 200, 202, 206
Wise, Rick 96
Wood, Alex 205
Wood, Kerry 183, 186–188
Wood, Smoky Joe 31–32, 34–35, 209
Woodeschick, Hal 88
Wrigley, Phillip K 89, 93
Wynn, Early 70–71

Yastrzemski, Carl 12, 112–113, 133
Young, Denton "Cy" 19
Young, Michael 176, 194–195
Yount, Robin 114

Zambrano, Carlos 187, 189

www.ingramcontent.com/pod-product-compliance
Ingram Content Group UK Ltd.
Pitfield, Milton Keynes, MK11 3LW, UK
UKHW041934140426
5217IPUK00014B/463